A HISTORY OF EVANGELICALISM
PEOPLE, MOVEMENTS AND IDEAS IN THE ENGLISH-SPEAKING WORLD

VOLUME 3

THE DOMINANCE OF EVANGELICALISM

The Age of Spurgeon and Moody

DAVID W. BEBBINGTON

InterVarsity Press
Downers Grove, Illinois

InterVarsity Press
P.O. Box 1400, Downers Grove, IL 60515-1426
Internet: www.ivpress.com
E-mail: mail@ivpress.com

Published in the United States of America by InterVarsity Press, Downers Grove, Illinois, with permission from Inter-Varsity Press Ltd. in Leicester, England.

InterVarsity Press® *is the book-publishing division of InterVarsity Christian Fellowship/USA*®*, a student movement active on campus at hundreds of universities, colleges and schools of nursing in the United States of America, and a member movement of the International Fellowship of Evangelical Students. For information about local and regional activities, write Public Relations Dept., InterVarsity Christian Fellowship/USA, 6400 Schroeder Rd., P.O. Box 7895, Madison, WI 53707-7895, or visit the IVCF website at <www.intervarsity.org>.*

All Scripture quotations, unless otherwise indicated, are taken from the Holy Bible, New International Version®*.* NIV®*. Copyright* ©*1973, 1978, 1984 by International Bible Society. Used by permission of Hodder and Stoughton Ltd. All rights reserved. "NIV" is a registered trademark of International Bible Society. UK trademark number 1448790. Distributed in North America by permission of Zondervan Publishing House.*

Cover design: Cindy Kiple

Cover image: Moody Bible Institute Archive

ISBN-10: 0-8308-2583-5
ISBN-13: 978-0-8308-2583-7

Printed in the United States of America ∞

Library of Congress Cataloging-in-Publication Data

Bebbington, D. W. (David William), 1949-
  The dominance of evangelicalism: the age of Spurgeon and Moody /
  David Bebbington.
    p. cm. — (A history of evangelicalism)
  Includes bibliographical references and index.
  ISBN 0-8308-2583-5 (cloth: alk. paper)
  1. Evangelicalism—History—19th century. I. Title. II. Series.
  BR1640.B44 2005
  270.8'1—dc22
                                                                      2005008306

P 15 14 13 12 11 10 9 8 7 6 5 4 3 2 1

Y 16 15 14 13 12 11 10 09 08 07 06 05

To friends in other

parts of the world

who have offered

invitations and hospitality

CONTENTS

ACKNOWLEDGMENTS

Material for this book has been assembled over many years in a wide range of places, and it is only by the kindness of those who invited me to teach, lecture or attend conferences in other parts of the world that the task has been possible. I am therefore glad to thank those who arranged visits to Sydney, Melbourne and Adelaide in Australia; to Acadia, Kingston and Toronto in Canada; to Christchurch in New Zealand; to Pretoria and Cape Town in South Africa; and to Wheaton College, together with Chicago, Notre Dame, Wake Forest and Baylor Universities, in the United States. To these people I want to dedicate the book.

I am also grateful for access to collections of primary material in Edinburgh, London, Cambridge, Oxford, Manchester, Bangor and Belfast. Friends who have been generous in providing information include Hoffie Hofmeyr, Peter Lineham and Wray Vamplew. As so often in the past, my wife Eileen and my daughter Anne have been indulgent companions on many of the research trips, and Eileen has proved a keen critic, especially of theological technicalities, in reading the text. I am profoundly in her debt for this as for many other reasons.

My colleagues in this project for writing a history of English-speaking evangelicalism have also been extremely helpful in reading the text: Mark Noll, Brian Stanley, Geoff Treloar and John Wolffe. Together with Larry Eskridge, who read the prologue, they have saved me from many errors, omissions and infelicities. Most particularly, my fellow general editor of the series, Mark Noll, has been a constant source of ideas, encouragement, useful references and constructive criticism. I must express both my gratitude to the readers and my apologies for the inadequacies that remain.

Perhaps I ought to note here that, in accordance with the general convention of the series, *evangelical* has a lower-case initial except where it applies to Anglican Evangelicals; and that *South Africa* has been used to describe the southern portion of the continent even though the political entity of that name did not come into existence until later.

PROLOGUE

The Setting

This volume, like the others in the series, takes the evangelical movement of the English-speaking world for its subject. The members of this international network professed the Christian faith in broadly the form that it had assumed during the evangelical revival of the eighteenth century. The movement was by no means confined to a single denomination, for the revival had transformed many older Protestant bodies as well as creating new ones. Evangelicalism had injected a fresh expansive dynamic into the church. It had given rise to the modern missionary movement that carried the gospel to many lands where it had hitherto not taken root. Although some attention is paid here to the missionary impulse, the "English-speaking" limitation is designed to focus the series not on missions themselves but on those who sent out the missionaries—in this period, the peoples of the United Kingdom, the United States and the settler communities of the British Empire. The range of territories where the movement flourished will be discussed in chapter two, but here it will be useful to indicate the broad social and political context in which the movement operated. Despite their otherworldly preoccupation, evangelicals did not live a life apart. They numbered in their ranks many of the merchants and artisans, wives and children, politicians and voters, who acted and suffered in the day-to-day events of society at large. The dominant place of their faith in the culture of the times, a central theme of this book, ensured that evangelicals engaged particularly closely with the trends of the day. So a brief review of the framework of circumstances that molded their lives during the later nineteenth century can help set the scene for a closer examination of the evangelical movement.[1]

POLITICS, NATIONAL AND GLOBAL

The political state of Britain is a suitable place to begin. The "Year of Revolutions" in continental Europe, 1848, had largely passed the country by. The Chartists, a radical working-class grouping whose efforts at insurrection had disturbed the previous decade, alarmed the government by its plans in that year, but managed only a minor demonstration and afterward withered away. Subsequent years in Britain were marked by constitutional stability. Queen Victoria, who had come to the throne in 1837, ruled to the very end of the century, but the crown no longer played a publicly partisan role in politics. Instead the parties held effective power through commanding a majority in the House of Commons. The Liberals, led by broad-minded peers and gentry but drawing support from new industrialists and many lesser folk, favored moderate measures of change. They had been responsible for the Reform Act of 1832 that greatly enlarged the franchise without threatening the influence of the landowners. It was, however, the Conservatives under Benjamin Disraeli who passed a further measure of parliamentary reform in 1867 with the aim of attracting the

---

[1]The sources for this prologue are standard works. Particularly helpful for the general circumstances of the later nineteenth century are:

On Britain: G. F. A. Best, *Mid-Victorian Britain, 1851-75* (London: Weidenfeld and Nicolson, 1971); Martin Pugh, *The Making of Modern British Politics, 1867-1945*, 3rd ed. (Oxford: Blackwell, 2002); F. M. L. Thompson, *The Rise of Respectable Society: A Social History of Victorian Britain, 1830-1900* (London: Fontana, 1988).

On the United States: Hugh Brogan, *The Pelican History of the United States of America* (London: Penguin, 1986); T. J. Schlereth, *Victorian America: Transformations in Everyday Life, 1876-1915* (New York: HarperCollins, 1991).

On Australia: Beverley Kingston, *The Oxford History of Australia*, Vol. 3, *1860-1900: Glad, Confident Morning* (Melbourne: Oxford University Press, 1988); Robert Lacour-Gayet, *A Concise History of Australia* (Harmondsworth, U.K.: Penguin, 1976).

On Canada: Margaret Conrad, Alvin Finkel and Cornelius Jaenen, *History of the Canadian Peoples*, 2 vols. (Toronto: Copp Clark Pitman, 1993); Kenneth McNaught, *The Penguin History of Canada* (London: Penguin, 1988).

Generally: Andrew Porter, ed., *The Oxford History of the British Empire*, Vol. 3, *The Nineteenth Century* (Oxford: Oxford University Press, 1999); Neville Williams, *Chronology of the Modern World, 1763-1965* (Harmondsworth, U.K.: Penguin, 1975).

new voters in the towns to their side. The Conservatives, who had previously been the party of upper-class traditionalists, the bulk of the professionals and the dependants of each, now mobilized a wider range of electors. Especially after a further round of reform in 1884-1885, the Conservatives attracted solid support from the middle classes. The Liberals under William Gladstone adopted increasingly radical measures, culminating in the proposal of Home Rule for Ireland in 1886. Nationalists in Ireland, often fired by memories of the devastating famine in their island of the 1840s, aspired to a separate state, and Gladstone believed that only the concession of a subordinate parliament in Dublin would keep the Irish within the United Kingdom. Home Rule, however, failed to pass, and the grumbling sore of the Irish question continued to afflict the body politic. In general, however, the people of the British mainland, the English, the Scots and the Welsh, were well content to live together in a secure and prospering United Kingdom.

Britain normally attempted to avoid continental entanglements during this period. There was widespread sympathy for Italians who were consolidating their land as a national unit, but Britain did not participate in the military side of the Risorgimento. Likewise Britain stood apart as Bismarck raised Prussia to a new eminence in Europe, sweeping aside the Austrians in a war in 1866, defeating the French in another war in 1870 and setting up the German Empire. By and large during the half century from 1850 onward Britain was at peace. In 1854-1856 the country joined France in an invasion of the Crimea in order to defend Turkey against Russia; and in 1899-1902 Britain fought a long and weary struggle against the two Dutch-speaking republics of southern Africa, the Orange Free State and the Transvaal. Otherwise, however, Britain confined itself to many small operations on the imperial frontiers. In November 1856, for instance, a campaign was launched against Persia and simultaneously the city of Canton in China was bombarded. Britain specialized in undertakings that could be accomplished by naval power, for the country exercised unchallenged authority at sea. The most prominent statesman of the middle years of the century, Lord Palmerston, declared in 1850 that, just as anyone in the ancient world could announce that he was a Roman citizen and the might of Rome's empire would protect him, so Britain's authority would shield all who could claim to be subjects of the crown wherever they might be. So high was the country's standing that when, in 1863, the Greeks decided to found a new ruling dynasty, it was natural for them to invite (unsuccessfully) a son of Queen Victoria to assume their throne. Britain was at the height of its worldwide prestige.

The area of the British Empire steadily grew during the half century. There was little or no deliberate plan for the extension of empire, but territory was acquired piecemeal because of wishes to protect commercial interests, requests for aid from adjacent peoples and decisions by local commanders. India, the jewel of the empire, underwent the catharsis of revolt in 1857-1858, when the so-called Indian Mutiny, or First War of Independence, threatened British authority. The mutiny was followed by the transfer of responsibility for the subcontinent from a primarily commercial organization, the East India Company, to the British government, a process several times replicated elsewhere. Extensive conflict also marred British expansion in other parts of the world such as New Zealand, which was riven by repeated struggles against the original Maori inhabitants down to 1870. Around that year there was an acceleration of territorial ambitions as other European powers began to take a more serious interest in imperial aggrandizement. In the era of "new imperialism," which lasted for the rest of the century, there was particular attention to Africa. In 1871 Britain annexed the diamond fields of Kimberley in South Africa; in 1873-1874 there was a war against the Ashanti people of West Africa; three years later the Transvaal was annexed; in 1879 there was a fierce struggle with the Zulus; in 1882 Britain occupied Egypt, ostensibly on a temporary basis; and the process continued in rivalry with other powers down to 1900 and beyond. There was the possibility of a similar carving up of China during the 1890s, but in that vast land the spheres of interest demarcated by the Great Powers never turned into swaths of empire. The strength of popular imperialism in the last few years of the century can be measured by the fact that the United States, born in revolt against empire, created its own version by the acquisition of Puerto Rico, Cuba, Hawaii and the Philippines in the wake of the Spanish-American War of 1898. The period was an age of empire.

Nevertheless there was a sustained effort to loosen the ties between Britain and her possessions in other parts of the world. This enterprise was not a campaign to dissolve empire, but an effort to save money on imperial defense and encourage self-reliance in the dependent territories. The new powers of self-government were not designed for peoples of other races, but were confined to areas of white settlement. Thus the Australian Colonies Government Act of 1850 granted large powers of legislative independence to New South Wales, South Australia, Van Diemen's Land (shortly to be renamed Tasmania) and Victoria (a new colony to be organized in the following year); two years later New Zealand received a constitution providing for representative government; and the Cape Colony opened a parliament in 1854. In British North America the two provinces now known as Quebec and Ontario, which had been consolidated in 1840, had effectively received responsible government in 1848. There constitutional development took a major forward stride when, in 1867, the Dominion of Canada was established containing the four provinces of Quebec, Ontario, New Brunswick and Nova Scotia. Subsequently other provinces joined, though Newfoundland was to remain separate long into the twentieth century. Similar federation was mooted for Australia, where Queensland and Western Australia were given responsible government in 1859 and 1890 respectively. It was not until 1901, however, that the Commonwealth of Australia was established to unite the former colonies, now called states, as a single nation. Except in Quebec, where the people were predominantly French-speaking, and the Cape, where many were of Dutch origin, the white population of each of these lands was drawn during this period overwhelmingly from the British Isles. Although some of the Irish-born were restive, most of the empire was well content to be British.

The United States, however, was proud of the independence it had won in the eighteenth century. The young republic had established a flourishing system of participatory democracy, electing a host of local officials, state and federal senators and congressmen, state governors and, every four years, a president. During the 1850s the pressing issue for politicians was how to accommodate competing sectional aspirations within the national framework. New territories acquired through the Louisiana Purchase and the Mexican-American War were being organized to the west: were they to be allowed to adopt slavery, a cornerstone of the economic life of the South? Many Northerners, some of them believing slavery to be intrinsically abhorrent, were totally opposed to any conciliation of the South. When in 1860 Abraham Lincoln, a Northern Republican pledged to prohibit the expansion of slavery, was elected president, most of the slave-owning states seceded from the Union to form the Confederacy. The ensuing Civil War, won by the North after four hard-fought years, led to the emancipation of the slaves but also to the subjection of the South to enforced reconstruction. Southerners, with Irish immigrants and other outsider groups, were stalwart supporters of the Democratic Party that struggled for national power against the Republicans over subsequent decades, creating elaborate party machines. By the 1890s, however, many small farmers began to think that the two-party system was no longer representing their interests and so launched the People's Party. Their champion, William Jennings Bryan of Nebraska, actually captured the Democratic Party nomination for the presidency in 1896. Before the end of the century a further wave of reformist zeal created another third force, the Progressives, that was to make a significant impact in the following decade. But the dominance of politics by the two main parties of state, Republican and Democrat, was not to be overturned.

SOCIETY AND ECONOMY

Although the political systems of Britain and America were different, some of the social developments in the two countries showed marked similarities. Rapid demographic growth was one of them, but because of immigration, America greatly outstripped Britain. Between 1851 and 1901 the population of the United Kingdom rose from twenty-seven million to forty-one million; from 1850 to 1900 the U.S. population increased from twenty-three million to seventy-six million. The American figures had already surpassed the British by 1860. The various areas of white settlement in the British Empire, by contrast, were only thinly populated except in very limited areas. Even at the end of the century Canada still had only some five million white inhabitants, Australia nearly four million, South Africa just over one million and New Zealand less than one. Britain was the source of many of the migrants to the empire, though America was consistently the most favored destination. Between 1853 and 1900, 56 percent of the emigrants from England and Wales traveled to the United States. The flow of immigrants into the United States from Germany and other parts of Europe, however, meant that only 11 percent of the foreign born in the country in 1900 were from Britain, though fully another 16 percent, a much higher proportion, had arrived from Ireland. The period was notable for the gradual spread of the American population westward, establishing new states, keeping up the frontier spirit and squeezing the Native Americans off their ancestral lands. The last territory to be opened to settlement was

Oklahoma, the former Indian Territory, in 1890. The half century witnessed a large-scale English-speaking diaspora.

It also saw the triumphant progress of industry. In 1851, the Great Exhibition was in London. The products of many nations were on display, but the overriding purpose was to celebrate the technical expertise of Britain, the first country to industrialize. The opening of the exhibition, said Queen Victoria, "was the greatest day in our history."[2] The subsequent advance of industrialism continued unabated. The record of cotton manufacturing, the cutting edge of earlier industrialization in Britain, speaks for itself. British cotton exports rose from 1,524 million yards in 1852 to 4,873 million yards forty years later. Likewise British coal production increased from 60 million tons in 1851 to 219 million tons fifty years later, much of it for export. The gradual removal of tariff barriers between nations had helped Britain establish its commercial dominance of the world, so that in the first year after the opening of the Suez Canal, 1870, 71 percent of the shipping passing through it flew the British flag. The strongest economic growth in Britain during the second half of the century was in the tertiary sector of trade, commerce and finance. It contributed 19 percent of the national income in 1851, but as much as 28 percent in 1907. The greatest success story of the later nineteenth century, however, was the industrial expansion of the United States. Though lagging behind Britain at the start of the period, America caught up at an astonishing pace. Between 1851 and 1901, for example, coal production in the United States mushroomed from 7 to 268 million tons. The statistics for iron production tell a similar story of the United States overtaking Britain as the greatest industrial power. The imposition of selected tariffs helped American industry profit from its vast natural resources and burgeoning internal market. Although, except for mining, industry remained marginal in the overwhelmingly agrarian lands of Australia, New Zealand and South Africa, it became a significant force in the cities of Ontario and Quebec. For many in the Anglo-Saxon world it was an era of manufacturing and commerce.

Industrial and mercantile development brought prosperity in its wake. For

---

[2]*Letters of Queen Victoria*, 1st series, Vol. 2 (London, 1907), p. 383, quoted by Francois Bédarida, *A Social History of England, 1851-1975* (London: Methuen, 1979), p. 3.

the first time many families had money to spend over and above what had to go toward subsistence. People enjoyed better clothes, a more varied diet and altogether a higher quality of life. Increasingly they lived in the great cities, London having over three million inhabitants and New York over one million by 1881. In the wake of sanitary improvements, city life was no longer as lethal as in the earlier phase of industrialization. Between 1860 and 1900 the average real wage of urban workers in Britain rose by more than 60 percent. Overall figures, however, disguise the uneven distribution of the new wealth. Entrepreneurs such as John D. Rockefeller, the creator of Standard Oil in the United States, could accumulate vast fortunes. At a lower level, skilled workers could command much higher wage rates than their unskilled contemporaries. In 1900, when the average weekly income of an industrial worker in the United States was $8.37, the average for the unskilled was only $5.50. So amidst the newfound plenty there were festering grievances. The growth of leafy suburbs for the rich, away from the inner-city slums of the poor, only served to accentuate the sense of exclusion among the badly paid and the unemployed. It was an era of periodic strikes. The London Dock Strike of 1889 shut down the greatest port in the world. Other strikes fostered serious unrest. In 1877, the Pullman railroad stoppage in the United States led to riots, twenty-six deaths and a reputed five million dollars worth of damage to property in Pittsburgh. Organized labor both reflected and aggravated class resentments. By the opening of the twentieth century, trade union membership in America had reached two million and Britain was only just behind. In Britain, Canada and Australia, though not in the United States, independent political candidates began to stand in the name of labor, with some of them winning seats in the New South Wales Legislative Assembly as early as 1891. If affluence was widespread in society, working-class leaders were often deeply aware that their families did not enjoy a sufficient share of it.

One of the conditions of economic progress was the growth of the railways. In 1850 there were already over nine thousand miles in operation in the United States and nearly seven thousand in Britain. Forty years later the figures had risen to a remarkable one hundred and twenty-five thousand miles in the United States together with twenty thousand in Britain. A line was opened between Melbourne and Sydney in 1883 and two years later, after enormous political wrangling, the Canadian Pacific Railway linking British Colombia in the west to the rest of Canada was finally completed. The railways were arteries for the commercial lifeblood of the era, opening up new towns, taking food to the cities and carrying manufactured goods everywhere. Nor were the railways the only revolutionary change in communications. A transatlantic telegraph cable was laid, allowing messages to be exchanged between queen and president in 1858 and establishing a permanent link across the ocean eight years later. Alexander Graham Bell patented the telephone in 1876 and four years later some fifty thousand private instruments were already in use in America. Steamships gradually replaced sailing vessels, greatly enhancing the speed and reliability of overseas trade and travel. The first Australian frozen meat, carried by sea in refrigerated storage, reached London in 1879. There were signs of future revolutions in the production of the earliest motor cars in the 1890s and the patenting of wireless telegraphy by Guglielmo Marconi in 1896. These inventions were to come into their own in the twentieth century, but already in the later nineteenth a great deal had been done to abolish distance. The various parts of the world were much more closely bound together in 1900 than in 1850.

It was also a time when people at large achieved higher standards of education. The Elementary Education Act of 1870 was a landmark for England and Wales. Whereas previously the training of the young had been left primarily to the churches and other forms of private initiative, now the state undertook to fill the gaps by providing schools for all children to attend. Although the earlier schools had been effective in promoting reading and writing skills, there were still social groups, especially miners and laborers, amongst whom illiteracy was common. Within fifteen years it had been almost eliminated. In 1870 only 57 percent of American children received any elementary education, but the proportion rose steadily afterward. The literacy level in the United States had reached 80 percent by 1876. In both lands, and also elsewhere in the English-speaking world, newspapers were widely read. From 1851 American weeklies could be mailed free to any address within the same county. In 1855 Britain abolished the stamp duty on newspapers and six years later the duty on paper, so the long resented "taxes on knowledge" were swept away. Hence news circulated freely in the period. Education, furthermore, was made available at a higher level than before. In Britain the so-called public schools catering to the middle classes grew or were founded during the period, and the government abolished most of the university tests that kept non-Anglicans out of positions at Oxford and Cambridge by 1871. Already by that date America possessed more colleges, medical schools and law schools than in the whole of Europe. Equivalent schools, newspapers and colleges were all to be found elsewhere in the English-speaking lands too. It was an era when the ideal of self-improvement, as classically set forth in Samuel Smiles's *Self-Help* (1859), beckoned industrious young men. Social convention was even relaxing sufficiently to allow some young women to be fired by similar aspirations. Learning, especially if it was useful, was widely respected.

Each of these characteristics of the age interacted with religion. In politics, for example, the place of Roman Catholicism in predominantly Protestant lands caused endless debate. The allegiance of some four-fifths of the Irish population at home and abroad to the Catholic Church ensured that interconfessional issues cropped up repeatedly. International affairs often had a Protestant-Catholic dimension, and how far imperial authorities should endorse Christian missions was another perennial question. Evangelicals strongly supported each side in the American Civil War, and the black slaves it emancipated, though continuing to suffer serious social restrictions, nonetheless used their freedom to build up their own denominations. Population growth meant more people to evangelize, while migration carried Christian allegiance from one continent to another. Those who prospered through industrialization often adopted a more cultivated taste and could afford to pay for its indulgence. Hence they built churches in a more elaborate style and expected more refined sermons from their preachers. The rising tide of respectability, in fact, was one of the forces that exercised the most influence over religion during the period. The plight of those who shared little in the new affluence, on the other hand, stirred the Christian conscience of those who turned to the social gospel at the end of the period. Better communications, together with widespread education, meant that the latest news and novel ideas spread rapidly. Evangelicals knew what was happening among their fellow believers on the other side of the globe and were often swayed by their opinions or inspired by their schemes. Hence there was a large-scale interchange between evangelicals in different lands. As we shall see, the movement possessed a high degree of unity across the world. Already during the later nineteenth century evangelicalism was contributing in a major way to globalization.

1

THE EVANGELICALS
OF THE WORLD

In 1846 the Evangelical Alliance was formed to bring together the Protestants all over the world who were the heirs of the awakening of the previous century. Its basis of faith, designed to express the "prominent characteristics of the designation evangelical,"[1] had been drawn up in the previous year by a subcommittee representing the British Isles alone, but it was approved unanimously at the founding conference that included a substantial American and continental presence. Its clauses therefore reveal what beliefs the founding evangelicals believed to be the common property of the movement around the middle of the nineteenth century. One clause, it is true, had occasioned considerable doubt because, by affirming the obligation of upholding the Christian ministry, baptism and the Lord's Supper, it had effectively excluded Brethren, who rejected the ministry, and Quakers, who repudiated the sacraments. Yet other evangelicals insisted that these institutions were of sufficient importance to incorporate them in the basis. The remaining clauses were less controversial. There were articles asserting the doctrines of the Trinity, of human sin and of the last things, but three other topics call for particular comment. There were two clauses on the Bible. One professed the inspiration and authority of the Scriptures and another the responsibility of private judgment in their interpretation. There were also two on conversion. The sinner was declared, in the manner of the Reformation, to be justified by faith alone, and

---

[1]J. W. Massie, *The Evangelical Alliance: Its Origin and Development* (London: n.p., 1847), p. 357, quoted by J. B. A. Kessler, *A Study of the Evangelical Alliance in Great Britain* (Goes, Netherlands: Oosterbaan & Le Cointre N.V., 1968), p. 31.

the Holy Spirit was identified as the agent of conversion (the word had originally been *regeneration*) as well as sanctification. Another clause confessed the
incarnation, atonement and mediatorial intercession of Christ. The work of
Christ in redemption was clearly regarded as central to the faith.[2] The Bible,
conversion and redemption were cardinal articles in the evangelical creed. If
the authors of the document had gone on to specify what Christians should
do alongside what they should believe, they would undoubtedly have put the
preaching of the gospel at the head of their list. Dedicated effort to the spread
of the Christian message was assumed to be the duty of believers. Activism, in
fact, was as much a feature of the evangelical world as what was specified in
the basis of the Alliance. Hallmarks of the evangelicals included a stress on the
Scriptures as the source of faith, conversion as its beginning, redemption as its
object and activity as its consequence.

The same four characteristics, albeit variously formulated, regularly appeared in evangelical statements about the kernel of Christianity. Evangelicals
were normally orthodox in the sense of sharing with other Christians—Eastern
or Roman Catholic, Lutheran or High-Church Anglican—an acceptance of
the beliefs expressed in the ancient creeds of the church. But it was not these
doctrines that they normally stressed. They usually preferred to dwell on what,
as a package, distinguished them from other orthodox Christians. Even the Anglicans amongst them, those who weekly recited the Apostles' Creed in church,
insisted that the supreme characteristics of vital Christianity were different
from the formal traditions of higher churchmanship. Thus a leading article in
the journal of the Evangelicals in the Church of England in Australia declared
in 1857 that they existed to maintain "the pure unadulterated Gospel of salvation by the blood of Christ, and of justification, only by faith in that blood, of
sanctification by the operation of the Holy Spirit, and of the supreme authority
of the inspired Word of God in all matters of faith and practice." "To us," it
went on, "emphatically belongs also to convey these truths to the ignorant, the
careless, the immoral, and all who are persisting in sin."[3] Like the framers of the
Evangelical Alliance basis, the writer wanted to lay down that the believer
should make spiritual progress through sanctification, but there is also insis-

---

[2] Kessler, *Evangelical Alliance*, p. 28.
[3] *Church of England Chronicle* (Sydney), January 1, 1857, p. 65.

tence on the birth of Christian life through justification, on the Bible as the Word of God and, with double emphasis, on the blood shed by Christ. The redeeming work of Christ is understood, as it normally was in evangelical professions of faith, as having been achieved by his atoning death on the cross. And there is an explicit avowal of the responsibility of the believer to take the gospel to the hitherto unconverted. Evangelicalism typically chose to give prominence to conversion, the Bible, the cross and missionary activity.

Nor did these features disappear during the second half of the nineteenth century. Although (as we shall see) some of them faded in certain quarters and all of them underwent unconscious change and deliberate adaptation, these qualities remained the defining features of evangelicalism down to the end of the century and beyond. In the 1880s the South African Methodists, in an annual address of their conference to the members, expressed very similar views. "We are determined, as ever, to know nothing among you save Jesus Christ and him crucified. . . . We invite you, and all men, to behold the Lamb of God, and by faith to realise a present, conscious pardon. . . . We cannot urge you too strongly to search the Scriptures. . . . Let the heathen of this Dark Continent have the gospel."[4] There were the typical emphases on the atoning work of Christ on the cross; the need for personal faith through conversion; the supreme value of the Bible; and the binding obligation of mission. What we can call crucicentrism, conversionism, biblicism and activism formed the enduring priorities of the evangelical movement throughout the English-speaking world.

THE BIBLE

The place of the Bible, always the supreme evangelical court of appeal, can be explored first. "There is," announced the newspaper of the American Free Methodists in 1884, "but one final standard of Christian living, or Christian doctrine. That standard is the Word of God, revealed to man in the Holy Scriptures."[5] Theology was therefore rooted in the Bible, often being little more than a pastiche of scriptural quotations. The consequences could be intellectually restrictive. Because the General Baptist was very much "a man of

---

[4]*Minutes of the Second Conference of the Wesleyan Methodist Church of South Africa* (Grahamstown: Richards, Slater & Co., 1884), pp. 60, 64.
[5]*Free Methodist* (Chicago), January 9, 1884, p. 1.

one book," the magazine of the English denomination admitted, he was often
"too neglectful of the theological writings of men."[6] That charge could rarely
be leveled at Anglican clergy, who were normally university men, but they nevertheless took the Bible as their single rule of faith. "God's Word Written, the
Sole and Sufficient Authority in Things Spiritual" was the title of a typical address at the annual Islington Clerical Conference of Evangelicals.[7] That did
not necessarily entail an obscurantist approach to the Bible, treating all its passages as of equal religious value. The New Testament, though much shorter
than the Old, was far more frequently used as the source of texts for sermons—in Ulster, for example, twice as often as the Old Testament during the
second half of the century as a whole.[8] Congregations, at least in Presbyterian
Scotland, were used to paying close attention to the scriptural passage chosen
for exposition. A visiting American recorded his experience of a church at
Lochearnhead in Argyll in 1857:

> The congregation all read with the minister. As soon as the text is read there is
> a rustle all over the church until the place was [sic] found and the Bible is laid
> down open before each one. When the preacher completes one head and takes
> another, all look at the text to see where he derived it.[9]

This critical approach, though evidently less familiar in America, could
hardly fail to be intellectually stimulating. In evangelical circles it was regarded
as a severe misfortune to be illiterate because the handicap denied the believer
direct access to the source of Christian teaching. That is one of the main reasons why illiteracy, still quite common in England at midcentury, was virtually
banished by 1900.[10] The Bible was expected to be the origin of the ideology of
the movement.

The Scriptures were also used for private devotion, usually on a daily basis.
One English Wesleyan Methodist woman made it her aim to go through the Bible once every year; a Canadian coreligionist was said to have read the whole of

---

[6]*General Baptist Magazine* (London), January 1854, p. 11.

[7]*Record* (London), January 18, 1889, p. 50.

[8]J. N. Ian Dickson, "More than Discourse: The Sermons of Evangelical Protestants in
Nineteenth Century Ulster" (PhD diss., Queen's University, Belfast, 2000), p. 111.

[9]*North Carolina Presbyterian* (Fayetteville, N.C.), January 15, 1858.

[10]David Vincent, *Literacy and Popular Culture: England, 1750-1914* (Cambridge: Cambridge
University Press, 1989).

it through fifteen times.[11] Standard advice was to read slowly, taking time to ponder, to assimilate the meaning and to learn the art of accurate quotation. The resulting familiarity with the text was a profound source of comfort, especially in adversity or illness. Philena Richmond, a Methodist woman of Columbia County, New York, was helpless for the last four years before her death in 1861, but she enjoyed a source of strength. "Her Bible was always near her, with leaves turned down and passages marked on its pages, impressing you with the feeling that there was the fountain of her happiness, her patience, her resignation."[12] Likewise a Virginia Baptist who died four years earlier clearly drew inspiration from the Scriptures. "Though fond of reading all good books, the Bible was his constant companion in health and in sickness. To him its promises were sweet."[13] The biblical promises, the assurances of divine help, were particularly cherished. Evangelicals would often emphasize favorite passages or else jot down thoughts in the margins of their Bibles. Thus the copy belonging to a New Zealand Methodist woman contained "numerous marks and underlinings," an indication, according to her obituarist, that she had been "a diligent student of the Blessed volume."[14] The family Bible lying on the parlor table became a Protestant icon, a testimony of religious allegiance as well as a means of spiritual guidance.[15]

The distribution of the Bible was one of the chief evangelical enterprises of the period. During the fifteen years from 1854 onward, the British and Foreign Bible Society, which had been founded in 1804 to print and disseminate the Scriptures, issued an average of nearly two million copies annually of Bibles, New Testaments or Scripture portions; by the end of the century the figure had risen to five million.[16] In 1873, when Colorado was still largely an empty tract of desert and mountain, the territory already contained nine auxiliary Bible societies, two branch Bible societies, two Bible committees and fourteen Bible depositories.[17] At intervals the American Bible Society undertook a general sup-

---

[11] *Wesleyan Methodist Magazine* (London), March 1860, p. 281. *Christian Guardian* (Toronto), February 11, 1880, p. 47.

[12] *Christian Advocate and Journal* (New York), January 16, 1862, p. 22.

[13] *Religious Herald* (Richmond, Va.), January 7, 1858.

[14] *Christian Observer* (Christchurch), February 1, 1870, p. 22.

[15] Colleen McDannell, *Material Christianity: Religion and Popular Culture in America* (New Haven: Yale University Press, 1995), chap. 3.

[16] William Canton, *The Story of the Bible Society* (London: John Murray, 1904), pp. 354-55.

[17] *Rocky Mountain Presbyterian* (Denver, Colo.), January 1873.

ply, aiming to use colporteurs to introduce the Scriptures into every home in
the land—even though in the effort that lasted from 1882 to 1890 it managed
to put copies in the hands of no more than 10 percent of the population.[18] It
was a cause that excited devotion and self-denial. Around 1860 a collector for
the American Bible Society in Florida approached an old bricklayer for a sub-
scription. When the man offered the considerable sum of ten dollars, the collector was going to put him down for only one dollar, thinking that was all he
could afford. But the bricklayer would have none of it. "He said No, he was
going to give the ten; that the Bible was the bread of life to him, and fed his
soul; that his old body that was almost worthless cost him a hundred dollars a
year. The old man talked about the Bible and giving until he got happy and
shouted."[19] The enthusiasm for the Bible sometimes resulted in stout defense
of its place in the schools provided for the mass of the people. As national education systems were put in place during the period, tensions often erupted. In
Prahran Town Hall in the Australian colony of Victoria, for example, there was
a protest meeting in 1890 under the auspices of the National Scripture Education League against the secular policy of excluding the Bible from state-aided
schools. An atheist had the temerity to move an amendment to the effect that
the Bible was an unfit and immoral book. "This, of course," according to the
press report, "aroused the hot indignation of the audience, who protested
against hearing another word in condemnation of the beloved Book."[20] More
will need to be said about how the popular biblicism was called into question
by intellectual challenges during the period, but here it needs to be registered
that allegiance to the Bible was one of the deepest convictions of evangelical
Christians of all stripes.

THE CROSS

The second distinctive aspect of the evangelicals was their attachment to the
doctrine of the cross. The sacrifice of Christ on Calvary was the way in which
the salvation described in the Bible was won for humanity. Preachers often dwelt

---

[18]Paul C. Gutjahr, *An American Bible: A History of the Good Book in the United States, 1777-1880*
(Stanford, Calif.: Stanford University Press, 1999), p. 33.
[19]S. P. Richardson, *The Lights and Shadows of Itinerant Life* (Nashville: Publishing House of the
Methodist Episcopal Church, South, 1900), p. 162.
[20]*Spectator and Methodist Chronicle* (Melbourne), January 16, 1891, p. 55.

on the Pauline manifesto of preaching "Jesus Christ, and Him crucified." If that was made the great object of their lives, avowed the journal of the emancipationist American Congregationalists at the new year of 1857, they would stem the decay of religion.[21] That was the text quoted in the address of the Australasian Methodist conference to its English superior in the following year as a summary of its conception of its mission.[22] When Andrew Murray, the son of a Scottish Presbyterian minister who had immigrated to the Cape to serve in the Dutch Reformed Church, returned from training in the Netherlands in 1848, his first sermon was on the nearby verse, "We preach Christ crucified," and when he was inducted in the following year, remarkably, he selected the identical text. He wrote to his father that the "one glorious central truth" that he intended to proclaim was "the amazing wonder of the love of a crucified Jesus."[23] In exactly the same way a preacher told the General Assembly of the Presbyterian Church in Ireland in 1861 that the "one grand prevailing principle of the Christian message" is "the redemption of a lost world through the sacrifice of Christ."[24] The Pastor's College created by Charles H. Spurgeon was said by its principal, George Rogers, to have the cross as "the centre of our system."[25] Even when, later in the century, more advanced thinkers began to broaden received teaching, they paid their respects to the doctrine of the atonement. When, in 1893, N. S. Needham, a Massachusetts Congregational minister, wanted to suggest that vicarious suffering was not just part of the story of Calvary but was also a theme of Christ's existence both before and after the incarnation, he conceded that the Scriptures "lay great emphasis on the death of Christ as the prevailing cause of pardon for sinners."[26] And when Henry Drummond, a prominent Scottish evangelist of broad sympathies, felt that, because the atonement was on the point of

---

[21] *American Missionary* (New York), January 1857, p. 11.

[22] *Minutes of the Methodist Conference* (London: John Mason, 1862), 10:148.

[23] Johannes du Plessis, *The Life of Andrew Murray of South Africa* (London: Marshall Brothers, 1919), pp. 76, 87, 91.

[24] S. M. Dill, *The Old Paths: A Sermon preached before the General Assembly of the Presbyterian Church in Ireland, on Monday, July 1st, 1861* (Belfast, 1861), p. 14, quoted by Dickson, "More than Discourse," p. 120.

[25] *Outline of the Lord's Work by the Pastor's College and its Kindred Organisations at the Metropolitan Tabernacle* (London: Passmore & Alabaster, 1867), p. 13.

[26] "The Vicarious Element in the Divine Government," *Bibliotheca Sacra* (New York), April 1893, p. 237.

being discredited, its underlying kernel of the law of sacrifice needed to be extracted from the shell, he readily admitted that it was "that central doctrine."[27] There was remarkable unanimity, among figures in all parties, that the cross of Christ was the focus of evangelical religion.

Evangelicals were accustomed to contrast their position on this question with the attitude of other groups. In a collection of essays on *Evangelical Principles* issued by members of the Church of England in 1875, W. R. Fremantle explained that there were two views of the atonement. There was the Reformation view that reconciliation was possible through the obedience of Christ to death; and there was the Rationalist view that God demands no atonement because of his eternal love. That was to set a stark contrast where in reality there were many gradations of belief, but the evangelical understanding did differ from more liberal ideas in insisting that, because of the gravity of sin, there was an imperative need for redemption. The means, according to Fremantle, was substitution, which he explained as the taking by Christ of the place of sinful humanity as its representative.[28] On the cross the Son of God bore the burden of sin so that believers might be forgiven. There were debates about the precise nature of substitution, but some form of the belief was the received opinion of evangelicals in this period. They also contrasted their convictions about salvation with the view that the incarnation was the way in which the Almighty had achieved reconciliation. This view, common alike among High and Broad Churchmen in Anglicanism, seemed to downgrade the uniqueness of Calvary. David Brown, a leading theologian of the Free Church of Scotland, declared that his fixed position was that "the propitiatory sacrifice of the Lord's death" was "the central article of Christianity—not the Incarnation."[29] Sometimes, it is true, evangelicals saw High Churchmen as allies against the creeping advance of theological laxity. The editor of the Sydney Methodist newspaper, for example, reprinted an extract on the atonement from one of the sermons of E. B. Pusey, the leader of the Anglo-Catholics, "as setting forth the orthodox view of a great Christian

---

[27] Henry Drummond, "The Method of the New Evangelism and Some of its Applications," in *The New Evangelism and Other Papers* (London: Hodder & Stoughton, 1899), p. 56.

[28] W. R. Fremantle, "Atonement," in *Evangelical Principles*, ed. Edward Garbett (London: William Hunt and Co., 1875), pp. 71, 82.

[29] W. G. Blaikie, *David Brown, D. D., Ll. D.: Professor and Principal of the Free Church College, Aberdeen: A Memoir* (London: Hodder & Stoughton, 1898), p. 265.

doctrine." Inevitably, however, he was challenged by one of his readers who claimed that Pusey had blundered by asserting that humanity could have been freed from sin by the physical power of God. The teaching of Paul, went on the correspondent, was that there was no way without the sacrifice of Christ.[30] He was claiming that the conviction of evangelicals, bolstered by Scripture itself, was unique. There was, in truth, normally a substantial difference between evangelicals and other Christians in the weight or the interpretation—or in both—that they put on the event of the crucifixion.

Teaching about the cross was therefore the supreme means by which souls were turned to Christ. In the journal published by the Presbyterian mission at Lovedale in southern Africa, one of the "messages about salvation" that it carried was that "the blood alone saves." "Stake your life for eternity on that blood," it urged, "on that death of Christ for you."[31] The atonement was equally central to ongoing spirituality, for it was the avenue to the regular forgiveness sought by evangelicals in the Calvinist tradition and the victory over temptation craved by those in the Methodist bodies. The importance of Christ's redemption was magnified as the end of life approached. A dying Congregational minister in England "thought of the efficacy of Christ's blood"; another, when a visitor noticed that the pillow of his deathbed needed adjusting, remarked, with more than a touch of banality, "*But*, comfortable thoughts arise from the bleeding sacrifice!"[32] A Merseyside Methodist was tempted as he lay dying to suppose that his religion was merely profession. But (his obituarist recorded) he was enabled to overcome the temptation and shout, "The conflict is over—I look to the Crucified—I rest in the atonement—Glory be to Jesus!"[33] Even if these were not the exact words, the notion that these would be the sentiments of a man *in extremis* reveals the expectation of the Methodist community about what would provide the most spiritual support. It was not the physical detail of the atonement that mattered—Catholic devotion had often made more of the nails or the crown of thorns—but the spiritual power of Christ the redeemer. Indeed, a committee of Canadian Methodism set up in 1874 revised its hymn book so as to exclude objectionable passages from hymns about the

---

[30] *Christian Advocate and Wesleyan Record* (Sydney), March 1, 1876, p. 188; June 2, 1876, p. 39.

[31] *Christian Express* (Lovedale, South Africa), February 1, 1876, p. 15.

[32] *Christian Witness* (London), 1852, pp. 370, 257.

[33] *Wesleyan Methodist Magazine*, March 1860, p. 283.

crucifixion if they were guilty of "extreme literalness."[34] Nor was the cross used
as a physical symbol by evangelicals in this period. No woman would have worn
a cruciform ornament, which was popish; no cross appeared on the holy table
of an evangelical church, even in the Anglican tradition, since that too savored
of Rome. The only New Testament symbols, thundered the *Irish Presbyterian* in
1853, were water, bread and wine. A cross might be seen on the spires of church
buildings—even on Presbyterian buildings in Scotland—but the practice was
deplorable, a form of "will-worship."[35] Yet, so long as it was held in heart and
mind alone, the cross carried potent Christian significance. "It is the symbol,"
declared Dr. John Miley, an American Methodist divine, in 1880, "of all that
is most vital in Christianity, the center of all that is deepest and dearest in our
religious consciousness."[36]

The prominence of the cross in evangelicalism could sometimes occasion
heart searchings. They are well illustrated by a letter from Ernest Coulthard, an
Anglican ordination candidate at Cambridge, to Handley Moule, the principal
of his theological college, Ridley Hall. Coulthard was one of the first set of
eight men to enter the college when it opened in 1881 to provide training for
intending Evangelical clergy. He was a man of some sensitivity, as Moule's later
description of him as a natural pastor suggests,[37] and in the letter, undated but
apparently written while he was still a student, he explains that he was having
difficulty in coming to terms with the doctrine of the atonement. It was not
that he doubted its truth; he had "no sympathy whatever with the invertebrate
style of modern teaching which practically ignores it." Yet he found that many
good and great men were giving the cross an exclusive position: "so much so
that preaching 'the gospel' has come to mean with many preaching the doctrine
of the atonement." Consequently, "a man is soon regarded as 'unsound' who
does not instantly & systematically press that doctrine to the front as the only
aspect of Salvation." There was a good deal of evidence, however, that it was
receiving disproportionate attention. The doctrine was not prominent in the

---

[34] Alexander Sutherland, *Methodism in Canada: Its Work and its Story* (London: Charles H. Kelly, 1903), p. 330.

[35] *Irish Presbyterian* (Belfast), December 1853, pp. 323-24.

[36] *Christian Advocate* (New York), January 29, 1880, p. 65.

[37] F. W. B. Bullock, *The History of Ridley Hall, Cambridge*, 2 vols. (Cambridge: Cambridge University Press, 1941-1953), I:174, 356.

Gospels, the book of Acts or even in some of the Epistles; other "good & earnest men" thrust it forward less; and some theologians (Coulthard was conscious of High-Church developments) believed that the incarnation was instead central to the divine purposes. Perhaps some Evangelicals were distorting the balance of the faith by reading the atonement into verses where it did not belong. Could Moule help? The reply does not survive, though from the subsequent long and fruitful ministry of Coulthard in the parishes it appears likely that his doubts were settled. But what the letter reveals is the recognition by a thoughtful individual that the tradition placed so great an emphasis on the cross that, in some hands, the very message of the Bible as a whole was being misrepresented. Yet before he finished writing, the young ordinand reaffirmed "how much I value the doctrine of the Atonement because I believe it is divinely given to appeal straight to the human heart."[38] Coulthard remained a loyal Evangelical.

CONVERSION

A third characteristic of the movement was that its members looked for conversions. A normal preliminary was a sense of despair. An Ontario teenager, the son of Congregationalist parents, reached the point in 1885 where he cried out, "Oh, God, I'm lost, there's no use of me trying to be good." It soon dawned on him, however, that, according to the Bible, Christ died for the ungodly, and, he recalled, "I passed from death unto life."[39] The actual change, it was believed, was the result of supernatural intervention in a person's life. "All that a man can do for himself religiously is to reform," wrote an Ohio Methodist in 1895; "but he can convert his soul no more than he can change the colour of his eyes."[40] So, as the *American Missionary* put it in 1858, "it is the instant and practicable duty of every sinner to yield to the Spirit, and become, by repentance and faith, a new creature in Jesus Christ."[41] Not all evangelicals would have phrased the idea in the same way, but nearly all would have agreed that the in-

---

[38]Ernest N. Coulthard to Handley C. G. Moule, March 17, [no year], inserted in Lecture Notebook, Handley Moule Papers, Ridley Hall, Cambridge.

[39]J. J. Rouse, *Pioneer Work in Canada Practically Presented* (Kilmarnock: John Ritchie, 1935), p. 15.

[40]*Methodist Review* (New York), January 1895, p. 131.

[41]*American Missionary*, July 1858, p. 159.

dividual had to exercise repentance, or a deliberate turning away from sin, and faith, or trust in Christ as Savior. The young were much more likely to undergo conversion than older people. Of a group of over a hundred converts who joined Thirteenth Street Presbyterian Church during the "businessmen's revival" in New York early in 1858, 56 percent were under twenty and 90 percent were under thirty.[42] Another sample at the end of the century, this time of a thousand people, yielded the information that at the time of their conversion 69 percent were under twenty and (again) 90 percent under thirty.[43] Hence evangelicals often made the conversion of children a paramount aim. How, asked a questioner in the *Rocky Mountain Presbyterian* in 1872, should a Sunday school teacher go to his class? "In God's strength," was the reply from the editor, "determened [*sic*] to get every one of his class interested in the salvation of his soul."[44] But the young were not the only ones targeted. Evangelicals never forgot that there were some in their pews who were strangers to vital religion. The English *Wesleyan Methodist Magazine* sounded an "Alarm to Unconverted Christians" in 1864:

> You give, it may be pleaded, your time, your wealth, your influence, and this in a hundred ways, for the furtherance of the cause of Christ in the world. Granted: and you perhaps even preach the Gospel to others, and you are ready to give your "body to be burned" in testimony of it. But what of this? Not a single prayer has yet ascended to God from our own renewed soul, yearning for the conversion of the world. . . . Christ has to do with you, to break your heart, to melt your soul, to bring you a happy captive to Himself.[45]

What was called "nominal Christianity" was not enough: there must be personal conversion.

The theological concept closest to conversion was regeneration. Those who were converted could equally be described as "born again." The two developments were sometimes described as identical, as they were by William Harrison, an Evangelical Anglican speaking at the Islington conference in 1860.[46] More

---

[42] *United Presbyterian Magazine* (Edinburgh), May 1858, p. 238.

[43] Arthur T. Pierson, *Forward Movements of the Last Half Century* (New York: Funk and Wagnalls, 1900), p. 207.

[44] *Rocky Mountain Presbyterian*, March 1872.

[45] *Wesleyan Methodist Magazine*, February 1860, p. 118.

[46] *Record*, January 16, 1860, p. 3.

often conversion was considered to be the human dimension of the process and regeneration its divine side. It was God who brought souls to new birth. In 1857, at a protracted meeting in Bracken County, Kentucky, for example, it was said that "The Lord was pleased to smile upon the means used, and beget sons and daughters."[47] Another theological term associated with conversion was justification. The part of the transaction called justification by faith, according to the widely traveled Methodist Episcopal bishop William Taylor, was when God sees sinners surrender and acquits them of their sin.[48] Believers subsequently trusted that they were treated by the Almighty as righteous even though they had previously been guilty. As the century wore on, this venerable Reformation principle faded from prominence. Although justification by faith might still be received by the heart, according to the English Congregationalist R. W. Dale in 1889, it was ceasing to be grasped by the mind of his contemporaries.[49] Conversion, as the doughty Irish Presbyterian theologian Robert Watts had complained a quarter of a century earlier, was understood in contrasting ways by different groups of Christians. Watts wanted to ensure that superficial ideas about the experience, including ones that it was a mere correction of views about God or a simple change of purpose, did not supplant more doctrinally freighted estimates. Properly, he claimed, conversion was the same phenomenon as the "effectual calling" described in the Shorter Catechism of the Westminster Assembly. "It comprises," he explained, "the entire change through which a sinner passes in his transition from the kingdom of Satan to the kingdom of God."[50] It was the start (and here all evangelicals would have agreed) of authentic Christian existence.

The biggest difference of opinion in the evangelical community over conversion related to its timing. Was it always the experience of a moment or could it be a long, perhaps unconscious process? The *Australian Evangelist* insisted in 1866 that a person is saved when he comes to Jesus: "Saved where I am, as I am, the very instant I know I am a sinner, the very instant I know Jesus Christ is the

---

[47] *American Missionary*, April 1857, p. 77.

[48] *William Taylor of California, Bishop of Africa: An Autobiography*, ed. C. G. Moore (London: Hodder & Stoughton, 1897), p. 204.

[49] Robert W. Dale, *The Old Evangelicalism and the New* (London: Hodder & Stoughton, 1889), pp. 51-57.

[50] *Evangelical Witness and Presbyterian Review* (Dublin), May 1863, p. 171.

sinner's friend."[51] Methodists traditionally favored the idea of a sudden change, expecting prospective converts to go through long agonies of soul before coming to the joy of salvation. "I have got it at last!" cried the young daughter of a Florida judge when she reached the end of her earnest quest for personal faith.[52] The crisis was momentous but also momentary. Revivalists, though often deprecating any need for a long search, favored an immediatist understanding of conversion. Although a Chicago journal associated with the revivalist Dwight L. Moody admitted in 1882 that many people were troubled by the notion of sudden conversion, it had a reply: "does not a man become a soldier when he enlists?"[53] Others, however, felt that the change was usually a long drawn out affair. "We find," declared an Anglican Evangelical in 1859, "very few sudden conversions recorded in the word of God."[54] The children of Christian homes, more respectable evangelicals tended to believe, would usually grow into believers without any crisis. Thus Frances Ridley Havergal, the future hymnwriter who was the daughter of an Anglican clergyman, could not fix the date of her conversion.[55] It was wicked and foolish, according to the Free Church of Scotland theologian James Denney, to expect a person to be able to assign a time to the event.[56] Only one in twenty Christians, estimated an article reproduced in the New York Baptist newspaper in 1865, could do so.[57] There was a trend over time for the expectation of instant conversion to weaken. There was less emphasis now, according to R. W. Dale in 1889, on a definite moment of transition from death to life.[58] Methodists echoed him. They still believed in the possibility of instant conversion, stated the English Methodist George Jackson in a lecture at Wesleyan University in Middletown, Connecticut, just after the close of the century, but they knew that they must not insist on any particular type of conversion.[59] Even a leading Methodist evangelist, Thomas Cook, ad-

---

[51] *Australian Evangelist* (Melbourne), July 3, 1866, p. 204.

[52] Richardson, *Lights and Shadows*, p. 141.

[53] *Evangelistic Record* (Chicago), May 1882, p. 3.

[54] *Christian Observer* (London), November 1859, p. 730.

[55] Maria V. G. Havergal, *Memorials of Frances Ridley Havergal* (London: James Nisbet, 1880), p. 38.

[56] James Denney, *On "Natural Law in the Spiritual World"* (Paisley: Alexander Gardner, 1885), p. 33.

[57] *Examiner and Chronicle* (New York), July 20, 1865.

[58] Dale, *Old Evangelicalism*, p. 43.

[59] George Jackson, *The Old Methodism and the New* (London: Hodder & Stoughton, 1903), pp. 37-38.

mitted that not all conversions must be sudden.[60] The experience tended to become less of a cataclysm and more of an evolution.

"Why," asked a Methodist itinerant from the American South in 1900, "are people not converted now as they were fifty years ago?"[61] Similarly in Britain the *British Weekly* carried a series of articles in 1896 on the dearth of conversions.[62] Fewer took place, fewer were looked for and fewer were drastic reorientations. Already in the late 1850s John Angell James, a leading English Congregationalist whose ministry went back to the early years of the century, was worrying that in many Dissenting pulpits "the necessity of an entire inward change of heart" was being "merged in vague general notions of a religious state, which implies no quickening from a death of sin to a life of righteousness."[63] By the later years of the century, however, matters had proceeded much further. In 1887, a correspondent asked the editor of the leading American Methodist weekly for help. "I joined the Church," the enquirer explained, "because I resolved to try and be one of Christ's followers. . . . Ever since I have tried, with God's help, to live a true Christian life. . . . Yet I am not at rest. I do not know that I have ever been converted. . . . What shall I do?" In the past a Methodist minister would have urged the writer to press on to salvation, but now the reply was different:

> Your experience may not be bright and clear; so there was a certain man who said: "Lord, I believe; help thou mine unbelief." . . . It is not the quantity, but the kind of faith that saves. Do you earnestly and truly repent of your sins, and do you trust in Christ? If so, "give to the winds thy fears, hope and be undismayed."[64]

Reassurance took precedence over trying to ensure authentic conversion. Even more cavalier attitudes were current. A member of Algonquin Congregational Church, Illinois, recounted in 1897 "how the minister had persuaded her to join the church, and when she told him she was not saved, he said, 'Never

---

[60] H. T. Smart, *The Life of Thomas Cook: Evangelist and First Principal of Cliff College, Calver* (London: Charles H. Kelly, 1913), p. 274.

[61] Richardson, *Lights and Shadows*, p. 142.

[62] du Plessis, *Andrew Murray*, p. 471.

[63] Robert W. Dale, *The Life and Letters of John Angell James* (London: James Nisbet & Co., 1861), p. 311.

[64] *Christian Advocate*, January 6, 1887, p. 4.

mind, you are as good as the rest of them.'"[65] Obituaries in the denominational press, which had once consisted largely of expanded conversion narratives, now often omitted the subject entirely. By 1903, less than half the candidates for the Wesleyan ministry in Britain could testify to a definite conversion experience, the majority preferring language about gradual enlightenment or conviction.[66] Conversion began to be subjected to psychological analysis, whether by William James in his classic study of 1902, *The Varieties of Religious Experience*, or in local gatherings, where older brethren shook their heads in dismay.[67] The more revivalist groups such as the disciples of Moody in America or the inheritors of Spurgeon's mantle in England suffered from no qualms about continuing to exhort sinners to repent and believe. Many of those in more broadminded sections of the diverse evangelical world were merely formulating the dawning of Christian allegiance in looser terms. But there is no doubt that the attachment to conversion was starting to be eroded in many of the mainstream denominations before the end of the nineteenth century.

ACTIVISM

The final mark of the evangelicals was an eagerness to be up and doing. This activism was in a sense a logical corollary of the awareness of having undergone conversion. "It is the duty," announced the chief American Baptist newspaper in 1868, "of every one who knows *the good news* of salvation through Christ to *tell* the good news, as he has opportunity and ability, to his companion who does not know it, that he too may be saved."[68] The theory was translated into sustained effort. "After it pleased the Lord to convert my soul," reported an elderly correspondent from Greene County, Pennsylvania, to the same newspaper, "I went to work in holding prayer-meetings, distributing tracts, and visiting the houses of the unconverted, to tell the people the glad tidings of salvation; I have lived to see a church of 218 members raised up."[69] Christian work, according to a leading article in the Irish Presbyterian magazine for 1873, was

---

[65]*Free Methodist*, January 11, 1898, p. 4.
[66]Kenneth D. Brown, *A Social History of the Nonconformist Ministry in England and Wales, 1800-1930* (Oxford: Clarendon Press, 1988), p. 53.
[67]*Religious Herald*, January 13, 1898, p. 2.
[68]*Examiner and Chronicle*, January 2, 1868.
[69]Ibid., April 27, 1865.

an element of strength in any church: "the great heart of humanity recognizes the pastors and church members that are self-denied, working hard, publicly and from house to house, Sabbath day and week day, in season, out of season."[70] The ideal was expressed in an obituary of Horace Clark, a Methodist layman who died in Amenia Union, New York, in 1861: "He was an active, ardent Christian, always at the post of duty; ready to work for God, and participating in and enjoying the means of grace."[71] Methodism gave particularly wide scope for lay responsibility, requiring a plethora of society stewards, class leaders, local preachers and prayer meeting leaders as well as Sunday school teachers, home visitors and practical handymen. The General Rules that formed one of John Wesley's legacies to his societies, it was still recalled in the 1880s, had warned against "softness and needless self-indulgence." What, asked a correspondent of the New York Methodist newspaper, did those words mean? The official reply was that they covered "over-feeding, over-sleeping, over-clothing, idleness, pampering the body, living an easy, idle life, regarding work as an evil, and gratifying the appetites and passions."[72] Inactivity was clearly a high crime and misdemeanor.

If hard Christian work was expected of laypeople, even more intense dedication was required in the ministry. *"Ministers of the Gospel!"* screamed an article in the Irish Presbyterian journal for 1864, "are you doing your utmost? You, of all men, are to be workers and labourers."[73] The ordination charge by the president of the Australasian Wesleyan conference three years later dwelt on the same point. "All true ministers are 'workmen.' Be ye 'workmen'—not idlers, not slothful men, not lovers of ease; but 'workmen'—labourers in the Lord's vineyard. Indolence never looks worse in any one than in a Christian minister."[74] Spurgeon, as was his wont, put it more pungently. "Brethren," he urged his students training for the ministry, "do something; do something; do something. While committees waste their time over resolutions, do something."[75] Such

---

[70]*Evangelical Witness and Presbyterian Review,* January 1873, p. 2.

[71]*Christian Advocate and Journal,* January 16, 1862, p. 22.

[72]*Christian Advocate,* September 20, 1883, p. 597.

[73]*Evangelical Witness and Presbyterian Review,* July 1864, p. 182.

[74]*Christian Advocate and Wesleyan Record,* April 30, 1867, p. 16.

[75]Charles H. Spurgeon, *Lectures to My Students* (London: Marshall, Morgan & Scott, 1954), p. 217.

maxims were zealously put into practice. Thomas Valpy French, sent by the
Church Missionary Society in 1850 to run an English-language college at Agra
in north India, frequently put in sixteen hours' work a day; Thomas Collier, as
superintendent of the Wesleyan Manchester Central Hall at the end of the century, usually managed to grab only three hours' sleep a night.[76] Ministers frequently wore themselves out. A Wesleyan minister stationed at St. Vincent in
the West Indies had to return to England in 1850 after a year's severe illness,
the result of overtasking himself. People, he sighed, might warn missionaries
not to work too hard. "But, Sirs," he went on, "when brands are so near the
eternal burnings, we must snatch them away."[77] Even when superannuated,
ministers would seize opportunities. At stops on the railroad, Samuel Howe, a
retired Methodist Episcopal minister, would move passengers to tears by addressing them on their souls' salvation.[78] Some ministers longed for the rest of
the future life; but perhaps it is not surprising that others should not think of
heaven as a place of the idleness they deplored. "The great attraction of heaven
to me," according to Michael Taylor, an English Wesleyan minister, on his
deathbed in 1867, "is, that I shall still serve Him; to cease to do that would be
deprivation indeed."[79] Sheer hard work was a hallmark of the ministry.

The effort put in by evangelicals in this period was by no means confined
to evangelism. As Timothy L. Smith has shown for the United States and
Kathleen Heasman for England, social work that carried over into pressure
for reform was equally characteristic of this period.[80] Among Presbyterians of
the American West in 1872 it was axiomatic that a profession of Christianity
meant not only "a *constant activity* in cooperating with the brethren in the up-
building of the cause of Christ" but also "*war against sin wherever found and war
to the death*."[81] Lord Shaftesbury, with his multitude of campaigns for the vic-
tims of an urban/industrial society, was also the leading Evangelical layman

---

[76]"Thomas Valpy French, D. D.," in *Brief Sketches: C.M.S. Workers* (n.p., n.d.), 1:4. George Jack-
    son, *Collier of Manchester: A Friend's Tribute* (London: Hodder & Stoughton, 1923), p. 151.
[77]*Wesleyan Methodist Magazine*, October 1850, p. 1113.
[78]*Christian Advocate and Journal*, March 18, 1858, p. 44.
[79]*Wesleyan Methodist Magazine*, November 1867, p. 513.
[80]Timothy L. Smith, *Revivalism and Social Reform: American Protestantism on the Eve of the Civil War*
    (Nashville: Abingdon Press, 1957). Kathleen Heasman, *Evangelicals in Action: An Appraisal of
    Their Social Work in the Victorian Era* (London: Geoffrey Bles, 1962).
[81]*Rocky Mountain Presbyterian*, October 1872.

in the Church of England.[82] But he was only one of the host of evangelicals of all denominations who attempted to redress the social conditions of Victorian Britain. Thomas Guthrie, a minister of the Free Church of Scotland in Edinburgh, was responsible for promoting a network of ragged schools, such as those backed by Shaftesbury in England, to provide free education, with food and clothing thrown in, for destitute children in Scottish cities.[83] Andrew Reed, a London Congregational minister who died in 1862, had founded in succession the London Orphan Asylum, the Infant Orphan Asylum, the Asylum for Fatherless Children, the Asylum for Idiots and the Royal Hospital for Incurables.[84] Spurgeon established his own flourishing orphanage at Stockwell.[85] Places of worship customarily maintained funds for the relief of the poor associated with their own congregations and many extended their philanthropy far wider. In the hard winter of 1867-1868 the sufferings of the poor of New York became acute. "The duty of lightening this terrible pressure of want," announced the Baptist paper published in the city, "lies on the Christian people of New-York. They cannot shirk responsibility and be held blameless before God."[86] A wealthy Methodist widow of the same city was typical of her class in supporting the Five Points Mission, the Home for the Friendless and the Methodist Old Ladies' Home. The backing was not only in gifts during her lifetime and bequests on her death in 1865, but also entailed personal involvement in "benevolence to the poor."[87] At the first semiannual business meeting of the Young Men's Christian Association of Collins Street Baptist Church in Melbourne, Australia, in September 1866, the committee felt the need to urge "practical action" on its members. They might, it was suggested, visit the Immigrants' Home where they could speak to the "wrecks of humanity."[88] It was a representative impulse to do good to

---

[82]See chap. 3, p. 99-100.

[83]D. K. Guthrie and C .J. Guthrie, *Autobiography of Thomas Guthrie, D.D., and Memoir*, 2 vols. (London: W. Isbister, 1874), vol. 2, chap. 7.

[84]Andrew Reed and Charles Reed, *Memoirs of the Life and Philanthropic Labours of Andrew Reed, D.D., with Selections from His Journals* (London: Strahan & Co, 1863), chaps. 5-6, 10, 16-17.

[85]Ian Shaw, "Charles Spurgeon and the Stockwell Orphanage: A Forgotten Enterprise," *Christian Graduate* 29 (1976): 71-9.

[86]*Examiner and Chronicle*, January 9, 1868.

[87]*Christian Advocate*, February 8, 1866, p. 46.

[88]*Australian Evangelist*, September 18, 1866, p. 288.

the less fortunate members of society, a symptom of the large-hearted sense of mission that motivated evangelicals of the Victorian era.

CHARLES HADDON SPURGEON

The Christians across the globe who adhered to the four emphases of Bible, cross, conversion and activism numbered many outstanding figures in their ranks, but preeminent among them during the second half of the nineteenth century were two men, an Englishman and an American. Not least because they earned enormous respect and widespread imitation, their careers help to illustrate the characteristics of evangelicalism in the period. The Englishman, who was not from the established order in church or state, was nevertheless—or perhaps in consequence—a personality of national standing. He was a versatile, witty and pugnacious man who was rarely out of the headlines. By common consent he was the greatest English-speaking preacher of the century. His name was Charles Haddon Spurgeon.[89] Born in 1834, he was the son of a coalyard clerk who doubled as a part-time Independent minister at small churches in Essex. Converted under the preaching of a Primitive Methodist local preacher at the age of fifteen, Charles was soon baptized as a believer and became the pastor of a village Baptist church near Cambridge. In what afterward became a famous episode, he missed an appointment to meet the principal of Stepney College, to which he had applied for training, and so received no formal preparation for the pulpit. He developed his own style of vivid declamation, homely and pungent, yet strongly doctrinal and probingly experiential. It recommended him to New Park Street Baptist Church in Southwark, south London, one of the premier causes in the denomination, where in 1854, before he was twenty, he began to create a stir in the capital. Was he an astonishing boy wonder, or merely a presumptuous rustic? Crowds rapidly outgrew the old meeting house, and so the congregation moved successively to the Exeter Hall in the Strand, the meeting place for the great Evangelical societies, to the Surrey Gardens Music Hall, where a false alarm caused a panic in which seven people died, and finally, in 1861, to the purposely built Metropolitan Tabernacle. There, in a huge auditorium that catered to almost six thousand hearers, Spurgeon reigned from the

---

[89]The standard modern appraisal is Patricia S. Kruppa, *Charles Haddon Spurgeon: A Preacher's Progress* (New York: Garland Publishing, 1982).

platform down to his death in 1892. Bearded, stocky and with a thickset jaw, he had a striking presence. A female admirer thought in 1857 that "the square forehead and magnificent dark eyes" redeemed him from ugliness, with "every line of his face and figure speaking of power." Eight years later she thought that he had deteriorated, becoming "coarse-looking even to grossness, heavy in form and features," but "as soon as he spoke, one felt the same power was there and that the man himself was unchanged."[90] The sonorous voice, supplemented by dramatic gesture, conveyed a message that induced 14,460 individuals to be baptized and added to the church during his ministry. Spurgeon was one of the sights of London.

The preacher maintained the Reformed faith of his East Anglian forebears. "I cannot sever Evangelicalism," he declared in 1884, "from Calvinism."[91] At the college for training students for the Baptist ministry that he created alongside the Tabernacle, the curriculum was unashamedly based on Calvinist texts when other institutions of his denomination had dropped them. There was, however, far less rigidity in Spurgeon's theological position than might be supposed. He modified his views so as to accept the idea that Christian ventures should be run on the basis that God would provide funds without any canvassing for them, a principle which he unsuccessfully urged on the Baptist Missionary Society.[92] He readily had non-Calvinists lecture at his college and occupy his pulpit—among them the General Baptist John Clifford and the Morisonian William Landels, both upholders of species of Arminianism.[93] Spurgeon recommended books by contemporaries with whom he did not see wholly eye-to-eye. He was, in fact, a very bookish man. He collected the works of Puritan divines, assembling a personal library of over twelve thousand volumes. He urged churches to assemble their own libraries for ministers, his wife organized a book fund to supply reading for Christian workers and he founded a colportage society to sell religious literature from door-to-door. He was a notable author in

---

[90] Mrs. F. Curtis, *Memories of a Long Life* (privately printed, n.p., 1912), pp. 141, 145.

[91] *Freeman* (London), April 25, 1884, p. 270.

[92] Brian Stanley, "C. H. Spurgeon and the Baptist Missionary Society, 1863-1866," *Baptist Quarterly* 29 (1982).

[93] *Annual Paper descriptive of the Lord's Work connected with the Pastors' College, 1873-1874* (London: Passmore & Alabaster, 1874), p. 9. *The Sword and the Trowel* (London), December 1865, p. 515. On Morisonianism, see chap. 4, p. 139.

his own right. His most substantial work, *The Treasury of David* (1870-1885), was a thorough commentary on the Psalms in six volumes. Yet there was a homely utilitarianism about his writing. The *Treasury* contains "Hints for Village Preachers" and *John Ploughman's Talk* (1868), his most popular book, was a collection of proverbs about everyday life. "It is hard to shave an egg," ran one of them, "or pull hairs out of a bald pate, but they are both easier than paying debts out of an empty pocket."[94] His *Lectures to My Students* (1875-1894), replete with similar vivid epigrams, were likewise designed to be a severely practical guide to the work of the ministry. Advising his students to shun "the foolish affectation of intellectualism,"[95] Spurgeon practiced what he preached. Although he could on occasion quote ten lines of Homer (albeit in English translation), he did not parade his learning. He could sometimes be heard disparaging the classics, and, unlike most other theological colleges, Spurgeon's did not require its members to learn Latin, Greek or Hebrew if they showed little aptitude for languages. His students, he remarked, were not to be "apostles of Plato and Aristotle, but ministers of Christ."[96] It is perhaps not surprising that Matthew Arnold, the poet, literary critic and upholder of classical ideals, should select Spurgeon as an epitome of all that Arnold considered wrong with English Nonconformity. For Arnold, Spurgeon was a boor, a despiser of culture, a Hebraiser who showed an obsession with religion to the exclusion of the humane values of ancient Greece.[97] The preacher, for all his love of Puritan theology, lacked the classical education that was deemed essential by the elite of English society.

Spurgeon bore the reproach gladly. We are not, he told his students, "to be the lackeys of those who affect gentility or boast refinement." He disliked propriety, etiquette and the conventions of the drawing room. Ministers of the gospel in Victorian England should be like Martin Luther, strong, forthright and courageous. Like Luther, Spurgeon was quite content to court controversy. In 1864 he criticized the Evangelical clergy of the Church of England for remain-

---

[94]Charles H. Spurgeon, *John Ploughman's Talk* (London: Passmore & Alabaster, 1868), p. 86.

[95]Spurgeon, *Lectures*, p. 232.

[96]*Annual Paper descriptive of the Lord's Work connected with the Pastors' College during the Year 1870* (London: Passmore & Alabaster, 1871), p. 9.

[97]Matthew Arnold, *Culture and Anarchy*, ed. J. Dover Wilson (1869; reprint, Cambridge: Cambridge University Press, 1935), p. 173.

ing in an institution whose official teaching included baptismal regeneration. Although he was forced to resign from the Evangelical Alliance for so unbrotherly an outburst, he refused to recant his opinions. At this time, in a gesture of contemptuous defiance, he erected a baptismal font in his garden as a bird bath. To the annoyance of Matthew Arnold, he persistently called for the disestablishment of the Church of England. Roman Catholicism was far worse, the cause of most of the miseries of Ireland and the continent. Spurgeon flaunted a hearty, John Bull style of patriotism that lauded his own country as a land of freedom. But, highly significantly, he associated not only the British colonies but also the United States with his own nation. The great republic had been swelled, he wrote, by "the people of England."[98] Spurgeon was profoundly imbued with an antielitism that he shared with America. So that nobody should be excluded because of poverty, trainees at his college did not have to pay for their education. When he recommended that his students should adapt their pulpit style to their audiences, he told them, paradoxically, to go up to the level of a poor man but down to the level of an educated person.[99] Spurgeon professed a version of egalitarianism that made him seem the champion of the common man.

His reputation became colossal. Some journals outside his own country initially picked up the condemnation of his irreverence in England. Noting reports that Spurgeon had preached about spending thousands of years in eternity peering into the wounds of Christ, the New York Methodist newspaper asked pointedly, "Is this religion?"[100] But, from an early stage, favorable comment overwhelmed criticism. In May 1857 a radical Congregational journal was already hailing this man of "extraordinary eloquence, genius and mind-power" as "the modern Whit[e]field."[101] Baptists in particular looked with astonishment on the rise of one of their own to a position of pulpit preeminence. In Nova Scotia, where Baptists predominated, their newspaper reported breathlessly at the start of 1858 that it had just received a fresh supply of Spurgeon's sermons, his first, second and third series, together with an account of his life and ministry. Two weeks later, it printed an account of a Lord's Day morning with Spurgeon; the next week it described a bazaar at the Surrey Gardens Music

---

[98] *Annual Paper* (1870), p. 16.

[99] Spurgeon, *Lectures*, p. 131.

[100] *Christian Advocate and Journal*, March 4, 1858, p. 33.

[101] *American Missionary*, May 1857, p. 102.

Hall to raise funds for the Tabernacle; in April it advertised his "greatest work,"
The Saint and his Saviour; in the next issue it recounted how Spurgeon had become
a Baptist; and a couple of months later it devoted the whole of the front page
and part of the next to a sermon of his on the revival that had broken out that
year.[102] Baptist periodicals elsewhere showed the same fascination. In Virginia,
the *Religious Herald* recorded in 1858 that the preacher gathered immense crowds
wherever he went.[103] In New York the *Examiner and Chronicle* reprinted in 1865
an astounded report that the Tabernacle now had no fewer than 2,881 members, and three years later, despite qualms about Spurgeon's lax views on admitting those not baptized as believers to Communion, it announced that it would
continue to publish his sermons regularly because they brought "spiritual comfort and strength to so many thousands of our readers."[104] The *Australian Evangelist* reported in 1866 that the Flinders Street Baptist Church in Adelaide was
distributing Spurgeon's tracts and that a man more than seventy-four years old
had been baptized through having read the preacher's sermons.[105] But the
standing of Spurgeon transcended his own denomination. The Presbyterians of
North Carolina were given accounts of the singing at the Tabernacle and Spurgeon's advice on evangelizing; the Methodists of New South Wales were told of
his views on eccentric preachers and on the faculty of impromptu speech.[106] At
Spurgeon's fiftieth birthday in 1884, the *Presbyterian Churchman* of Dublin concluded without any sense of hyperbole that he was the "greatest preacher of
modern or even of ancient times."[107]

The influence of the man was correspondingly immense. An indication of his
sway was the trouble taken by advertisers to claim that Spurgeon's communicants
had used their brand of unfermented wine or that he recommended a High Class
School for Young Ladies in Clapham Rise.[108] One of his most potent legacies was

---

[102] *Christian Messenger* (Halifax, Nova Scotia), January 6, 1858, p. 7; January 20, 1858, pp.
20-21; January 27, 1858, p. 29; April 14, 1858, p. 120; April 28, 1858, p. 129; June
23, 1858, pp. 193-94.

[103] *Religious Herald,* January 7, 1858.

[104] *Examiner and Chronicle,* March 30, 1865; January 9, 1868.

[105] *Australian Evangelist,* August 18, 1866, p. 255.

[106] *North Carolina Presbyterian,* February 5, 1858; January 3, 1872. *Christian Advocate and Wesleyan
Herald,* July 1, 1876, p. 63; August 2, 1876, p. 77.

[107] *Presbyterian Churchman,* July 1884, p. 194.

[108] *Freeman,* January 6, 1888, p. 16; January 13, 1888, p. 26.

transmitted through the men he trained, who, it was said, had a loyalty to the preacher "akin to the many-sided feeling of the clansman for his chief."[109] His greatest impact was in London, where at the end of the century a majority of serving Baptist ministers had been trained at Spurgeon's college.[110] In his denomination within Britain, of the twenty-nine ministers who rose to the presidency of the Baptist Union between 1897 and 1933, ten were Spurgeon's men.[111] But the trainees also went abroad in significant numbers. Of the 511 students educated in the college during its first twenty-three years down to 1880, twenty-nine went to North America, twenty went to Australia and New Zealand, five went to India, four went to the West Indies and eight went elsewhere in the world.[112] South Africa was also deeply affected, twenty men going out before 1915 and the Baptist Union having a Spurgeon's man as its secretary from 1890 to 1902.[113] At a festival to mark the publication of Spurgeon's two thousandth weekly sermon in 1888, it was said that the explorer David Livingstone possessed one of the sermons marked with his initials when he died in Africa; that the Russian ecclesiastical authorities had approved several for circulation; and that the Serbian government had required three of them to be preached by the priests on specified occasions.[114] Spurgeon was a man who bestrode the globe.

DWIGHT L. MOODY

One of Spurgeon's most ardent admirers in the United States was a New Englander who turned into another outstanding figure in world evangelicalism. In 1867, when the American initially traveled to Britain, the first place he made for was the Metropolitan Tabernacle.[115] He became the most celebrated

---

[109] *Annual Paper* (1876-1877), p. 13.

[110] *British Weekly* (London), January 24, 1901, p. 399.

[111] J. C. Carlile, *C. H. Spurgeon: An Interpretative Biography* (London: Religious Tract Society, 1933), p. 185.

[112] *Annual Paper* (1879-1880), p. 3.

[113] M. S. Blackwell, Sr., "The Influence of Charles Haddon Spurgeon on the Church in South Africa between 1870 and 1930" (master's thesis, University of South Africa, 1994), p. 31. K. E. Cross, *Ours is the Frontier: A Life of G. W. Cross, Baptist Pioneer* (Pretoria: UNISA, 1986), p. 86.

[114] *Freeman*, January 13, 1888, p. 17.

[115] Robert Shindler, *From the Usher's Desk to the Tabernacle Pulpit: The Life and Labours of Pastor C. H. Spurgeon* (London: Passmore and Alabaster, 1892), p. 208.

evangelist of the age on both sides of the Atlantic. His name was Dwight L. Moody.[116] Born in 1837, three years after Spurgeon, Moody came from Northfield in rural Massachusetts, where his resourceful mother brought him up after the early death of his father, a bricklayer. Moving to Boston at the age of seventeen to join his uncle's shoe shop, he was converted and joined a Congregational church. After only two years he went out to Chicago, where he prospered as a shoe salesman, threw himself into the revival of 1857 and served as a full-time employee of the Young Men's Christian Association, whose national president he eventually became. Sunday school work with children led to the creation, in 1864, of the nondenominational Illinois Street Church with Moody as pastor. The Chicago fire of 1871, however, destroyed his home, church and the Y.M.C.A. building, and Moody was glad to accept an invitation to conduct a series of evangelistic missions in the British Isles over two years from 1873. There he discovered his calling. Accompanied by the performer of popular sacred songs Ira D. Sankey, he stirred the towns he visited with enthusiasm for his simple gospel messages. In Glasgow in 1874 there were perhaps as many as three thousand converts; in London in the following year the American evangelists regularly drew audiences of twelve thousand to just one of the four preaching places. On their return to the United States, Moody and Sankey ran a succession of similar city missions, beginning with Brooklyn in 1875. They were carefully planned, advertised in the press, preceded by house-to-house visitation and run on similar lines to the contemporary music hall, which, with Sankey's solos and congregational singing, they much resembled. The great innovation was the enquiry room. After the evangelistic meeting, seekers of salvation would be given personal counseling, from which, it was estimated, some four-fifths of the results flowed.[117] Moody was brisk in manner but attractive in personality. A short, stocky, bearded man not unlike Spurgeon in physique, the evangelist could be outspoken, but he enjoyed boyish practical jokes as much as inspiring prayer meetings. He showed genuine humility, refusing to countenance any person-

---

[116]James F. Findlay, Jr., *Dwight L. Moody: American Evangelist, 1837-1899* (Chicago: Chicago University Press, 1969), and Lyle W. Dorsett, *A Passion for Souls: The Life of D. L. Moody* (Chicago: Moody Press, 1997) are thorough biographical studies.

[117]A. W. W. Dale, *The Life of R. W. Dale of Birmingham* (London: Hodder & Stoughton, 1898), p. 319.

ality cult and so forbidding the publicity of photographs of himself. From 1875, Moody made his home once more in Northfield, where he took up farming on the side, but he retained a special bond with Chicago, where he founded an Evangelization Society in 1887, and twice more, in 1881-1883 and 1891-1892, he traveled to Britain for evangelistic campaigns. He died in 1899 while conducting a mission in Kansas City.

Moody's platform manner, shaped by his early experience of addressing children, gave a large place to storytelling. Bible characters came to life on his lips. He also characteristically chose a theme from the Bible for each of his addresses, going through the Scriptures to find the various relevant passages. His preparation entailed carrying large linen envelopes about with him on his travels, each devoted to illustrations for one of the themes. Whenever he came upon a relevant idea, a sheet or cutting would be added to the appropriate envelope. Before speaking, he would select a few of the items, set them in order and jot down a few connecting thoughts. The result was that sermons on the same topic were often very different. Even though an address might be delivered many times (the one on "The New Birth" was given one hundred and eighty-four times between 1881 and 1899), it was always fresh.[118] He was criticized by Calvinists such as John Kennedy, the Free Church of Scotland minister at Dingwall, for preaching the Arminian message that all could be saved. It is true that Moody emphasized human ability to believe the gospel, but he did not reject the Reformed doctrine of election. He merely believed that it was not suitable for evangelistic addresses. Moody knew that he had to avoid putting obstacles in the path of either Arminians or Calvinists if he was to retain widespread confidence, and so avoided controversial topics. "I don't try," he once remarked, "to reconcile God's sovereignty and man's free agency."[119] He strove to assimilate wisdom from those with more theological training than himself such as another minister of the Free Church of Scotland, Andrew Bonar, in whose honor Bonar Hall and Bonar Glen at Northfield were named.[120] From Bonar and others Moody imbibed the premillennial teaching about the last things that became

---

[118]Henry Drummond, *Dwight L. Moody: Impressions and Facts* (New York: McClure, Phillips and Co., 1900), p. 70. Stanley L. Gundry, *Love Them In: The Life and Theology of D. L. Moody* (Chicago: Moody Press, 1999), p. 126.

[119]Gundry, *Love Them In*, p. 141.

[120]T. Shanks, *D. L. Moody at Home* (London: Morgan and Scott, n.d.), pp. 14, 17.

characteristic of the Northfield conferences which he began in 1880. Perhaps
most typical of Moody's platform addresses, however, was an emphasis on the
love of God. His preaching did not dwell on hell, but concentrated on the
drawing power of the God who was a kindly Father. Reinforced by Sankey's
rather sentimental lyrics, Moody's message was a gospel well suited to an age
that delighted to celebrate the domestic virtues.

There have been attempts to present Moody's career as an exercise in social
control. He was associated with the elite, in America with businessmen and
in Britain with aristocrats as well. They provided the funding for his campaigns, and in return, it is suggested, Moody was expected to teach social
subordination.[121] It is true that in 1887, Chicago businessmen regarded his
evangelistic training school as a cheap way of counteracting socialism, but
Moody did not set out to keep the workers in their place. In Britain, in fact,
he was thought to be a dangerous subversive, championing the common man
against his natural superiors. Part of the social control interpretation is that
working people saw through the scheme to manipulate them and so avoided
Moody's campaigns. It has been shown, however, that the lower classes did
attend his rallies. At Liverpool in 1875, for example, it was reported that "ill
clad working men were there."[122] Furthermore, Moody showed a persistent
concern for the welfare of the masses of the people. The legacy of his Glasgow mission included free morning breakfasts for down-and-outs, free Sunday dinners for destitute children and an orphanage by the sea. He identified
wholly with the temperance campaign, the supreme progressive cause of the
day. He did not, as has been alleged, turn away from social issues in his later
career toward an exclusively conversionist policy. It is true that in 1898, he
declared that he was sick and tired of hearing about reform since what human
beings needed was not a patching up job, but regeneration. But what he was
objecting to was treating reform as an alternative to the gospel rather than as
its partner. In the previous year, he had criticized American employers as

---

[121]John Kent, *Holding the Fort: Studies in Victorian Revivalism* (London: Epworth Press, 1978),
   chaps. 4-6, 9.
[122]John Coffey, "Democracy and Popular Religion: Moody and Sankey's Mission to Britain, 1873-1875," in *Citizenship and Community: Liberals, Radicals and Collective Identities in the
   British Isles, 1865-1931,* ed. Eugenio F. Biagini (Cambridge: Cambridge University Press,
   1996), p. 97.

sharply as any social gospeler for paying their employees starvation wages.[123]
Moody was committed to promoting social progress. There is no doubt that
he would always have said that conversion was the key to advance, but, as the
schools for young women and men (in that order) that he founded at Northfield illustrate, he was not averse to using complementary methods. The evangelist wanted to help the mass of the people, not to make them submit to
their masters.

Moody had his critics at the time. The editor of the *Christian Advocate* in
New York, a Methodist Doctor of Divinity, expressed the view in 1887 that
at Moody's missions the way of salvation was made "a little too easy" because
repentance was unduly neglected.[124] A contributor to the same journal later
showed statistically that, after gains during the Boston mission of 1877, the
churches were able to recruit a smaller number of new members over the next
five years than over the previous quinquennium.[125] But most reports were
much more favorable. Moody had the gift of engineering the revival that
worldwide churches craved. In South Australia news of his Scottish campaign
in 1874 was eagerly received; imitative special services were held in Adelaide
Town Hall; the Liverpool mission in the following year was described enthu-
siastically; and the story of the lives of Moody and Sankey became a front-
page feature.[126] In 1877 a conference at which all the attenders approved of
their work considered inviting the pair to South Africa; the Irish Presbyterian
magazine was amazed that, after the Chicago mission of that year, the sum of
eighty thousand dollars was raised for the Y.M.C.A., "doubtless the largest
collection ever realised in a Christian assembly"; and the doings of the evangelists in America, such as the erection of a giant tabernacle for their Louisville mission of 1888, provided constant copy for British periodicals.[127] The
global sway of Moody and Sankey was immense. Much of it was exercised
through Sankey's hymns, first published in 1873 and soon sung all over the

---

[123]Gundry, *Love Them In*, pp. 97, 155.

[124]*Christian Advocate*, January 13, 1887, p. 25.

[125]Ibid., January 28, 1892, p. 53.

[126]*Methodist Journal* (Adelaide), July 11, 1874; September 5, 1874; May 7, 1875; May 21,
1875.

[127]*Christian Express*, August 1, 1877, p. 2. *Presbyterian Churchman*, April 1877, p. 77. *Freeman*,
January 13, 1888, p. 23.

world, but there were many other aspects. Andrew Murray, revisiting Scotland after the Moody campaign of 1873-1874, felt that "the whole religious tone" of the country had been transformed, so that afterward there was much less reticence about spiritual matters. Returning to South Africa, Murray introduced after-meetings, where, on the Moody model, seekers of salvation stayed for further guidance, to the consternation of many of his more inhibited colleagues in the Dutch Reformed Church.[128] In England just one of the effects of Moody's first visit was the training in urban evangelism of Wilson Carlile, subsequently the founder of the Church Army that brought fresh impetus to the home mission of the Church of England in the twentieth century.[129] A veteran of Moody's Liverpool campaign immigrated to Sydney, where he set about mobilizing the young men for personal evangelism.[130] "It was at the close of Mr. Moody's late Mission in London," testified Jennie Jay, a missionary to Morocco, "that I first felt a desire to devote myself wholly to work for God."[131] The Student Volunteer Movement that took up foreign missions from 1888 under the banner of "the evangelisation of the world in this generation" emerged from the Northfield conferences with the same spirit of dedication. In America, through his sermons, the Northfield circle and the Christian workers he trained, Moody shaped the trajectory of conservative evangelicalism long into the twentieth century. His chief institutional legacy, the Bible Institute in Chicago that took his name after his death, was to be the redoubt of fundamentalism between the wars. But Moody was not merely an American evangelist: he exercised a profound and lasting influence over the course of evangelicalism throughout the world.

The movement represented by Spurgeon and Moody possessed a vigorous dynamic. Its adherents were stirred by the teaching of the Scriptures; they were eager to proclaim the message of Christ crucified; and they were unflagging in their quest for conversions. Hence they were dedicated activists in the spread of the gospel. "Christianity," declared Robert Young, a senior Wesleyan minis-

---

[128] du Plessis, *Andrew Murray*, pp. 303, 437. W. M. Douglas, *Andrew Murray and His Message: One of God's Choice Saints* (London: Oliphants, n.d.), pp. 130-31.

[129] George E. Morgan, *"A Veteran in Revival": R. C. Morgan: His Life and Times* (London: Morgan & Scott, 1909), pp. 184-85.

[130] *Christian Advocate and Wesleyan Record*, October 3, 1876, p. 108.

[131] *Christian* (London), March 4, 1886, p. 2.

ter, in 1854, "is essentially aggressive."[132] Evangelicalism had grown from a
small beginning just over a century before to become a powerful force. The
middle year of the nineteenth century, according to the newspaper of the Evangelicals in the Church of England, was totally different from the equivalent year
in the eighteenth century. "Then all was dead," it observed, "—now all is
life."[133] The transformation is evident in the membership figures for Methodism, the movement that most embodied the vibrant spirit of the eighteenth-
century revival. In 1767, when Methodist statistics were first collected, there
were 22,000 members in the English movement. By 1800 there were 96,000
and by 1850 as many as 518,000.[134] In the United States, where Methodism
was organized only in 1784, there were 65,000 members by 1800 and half a
century later there were over one and a quarter million.[135] Although other denominations were less careful in keeping statistics, it is clear that there had also
been marked growth among Evangelical Anglicans, Scottish Presbyterians and
English Dissenters. Each grouping had its representatives in Canada, Australia,
New Zealand and South Africa as well as in America. Already by 1850 society
was being permeated by the values of the movement. The subsequent half-
century, as this book will try to show, was a time when the gospel was deeply
rooted in the English-speaking world.

---

[132]Robert Young, *The Southern World: Journal of a Deputation from the Wesleyan Conference to Australia
and Polynesia; including Notices of a Visit to the Gold Fields* (London: Hamilton, Adams & Co.,
1854), p. 1.

[133]*Record*, January 3, 1850.

[134]Robert Currie, Alan Gilbert and Lee Horsley, eds., *Churches and Churchgoers: Patterns of
Church Growth in the British Isles Since 1700* (Oxford: Clarendon Press, 1977), pp. 139-41.
The figures are rounded to the nearest thousand.

[135]E. S. Gaustad, *Historical Atlas of Religion in America* (New York: Harper & Row, 1962), p. 78.

2

VARIETIES OF
EVANGELICALISM

The common features of the whole evangelical movement undergirded an immense variety of expressions. If the movement was recognizably one, it was also in several respects diverse. Evangelicals differed in theology, denomination, social characteristics and geographical location. While the first of these topics is reserved for fuller consideration in subsequent chapters, the other three are covered here. Denominational divisions are sometimes underestimated by historians who group evangelicals together as a single entity. In reality, however, there was a marked difference, reinforced by a sense of rivalry, between two residents in an American frontier town who belonged to different Christian bodies, even though both were evangelicals. A Colorado Methodist, for instance, might pride himself on belonging to the most effective evangelistic organization. His Presbyterian neighbor, however, knew that numerical strength was not everything, and that, if wealth and intelligence were also taken into the reckoning, his own church was "the most commanding of all our denominations."[1] Contrasts between inherited principles and patterns of church government ensured that individuals equally dedicated to Christian mission did not see eye-to-eye. Likewise social characteristics, as the Colorado comment on wealth and intelligence illustrates, set evangelicals apart from one another. The inhabitants of great Victorian mansions were unlike their humbler contemporaries who lived in tiny cottages. Industrialization was creating new styles of living in the later nineteenth century. Alongside

---

[1] *Rocky Mountain Presbyterian* (Denver, Colo.), April 1872.

traditional denominational divisions, the novel wealth of the English-speaking world necessarily had an impact on the members of the churches. So factors external to church life as well as factors internal to it created variety among evangelicals.

The other main way in which evangelicals were sundered from one another was by geographical location. They lived in contrasting regions from the Arctic to the Tropics; and, although a high proportion owed allegiance to Queen Victoria, they paid their taxes to different governments. Historians have been well aware of this cause of evangelical separation. It has been customary to organize ecclesiastical history by country, tracing events in one land to the exclusion of developments in another. Normally the only exceptions are accounts of when an individual from one nation played an undeniable role in another, as when Dwight L. Moody ran evangelistic campaigns in Britain or the English Congregational leader Thomas Binney visited Australia. But in general evangelicalism has been split up for study into national units, or else into units smaller than a country, whether state, area, city or village. This is far from a mistaken strategy, because nations—and smaller areas—have certainly possessed distinctive religious complexions. The specificity of evangelical experience in particular lands will therefore be addressed in this chapter. Yet the unity of the evangelical world, considered in the previous chapter and embodied in the global fame of Spurgeon and Moody, raises the question of whether the division by nation is as exclusively significant as historians have generally assumed. Normally, for example, the church history of Scottish Presbyterians has been written as though Scotland were the only natural unit for study. Equally, however, the Reformed tradition in different lands during the Victorian era, as a recent volume has shown, forms a suitable topic for investigation. The book includes Scottish congregations but highlights their similarities to Presbyterians in America and Congregationalists in England.[2] It will be worth asking how far national historiographies have done insufficient justice to the religious bonds between the countries of the English-speaking world. The denominational and social differences may turn out to have been no less salient than the national contrasts.

---

[2]Charles D. Cashdollar, *A Spiritual Home: Life in British and American Reformed Congregations, 1830-1915* (University Park: Pennsylvania State University Press, 2000).

THE MAIN DENOMINATIONAL FAMILIES

The denominational variety may be examined first. The Anglican communion, itself becoming globally conscious with the inauguration of the Lambeth conferences of its bishops in 1867, possessed churches in virtually every English-speaking land. Its distinguishing feature was the possession of bishops in communion with the see of Canterbury. In England and Wales, and in Ireland down to 1870, Anglicanism had the advantage of constituting the established church. Elsewhere in the British Empire at the opening of the period it possessed some vestiges of established status, but the Episcopal Church of the United States was just one denomination among many. There were three tendencies amongst Anglican clergy. High Churchmen put greater stress than Evangelicals on the doctrines of the church, the ministry and the sacraments; Broad Churchmen believed in bringing doctrine up to date, sometimes to the extent of modifying scriptural teaching by assimilating the discoveries of modern research.[3] Some Evangelicals were drawn toward each of these sections of opinion, so adopting certain High-Church or Broad-Church characteristics, but the Evangelical party formed a distinct force in almost every Anglican body throughout the period. Within the Church of England the Evangelical clergy, only some five hundred at the start of the nineteenth century, had grown by its middle to number no fewer than sixty-five hundred, that is well over a third of the whole.[4] In 1860 nearly half the English episcopal bench was aligned with the party.[5] Evangelicals never formed a majority of the parish clergy because during the second half of the century the chief growth in numbers was among the High Churchmen who drew inspiration from the Oxford movement. The proportion of Evangelicals among bishops and lower clergy alike declined, though they claimed, with much plausibility, to possess the allegiance of the majority of the laity. Outside England the balance between Evangelicals and other parties in the Anglican communion varied. In Scotland the proportion of Evangelicals was low; in Ire-

---

[3]The classic study of the Church of England in the period is W. Owen Chadwick, *The Victorian Church*, 2 vols. (London: Adam and Charles Black, 1966-1970).

[4]David W. Bebbington, *Evangelicalism in Modern Britain: A History from the 1730s to the 1980s* (London: Unwin Hyman, 1989), pp. 106-7.

[5]Nigel Scotland, *"Good and Proper Men": Lord Palmerston and the Bench of Bishops* (Cambridge: James Clarke 2000), p. 176. According to Scotland, ten of the twenty-three sees were occupied by Evangelicals, but to his list should be added John Graham, bishop of Chester.

land, by contrast, it was high. In the United States and southern Africa it was low; in Australia it was very high indeed. In Canada, where there were reputedly no Broad Churchmen, the balance between Evangelicals and High Churchmen was roughly equal. In some lands the sense that Evangelicals were a threatened species led to a series of small splits—there was a secession from the Episcopal Church of Scotland in 1843, a Free Church of England emerged in the 1840s, a Reformed Episcopal Church was established in America in 1873 and a (confusingly named) Church of England, largely Evangelical in tone, separated gradually during a series of legal tussles from the Church of the Province of South Africa. But Evangelical Churchmen, among whom Bishop J. C. Ryle of Liverpool was preeminent during the period, insisted on their conformity with the principles of the Reformers who had broken with Rome in the sixteenth century. They therefore claimed to be the most authentic Churchmen of all.[6]

A second grouping of evangelicals consisted of the Presbyterians. They inherited the Reformed tradition stemming from John Calvin, formally accepting the version of his theology embodied in the Westminster Confession of the seventeenth century. Against the Anglicans, they claimed that there should be no bishops, all ministers being equal and supervision being exercised by church courts. Presbyteries, which included elders drawn from the laity as well as ministers, exercised authority over congregations. Above the presbyteries were usually synods, and above them, in most lands, a General Assembly was the capstone of the system. In Scotland the established church was Presbyterian, which meant that when Queen Victoria crossed the River Tweed from England she became an ordinary member of the Church of Scotland. Alongside the established church, however, there was also the Free Church of Scotland, created in the Disruption of 1843 in order to assert the right of congregations to choose their own ministers, and the United Presbyterian Church, formed four years later from the main bodies that had seceded from the Church of Scotland over similar issues in the previous century. Smaller, fragmentary denominations maintained the principles of the Covenanters of the seventeenth century and the Seceders of the eighteenth. At the very end of the period, in 1900, the Free Church combined with the United Presbyterian Church to form the United

---

[6]On Anglican Evangelicals, see especially Kenneth Hylson-Smith, *Evangelicals in the Church of England, 1734-1984* (Edinburgh: T & T Clark, 1988).

Free Church of Scotland, though its most tenacious adherents in the Highlands remained resolutely separate. Each of these bodies, though differing in their degree of theological conservatism, formed part of the evangelical mosaic. Echoes of the debates in Scotland were heard elsewhere in the English-speaking world, so that, for instance, the Scottish splits were temporarily reproduced in Canada and Australia. There was nevertheless a tendency in the later nineteenth century for Presbyterians to consolidate: most crucially, the Northern branch of American Presbyterianism, divided since 1837-1838 into the Old and New Schools over the degree to which revivalist faith and practice should be accommodated, reunited in 1869. The Cumberland Presbyterians, the most revivalist of all, however, continued to remain a separate body, and the Civil War created a fresh division between Northern and Southern Presbyterianism that was to endure for over a century. The descendants of Dutch immigrants worshiped in the Reformed Church in America, which dropped the word *Dutch* from its title in 1867; more recent immigrants from the Netherlands were in the process of forming the Christian Reformed Church; and there was an equivalent, though smaller, German Reformed Church. In Wales the Calvinistic Methodists, the largest denomination outside the Church of England, were well on their way to becoming the Presbyterian Church of Wales, a title not officially assumed until the following century, and in Ireland the Presbyterians were the strongest Protestant denomination in Ulster. Insisting on a theologically trained ministry, the Presbyterian and Reformed family of churches formed an intellectually gifted strand within the evangelical movement.[7]

The Congregationalists shared much in common with the Presbyterians. So close were they that on the American frontier the New School Presbyterians, during the period of the Presbyterian division, usually worked in comity with

---

[7]Scottish Presbyterianism is analyzed in A. C. Cheyne, *The Transforming of the Kirk: Victorian Scotland's Religious Revolution* (Edinburgh: Saint Andrew Press, 1983). Richard W. Vaudry, *The Free Church in Canada, 1844-1861* (Waterloo, Ontario: Wilfrid Laurier University Press, 1989); M. D. Prentis, *The Scots in Australia: A Study of New South Wales, Victoria and Queensland, 1788-1900* (Sydney: Sydney University Press, 1983), chaps. 10-11; and Dennis McEldowney, ed., *Presbyterians in Aotearoa, 1840-1990* (Wellington: Presbyterian Church of New Zealand) are valuable for their respective lands. The American denominations in this and succeeding paragraphs are conveniently catalogued, with references, in Daniel G. Reid, Robert D. Linder, Bruce L. Shelley and Harry S. Stout, eds., *Dictionary of Christianity in America* (Downers Grove, Ill.: InterVarsity Press, 1990).

them. Like the Presbyterians, the Congregationalists inherited the Reformed theology of the Puritans. Unlike them, however, they contended that that no external body should wield authority over the local church. Hence every congregation was independent, a principle that in many lands gave the denomination its alternative title of Independents. A church meeting, which all members were entitled to attend, was the supreme earthly authority, responsible for choosing the church's own minister and deacons. Although each congregation ran its internal affairs, churches were grouped in broader bodies, usually called associations, for mutual support and joint mission. Among such an independently minded people, however, common ventures, such as the national Unions that developed during the nineteenth century, were often weak enterprises. New England, the seat of the Puritan settlement in North America, was where the denomination had its greatest strength, and as recently as 1833 it had enjoyed the status of being the established religion of Massachusetts. In England and Wales, however, Congregationalists took the lead in the movement of the separation of church and state, and their militancy was imitated elsewhere. Other bodies closely associated with the denomination included, in England, the Countess of Huntingdon's Connection, a grouping of congregations established by the great patron of the eighteenth-century revival, and, in Scotland, the Evangelical Union, which followed revivalism further in modifying its theology than mainstream Congregationalists. In America Henry Ward Beecher, a progressive theological preacher in the suburbs of New York, was the best known figure in the denomination,[8] and a man of equivalent influence in England was R. W. Dale, the lucid and thoughtful minister of Carr's Lane Church in Birmingham. His brand of broader evangelicalism was typical of the Victorian denomination throughout the world.[9]

The Baptists were identical in church organization to the Congregationalists, entrusting authority to church meeting, in America usually called the conference, and being served by a minister and deacons. They differed, however, in restricting baptism to those with conscious faith and practicing the rite by total immersion. The largest section amongst them, the Particular or Regular Baptists, stood in the Calvinist tradition, believing in the redemption of a particu-

---

[8]See chap. 5, pp. 164-65.
[9]On English Congregationalism, see R. Tudur Jones, *Congregationalism in England, 1662-1962* (London: Independent Press, 1962).

lar part of humanity, the elect. Some of them felt that too many theological and practical concessions were being made to the newer influences of the times and so turned into separate communities, called Strict and Particular Baptists in England and Primitive, Hard-Shell or Anti-Mission Baptists in America. Most Particular Baptists, however, were prepared to modify traditional ways for the sake of evangelistic effectiveness, a majority in England, Canada and elsewhere even opening the Lord's Table to those not baptized as believers. In America the same practice, though not unknown, was stoutly resisted as a heresy. Except among white churches in the South, where the Southern Baptist Convention coordinated denominational affairs, there was a deep-seated wariness of centralization in America that prevented the emergence of a Northern Convention until the twentieth century or a national structure for the numerous black Baptists until 1895. Another feature of firmness in Baptist principles, though in this case chiefly in the South, was the emergence of Landmarkism, the assertion of the exclusive validity of immersion practiced by Baptist churches, which, it was claimed, had enjoyed an unbroken succession since New Testament times. Alongside the Particular Baptists were the General or Freewill Baptists, who rejected Calvinism in favor of Arminianism, maintaining that redemption is general and so available to the whole of humanity. Another distinct grouping, the descendants of the followers of Henry Alline, a powerful revivalist preacher in Nova Scotia, had gradually approximated to the prevailing Baptist patterns elsewhere. The largest expansion of the Baptists was in the American South; but their greatest figure was undoubtedly the Englishman Charles H. Spurgeon.[10]

The Methodists formed the largest single contingent of evangelicals in the period. Springing primarily from the ministry of John Wesley in the eighteenth century, Methodism had grown until it was the largest Protestant body both in the United States and Canada, and the second largest, after the established church, in England. The South African Methodists congratulated themselves in 1885 that their churches formed "the largest protestant denomination on the face of the globe."[11] Methodism operated partly through traveling preachers, often in America called circuit riders, who carried the gospel to outlying places that other religious bodies failed to reach. They were essentially evange-

---

[10]On the English Baptists, see John H. Y. Briggs, *The English Baptists of the Nineteenth Century* (Didcot: Baptist Historical Society, 1994).

[11]*South African Methodist* (Grahamstown), January 20, 1885, p. 1.

lists, moving on after two or three years to another sphere for soul winning. These men, who were ordained, gathered converts into societies that functioned as local worshiping communities and into classes of some ten or twelve who, at least in theory, met weekly for the exchange of spiritual experience. Laypeople, however, led most of the classes and also did by far the greatest proportion of the preaching, allowing Methodism to become an embodiment of lay initiative. Yet the network—in Britain called a "connection"—of societies was tightly disciplined by the ministry, whose members wielded authority in virtue of their ability to refuse to renew the quarterly class ticket which was the sign of Methodist membership. Ministers met annually in a conference, which gave them a strong sense of cohesion. Senior figures in the British conference dominated connectional policy. At the very beginning of the period, Jabez Bunting, "the Methodist pope," was drawing to a close the years when he exercised an authority over Wesleyan Methodism, the main body, scarcely less than that once wielded by John Wesley himself. The conference insisted on its policies being enforced lest the whole agency for winning souls should disintegrate. There were subordinate conferences in Ireland, Australia, Canada and South Africa that, while autonomous in many ways, were kept in line by directives from England. In the United States, however, the two Methodist Episcopal Churches, operating apart in North and South since 1844, were wholly independent. As their name implied, their leadership consisted of bishops, who directed the affairs within the territories of many separate conferences. Worldwide Methodism was nevertheless bound together by a common ethos: insisting on the need for experienced faith, professing the Arminian theology of John Wesley and singing the hymns of his brother Charles.[12]

The high degree of direction from above in mainstream Methodism proved irksome to many members and led to breakaway movements on both sides of the Atlantic. The largest body in England was Primitive Methodism, so called because it wished to reassert what it took to be the original flexibility of the move-

---

[12]On British Methodism, see Rupert Davies, A. Raymond George and Gordon Rupp, eds., *A History of the Methodist Church in Great Britain*, vol. 3 (London: Epworth Press, 1983). Canada has been well served by Neil Semple, *The Lord's Dominion: The History of Canadian Methodism* (Montreal & Kingston: McGill-Queen's University Press, 1996); and South Australia by Arnold D. Hunt, *This Side of Heaven: A History of Methodism in South Australia* (Adelaide: Lutheran Publishing House, 1985).

ment. It therefore held camp meetings on the American model, huge outdoor gatherings for prayer and preaching; it allowed laypeople to participate in conference; and it encouraged a more populist style of revivalism that attracted the nickname of Ranters. The Methodist New Connection and the United Methodist Free Churches were both bodies that believed in greater local lay control than the Wesleyan conference permitted. There were also smaller denominations: the Bible Christians of southwest England, the Independent Methodists, chiefly in the northwest, and the Wesleyan Reformers, concentrated primarily around Sheffield. They all had their distinctive reasons for not being ordinary Wesleyan Methodists. In Ireland, oddly, the justification for the separate existence of the Primitive Wesleyan Methodists down to the 1870s was their wish to retain stronger links with the Anglican established church. There was similar fragmentation in America, where the African Methodist Episcopal Church and the African Methodist Episcopal Zion Church both catered to the black community. The Wesleyan Methodists had seceded from the Methodist Episcopal Church over official tolerance of slavery and the Free Methodists broke away in 1860. They were particularly concerned that official Methodism was losing its grasp on the doctrine of holiness. Wesley had taught that entire sanctification is possible in this life, but the message was fading from most pulpits. Free Methodists reasserted it, claiming to be the champions of "old-time religion." Before the end of the century, however, others began to think that the Free Methodists had not gone far enough. Separate groups sprang up in America and Canada to propagate a more radical holiness message and it was chiefly in these circles that, in the 1890s, there were the initial stirrings of Pentecostalism. In England the Salvation Army, though rapidly evolving into a disciplined force fighting the sins of the cities, emerged from the same matrix.[13] Methodism therefore became the seedbed of movements within evangelical Christianity that in the twentieth century were to sweep across the world.

Other bodies with pre-nineteenth-century origins formed pieces in the evangelical mosaic. Lutherans, inheriting the legacy of the sixteenth-century Reformer Martin Luther, existed in various parts of the English-speaking world, often bearing the title evangelical in their denominational title. That, however, indicated loyalty to the principles of the Reformation rather than any partici-

---

[13]On the developments outside Methodism, see chap. 7.

pation in the world created by the evangelical revival. Although some Lutherans were influenced by Anglo-Saxon revivalism, most maintained a scrupulous distance from other Christian bodies. In any case Lutherans, as immigrants or descendants of immigrants from Germany or Scandinavia, normally retained a language other than English for worship down to the First World War or even beyond.[14] Mennonites and their Amish cousins, who trickled into North America from Switzerland, the Netherlands, Germany and Russia over the centuries, were also usually insulated by language and customary ways from their evangelical neighbors.[15] Another continental group, however, was more obviously part of the broader evangelical coalition. The Moravians, with antecedents in fifteenth-century Bohemia but reorganized by Count Zinzendorf in the 1720s, had been the pioneers of evangelical missions. Although few in numbers, in the later nineteenth century they retained several of their characteristic Christian communities on both sides of the Atlantic such as Bethlehem in Pennsylvania.[16] The other body with early origins was the Religious Society of Friends, more commonly called Quakers. Begun in England in the mid-seventeenth century by George Fox, they were traditionally highly sectarian, worshiping in silence, wearing plain clothes and marrying only within their own ranks. In 1860, however, the distinctive forms of witness became optional in Britain, partly because sections of the Society had been permeated by evangelicalism. American Quakers divided institutionally between traditionalists, rationalists and evangelicals, the last group sometimes adopting sung hymns, formal sermons and a paid ministry. Quakers therefore played a full part in the evangelical enterprises of the later nineteenth century, frequently taking the lead in anything of a philanthropic nature.[17]

---

[14]E. Clifford Nelson, ed., *The Lutherans in North America* (Philadelphia: Fortress, 1980). An English congregation is the subject of B. M. Robinson, *The Hull German Lutheran Church, 1848-1998* (Beverley, U.K.: Highgate, 2000).

[15]Theron F. Schlabach, *Peace, Faith, Nation: Mennonites and Amish in Nineteenth-Century America* (Scottdale, Penn.: Herald Press, 1988).

[16]J. Taylor Hamilton and Kenneth G. Hamilton, *History of the Moravian Church: The Renewed Unitas Fratrum, 1722-1957*, 2nd ed. (Bethlehem, Penn.: Interprovincial Board of Christian Education, Moravian Church in America, 1983).

[17]Elizabeth Isichei, *Victorian Quakers* (Oxford: Clarendon, 1970). Margaret H. Bacon, *The Quiet Rebels: The Story of the Quakers in America* (Philadelphia: New Society Publishers, 1988).

DENOMINATIONAL NOVELTY, DIVISION AND COOPERATION

New groupings also assumed a prominent role in evangelicalism. The impulse to restore the characteristics of the primitive church had recently given rise to two bodies with strikingly novel features. The Disciples (or Churches) of Christ, created by Thomas and Alexander Campbell and Barton Stone on the American frontier during the earlier nineteenth century, upheld weekly communion, lay ministry and congregational independence. They practiced believer's baptism by immersion, but because they taught that it was an act of obedience essential to salvation they were excluded from the Evangelical Alliance as rejecting justification by faith. Yet their style was virtually identical with that of evangelicals, and many of them were gradually drawn into the pan-evangelical network. Their commitment to Christian unity led their more progressive American section, increasingly distinguished as Disciples, to take the lead in ecumenical cooperation by the end of the century.[18] Another new body was the Brethren, often called Plymouth Brethren from one of their early points of strength in England. They, too, were eager to restore the primitive church, reaching identical conclusions to the Churches of Christ about weekly communion, lay ministry and congregational independence. They almost always practiced believer's baptism, but did not hold it to be essential to salvation. Their "open" wing was more willing to cooperate with other evangelicals; they gathered in many of the converts of nondenominational revivalism in Britain from the 1850s onward. Normally ardent premillennialists, their more fissiparous "closed" wing was dominated by J. N. Darby, the first exponent of the dispensational teaching that was to spread widely in American fundamentalism during the twentieth century.[19] The ideal of restoring the pattern of the earliest church was a living ideal in these movements.

Some new evangelical bodies were actually founded within the period. They were sometimes designed to meet particular needs of the hour. The Christian

---

[18]Richard T. Hughes, *Reviving the Ancient Faith: The Story of Churches of Christ in America* (Grand Rapids: Eerdmans, 1996). Michael W. Casey and Douglas A. Foster, eds., *The Stone-Campbell Movement: An International Religious Tradition* (Knoxville: University of Tennessee Press, 2002). David M. Thompson, *Let Sects and Parties Fall: A Short History of the Association of Churches of Christ in Great Britain and Ireland* (Birmingham: Berean Press, 1980).

[19]F. Roy Coad, *A History of the Brethren Movement* (Exeter: Paternoster Press, 1968). There is now an excellent national study: Neil W. Dickson, *Brethren in Scotland: A Social Study of an Evangelical Movement* (Carlisle: Paternoster Press, 2003).

and Missionary Alliance is a case in point. Consolidated in 1897 by A. B. Simpson, a former Presbyterian minister in New York, it was designed to link those wanting fellowship in gospel work at home and abroad. Teaching holiness and even divine healing, it was originally a parachurch organization, having branches rather than churches, but it was to evolve into a denomination alongside others.[20] There were congregations without denominational affiliation, a common phenomenon in the period, sometimes targeting particular occupational groups. There were, for example, halls set up by the various City Missions that effectively functioned as local churches; there were many stand-alone black congregations in the American South; and there were missions for railwaymen and fishermen in towns where they congregated.[21] In New York a freshly established Hebrew Christian church of converted Jews was reported in 1882.[22] There were also small local groupings of churches with distinctive principles that never achieved the limelight. An intriguing example in England was the Society of Dependants, often (for obscure reasons) called Cokelers. Springing up in hamlets on the Sussex/Surrey border in the 1850s under the preaching of John Sirgood, a former bootmaker, they grew to around two thousand people, largely agricultural laborers, by their founder's death in 1885. Their theology approximated to that of Wesley, but they had no affiliation to Methodism. Cokelers specialized in artless testimonies during their services and composed simple hymns that were handed down through the generations in manuscript. They believed that union with Christ meant economic as well as spiritual solidarity and so operated village stores on the cooperative principle. One of their hymns ran:

> Christ's combination stores for me
> Where I can be so well supplied,
> Where I can one with brethren be
> Where competition is defied.[23]

---

[20] Charles Nienkirchen, *A. B. Simpson and the Pentecostal Movement: A Study in Continuity, Crisis and Change* (Peabody, Mass.: Hendrickson, 1992).

[21] The international work for seamen has been chronicled in Roald Kverndal, *Seamen's Missions: Their Origin and Early Growth: A Contribution to the History of the Church Maritime* (Pasadena, Calif.: William Carey Library, 1986).

[22] *Evangelistic Record* (Chicago), March 1882, p. 12.

[23] Roger Homan, "The Society of Dependents: A Case Study in the Rise and Fall of Rural Peculiars," *Sussex Archaeological Collections* 119 (1981).

Union with Christ, however, was also interpreted as discouraging marriage, which goes a long way toward explaining why the group soon went into rapid decline. The upholding of cooperative retailing and principled celibacy meant that the Cokelers were highly unusual, but they may stand as an example of a sectarian body, strong in a restricted locality, that formed one of the enduring features of evangelical life.[24]

The sheer heterogeneity of the evangelical denominations, ranging from urbane Episcopalians to rustic Cokelers, means that rivalry could often become intense. The principle of establishment erected a barrier that divided Anglicans from Nonconformists in England and Wales and even Presbyterians from other Presbyterians in Scotland. Residual features of establishment, such as government grants for Anglicans, caused problems in various British colonies too. Since those outside the established churches often sought their disestablishment, the tension was political as well as spiritual. Although there were some Evangelical clergy of the Church of England who were prepared to conduct sevices for other denominations, prebendary William Cadman drew cheers in 1876 at the Islington conference, the annual gathering of the Evangelical party, by declaring that, since cooperation was impossible, there was no point in preaching in other pulpits.[25] Church against chapel was probably the sharpest social division of all in Victorian England and Wales. But throughout the world there was a competitive market for souls. The desire to spread the gospel was given added edge by each denomination's desire to vindicate its own principles through successful recruitment. In 1850 Simon Richardson, a Methodist circuit rider, was delighted when, as a result of his meetings at St. Mary's, Florida, all the Episcopal families except one joined his own church. "I have always proselyted any one I could," he recalled half a century later, "because I felt that I was giving them a better Church and better religion in return."[26] There were controversies over church government, over doctrine and especially over baptismal practice. The early days of Brisbane in Australia were enlivened at the end of the 1850s by a fierce debate following the arrival of the first Baptist minister.

---

[24]Peter Jerrome, *John Sirgood's Way: The Story of the Loxwood Dependants* (Petworth, U.K.: Window Press, 1998).

[25]*Record* (London), January 21, 1876.

[26]S. P. Richardson, *The Lights and Shadows of Itinerant Life* (Nashville: Publishing House of the Methodist Episcopal Church, South, 1900), p. 101.

His Methodist counterpart circulated a small work defending infant baptism; a visiting Baptist grandee delivered three lectures in reply; and an opponent tried to tar the Baptists with the crimes of the Anabaptists at Munster in 1534. "These are stirring times in Brisbane," a correspondent reported. "The discussion goes on in the shop, in the street, in the office, on the wharf, on the road, on the farm, on the river, in the parlour, in the drawing-room, and, I believe, in the bedroom."[27] Divisions between different denominations, equally committed to the evangelical faith, could often flare up into heated controversy.

Yet cooperation among evangelicals was also widespread. The Bible Societies of the world, together with many other publishing agencies such as the Religious Tract Society in England, normally operated on the pan-evangelical principle. The committee of the British and Foreign Bible Society was constitutionally required to contain equal numbers of Churchmen and Nonconformists.[28] The Evangelical Alliance brought together the various denominations. In Kingston, Jamaica, for instance, at the start of the period there were monthly prayer meetings supplemented with public addresses that attracted Independents, Baptists, Wesleyans and members of the separate Wesleyan Association.[29] Every year the Alliance sponsored a week of united and universal prayer, with prayer meetings on specified topics every evening. "A stranger coming into any of the various meetings," it was said of the 1870 week of prayer in Halifax, Nova Scotia, "would have been unable to say who were Episcopalian, or who Methodist, or whether the meeting was presided over by a Presbyterian, a Congregationalist or a Baptist."[30] In Toronto, as in many other places, there was an annual exchange of pulpits organized by a local Ministerial Association.[31] City Missions, designed to grapple with the irreligion and destitution of the urban masses, were also run on the principle of interdenominational cooperation. At the tenth annual meeting of the Melbourne City Mission in 1866, it is true, the organization was reported to be experiencing hard times. "In a new country," admitted the reader of the annual report, "where churches had heavy local

---

[27] *Christian Pleader* (Sydney), May 14, 1859, p. 79.

[28] Leslie Howsam, *Cheap Bibles: Nineteenth-Century Publishing and the British and Foreign Bible Society* (Cambridge: Cambridge University Press, 1991), p. 21.

[29] *Wesleyan Methodist Magazine* (London), April 1850, p. 446.

[30] *Christian Messenger* (Halifax, Nova Scotia), January 17, 1872, p. 18.

[31] *Christian Guardian* (Toronto), March 10, 1880, p. 76.

claims and demands for denominational objects upon them, it was difficult to get up collections for an object of a catholic nature."[32] Yet the principle was often reversed in areas of new settlement. The American frontier and the newly settled areas of the British Empire were dotted with Union Churches catering for the variety of Christians who happened to be thrown together there. A church in Buffalo Grove, Illinois, in 1857, for example, contained mostly Methodists, with some Presbyterians and United Brethren and two Congregationalists.[33] Likewise a church opened in Kyeburn Diggings in New Zealand in 1869 was explicitly nondenominational and open to preachers of every section of Christianity.[34] Revival, as in America in 1857-1858, tended to dissolve denominational differences. So did the organized missions of Moody and Sankey. In Glasgow their greatest triumph in Britain was followed by the creation of the Glasgow United Evangelistic Association. In such ventures the common purpose of winning fresh converts eclipsed confessional boundaries. The gospel could create its own bond of unity, transcending the immense diversity of evangelical denominations.

SOCIAL DIVISIONS

There were also, however, great social contrasts between different adherents of the evangelical movement.[35] H. Richard Niebuhr suggested in 1929 that socioeconomic realities were the true foundation of denominational differences. Although religious factors do sometimes generate denominations, he argued, "the divisions of the church have been occasioned more frequently by the direct and indirect operation of economic factors than by the influence of any other major interest of man."[36] The origin and persistence of denominational rifts, on this analysis, are largely attributable to the different social strata occupied by the adherents of the various religious bodies. The phenomenon to which Niebuhr points was apparent within the evangelical movement of the later nineteenth

---

[32] *Australian Evangelist* (Melbourne), November 3, 1866, p. 335.

[33] *American Missionary* (New York), January 1858. p. 19.

[34] *Christian Observer* (Christchurch), January 1, 1870, p. 15.

[35] The social gulf based on race, perhaps the deepest of all, is left for discussion in chapter 7, pp. 227-33.

[36] H. R. Niebuhr, *The Social Sources of Denominationalism* (1929; reprint, New York: Meridian Books, 1957), p. 26.

century. Some denominations, and supremely the Anglicans/Episcopalians, associated as they were with traditional authority, attracted those of higher status than did others, such as the Baptists, who were in most places felt to be inferiors. It would be wrong, however, to suppose that the distinction between the denominations was always grounded in differing socioeconomic characteristics. It used to be supposed that English Methodism, for example, fragmented on social grounds, the Wesleyans appealing to the middle classes and the Primitives to the working classes. Careful examination of the range of available evidence, however, reveals that throughout the later nineteenth century the Wesleyans held the allegiance of large numbers of working people, and that the Primitives, though on average lower in the social scale, were tending to rise in status and numbered many middle-class families in their ranks.[37] There was far more contrast between particular congregations in the same denomination than there was between the denominations as a whole. Varying economic circumstances necessarily molded the characteristics of local churches. In particular the advance of industry during the later nineteenth century was closely associated with the growth of cities. By the middle of the century over half the British population, together with nearly a quarter of the American population, was already urbanized. There developed striking contrasts between urban and rural styles of congregation while class segregation became the normal pattern of the late Victorian city.[38] The congregations established in different areas inevitably reflected their settings.

There were, consequently, enormous disparities in wealth between congregations. The new wealth arising from the growth of manufacturing and trade was by no means evenly distributed. The poor shared in a rising standard of living, but the improvement in their resources was tiny by comparison with the advances of the rich. In England, for example, Samuel Morley rose through the hosiery trade to become a millionaire. His Congregational chapel, the King's Weigh House, was one of the wealthiest in London. Such urban congregations went in for pew rents, selling the right to occupy a particular seat for specified periods. The effect, according to critics, was to restrict the attenders to the well-to-do. Large congregations increasingly advertised their affluence by publishing

---

[37]Clive D. Field, "The Social Structure of English Methodism: Eighteenth-Twentieth Centuries," *British Journal of Sociology* 28 (1977).

[38]Hugh McLeod, *Class and Religion in the Late Victorian City* (London: Croom Helm, 1974).

annual accounts in elaborate yearbooks. By contrast, there were places of worship in deprived parts of the great cities, in agricultural regions fallen on bad times or in newly opened areas of settlement that, like their members, were utterly impoverished. Some could barely afford a minister, paying him only a pittance so that he had to take on a secular job to support his family. Others simply dispensed with a minister altogether. Congregations, furthermore, could be heavily burdened with debt. Their inability to pay off the cost of erecting their buildings often prevented fresh initiatives in mission. Thus in 1864 a group of desperate North Welsh chapels approached Samuel Morley to help them reduce their debts, being rewarded with between £50 and £100 each.[39] Throughout the period there remained a sharp difference between the richer and the poorer congregations.

The consequences were visually striking. Humble congregations might be content with spontaneous services in rude brick chapels, tin tabernacles (in the later part of the period) or even (on the frontier) log cabins. Congregations containing the nouveaux riches, however, would not remain content with primitive surroundings. They wanted to demonstrate their respectability in their buildings and their style of worship. In England, there was a model for all denominations in the medieval parish churches that seemed the epitome of good ecclesiastical taste. The trend toward raising standards of public worship, however, was global. At Port Elizabeth in the Eastern Cape in 1850, the Wesleyans put up a new ceiling, introduced an "organ-seraphine" and established a choir to ensure "greater propriety and effect."[40] In Sydney, New South Wales, eight years later the official Methodist newspaper was condemning mean buildings and expressing a preference for Gothic.[41] In New York in 1865 the Fifth Avenue Baptists opened "a neat and commodious structure in the Gothic style" at a cost of forty thousand dollars. It included a pastor's study, robing and committee rooms, no ugly galleries, but fourteen stained glass windows.[42] There was in the earlier stages of the process a consciousness that the change required justification. If elegant buildings and harmonious organs attracted larger numbers,

---

[39]Edwin Hodder, *Life of Samuel Morley* (London: Hodder & Stoughton, 1888), p. 230.

[40]W. B. Boyce, ed., *Memoir of the Rev. William Shaw* (London: Wesleyan Conference Office, 1874), p. 210.

[41]*Christian Advocate and Wesleyan Record* (Sydney), September 21, 1858, p. 43.

[42]*Examiner and Chronicle* (New York), June 22, 1865.

it was contended, then more would hear the gospel.[43] Others, however, believed that the more elaborate structures were a symptom of the gospel's decay. When in 1857 William Taylor, a fervent Methodist revivalist, visited the Cheshire Street Church, Baltimore, renowned as the only Methodist church south of the Mason-Dixon Line to possess pews, he found the merchants and bankers of the congregation reluctant to leave their counting houses for revival meetings. Their taste, he concluded, had been allowed to quench their zeal.[44] In the next generation the Free Methodists of America poured the vials of their holy indignation on the various signs that religion was at low ebb in cold, fashionable Methodist Episcopal congregations. In particular worshipers were taken to task for bowing their heads on the back of the seat in front rather than exerting themselves to kneel for prayer.[45] There was a gulf between those who wanted services to be more genteel and those who wanted a more populist style. Differing status dictated contrasts in the setting and pattern of worship.[46]

Similar contrasts were to be found in the field of education. Some who treasured memories of a heroic age when little was valued but strenuous preaching of the gospel thought that schooling was spoiling the simple earnestness they recalled. Thus in 1880 an elderly Methodist itinerant in Canada numbered education and "talent-worship" among the forces sapping reliance on the Holy Ghost.[47] A few, such as sections of the Primitive Baptists of the American South, consequently decried altogether any application of human learning to religious affairs. More merely neglected schooling because it seemed irrelevant either to life or to eternity. There was, after all, no national system of elementary education in England and Wales until 1870, so that many churchgoing children never had their minds stirred. The commanding trend of the period, however, was toward higher scholastic attainments for all. There were schools attached to many places of worship; there was greater training for Sunday school teachers, lay preachers and class leaders; and many a larger church possessed a mutual improvement society for young men. Denominations began to

---

[43]E.g., *Religious Herald* (Richmond, Va.), February 11, 1858.

[44]*William Taylor of California, Bishop of Africa: An Autobiography* (London: Hodder & Stoughton, 1897), pp. 141-42.

[45]*Free Methodist* (Chicago), January 9, 1884, p. 4.

[46]Worship is covered more fully in chapter 3, pp. 89-96.

[47]Benjamin Sherlock in *Christian Guardian*, April 21, 1880, p. 126.

pride themselves on their educational institutions. In 1856 the Methodist Episcopal Church in the United States could list nineteen colleges and universities and sixty-eight academies run under its auspices,[48] and yet still trailed well behind the Presbyterians in its educational provision. Even in New South Wales a Wesleyan Collegiate Institution teaching Latin and Greek, modeled on similar schools in England, was founded in 1863 on the Paramatta River.[49] There were soon equivalents for girls: ten years later, for example, a school, partly to train lady teachers, was established at Wellington in the Cape, this time taking the American Holyoke Girls' School as exemplar.[50] The belief grew that ministers must keep one step ahead of their people. "If there *ever* was a period," ran an article in the leading American Methodist magazine in 1853, "that demanded intense intellectual application in the ministry, the present is such a period. In order to be extensively and permanently successful in our mission, we *must* keep pace with the age in literature and science."[51] Hence, for instance, between 1870 and 1901 the proportion of the Baptist ministry in England having no formal education fell from a half to a mere 18 percent.[52] The Anglican ministry had always been preponderantly graduate, but in other denominations many of the theological colleges either forged links with universities or (in America in particular) turned themselves into universities. The tendency of the times to push up educational standards, and so to extend the range of different scholastic attainments, reinforced the social variation within the evangelical movement.

The cumulative effects of commercial growth, status aspirations and educational advances on evangelical religion can be illustrated from the development of the American camp meeting tradition in the period. Originally exuberant and noisy affairs on the frontier where soul saving was the norm, camp meetings were revived in a new form after the Civil War. On the east coast there were

---

[48]Richard Carwardine, "Charles Sellers's 'Antinomians' and 'Arminians': Methodists and the Market Revolution," in *God and Mammon: Protestants, Money and the Market, 1790-1860,* ed. Mark A. Noll (New York: Oxford University Press, 2002), p. 78.

[49]*Christian Advocate and Wesleyan Record,* June 22, 1867, pp. 35, 37.

[50]Johannes du Plessis, *The Life of Andrew Murray of South Africa* (London: Marshall Brothers, 1919), pp. 274-89.

[51]*Christian Advocate and Journal* (New York), January 20, 1853, p. 9.

[52]J. E. B. Munson, "The Education of Baptist Ministers, 1870-1900," *Baptist Quarterly* 26 (1976): 321.

larger gatherings nearer to centers of population where, often under official Methodist sponsorship, the obligations of holiness were urged on the people. At Sing Sing camp meeting, just north of New York City, in 1866 there were already significant indications of change. Methodist families arrived two to three weeks early, pitching their tents to enjoy a summer holiday. Their comfort was taken into account by the provision of permanent seating. A sermon was partly read and there were fewer converts than in the past, a deficiency partly attributed by an observer to "the picnic style of gathering."[53] Six years later a new meeting ground, at a spot called Sea Cliff, was said to have a "Tabernacle," capable of seating six thousand, where the service was conducted much as in a church. In fine weather the attenders went fishing, boating and bathing.[54] The organization sponsoring holiness camp meetings felt compelled to ban tobacco, soda water, nuts and confectionery.[55] At the same time the denominational newspaper was critical of more traditional camp meetings in Maine and New Jersey where brothers and sisters in the Lord exchanged a holy kiss and where jumping, falling and shouting were common. The managers, the editor laid down, must guard against such "offenses against propriety and good taste."[56] Another eleven years later it was regretted that at camp meetings "sentimentalism is taking the place of conviction, and taste is more considered than truth, and the utterance of strong emotions . . . is condemned as very coarse and unrefined."[57] At the same time as the affluent were turning camp meetings into comfortable holidays, the older style was condemned as dated and vulgar. Respectability had been married to religion.

It was Charles H. Spurgeon who, more than any other individual in the period, objected to the union. He delivered a sustained onslaught against respectability in the lectures he delivered to the students at his college on a Friday afternoon. It was a force, in his view, that enfeebled true religion. He delighted in a piece of advice said to have been given by an experienced minister to his son, but in reality a satire on genteel pastoral practice by Paxton Hood, a Congregationalist:

---

[53] *Christian Advocate* (New York), August 30, 1866, p. 276.

[54] *Christian Advocate*, August 29, 1872, p. 276.

[55] *Christian Advocate*, September 26, 1872, p. 307.

[56] *Christian Advocate*, August 22, 1872, p. 268.

[57] *Christian Advocate*, January 25, 1883, p. 57.

Keep also a watchful eye on all likely persons, especially wealthy or influential, who may come to your town; call upon them, and attempt to win them over by the devotions of the drawing-room to your cause. . . . And I would say to you, be a gentleman. . . . We must show that our religion is the religion of good sense and good taste . . . If I were asked what is your first duty, *be proper;* and your second, *be proper;* and your third, *be proper.*[58]

Spurgeon loathed the expected attributes of a "gentleman"—polish, kid gloves, classical knowledge, "culture." Against the image of a gentleman he set his conception of a man. Ministers must be manly, talk like ordinary men and not be effeminate in manner. Like many Broad Churchmen, Spurgeon was an exponent of "muscular Christianity." Even the good manners of everyday society were anathema to him, for they savored too much of hypocrisy to his gruff, no-nonsense personality. "As a general rule," he wrote, "I hate the fashions of society, and detest conventionalities, and if I conceived it best to put my foot through a law of etiquette, I should feel gratified in having to do it."[59] All that flowed from the rising sense of decorum was to be dismissed as a rival ideal to the egalitarian challenge of the gospel. The very vigor of Spurgeon's critique is an indication of the potency of the social tide he was trying to hold back. It was in vain: the advance of respectability in the period was inexorable. It meant that, though certain sections of the evangelical world continued to uphold Spurgeonic values, the proportion aspiring to comfort and refinement was steadily rising.

THE INTERNATIONAL GEOGRAPHY OF EVANGELICALISM

Even if denominational and social variations deserve more weight than they are commonly given in accounts of the evangelical experience, the national distinctions must not be neglected. There were clear geographical differences between the lands where the gospel had put down roots. A survey may begin with England, which contained, in London, the largest city of the era. Exeter Hall in the Strand was the epicenter of the global movement. Its May Meetings, the annual gatherings of the evangelical missionary and philanthropic agencies, formed a magnet that drew visitors from all over the world. Metropolitan religion tradi-

---

[58]Charles H. Spurgeon, *Lectures to my Students* (London: Marshall, Morgan & Scott, 1954), pp. 172-73.
[59]Ibid., p. 21.

tionally set the tone for Christian practice elsewhere, both erecting a high standard of decorum and generating novel developments. Thus a visitor to London from Nova Scotia commented in 1850 that, contrary to his experience of home, it was rare for many tears to be shed in worship.[60] And it was in West London that the great late nineteenth-century Wesleyan experiment in urban missions launched its most ambitious venture.[61] The English provinces showed immense variety, not least because the denominational balance differed from place to place. Preston in Lancashire, where there was a roughly equal threefold split between the Church of England, the Roman Catholic Church and Nonconformity, was totally unlike Stoke-on-Trent in Staffordshire, where Methodism by itself enjoyed the support of a majority of churchgoers.[62] In most parts of the country, however, the established church was the strongest force. Its divisions shaped the religious life of the nation. During the Victorian era the rise of High Churchmanship meant that Evangelicals were squeezed out of the leadership of the church and that there were increasingly daring innovations in ritual by Anglo-Catholic clergy. At the same time Broad Churchmen, though fewer in number, were taking the intellectual initiative. Consequently Evangelicals within the church were thrown on the defensive, differing among themselves on how publicly to resist the novelties and how far to concentrate instead on simple parish work. Evangelical Nonconformists, equally dismayed by the advances of sacerdotalism, feared for their young people. Consequently England did not appear to insiders to be the bastion of the gospel that outsiders often imagined it to be. The country might be the heartland of English-speaking evangelicalism, but hostile forces seemed to be ravaging it.

The religious complexion of the rest of the British Isles differed significantly from that in England. Wales was most like England, having the same established church and branches of Nonconformity that were largely integrated with their English equivalents. The balance between church and chapel, however, was by no means the same. Whereas in England chapel attendance was just behind

---

[60] *Christian Messenger*, April 26, 1850, p. 134.

[61] Philip S. Bagwell, *Outcast London: A Christian Response: The West London Mission of the Methodist Church, 1887-1987* (London: Epworth Press, 1987).

[62] The figures for English towns in 1851 are usefully tabulated in Bruce I. Coleman, *The Church of England in the Mid-Nineteenth Century: A Social Geography* (London: Historical Association, 1980), p. 41.

Church of England attendance at the religious census in 1851, in Wales there were roughly four times as many Nonconformists as Anglicans. Although there were a few Unitarians, the chapels were overwhelmingly evangelical. The other great distinctive in the principality was the Welsh language, still spoken by over half the population in 1891.[63] The trend over time, largely a symptom of rising respectability, was for English to be used more, but affection for the indigenous tongue as the vehicle for worship was deeply rooted in many congregations. Scotland, however, was totally distinct from England in denominational patterns. The three largest denominations were all Presbyterian, together taking 83 percent of the worshiping population in 1851.[64] The consequence was a high degree of conformity to strict Calvinist norms. The sabbath, for example, was observed with particular punctilio, a future English Nonconformist minister finding himself rebuked by a Glasgow policeman for whistling the last hymn on the street after morning service.[65] The Highlands, still largely Gaelic-speaking, constituted a distinct religious culture, overwhelmingly adhering to the Free Church of Scotland.[66] By contrast Ireland, still a part of the United Kingdom, was four-fifths Roman Catholic in allegiance. The Church of Ireland, the establishment down to 1870, had a period of Evangelical ascendancy from around 1845 to 1895;[67] and in the northern province of Ulster there was a vigorous Presbyterian community.[68] Many Protestants, however, felt themselves, especially after the proposal to grant Ireland a separate parliament in 1886, to form a beleaguered evangelical outpost. But northern Ireland in particular bred men who gave stalwart leadership to the churches throughout the English-speaking world.

---

[63]E. T. Davies, *Religion and Society in the Nineteenth Century: A New History of Methodism* (Llandybie, Dyfed: Christopher Davies, 1981), p. 89. The Evangelicals in the established church are discussed in Roger L. Brown, *The Welsh Evangelicals* (Tongwynlais, U.K.: Tair Eglwys Press, 1986).

[64]Callum G. Brown, *The Social History of Religion in Scotland since 1730* (London: Methuen, 1987), p. 61.

[65]Arthur Mursell, *Memories of My Life* (London: Hodder & Stoughton, 1913), p. 63.

[66]Douglas Ansdell, *The People of the Great Faith: The Highland Church, 1690-1900* (Stornoway: Acair, 1988), chaps. 10-11.

[67]Alan Acheson, *A History of the Church of Ireland, 1691-1996* (Dublin, Ireland: Columba Press, 1997), p. 182.

[68]R. Finlay G. Holmes and R. Buick Knox, eds., *The General Assembly of the Presbyterian Church in Ireland, 1840-1990* (Belfast: Presbyterian Historical Society of Ireland, 1990).

The United States, occupying half a continent, could not avoid being a scene of infinite internal variety. New York commanded almost as much prestige within American religion as London within its British counterpart, being home, for example, to the chief organs of the denominational press. Nevertheless Boston, with the rest of New England, though powerfully swayed by Unitarianism, retained some of its colonial standing as a center for Congregationalists. The east coast as a whole was the source of inspiration and largesse for much of the rest of the country. A new Presbyterian church at Colorado Springs dedicated in 1873 was grateful for presents of an organ, chandeliers and a bell from "friends East."[69] Evangelicals participated fully in the shift of the population westward. Before the end of the century, Chicago, the scene of Moody's urban ministry, was feeling itself to be the fulcrum of the country. Meanwhile the South was content with the distinct version of Christian civilization it had created.[70] Its Methodist and Baptist denominations were separate entities from their Northern counterparts before the middle of the century; they were joined by a separate Presbyterian Church after the Civil War. That conflict also gave rise to a mass exodus of black members from predominantly white churches to create monochrome congregations and ultimately separate denominations. The South, however, was no different from other sections of the United States in being dominated by the popular evangelicalism of the Methodists and Baptists. In 1850, it has been calculated, the Methodists enjoyed the support of 34 percent of religious adherents, the Baptists 20 percent. Methodism retained its strength for much of the century, but was overtaken by the Baptists in the South before 1890 and in the nation overall by 1906. Even more significantly, by 1890 the proportion of Methodists in the population was smaller than that of the immigrant Roman Catholics.[71] The evangelical hegemony over the United States, a reality in the middle years of the century, was fading before its end.

---

[69] *Rocky Mountain Presbyterian*, February 1873.

[70] Samuel S. Hill, "Northern and Southern Varieties of American Evangelicalism in the Nineteenth Century," in *Evangelicalism: Comparative Studies of Popular Protestantism in North America, the British Isles and Beyond, 1700-1990*, ed. Mark A. Noll, David W. Bebbington and George A. Rawlyle (New York: Oxford University Press, 1994), pp. 275-89. Samuel S. Hill, ed., *Religion in the Southern States: A Historical Study* (Macon, Ga.: Mercer University Press, 1983), catalogues the experience of the various states.

[71] Roger Finke and Rodney Stark, *The Churching of America, 1776-1990: Winners and Losers in our Religious Economy* (New Brunswick, N.J.: Rutgers University Press, 1992), pp. 55, 145-46.

The main territories of white settlement within the British Empire—
Canada, Australia and New Zealand—were naturally home to the range of
British denominations and so to a strong evangelical presence. Quebec, originally French and still largely francophone, was the exception, being overwhelmingly Roman Catholic. In Ontario, by contrast, in 1891 only 17 percent of population were Catholics, but 31 percent were Methodists, 21
percent Presbyterians and 18 percent Anglicans. Toronto was an evangelical
citadel, with Anglican Evangelicals enjoying extensive, though not uncon-
tested, social influence. In the Maritime Provinces to the east, Methodism
was weaker, but the Baptists had the allegiance of 19 percent of the population. On the prairies and in British Columbia to the west there were also
rather fewer Methodists relative to Presbyterians and Anglicans.[72] Canadian
confederation in 1867, forging national unity for the first time, was followed by the Methodists creating a dominionwide church (1874 and 1884);
the Presbyterians similarly healed their divisions in 1875. The equivalent
step of nation-building in Australia, federation, did not occur until 1901,
and so the colonies retained a separate existence and character. Tasmania,
South Australia, Western Australia and Queensland were each very thinly
populated; but Victoria, containing the largest city, Melbourne, and New
South Wales, with Sydney, possessed significantly more people. The balance
between the denominations differed considerably from colony to colony.
Thus in 1891 whereas in New South Wales the Methodists had only some
10 percent of the population, in South Australia they claimed 23 percent.[73]
Among Anglicans, the Sydney diocese was already emerging as the strong-
hold of Evangelical faith that it was to remain during the twentieth century.[74] Missions to indigenous peoples were a feature of both Canada and
Australia, but even more so of New Zealand, where initially they proved
more successful. There, however, the land wars drastically reduced the number of Maori associated with the churches, which became predominantly set-

---

[72]Semple, *The Lord's Dominion*, p. 182. The figures are from census professions of allegiance.

[73]Walter Phillips, *Defending "A Christian Country": Churchmen and Society in New South Wales in the
1880s and After* (St. Lucia, Australia: University of Queensland Press, 1981), p. 6. Hunt,
This Side of Heaven, p. 105.

[74]Stephen Judd and Kenneth Cable, *Sydney Anglicans* (Sydney: Anglican Information Office,
1987).

tler institutions.[75] In the later nineteenth century the largest city was Dunedin, designed as the counterpart of Presbyterian Edinburgh in the southern hemisphere. In all these lands the British influence was strong, sometimes reinforced by a desire to avoid being, as one South Australian Methodist put it in 1881, *"Americanised."*[76] Imperial loyalties, as in other spheres, were a potent force in religion.

Elsewhere in the empire a similar pattern was reproduced on a minor scale. The extent to which the South African church scene was assimilated to Anglo-Saxon models has often been underestimated. The British-derived denominations were closely tied to the home country; and even the Dutch Reformed Church, which sometimes held services in English as well as in Dutch, was drawn into joint evangelical enterprises, especially under the leadership of Andrew Murray.[77] In India, Anglican bishops and chaplains to the main European communities were maintained at government expense and the numerous missionaries often took pains to serve the local expatriates. The Wesleyans, for example, paid special attention to the British troops stationed in the country. Indian missions, furthermore, had adopted the strategy of evangelizing the land through teaching the values of Western civilization in English. In 1852, it was reported, there were one hundred and twenty-six superior English-language day schools in the country, almost all attached to missions.[78] In the Caribbean many missions had turned into settled churches, the diocese of Jamaica, like many other colonial sees, having as its bishop from 1880 a strong Evangelical, Enos Nuttall.[79] In other parts of the empire, where British settlement was even sparser, there was nevertheless English-speaking worship. Sierra Leone, a small settlement for freed slaves on the west African coast, had services in English under the auspices of the various evangelical denominations.[80] At Lagos, further east on the same coast, there were in 1868 four Anglican churches, one with services in Yoruba only, two with a mixture of Yoruba and English, and one, attended by the gov-

---

[75]E. W. Hames, *Out of the Common Way: The European Church in the Colonial Era, 1840-1913* (Auckland: Wesley Historical Society of New Zealand, 1972), pp. 51-52.

[76]*Methodist Journal* (Adelaide), March 18, 1881, p. 8.

[77]du Plessis, *Andrew Murray,* n.p.

[78]*Irish Presbyterian* (Belfast), July 1853, p. 198.

[79]Frank Cundall, *The Life of Enos Nuttall, Archbishop of the West Indies* (London: SPCK, 1922), pp. 45, 52.

[80]Christopher Fyfe, *A History of Sierra Leone* (London: Oxford University Press, 1962).

ernor and his entourage, with English only.[81] On Fiji in the Pacific, Wesleyan
missionaries catered to the European farmers.[82] Outside the empire similar facilities for English-speaking residents, often provided by Americans, were scat-
tered around the world. Thus the Copt Mission in Cairo ran an afternoon English service, attracting in 1857 over forty worshipers; and the missionaries
stationed in Bankok, Siam, took turns preaching to Europeans and Americans
in the city.[83] Liberia, founded as a haven for freed slaves from America on the
west coast of Africa in 1822, attracted Baptists and Methodists among its black
settlers as well as sustaining missions to the indigenous peoples.[84] China and Ko-
rea, often the preferred missionary destinations by the end of the century, contained cities where the gospel could be heard in the tongue of the missionaries
themselves. In all these lands there was a mingling of evangelistic activity among
users of other languages with preaching through the medium of English. These
territories added a further element of diversity, often vigorous though frequently
small in scope, to the international evangelical movement.

INTERNATIONAL EVANGELICAL BONDS

Yet what is most striking about the movement is less its heterogeneity over
space than its internal connections. Improvements in communications during
the period—the railway, the steamship, the telegraph, the spread of magazines
and newspapers—revolutionized contact between different parts of the world.
The transatlantic linkages were particularly strong. Many of the immigrants to
America from the United Kingdom carried their faith with them across the
ocean. Consequently there was a steady flow of ministers, such as many of Spurgeon's trainees, from Britain to America. Many ministers also paid visits to the
United States for the sake of cementing relations between the churches on the
two sides of the Atlantic. At a meeting of Stockwell Orphanage in 1883, Spurgeon's son Charles proudly exhibited eighty-three views taken on a recent tour
of America.[85] Some visitors were treated with great honor. On a triumphal

---

[81] *Religious Herald*, April 2, 1868.
[82] *Wesleyan Methodist Magazine*, August 1850, p. 880.
[83] *American Missionary*, July 1857, p. 152; December 1852, p. 268.
[84] Walter L. Williams, *Black Americans and the Evangelization of Africa* (Madison: University of
Wisconsin Press, 1982).
[85] *Freeman* (London), April 20, 1883, p. 245.

progress in 1867, the Congregationalist Newman Hall, celebrated as the author of the immensely popular tract *Come to Jesus* (1848), preached to members of both houses of Congress and had a private interview with the president. At the home of the lieutenant governor of Massachusetts, Hall prayed for blessings on "both sections of the one great English family."[86] Writings and ideas from the British Isles circulated widely in America. Thus the tract *Seek Riches* by J. C. Ryle was reproduced in the Virginia Baptist newspaper in 1858.[87] The first article written by the New England Congregationalist Henry Trumbell in the *Sunday School Times*, which he was later to edit, was an account of a house-to-house visitation in London.[88] There was also a significant reverse flow of personnel across the Atlantic. American Christians visited Britain for tourism and health, picking up observations and sometimes more—as when a North Carolina Presbyterian delightedly carried home from Stirling Castle a piece of the pulpit once used by John Knox.[89] C. P. McIlvaine, bishop of Ohio and leader of the Evangelical Episcopalians, crossed the Atlantic nine times;[90] Charles Finney, Phoebe Palmer and other prominent exponents of holiness spent extended periods in Britain; and the visits of Moody and Sankey were key episodes in the national life of the United Kingdom. Henry Ward Beecher, the leading American Congregationalist, who was feted during a British tour in 1886, declared at a London reception that "I am of England, although I live in America."[91] Many others could have said the same.

A similar web was woven between the various parts of the evangelical diaspora. Emigration again laid the foundation on which a religious superstructure could be built. In the first issue, published in January 1870 at Christchurch, New Zealand, of the interdenominational *Christian Observer*, the obituarist of a colonist who had lived successively in South Australia, the North Island of New Zealand, Victoria and finally the South Island of New

---

[86]Newman Hall, *From Liverpool to St. Louis* (London: George Routledge & Sons, 1870), pp. 198, xviii, 27.

[87]*Religious Herald*, March 4, 1858.

[88]P. E. Howard, *The Life Story of Henry Clay Trumbell* (Philadelphia: Sunday School Times Co., 1905), p. 167.

[89]*North Carolina Presbyterian* (Fayetteville, N.C.), January 22, 1858.

[90]William Carus, *Memorials of the Right Reverend Charles Pettit McIlvaine, D.D., D.C.L.* (London: Elliot Stock, 1882).

[91]*Henry Ward Beecher in England, 1886* (London: James Clarke & Co., n.d.), p. 8.

Zealand, mused on the wider significance of his subject.

> The providence of God has evidently been at work in leading pious families to
> these new countries; with the stream of emigration flowing, God has taken care
> to send out some of the piety of the fatherland, that Christianity might go hand
> in hand with commerce, and colonization might be the means of spreading the
> Redeemer's Kingdom.[92]

Preachers, particularly if well known, traveled back and forth around the
world. William Taylor, an American Methodist Episcopalian whose early service was in California and who subsequently was elected bishop of Africa, was
on one occasion asked by a friend in Sydney to call on his nephew near
Southampton on the south coast of England; mistaking his quarry, he struck
up an acquaintance with a man of the same name who later opened the way for
Taylor to conduct a mission at Cawnpore in India.[93] Literature was similarly
widely dispersed. Andrew Murray in South Africa subscribed to the *Revival*,
continuing to read it when it turned into the *Christian*, and also received the *Life
of Faith* and the *British Weekly*.[94] He must have been as well informed about ecclesiastical developments in Britain, where all these titles were published, as any
Briton. Likewise Nova Scotia Baptists were kept up to date on denominational
progress in Melbourne,[95] and conversely Sydney Christians were presented with
the text of one of Henry Ward Beecher's latest sermons from Brooklyn, New
York.[96] The *Irish Presbyterian* was proud in 1854 that, because its subscribers
could send copies abroad for four shillings a year, it reached almost every part
of Britain's colonial possessions.[97] It was no idle boast. The English-speaking
evangelical network straddled the globe.

In any overall assessment of evangelicalism in the later nineteenth century,
the diversity of the movement must loom large. The denominations could be
extremely different: large or small, authoritarian or libertarian, traditional or in-
novating. The social tone could vary: rich or poor, respected or obscure, educated or ignorant. And the geographical location could contrast sharply: north-

---

[92] *Christian Observer* (Christchurch), January 1, 1870, p. 7.
[93] *Taylor of California*, p. 303.
[94] du Plessis, *Andrew Murray*, pp. 438, 448, 494.
[95] *Christian Messenger*, January 6, 1858, p. 7.
[96] *Christian Pleader*, March 10, 1860, p. 75.
[97] *Irish Presbyterian*, April 1854, p. 107.

ern or southern, long established or newly settled, part of the British Empire or out of it. The picture was further complicated by the intertwining of the three variables. Differences between evangelical communities in the various lands were themselves partly a product of the denominational balance. Contrasts in social tone were often related to denomination, Anglicans being superior and Baptists inferior in almost every part of the world; and they were rooted in the differing locations of the congregations, whether urban or rural. Nevertheless the national—as opposed to the urban-rural—differences were in the last resort probably of less significance for lived experience than the social and denominational contrasts. A Cornish Methodist miner moving to South Australia soon found himself a spiritual home virtually indistinguishable from the chapel life he had left behind.[98] It may be convenient to split up evangelicals into separate national units, but there is a danger of forgetting that in reality other differences might have loomed larger for contemporaries. In every respect, furthermore, the diversity of the evangelical movement was reduced by other factors. Denominations, for all their variety, cooperated in many and various ways; the social trend was upward, toward greater respectability, for nearly everybody during the period; and groups that were geographically remote from each other were nevertheless in closer touch than might be imagined. Although some divisions, such as that between church and chapel in England and Wales or between North and South in America, were deep and enduring, there was a sense in which the prevailing tendency of the times was toward greater homogeneity within the global movement. The denominational, social and national divisions persisted, but they were weaker at the end than at the start of the period. In the last resort the internal contrasts, however vivid, were less important than the unity of the evangelical movement.

---

[98]Oswald Prior, *Australia's Little Cornwall* (Adelaide: Rigby, 1962), chap. 12.

3

THE PRACTICE OF FAITH

How did evangelicals express their faith in the later nineteenth century? The chief ways were in spirituality, worship and mission, and yet these fundamental aspects of religion, and especially the first two, have been extraordinarily neglected by historians. The theological convictions and social activities of evangelicals are much better understood than the inner dynamic that gave meaning to their personal and corporate life. Yet it is evident that the defining characteristics of the movement, its concern with conversion, Bible, cross and activism, supplied a framework for its spirituality. A person could not enter authentic spiritual experience without conversion. Thereafter the process described by theologians as sanctification, or growth in grace, was nourished by the Scriptures, focused on the atonement and demonstrated in Christian service. Sanctification, at least in the churches indebted to the Reformed tradition, was a gradual process that turned the soul into a fit occupant of heaven. Methodists might hold that there was the opportunity of leaping ahead into a state of entire sanctification, but they too believed that there was much scope for steady spiritual improvement. The whole of life was, at least ideally, a self-conscious training for eternity. Thus a sick sixty-eight-year-old Wesleyan woman from an English village near Stockport, when asked at midcentury whether she was afraid of death, replied, "Why should I fear? More than forty years I have been preparing for this."[1] The constant quest for a closer approximation to the character of Christ was the heartbeat of the movement. Many individuals would lapse into sin, so becoming "backsliders"; others would make no discernible progress, always remaining among the least committed. But others took their

---

[1] *Wesleyan Methodist Magazine* (London), March 1850, p. 319.

obligation to heart, and so pursued their pilgrimage with increased dedication. Their personal devotion underlay the vigorous missionary temper that marked the movement.

EVANGELICAL SPIRITUALITY

Prayer was the most obvious way in which evangelicals practiced their faith. There existed, as an American textbook on prayer meetings admitted, "prayer-less Christians."[2] But to allow others to do the praying on one's behalf seemed anomalous, a symptom of serious spiritual declension. Prayer, it was held, should be a joy. Elizabeth Eacott, a Wesleyan married woman from near Buckingham in England who died in 1869, was said to have "delighted in devotional exercises."[3] The American textbook recommended the setting aside of half an hour a day for private prayer, together with devotional Bible reading. Half an hour, it explained, would not be too little, "but when the half-hour becomes a habit, the season will prove so precious and be found so necessary to the support of Christian life that the full hour will be approximated."[4] The book was typical in recommending that the first half hour of the day should ideally be used in this way. This standard advice was the chief reason why evangelicals became known for their custom of early rising. It was not so much an arbitrary form of self-discipline as a means of ensuring freshness for devotional practice. But whatever time of day was chosen, private prayer, according to all the authorities, must be observed at least daily. Some more exemplary souls would seek communion with God more frequently, sometimes at two, three or more fixed points in the day. The task of finding time was often difficult, especially for servants and mothers. "How," asked a meeting of the London Maternal Association in 1850, "may the Christian mother best attain and preserve a high degree of piety amidst the numerous duties which daily and hourly devolve upon her?"[5] Regularity, it seems, was easier for women in Congregationalism, a more affluent denomination whose members would commonly enjoy domestic help,

---

[2]L. O. Thompson, *The Prayer-Meeting and its Improvement* (Chicago: F. H. Revell, 1881), p. 41.

[3]Linda Wilson, *Constrained by Zeal: Female Spirituality amongst Nonconformists, 1825-1875* (Carlisle: Paternoster Press, 2000), p. 106. This book is a penetrating study of evangelical spirituality, making comparisons across the genders as well as across denominations.

[4]Thompson, *Prayer-Meeting*, p. 43.

[5]Wilson, *Constrained by Zeal*, p. 112.

than in many of the others. Printed guidance was increasingly available for those who wanted it: from 1878, for example, there existed in England a Methodist Bible and Prayer Union that issued suggestions for daily prayer and praise.[6] Private prayer was an essential feature of evangelical spirituality.

Corporate prayer was felt to be barely less essential to a congregation. "The weekly prayer-meeting" it was said, "is the pulse of the church."[7] If the prayer meeting was enthusiastic and well attended, the vitality of the congregation could be guaranteed. Normally held on a weeknight evening, it offered an opportunity for lay members to offer spontaneous prayers. It was often the humbler classes who were the best supporters, with many Sunday worshipers staying away. Attendance among Sydney Wesleyans in 1867 was reported to be poor, with only the church officers and a few devout women being regular.[8] A perennial problem was that veteran prayer warriors would give voice to comprehensive petitions for so long, perhaps fifteen or twenty minutes, that younger people would despair of finding anything to say and so give up attending. Reform was essential, it was urged in America in 1876, "or the prayer-meeting will soon be as withered and dead as an Egyptian mummy."[9] Possible remedies were redecorating the room, sitting close together, singing heartily, all participating and, crucially, saving long prayers for private use. The pastor had the remedy in his hands, by keeping his own address (which was standard) brief and by insisting on prayers of no more than five minutes. There was a flurry of prayer meeting remodeling along these lines in the later 1870s, much of it owing to the example of Moody. Where his influence was felt in Scotland, long prayers were abandoned in favor of the five-minute variety. Elsewhere, too, prayer meetings were sometimes revitalized by making them brighter and brisker, with beneficial results for attendance, volume of intercession and the general tenor of church life. Prayer meetings were a good index of evangelical esprit de corps.

Prayer also normally hallowed evangelical families. Daily prayers, usually conducted by the head of the family, were the focal point of life for the whole household, encompassing servants and visitors as well as relations. The master of the house, especially if an Anglican, might use a book of orders of service

---

[6] *Methodist Bible and Prayer Union Monthly Letter*, January 1881.
[7] A. E. Kittredge in Thompson, *Prayer-Meeting*, p. ix.
[8] *Christian Advocate and Wesleyan Record* (Sydney), May 28, 1867, p. 30.
[9] *Christian Advocate* (New York), August 31, 1876, p. 278.

such as *Family Prayers* (1834), compiled by the doughty member of the Clapham Sect Henry Thornton and published posthumously. So popular was this work that within twenty years it had gone through thirty-one editions.[10] In many households none but the father of the family spoke, yet sometimes there was scope for audible participation by others. There could be an element of display about these occasions, a desire to exhibit evangelical credentials. Thus the members of a household might conduct morning and evening prayers only when entertaining visiting ministers or Christian workers. Then, as it was put in America, "they dust their Bibles, oil their knees, and kindle a fire upon the family altar."[11] On the other hand, there might be regular prayer more than once or twice a day. Holiness zealots in Canada toward the end of the century, for example, were arranging three daily prayer sessions in the home.[12] Holding prayer each day in the household was certainly regarded among evangelicals, by contrast with the prevailing view among High Churchmen, as preferable to attending a daily service in church. The household was marked by various forms of abstention, especially on the sabbath, but the gatherings for prayer were designed to consecrate the home, which in so many ways was the power house of evangelical religion.

The kernel of the spiritual life was the practice of fellowship with God. Thus an elderly Welsh Baptist minister talked of enjoying "much rich communion with God."[13] Evangelicals tended to emphasize their relationship with Jesus rather than with the Father. A sample of Nonconformist obituaries from England for the period 1850-1875 reveals that only 8 percent of the male instances and 11 percent of the female equivalents mention God the Father. By contrast there were references to Christ for 40 percent of the men and for 52 percent of the women. The number of allusions to the Holy Spirit was roughly at the frequency of the references to the Father.[14] It is clear that the piety, though definitely trinitarian, was emphatically Christocentric. There are indications, in fact, that this pattern became more marked as the

---

[10]Elisabeth Jay, *The Religion of the Heart: Anglican Evangelicalism and the Nineteenth-Century Novel* (Oxford: Clarendon Press, 1979), p. 145.

[11]Thompson, *Prayer-Meeting*, p. 40.

[12]*Christian Guardian* (Toronto), February 15, 1893, p. 99.

[13]*Baptist Magazine* (London), March 1850, p. 138.

[14]Wilson, *Constrained by Zeal*, pp. 101-6.

century wore on. An observer noted in 1895 that there was an increasing tendency for prayer to be addressed to the Lord Jesus rather than to the Father through the Son.[15] Because the comment was made about Bible readings and conventions, which were much more likely to be attended by members of the Church of England, it may well be that this process was most evident among Anglicans, perhaps because others had long observed the more exclusively Christocentric approach. For evangelicals in general, however, Christ was "the rock," "the all," "the panacea." Perhaps most commonly, with an allusion to I Peter 2:7, he was said to be "precious." Evangelicals cherished the conviction that Jesus was their personal Savior.

If growing appreciation of closeness to Christ was one dimension of the devotional life, another was the conflict with sin. A standard symptom of sanctification was humiliation, a deep-seated loathing of the sinfulness that believers discovered within themselves. Thus an elderly Baptist minister felt himself to be "a poor creature" and a prominent Leeds Congregational layman spoke of his "self-distrust."[16] It was not only the self in its weakness but also Satan in his power that threatened the welfare of the soul. Obituaries of ordinary Christians at midcentury, especially Methodists, often refer to struggles against "the enemy," "the adversary" or "the powers of darkness." Temptation came, too, from the world, the attractions that might draw the believer into wrongdoing. Thus in the 1890s holiness people, who, as we shall see, took this teaching further than others, condemned "superfluities of dress" together with "tobacco, snuff and drama."[17] Doubt, to which evangelicals were often remarkably willing to admit, was another trial to be endured. After making several pious affirmations, the wife of a Baptist pastor in Devon paused to ask, "But suppose it should all be a delusion?"[18] Likewise a Congregational minister confessed to having many dark clouds in his room. "Lord, I believe!" he cried, "help thou my unbelief!"[19] There were also worries, most common among the more conservative Presbyterians, about whether they were numbered among the elect. Assurance of salvation was by no means automatic, and its absence could cause

---

[15] *Christian* (London), July 18, 1895, p. 16.

[16] *Baptist Magazine*, July 1850, p. 402. *Christian Witness* (London), 1851, p. 319.

[17] *Christian Guardian*, February 15, 1895, p. 99.

[18] *Baptist Magazine*, February 1850, p. 101.

[19] *Christian Witness* (London), 1852, p. 256.

prolonged anxiety. Suffering was another cause of trouble. In an age without analgesics, pain could often be acute, but it was commonly interpreted as intended for the good of the soul. A Wesleyan woman saw her sufferings as "the chastening of her heavenly Father, designed to make her a partaker of his holiness."[20] So life was a demanding business, a pilgrimage with many a danger lurking on either side of the narrow way. It is not surprising that John Bunyan's *Pilgrim's Progress* (1678) was still widely used as a medium for interpreting the pattern of Christian experience. The Slough of Despond and Castle Doubting were as real in the nineteenth as in the seventeenth century.

A stern test of spirituality came with the approach of death. Evangelicals nurtured the ideal of a "good death," a bedroom scene in which the dying saint made an unhurried disposition of affairs and testified to a calm assurance of faith. Pat Jalland has shown that the ideal often differed from reality, with published accounts often being edited so as to eliminate any discreditable behaviour.[21] There is evidence from circles other than those of the upper- and middle-class Anglicans whom Jalland has examined that this practice was widespread. Nevertheless reports of deathbed scenes, which were a staple feature of evangelical literature down to the 1870s, often have an authentic ring to them. They sometimes show venerable figures making their farewells and appropriate arrangements for the welfare of their families. Thus Edward Baines, the Congregational proprietor of the *Leeds Mercury* and a former Member of Parliament, called the members of his family together and spoke individually to each of them with "patriarchal dignity."[22] Again, particular remarks can hardly have been wholly invented. The wife of a minister who took an early Presbyterian charge in Australia, for instance, seems to have had a sense of reaching heaven but then returning. "What a pity I lost the glory!" she exclaimed.[23] The overall impression is of natural apprehension about death mingling with varying degrees of confidence about what lay beyond, but often including a high degree of serenity or a vivid sense of triumph. Last words were carefully recorded: "All is right" or "The Lord is faithful." But it is notable that after the 1870s there was a reaction against recording such scenes. Jalland has attributed the change

---

[20] *Wesleyan Methodist Magazine*, February 1850, p. 203.

[21] Pat Jalland, *Death in the Victorian Family* (Oxford: Oxford University Press, 1996), chap. 1.

[22] *Christian Witness*, 1851, pp. 319-21.

[23] Ibid., p. 593.

partly to the decline of Evangelicalism among well-to-do Anglicans, but the same shift took place among non-Anglicans who remained evangelicals. Respectability was forcing its way into the treatment of death. In 1880 a contributor to the *Baptist Magazine* declared that it was "very repugnant to refinement of feeling for the still utterances of the chamber of death to be noised abroad and made the theme of rude religious declamation."[24] Reticence in the face of death now seemed more appropriate.

One of the chief topics on the lips of dying believers was the afterlife. Heaven has recently been recognized as a central theme of evangelical piety in the period.[25] African American devotion, as Negro spirituals suggest, had a special place for anticipation of the release from bondage that would come to the believer after death. But Alexander Raleigh, a fashionable London Congregational preacher, was equally concerned during the 1870s to dwell in his sermons on what his wife called "the mystic attraction of heaven."[26] The afterlife was portrayed in a variety of ways. By contrast with the present, it was bright, light or glorious. The inhabitants of heaven could enjoy rest, peace and happiness. Spurgeon, however, embraced what has been called the "modern" idea of the future state when, in his vigorous youth, he spoke of heaven not as a place of rest suited to the indolent but as "a place of uninterrupted service."[27] Another "modern" aspect of the afterlife commonly anticipated by evangelicals was reunion with friends and family. "I shall never again see her this side of Jordan," said a dying Welsh Baptist minister of a church member, "but we shall soon meet in heaven."[28] This expectation was more than a sanctified version of Victorian domesticity, for it was an expression of the solidarity of the fellowship of believers that would endure beyond the grave. But the most common feature of anticipation of the afterlife was looking forward to being in the divine presence. Sometimes the central theme was a welcome from the Father; more often it was dwelling with the Savior. The prayer "Come, Lord Jesus" was

---

[24] *Baptist Magazine*, January 1880, p. 34.

[25] Wilson, *Constrained by Zeal*, pp. 59-63.

[26] Mary Raleigh, *Alexander Raleigh: Records of his Life* (Edinburgh: Adam and Charles Black, 1881), p. 271.

[27] Colleen McDannell and Bernhard Lang, *Heaven: A History* (New Haven: Yale University Press, 1988), pp. 278-79.

[28] *Baptist Magazine*, March 1850, p. 138.

customarily applied not to the second advent but to Christ fetching the believer at death. Heaven seemed close to evangelicals: while groping through London fogs or farming the American plains, they could already catch glimpses of Beulah land.

PATTERNS OF WORSHIP

Worship, though rarely approximating to the ideal of a foretaste of heaven, was assumed to be a regular part of Christian duty. Certain denominations had their own particular ways. Most obviously distinctive was the liturgical worship maintained by those in the Anglican communion through the use of the *Book of Common Prayer*. Evangelicals within the Church of England and its sister bodies, however, did not simply conform to the pattern of worship followed by other Anglicans in their day. They were marked out by resistance to the innovations steadily introduced during the period by the disciples of the Oxford movement. Evangelical clergy long refused to permit robed choirs, wear the surplice for sermons or adopt the eastward position at Holy Communion. Other evangelical groups, on the other hand, were noted for their total opposition to formal liturgy. Quakers maintained their traditional meetings for worship in which silence was broken only as attenders were moved by the Spirit to speak; and Brethren adopted a similar pattern, though focused on the Lord's Supper, whereby individuals could contribute a prayer, a hymn or an exhortation as they felt guided. Both bodies, however, also held evening services virtually undistinguishable from those of the Methodists, Presbyterians, Congregationalists or Baptists. A typical order of service among these Free Churches was reported by a Methodist in or about Adelaide in 1875: hymn (seven to ten minutes), prayer (fifteen minutes), choir anthem (long), two Bible readings, hymn, announcements (long), sermon (forty-five minutes), hymn, prayer.[29] Some made a point of restricting the service to a single hour, since the brevity appealed to less regular churchgoers, but often the whole—as these comments on length suggest—would continue for an hour and a half or longer. At midcentury the morning service was usually complemented by an afternoon meeting of similar character, but gradually during the period there was a trend to replace the afternoon gathering, when relatively few strangers attended, with one in the evening. The

---

[29]*Methodist Journal* (Adelaide), April 16, 1875.

change was gradually creeping over New England towns, it was noted in 1871, but it was being resisted in some urban congregations and all those in the countryside.[30] The motive for the alteration was to provide a service designed for evangelistic purposes at a time when young people, and especially domestic servants, would be more likely to attend. Its style might be slightly less formal and the sermon would target nonbelievers. The result was a pattern of worship bequeathed to the twentieth century, with saints catered to in the mornings and sinners in the evenings.

There were many other adaptations in worship during the period. On the one hand, the informality of Methodism gradually became more disciplined. Worshipers were dragooned into arriving punctually, falling to one's knees to pray became less common and pious ejaculations became rarer. At Saul Street Primitive Methodist Chapel, Preston in Lancashire, for example, an observer remarked in 1869 that cries of "Amen," "Yes" and "Praise the Lord," though frequent in the past, were now voiced by "only a few of the old-fashioned and more passionately devoted members."[31] At the same time liturgical elements gradually crept into the services of denominations in the Reformed tradition that had looked askance at anything not prescribed in Scripture. Especially in prosperous urban congregations, there were printed prayers, congregational responses and a larger number of musical items. At a time of growing recreational opportunities and the rise of the music hall, churches had to adapt if they were to draw in the people they wished to see converted. The relative weight given to the sacraments also increased in some bodies. The Free Church of Scotland, from its inception in 1843, had doubled the number of Communion services offered each year from two to four. Both trends—toward less spontaneity and toward more liturgical worship—were undergirded by the same cultural developments, what an American Methodist commentator identified in 1892 as "the opinions and tastes of so-called refined and cultivated society."[32] The advance of respectability, especially in the middle classes, meant that shouting in services was out and more decorous services were in. The introduction of flowers into places of worship was a symbol of the process. Previously they had been excluded as a diversion from the spiritual, but in 1852 Henry Ward Beecher, a

---

[30]*Examiner and Chronicle* (New York), January 5, 1871.
[31]Anthony Hewitson, *Our Churches and Chapels* (Preston: Chronicle Office, 1869), p. 74.
[32]*Christian Advocate,* January 14, 1892, p. 17.

broad-minded Congregational minister in Brooklyn with a passionate Romantic love for nature, placed a vase of flowers beside him for the morning service. Despite denunciation, he insisted on their remaining and his genteel congregation soon came to love them.[33] The practice of having flowers in church gradually spread. Worship was being adapted to the preferences of the times.

The sermon was in almost all evangelical bodies the climax of worship. The preaching of the Word was what explained the Bible, proclaimed Christ crucified and led to conversions. There could be complaints, as among South Australian Methodists in 1875, that all else was eclipsed:

> The sermon is the most prominent part of the service; everything is made to bend to this; praise and prayer, and the reading of the Scriptures, are sometimes so curtailed as to make the impression on the mind that they are regarded as very insignificant and comparatively unimportant parts of public worship.[34]

But preaching was what most people came for, so that they often drifted in during the sections of the service before the sermon, what were often called "the preliminaries." The sermon was accorded a space of time appropriate to its preeminence. Robert Bickersteth, the Evangelical bishop of Ripon from 1857 to 1884, usually preached for fifty minutes.[35] At Gideon Congregational Church, Bristol, in 1880, the morning sermon lasted thirty-seven minutes and the evening sermon forty.[36] A South Australian Methodist proposal for reform in 1875 suggested that, with a little extra study, ministers could compress their thoughts into thirty minutes, but sixteen years later another would-be Australian shortener of services still expressed a preference for sermons lasting forty-five to fifty minutes.[37] An address of twenty-five minutes was dismissed by an English Baptist in 1888 as a mere "pulpit talk," not a "real sermon" at all.[38] In 1896 Robertson Nicoll, the enterprising editor of the *British Weekly*, an interde-

---

[33] Charles D. Cashdollar, *A Spiritual Home: Life in British and American Reformed Congregations, 1830-1915* (University Park: Pennsylvania State University Press, 2000), p. 41. Chapter 3 of this book is a valuable discussion of changes in worship.

[34] *Methodist Journal*, April 9, 1875.

[35] M. C. Bickersteth, *A Sketch of the Life and Episcopate of Right Reverend Robert Bickersteth, D.D., Bishop of Ripon, 1857-1884* (London: Rivingtons, 1887), p. 45.

[36] R. D. Robjent, *The Bristol Nonconformist Sunday Services* (Bristol, n. d.), pp. 10-11.

[37] *Methodist Journal*, April 23, 1875; *Spectator* (Melbourne), January 23, 1891, p. 94.

[38] *Freeman* (London), January 13, 1888, p. 17.

nominational newspaper that circulated mainly among English Nonconformists and Scottish Presbyterians, published a survey of sermon lengths reported
by its readers. The shortest, preached by the Rev. G. Bicheno at Clitheroe Primitive Methodist Chapel in Lancashire, took only 5.75 minutes; the longest, delivered by a Mr. E. W. Bishop at Clay Cross Methodist New Connection
Chapel in Derbyshire lasted an astonishing one hour and twenty-eight minutes.[39] Hearers were expected to develop remarkable powers of concentration.

There was agreement among evangelicals on some basic points of sermon
technique. Henry Gaud, the President of the Australian Wesleyan conference,
spoke for most of them in recommending at an ordination service in 1867 the
preaching of the Word, that is "God's truth" rather than "fancies and speculations," a concentration on the gospel, a "*plain* and *perspicuous* style" and an effort
to stir the consciences of hearers.[40] Not all the preachers in the movement, however, managed to achieve great things in the pulpit. William Butler, for example,
an English General Baptist minister who died in 1850, possessed (even according to his sympathetic obituarist) talents that were "decidedly respectable, but
not of a high order." His sermons lacked "originality of thought or arrange-
ment"; his delivery was occasionally "somewhat heavy"; and he spoke with "a
degree of loud monotony."[41] Part of the problem for such weaker brethren was
that many congregations objected to written discourses or sometimes even to
notes in the pulpit, considering them a denial of the help of the Holy Spirit in
delivery. At midcentury, American Methodism was especially hostile to reading
a written text, though some preachers defied convention. "If a man . . . cannot
preach a sermon without writing it," a note in the main denominational paper
declared in 1872, "he has reason to fear he has mistaken his calling."[42] In general, however, there does not seem to have been any deliberate obscurity in the
choice of biblical texts to expound. The same *British Weekly* survey in 1896 discovered that of the sermons delivered on a particular Sunday, three-quarters
were based on texts from the New Testament, with the Gospel of John being
the favorite source, the first letter of John coming next, and the other three Gospels following. One-fifth of the Old Testament texts were from the book of

---

[39] *British Weekly* (London), March 19, 1896, p. 356.
[40] *Christian Advocate and Wesleyan Record*, April 10, 1867, p. 16.
[41] *General Baptist Magazine* (London), October 1850, p. 446.
[42] *Christian Advocate*, August 29, 1872, p. 275.

Psalms.[43] In terms of style, the most respected exemplars of pulpit eloquence at midcentury such as the Methodist William Morley Punshon were distinctly florid. Punshon spoke in elaborate sentences, possessing (it was said) "the literary faculty" that appealed to "the cultured congregation."[44] But the trend was thereafter toward simpler diction, as exemplified in the addresses of the Methodist pulpit star of the end of the century Hugh Price Hughes, whose plainness had a more modern ring. The manner might alter, but the aim was always to secure a hearing for the gospel.

The musical dimension of worship tended to become livelier during the period. The development had already taken place in some quarters. The Methodists had led the way in vigorous hymn singing and Evangelical Anglicans had followed by adding a repertoire of hymns to the traditional diet of metrical Psalms. In the later nineteenth century the Evangelicals of the Church of England persisted, against High Churchmen, in their preference for "a hearty service and congregational hymnody."[45] African Americans could hardly increase the uninhibited exuberance in their services:

> The perfect *abandon* of their worship is wonderful. . . . In singing, one of their number steps out and repeats, in a perfect sing-song, one or two lines of a hymn, when all fall in and sing an *impromptu* sort of tune. . . . Some one seizes the hand of another and begins to shake it, and this goes on till the whole audience becomes thus engaged—the singing still proceeding, and at the same time each one moving from side to side in a measured manner, as if to beat the time, or convert music into motion.[46]

Amongst those strongly influenced by the Reformed tradition, and supremely among Presbyterians, however, there was a transformation of worship style. Their custom had been to admit into their services only what had Scripture warrant, the explicit sanction of the New Testament. That principle, apparently dictating the exclusion of instrumental music and the limitation of singing to biblical passages, which in practice meant the Psalms, came under increasing pressure for change during the period. Thus in 1869 in New Zealand the Pres-

---

[43]*British Weekly*, March 26, 1896, p. 379.

[44]*Methodism in 1879* (London: Haughton & Co., 1879), p. 30.

[45]Bickersteth, *Bickersteth*, p. 79.

[46]*Examiner and Chronicle*, April 27, 1865 (on the "colored" Baptists of Richmond, Va.).

bytery of Dunedin requested permission from its superior court, the Synod of Otago and Southland, to introduce "well-selected hymns." Despite resistance from one minister who defended the church's "time-honoured psalmody," the request was granted.[47] As a result of such decisions, the rich stock of English hymns, including the inspirational but profound compositions of Isaac Watts and Charles Wesley, became the common property of evangelicals at large.

Many churches also altered their manner of singing. The custom in denominations with a strong Calvinist inheritance had been for a psalm to be started by a precentor with a tuning fork to pitch the note. Prosperous churches, such as many in Edinburgh, had begun to hire paid precentors with particular musical ability, or even a band of singers. In New York churches it became the norm to employ a "fashionable quartette" to lead the praise.[48] There was also an attempt to encourage church members to practice their singing in musical associations on a weeknight evening. In recommending the general formation of such groups, the Psalmody Committee of the Presbyterian Church of Ireland urged in 1866 that their organizers should sanction "nothing but the best sacred music, rigidly excluding all the light, irreverent rants in which many delight."[49] The traditional posture of sitting to sing, though standing to pray, was reversed in most congregations, partly because hearty singing was easier for those on their feet. This development, which gathered pace in the middle years of the century, was not universally welcomed. When the minister tried to introduce it at the Free High Church in Inverness, a protest from a section of the congregation was upheld after eleven hours' discussion by the local presbytery.[50] Another alteration, however, was accepted by nearly all the churches during the period. The traditional custom, catering for the illiterate, was to "line out" hymns by reading a sentence or two, whatever a congregation could remember, before they were sung. As the ability to read increased, however, the practice was modified or dropped. In America it had largely disappeared before midcentury, but at the Metropolitan Tabernacle in 1868 each hymn was still read through and then in addition each verse was read before it was sung.[51] In

---

[47] Christian Observer (Christchurch), January 1, 1870, p. 14.

[48] Examiner and Chronicle, January 9, 1868.

[49] Evangelical Witness and Presbyterian Review (Dublin), December 1866, p. 331.

[50] Presbyterian Churchman (Dublin), May 1877, p. 95.

[51] Examiner and Chronicle, February 6, 1868.

South Australia lining out persisted well after that point. There it was first challenged by a Methodist minister fresh from England who copied younger men
in the homeland by giving out a whole verse rather than a line or two at a time.
Only by the early 1880s was there a demand in the colony to sing the hymn
without any spoken interruption at all.[52] When, toward the end of the century,
it became normal for churches to buy a set of hymn books for the pews, the old
custom faded away entirely. It must have been a great relief to be able to sing a
hymn straight through.

One factor encouraging the adoption of a brisker method of singing was
the arrival of gospel songs.[53] Although Moody's partner Ira D. Sankey was by
no means the only exponent of the genre, he was by far the most popular.
Sankey's *Sacred Songs and Solos* achieved an immediate worldwide impact, being
adopted, for instance, by the Evangelical Alliance prayer meetings in South
Australia only two years after their first publication in 1873.[54] Maria Havergal, the sister of Frances the hymnwriter, admitted that the harmonies in Sankey's tunes were weak, but, she claimed with justice, "they move the masses
in England."[55] The song "There were ninety and nine that safely lay," with its
insistent rhythm and welcome message that Christ the good shepherd came
to seek the wandering sheep, was just one of Sankey's compositions that became part of the staple of the Sunday school repertoire. Yet the prevailing direction of change in the period was toward more dignified music, with better
trained choirs and more demanding anthems. In England and Australia during the 1850s and 1860s even chanting in the High-Church manner was introduced in some of the most fashionable Nonconformist churches on the
ground that it ensured greater participation. The greatest musical change of
all, however, was the introduction of organs. The process had begun before
1850 in a number of larger urban congregations, but even in English parish
churches, where instrumental music had long been admitted, it had normally
been provided by an amateur band. Initially Calvinist inhibitions ensured a

---

[52]Thomas Lloyd in *Methodist Journal*, February 25, 1881, p. 7.
[53]Sandra S. Sizer, *Gospel Hymns and Social Religion: The Rhetoric of Nineteenth-Century Revivalism*
    (Philadelphia: Temple University Press, 1978).
[54]*Methodist Journal*, May 21, 1875, p. 2.
[55]*The Autobiography of Maria Vernon Graham Havergal, with Journals and Letters*, ed. J. Miriam Crane
    (London: James Nisbet, 1888), p. 190.

spirited resistance to the new instrument. Thus in Canada a Free Church congregation brought in an organ in 1855 only to be directed to remove it immediately.[56] Scottish opposition was fierce and, in the Highlands, unyielding.
Nevertheless in most lands an organ, whether an elaborate instrument with
an array of pipes or a humble harmonium, was introduced into the great majority of places of worship at some point in the later nineteenth century. An
organ supported congregational singing, allowed virtuoso performances by
the organist and confirmed the good taste of the attenders. Once again the
predominant tendency of change was toward catering for the growing respectability of the worshipers.

METHODS OF OUTREACH

There was equally a great deal of flexibility in the methods of evangelism used
during the period. Much of the responsibility fell upon the ministers. "A
house-going parson," recalled a South Wales clergyman in 1878, "makes a
church-going people."[57] Ministers might also penetrate into places other than
homes, though with varying degrees of success. In 1858 an incumbent reported
that he and his curate had visited a public house in Manchester to expostulate
with the landlord for opening on a Sunday evening. The landlord proved remarkably civil, explaining that they were playing *The Messiah*. "I told him," went
on the incumbent, "that sacred music was a fitting introduction to a sermon,
and with his permission I would go and preach them one. He would rather I
did not, so I left him."[58] What was remarkable about the period, however, was
the capacity of the churches to mobilize laypeople as well as ministers for mission. Thus a Baptist church in New York organized some of its young people
into a society of "Pastor's Helpers" who distributed tracts and visited the poor
in the district of the church.[59] Calling on people in their homes for spiritual
purposes was turned into a regular feature of Christian duty in the rising cities.
Ideally an Anglican parish might be divided into small areas of no more than
twenty households, each of which was to be visited weekly by a member of the

---

[56] Richard W. Vaudry, *The Free Church in Victorian Canada, 1844-1861* (Waterloo, Ontario: Wil-
    frid Laurier University Press, 1989), p. 93.

[57] *Occasional Paper*, 113 (London: Church Pastoral Aid Society, 1878), p. 11.

[58] *Occasional Paper*, 53 (London: Church Pastoral Aid Society, 1858), p. 5.

[59] *Examiner and Chronicle*, March 19, 1868.

congregation. This vast army of volunteer district visitors might be supplemented by paid laypeople on the church staff. Thus alongside the seven clergy at St. Giles, Bloomsbury, in central London, in the mid-1850s, there were eleven Scripture readers and city missionaries.[60] These employees were often charged with the supervision of a wide range of organizations, many of them targeting the young. During the 1890s St. Mary's, Islington, provided Bands of Hope, a Church Lads' Brigade, a midweek Bible class for young women, an institute offering recreation, instruction and the benefits of a club for the same group, a Bellringers' Guild, a football club, a choral society and other organizations.[61] At the same time Union Chapel, Islington, a Congregational church just up the road, supported three branch mission churches in more deprived parts of the area.[62] The spread of the gospel in the vicinity was regarded as the task of every congregation.

Home missionary work, however, extended far beyond the neighborhood of the church. In cities there were open-air meetings, missions in hired halls and theater services. In rural and freshly settled regions there were other methods. Methodists in America had pioneered camp meetings to bring the people of sparsely occupied areas together for preaching.[63] Such gatherings, often more planned but still marked by an intensely revivalist spirit, continued in the period. They were also extended to other parts of the world—to England, where they were run by Primitive Methodists, and to Australia, where Wesleyans as well as Primitives participated. Ingenious methods were contrived to attract interest in remote areas. Sensing a demand for instruction in song, a Baptist preacher in Tennessee would organize a singing school in an area, turn it into a prayer meeting "and the usual result was a fruitful revival."[64] The earliest preachers in a new territory would often arrive soon after the first settlers. They might, as in the Eastern Cape at midcentury, need to travel long distances to hold services in the homes of the people because there was no hope of gathering

[60]Bickersteth, *Bickersteth*, p. 68.

[61]Margaret Barlow, ed., *The Life of William Hagger Barlow, D. D.* (London: George Allen & Sons, 1910), p. 74.

[62]W. H. Harwood, *Henry Allon, D. D.: Pastor and Teacher* (London: Cassell & Co., 1894), pp. 28-29, 63.

[63]C. A. Johnson, *The Frontier Camp Meeting: Religion's Harvest Time* (Dallas: Southern Methodist University Press, 1955).

[64]*Examiner and Chronicle*, February 27, 1868.

them into congregations.[65] Or ministers might find, as in Minnesota in the 1850s, that attendance at services was limited by the danger of Indian attack.[66] Frontier conditions often dictated that the pioneer preachers should be bivocational, turning their hands to teaching or farming to provide for their families. Circumstances might also induce them to adopt desperate measures, as when Simon Richardson, a Florida circuit rider, planned to kill as many as he could of a party lying in wait to ambush him before they disposed of him.[67] Such rough-and-ready characters, thoroughly integrated into the way of life of their neighbors, carried the gospel into every nook and corner of the English-speaking world.

Many organizations existed to spread the faith during the period. Hay Aitken, an Anglican clerical evangelist, set up the Church Parochial Missions Society in 1881 to coordinate the work of men like himself who were willing to visit a parish for a special evangelistic effort. A similar body that branched off from the C.P.M.S. four years later, the Church Army, deliberately included non-Evangelicals on its committee in order to give the organization broader appeal.[68] The Wesleyans had started appointing district missionaries shortly before, and soon Thomas Champness was creating a network of evangelists associated with his newspaper *Joyful News*. By 1889 there were eighty-nine of them.[69] Samuel Morley, the millionaire hosier, was responsible from 1858 for reactivating the Congregational Home Missionary Society. Under his patronage, the organization specialized in employing lay evangelists and colporteurs, who often served with county associations.[70] Spurgeon's Pastors' College spawned successively a Home Visitation Society, a Society of Evangelists and a Pioneer Mission. The college could very reasonably claim to be itself a type of home mission concerned with "the breaking up of new ground, and the gathering of

---

[65] *Wesleyan Methodist Magazine*, February 1850, p. 216.

[66] *American Missionary* (New York), January 1857, p. 6.

[67] S. P. Richardson, *The Lights and Shadows of Itinerant Life* (Nashville, Tenn.: Publishing House of the Methodist Episcopal Church South, 1900), p. 129.

[68] Anne Bentley, "The Transformation of the Evangelical Party in the Church of England in the Later Nineteenth Century" (PhD diss., Durham, 1971), pp. 311, 324-25, 328.

[69] Eliza M. Champness, *The Life-Story of Thomas Champness* (London: C. H. Kelly, 1907), pp. 189, 215, 243.

[70] Edwin Hodder, *Life of Samuel Morley* (London: Hodder & Stoughton: 1888), pp. 95-98.

new churches."[71] Even the Strict Baptists, who disdained many organizations beyond the local church, founded a London Gospel Mission Association in 1851 and a Gospel Home Mission nine years later.[72] Apart from denominational ventures, there was a host of cooperative organizations that straddled confessional boundaries. The London City Mission and its equivalents in other cities that concentrated on reaching the working people through strategically placed agents were perhaps the most prominent of the interdenominational organizations.[73] All the bodies mentioned here were in England, but there were similar agencies elsewhere—often replicas of the English bodies, but sometimes, as with the Bible Christians' Gospel Van Mission established in South Australia in 1895, an initiative adapted to local conditions, in this case the inhospitable outback that did not permit travel by horse.[74] It was an era of vigorous home missionary activity.

Evangelistic work was intimately associated with social concern in the period. The great exemplar was Lord Shaftesbury, at once the leading Evangelical Anglican layman of his day and the preeminent social reformer.[75] The cause with which he is most commonly associated, the campaign for the limitation of working hours in the factories to ten hours a day, already lay in the past: he had won a notable triumph in 1833 by carrying a parliamentary measure to enforce this restriction for children and he had continued to champion the crusade until its success in 1847. But Shaftesbury was a leader on a range of other issues. He promoted sanitary reforms, introduced the inspection of lodging houses and ensured the regulation of homes for the mentally ill. He was the most celebrated proponent of improved housing for the working classes. He was the pa-

---

[71] *Historical Tablets of the College founded by Charles Haddon Spurgeon in 1856 and first called the Pastor's College*, ed. G. W. Harte (Southport: Thomas Seddon, 1951), pp. 39, 45, 51. *Annual Paper descriptive of the Lord's Work connected with the Pastors' College, 1879-1880* (London: Alabaster & Passmore, 1880), p. 3.

[72] Ian J. Shaw, *High Calvinists in Action: Calvinism and the City: Manchester and London, 1810-1860* (Oxford: Oxford University Press, 2002), pp. 265-66.

[73] Donald M. Lewis, *Lighten Their Darkness: The Evangelical Mission to Working-Class London, 1828-1860* (Westport, Conn.: Greenwood Press, 1986).

[74] Arnold D. Hunt, *This Side of Heaven: A History of Methodism in South Australia* (Adelaide: Lutheran Publishing House, 1985), p. 114.

[75] The standard biography is Geoffrey B. A. M. Finlayson, *The Seventh Earl of Shaftesbury* (London: Eyre Methuen, 1981).

tron of an array of voluntary societies, of which the two nearest his heart were the Ragged Schools that catered to destitute children and the Golden Lane Mission to Costermongers (sellers of fruit and fish), for whose use he provided a street barrow emblazoned with his coat of arms. There was no more frequent speaker at the May Meetings in the Exeter Hall, the annual gatherings of the missionary and philanthropic societies of the evangelical world. Shaftesbury's motives were mixed. Part of his purpose, as he had avowed to Sir Robert Peel in the 1840s, was to conciliate "thousands of hearts to our blessed constitution."[76] It was as explicit a statement of the aim of social control as a Marxist could wish. Shaftesbury, as a Conservative peer, inevitably upheld the traditional aristocratic values of the day that endorsed social rank, inequality and deference. Yet there was a powerful sense of Christian obligation too. He noted in his diary for 1857 that in the scene of judgment in Matthew 25 the goats are condemned "not for sins they have *committed*, but for duties they have *omitted*." Christ asked in effect, "Have you labored for the physical and spiritual welfare of your fellow sinners?" "Therefore," Shaftesbury concluded in the words of James 4:17, "to him that knoweth to do good and doeth it not, to him it is sin."[77] The peer gave himself to unremitting labor on behalf of the disadvantaged because he was stirred by a conscience sensitive to Scripture.

Nor was Shaftesbury unusual in the evangelical community of his day. Other prominent figures also promoted major charitable projects. George Müller in Bristol, Thomas Barnardo in London and William Quarrier in Glasgow were all responsible for creating large-scale orphanages. So, as we have seen, was Spurgeon. Likewise Dwight L. Moody encouraged ventures of social concern among those who looked to him for guidance. He spoke in favor of better housing for the poor and a wave of social reform followed his visit to Glasgow.[78] In America the Young Men's Christian Association undertook welfare work, during the Civil War the Christian Commission embodied compassion for the troops and from the 1870s independent rescue missions in the slums combined free food and lodging with earnest evangelism. A plethora of churches and church-sponsored

---

[76]D. L. Edwards, *Leaders of the Church of England, 1828-1944* (London, 1971), p. 129.

[77]Lord Shaftesbury's Diary, October 1, 1857, quoted by G. F. A. Best, *Shaftesbury* (London: B. T. Batsford, 1964), pp. 54-55.

[78]I. G. C. Hutchison, *A Political History of Scotland, 1832-1924: Parties, Elections, Issues* (Edinburgh: John Donald, 1986), pp. 136-38.

organizations throughout the English-speaking world tackled aspects of social destitution.[79] The ideal pattern of an urban parish, as outlined by Charles Kemble in 1859, included relief in meat, bread, coal, wine, beer, arrowroot, sago, rice and tea, all being supplied through tradesmen who closed on Sundays; access to hospital facilities; a Provident Fund providing interest on deposits; cheap soup and loaned blankets in winter; and tin boxes for expectant mothers, each containing a Bible, a Prayer Book, oatmeal, sugar, soap and sometimes linen.[80] The underlying premise was articulated by Bishop Bickersteth in an address to the Leeds Philosophical Society in 1860. The poor, he urged, needed help in their physical circumstances. Wretched dwellings could paralyze the work of the clergyman. "Mind and matter are closely connected," he concluded; "and the moral constitution, like the mental, may be elevated and depressed according to the material influences to which it is constantly exposed."[81] Human beings, that is to say, form a unity. Holistic mission, combining care for the body with nourishment for the soul, seemed the natural response.

Literature was another means by which evangelicals engaged in outreach to their contemporaries. The tract, a brief booklet or even a single sheet, was widely used to disseminate the gospel. The chief aim of district visitors was often to take a weekly tract to each home. The volume of material handed out in this way was immense. Thus the Tract Society of Collins Street Baptist Church, Melbourne, working chiefly in "the most neglected portions of the city," reported in June 1861 that during the past year it had distributed, together with 540 copies of the *Australian Evangelist* and 120 Chinese Testaments and tracts, no fewer than 63,500 ordinary tracts. In addition there was an average weekly circulation of three hundred tracts on loan. Five years later the same organization had pushed up its tract total to 96,000.[82] In Britain the minister of two small Northamptonshire churches acknowledged receipt in December 1887 of three dozen copies of tracts called *On Growing Older*, two dozen of *Wayside Chimes*, eight

[79]On America, see Norris Magnuson, *Salvation in the Slums: Evangelical Social Work, 1865-1920* (Grand Rapids: Baker, 1990); and on England, Kathleen Heasman, *Evangelicals in Action: An Appraisal of their Social Work during the Victorian Era* (London: Geoffrey Bles, 1962).

[80]Charles Kemble, *Suggestive Hints on Parochial Machinery* (London: David Batten, 1859), pp. 24-26.

[81]Bickersteth, *Bickersteth*, p. 61.

[82]*Australian Evangelist* (Melbourne), June 18, 1861, p. 43; December 18, 1866, p. 380.

dozen of *Home Words for Christmas*, four numbers of the *Tablet Almanac for 1888*, two copies of the *Fireside* Christmas number and one dozen *Songs of Cheer for Hours of Pain*.[83] "Do you want to see souls saved [?]", asked an American advertisement in 1898. "Then order ten thousand 'Arrows' and scatter broadcast. They are soul winners. 10,000: $5."[84] Increasingly, as the Northamptonshire instance suggests, magazines supplemented and began to supplant the tract. Already in 1858 *Sunday at Home* and *Leisure Hour* were being seen as remedies for infidel and demoralizing literature.[85] More substantial books were also used for evangelistic purposes. A work by an English Congregational minister circulating at midcentury recommended Alleine's *Alarm to the Unconverted*, Baxter's *Call to the Unconverted*, Baxter's *Now or Never*, *Jesus showing Mercy*, Pike's *Eternal Life*, Doolittle's *Call to the Unconverted*, James's *Anxious Enquirer* and Doddridge's *Rise and Progress of Religion*—a list that is intriguing because half of the items came from the seventeenth century.[86] Alongside Bibles and Testaments, this vast body of literature must go a long way toward explaining the cultural ascendancy of evangelical faith in the period.

MISSION TO THE YOUNG

Another explanation lies in dedicated work among the young. There were places, not only in the Scottish Highlands, where the traditional technique of catechizing children was employed. Among the Presbyterians of North Carolina the Shorter Catechism of the seventeenth-century Westminster Assembly was still being recited to the minister at the end of the century and indeed long afterward.[87] The chief method of inculcating the faith among the young in the later nineteenth century, however, was the Sunday school.[88] Nearly all urban

---

[83] *Freeman*, January 6, 1888, p. 14.

[84] *Evangelistic Record* (Chicago), June 1898, p. 282.

[85] *Occasional Paper*, 53 (London: Church Pastoral Aid Society, 1858), p. 4.

[86] George Redford, *The Great Change: A Treatise on Conversion* (London: Religious Tract Society, n. d.), p. 42.

[87] *North Carolina Presbyterian* (Charlotte, N.C.), January 13, 1898, p. 6.

[88] On England, despite its covering an earlier period, the basic work is Thomas W. Laqueur, *Religion and Respectability: Sunday Schools and Working Class Culture, 1780-1850* (New Haven: Yale University Press, 1976). It is supplemented by Philip B. Cliff, *The Rise and Development of the Sunday School Movement in England, 1780-1980* (Nutfield, Redhill, U.K.: National Christian Education Council, 1986). For the United States, there is Anne M. Boylan, *Sunday School: The Formation of an American Institution* (New Haven: Yale University Press, 1982).

churches and many rural congregations held a regular Sunday school where volunteers would teach children from the Bible. These organizations became extraordinarily popular. In Connecticut in 1857, about 38 percent of the age group from five to twenty was enrolled.[89] In Glasgow in 1891, 52 percent of children aged five to fifteen were on the books of Presbyterian Sunday schools alone.[90] These institutions, that is to say, might gather a much higher proportion of the targeted age group than the churches drew in from the population at large. In areas of new settlement, such as Minnesota in the 1850s and the Rocky Mountain states twenty years later, Sunday schools were often founded before worship was begun.[91] The popularity had originally been based in part on the provision in the Sunday schools of a free training in reading and writing at a time when day schools were rudimentary and charged fees, but by the 1870s, with the improvement of public educational facilities, the secular content in the curriculum had virtually disappeared. Sunday schools no doubt appealed to parents as a means of training children in basic morality; and they drew in children because of the special attractions. At the opening of a Queensland Baptist church in 1861, for example, there was a Wednesday evening Sunday school treat, when "the juveniles . . . disposed of a vast quantity of the good things provided for them."[92] There were rewards for good attendance and annual outings into the country or to the seaside that were enormously enjoyable for children trapped for the rest of the time in urban squalor. Above all the Sunday school anniversary was the high point in the year. There were songs and recitations, new dresses and public applause, special speakers, grand efforts in fundraising and the return of old friends. For three or four days the Sunday school far eclipsed the church in importance. The anniversary did much to confirm the allegiance of the young.

The regular pattern of Sunday school was much less exciting. Normally there would be a session before morning service and a second session at two or three o'clock in the afternoon. In the morning there might be the repetition of a hymn

---

[89]P. E. Howard, *The Life Story of Henry Clay Trumbull* (Philadelphia: Sunday School Times, 1905), p. 155.

[90]Callum G. Brown, *The Social History of Religion in Scotland since 1730* (London: Methuen, 1987), p. 85.

[91]*American Missionary*, January 1851, p. 6. *Rocky Mountain Presbyterian*, March 1872.

[92]*Australian Evangelist*, December 3, 1861, p. 224.

and text previously learned by heart, together with instruction in an Old Testament lesson in small classes. In the afternoon there might be (in an Anglican school) the recitation of a collect, the teaching of a New Testament lesson and a half-hour examination of the whole school by the superintendent on what had been learned.[93] A correspondent from Atlanta, Georgia, to a Baptist newspaper urged in 1868 that singing should be animated and prayer short. The introduction of a blackboard would enliven proceedings. "The habit of compelling the children to sit for an hour under the Question Book lesson is not a good one."[94] Those in charge, since they lacked professional training, were often notably less effective than the teachers children encountered on weekdays. Yet there were efforts at raising standards, notably through the Sunday School Union in Britain and its equivalent in the United States, both of which printed uniform lessons that became widely used. Denominational agencies such as the Church of England Sunday School Institute, founded under episcopal patronage at Sydney in 1857, also exerted themselves to improve the quality of Christian education.[95] Although in evangelical Sunday schools the aim was to lead the children to the point of conversion, there were complaints that efforts were unsuccessful. A zealous member of the Brethren attending a Sunday school workers' convention at London, Ontario, in 1871 felt that it was strong on the machinery of the schools but overlooked conversions.[96] Certainly there were constant worries that the schools were not bringing their charges, and especially the boys, into the churches themselves. In teenage years their attendance would fall away. Consequently Sunday schools probably did more to instill Christian values in the population at large than to draw young people into church membership.

There were, however, other agencies that had an impact on the young. Day schools in many parts of the world were media for the communication of Christian teaching. Many of them were provided by the churches. In the diocese of Ripon in 1867 as many as 407 of the parishes had a church elementary school while only 23 did not.[97] The parish clergyman visited on a weekly or

---

[93]Kemble, *Parochial Machinery*, p. 20n.

[94]*Religious Herald* (Richmond, Va.), April 23, 1868.

[95]*Church of England Chronicle* (Sydney), May 1, 1857, p. 153.

[96]*Donald Munro, 1839-1908: A Servant of Jesus Christ* (Glasgow: Gospel Tract Publications, 1987), p. 60.

[97]Bickersteth, *Bickersteth*, p. 221.

even daily basis to supply religious instruction. Even when, after the passing of the Elementary Education Act three years later, England for the first time possessed a national education system, the board schools provided under the act continued to include Christian teaching in their curriculum. They were prohibited from inculcating the distinctive doctrines of any denomination, but the scripturally based instruction that was offered approximated to the common message of the evangelical churches. Likewise nonsectarian Christian teaching was regularly included in the curriculum of American public schools. Consequently what children learned on weekdays reinforced their lessons on Sundays. The churches, furthermore, created fresh organizations to teach and mobilize the young. In 1881 Dr. Francis E. Clark, a Congregational minister of Portland, Maine, launched the Christian Endeavor Society, a movement that quickly spread around the world. Operating under the motto "For Christ and the church," it was designed to train young people in Christian discipleship by giving them responsibility for various aspects of its work.[98] Thus at Yarra Street Wesleyan Sunday School in Geelong, Victoria, in 1891 the Christian Endeavour Society appointed eight committees apart from the executive: lookout (for visitors and absentees), prayer meeting, social, Sunday school and calling (to look after absentees and bring new scholars), temperance, good word (fining its members a halfpenny for idle or unkind words), relief (for visiting the sick) and literature.[99] The Children's Special Service Mission, founded in 1867, organized seaside missions in England; its offshoot the Scripture Union published Bible study notes; and the Boys' Brigade, established in Glasgow in 1883, set a new pattern by giving its members drill and uniforms. Throughout the period the Young Men's Christian Association gave facilities for self-improvement in a Christian atmosphere. All these organizations, together with others, fostered Christian life and effort among young people.

REVIVALS

Another way in which church growth was generated was the revival, a time of intense religious excitement dear to evangelicals in the period. "A revival of religion," explained the *Irish Presbyterian* in 1853, "takes place whenever religion be-

---

[98]W. K. Chaplin, *Francis E. Clark: Founder of the Christian Endeavour Society* (London: British Christian Endeavour Union, n. d.).

[99]*Spectator and Methodist Chronicle* (Melbourne), February 13, 1891, p. 154.

comes more flourishing than for some time it has been. It consists in the impartation of spiritual life to the dead in sin, and the quickening and invigorating of the graces of believers."[100] There was a traditional form of revival associated with the Presbyterian Communion season, an infrequent event when thought was concentrated on the ultimate issues of sin and salvation, so stirring many attenders to fresh commitment. Ministers would offer personal guidance, organize prayer meetings and hold additional weekday services for long stretches of time.[101] Revivals prompted by the holding of Communion still sometimes broke out in the middle years of the century, as among the Congregationalists of Strait Creek Church, Ohio, in December 1857.[102] The Methodists had introduced a novel style of revival—emotional, often lay-led, commonly going on deep into the night and throwing propriety to the winds. Nine-tenths of Methodists, according to a Georgia circuit rider, owed their conversions to a revival.[103] Consequently the growth of Methodism was marked by a pattern of pulsation, with high rates of growth in years when revival was common. In England there were such peaks in 1848-1850, 1858-1860, 1875-1877, 1881-1883 and 1904-1906.[104] In the earlier years of the century Charles Finney had added a third approach, teaching that a revival, as a natural phenomenon in an orderly universe, could be understood scientifically. Hence if special measures were properly planned, a revival would infallibly follow. Revivalism, especially of the Methodist and Finney types, attracted criticism from within as well as without the evangelical camp. "Singing, shouting, jumping, talking, praying, all at the same time . . . in a crowded house, filled to suffocation," according to a more sober Congregational missionary, led to people having fits and giving in their names as converts but, as soon as the excitement was over, falling away.[105] It is true that the commitment of those professing conversion by this method often proved transient, but it is equally the case that these events brought evangelical faith prominently before the eyes of whole communities and frequently effected deep-seated moral change.

---

[100] *Irish Presbyterian*, June 1853, p. 145.

[101] Leigh E. Schmidt, *Holy Fairs: Scottish Communions and American Revivals in the Early Modern Period* (Princeton: Princeton University Press, 1989).

[102] *American Missionary*, March 1858, p. 62.

[103] Richardson, *Lights and Shadows*, p. 143.

[104] R. B. Walker, "The Growth Rate of Wesleyan Methodism in Victorian England and Wales," *Journal of Ecclesiastical History* 24 (1973): 268.

[105] J. H. Jones in *American Missionary*, June 1858, p. 136.

The greatest stir of the period took place between 1858 and 1860. Edwin Orr contended that the revival at this point inaugurated a half century that, at least in the British Isles, can properly be called the "Second Evangelical Awakening."[106] Even if that claim is exaggerated, the revival of 1858-1860 was remarkably broad in its scope and powerful in its impact. Around the new year of 1858 there was an unusual number of local awakenings in the northern United States and then, from late February, the revival seized hold of New York. Its salient characteristics were listed by the city's Methodist newspaper: the revival was started not by special revivalists but in ordinary services; it was widespread in the North of the country; it drew in "the practical businessmen of the cities"; it was calm, with scarcely any physical phenomena; and it was marked by Christian charity, so that there were united meetings.[107] The pattern, at least in places such as New York, was altogether more organized, more sober and more irenical than backwoods revivals had traditionally been. Businessmen, deeply troubled by an economic recession that had caused a spate of bankruptcies, crowded to midday prayer meetings, timed to last exactly one hour and compatible with a full diary. The whole episode became known as "The Businessmen's Revival."[108] Young men were deeply involved: the Y.M.C.A. often provided a cadre of dedicated workers, and at Yale one hundred and eleven professed conversion.[109] In the following year, partly inspired by news from America, revival broke out in Ulster.[110] Again it was marked by dedicated prayer, evangelical cooperation and the support of young men. In Ulster, however, there were rather more instances of "physical prostrations" associated with conviction of sin. Some used these phenomena to discredit the whole provincewide revival as an outburst of hysteria, but others contended that it was merely an accidental accompaniment. From Ulster the revival passed to Wales and Scotland, where it was particu-

---

[106]Edwin Orr, *The Second Evangelical Awakening in Britain* (London: Marshall, Morgan & Scott, 1949), pp. 262-63.

[107]*Christian Advocate and Journal* (New York), March 11, 1858, p. 38.

[108]Kathryn T. Long, *The Revival of 1857-58: Interpreting an American Religious Awakening* (New York: Oxford University Press, 1998), stresses the image building that went on at the time and afterward.

[109]*Christian Advocate and Journal*, April 22, 1858, p. 63.

[110]David Hempton and Myrtle Hill, *Evangelical Protestantism in Ulster Society, 1740-1890* (London: Routledge, 1992), chap. 8.

larly varied,[111] though hardly at all to England. The tide of revival eventually reached even Madras in India and Monrovia in Liberia.[112] Not only were there many thousands of conversions; there was also a distinct quickening of the pace of global efforts to spread the gospel.

Thereafter, however, there was no similar international awakening during the later nineteenth century. Instead there were many local outbreaks, especially among fishermen and miners, both occupational groups in which the risk of death was ever present. Within England the county most given to revivalism was Cornwall, where fishing and mining were both strong. There and elsewhere revivals continued to be spontaneous affairs, usually associated with prayer and expectation.

> A revival [it was said in South Australia] generally commences in the church. A few or many unite together, and with deep humiliation of soul, and true sincerity of heart, plead with God for "power from on high." They rest upon His promises, and persevere in their supplications, and God hears and answers.[113]

Prostrations were still known toward the end of the century, in the holiness revival movement of Ontario, for example,[114] but in general the tendency was toward greater self-restraint. Increasingly revivals were preplanned by traveling speakers who became semiprofessional, sometimes in imitation of Moody. In 1874 the American press carried advertisements for a *Hand-Book of Revivals*, by Henry C. Fish, "a book for every Christian worker."[115] By 1888 a Virginia evangelist was commended as "absolutely free from trickery" as though manipulative techniques had become all too common.[116] In some parts of America, and especially the South, it became the standard practice to announce and hold an annual organized revival.[117] It was not until 1904-1905, with the bursting into

---

[111]Kenneth S. Jeffrey, *When the Lord Walked the Land: The 1858-62 Revival in the North East of Scotland* (Carlisle: Paternoster Press, 2002).

[112]J. E. Orr, *Evangelical Awakenings in Southern Asia* (Minneapolis: Bethany Fellowship, 1975), pp. 59-60. *Wesleyan Methodist Magazine*, January 1860, p. 77.

[113]*Methodist Journal*, July 11, 1874.

[114]S. Crookshanks on the ministry of R. C. Horner, an Ontario holiness revivalist in *Christian Guardian*, September 30, 1891, p. 612.

[115]*Examiner and Chronicle*, February 5, 1874.

[116]R. H. Pitt on J. E. Huttton in *Religious Herald*, April 5, 1888.

[117]*Christian Advocate*, January 28, 1897, p. 59. *Free Methodist*, January 4, 1898, p. I. Helen C. A. Dixon, *A. C. Dixon: A Romance of Preaching* (New York: G. P. Putnam's Sons, 1931), p. 55.

flame of the Welsh Revival, that the tendency to routinization was broken up.[118] Although local revivals still functioned as an occasion when souls could be harvested, by the end of the nineteenth century the spontaneity had faded from most of them.

OVERSEAS MISSION

The impulse to spread the message of salvation was not limited by language, race or distance. Foreign missions formed a salient feature of evangelical life in the later nineteenth century. Part of the British, and even some of the American, effort was directed toward continental Europe. The January 1850 issue of the periodical of the Evangelical Alliance documented missionary work in France, Belgium, Switzerland, Bavaria, Schleswig, Austria and Hungary.[119] Much of the aim was to supply local evangelists with literature, money and (when necessary) diplomatic protection, but sometimes English-speaking personnel were also involved. The most celebrated figure was probably Lord Radstock, an authentic English peer, who carried the gospel in the 1870s to "the very *élite* of the Russian aristocracy" in St. Petersburg, planting some of the seeds for the subsequent flowering of evangelical communities in that land.[120] But the bulk of the overseas missions enterprise concentrated on the tropical world. The 1850 issue of the magazine of the Baptist Missionary Society, the first of the Anglo-American missionary organizations that had been founded in 1792, contained reports on activities on a global scale. Only one center, at Morlaix in Brittany, was in Europe. In Africa, missionaries served in the Cameroons, Fernando Po and Bimbia. In Asia, they were located in Barisal, Benares, Calcutta, Ceylon, Chitoura, Dacca, Delhi, Dinagepore, Dum Dum, Howrah, Intalvy, Jessore, Madras, Monghir, Narsigdarchoke, Sagor, Serampore and Sewry. In the West Indies, they were in the Bahamas, Haiti, Jamaica and Trinidad.[121] At the same time the Church Missionary Society, supported by Evangelical Anglicans since

---

[118]R. Tudur Jones, *Faith and the Crisis of a Nation: Wales, 1890-1914* (Cardiff: University of Wales Press, 2004), chaps. 12-14.

[119]*Evangelical Christendom* (London), January 1850, pp. 8-28. Cf. N. M. Railton, *No North Sea: The Anglo-German Evangelical Network in the Middle of the Nineteenth Century* (Leiden: Brill, 2000).

[120]*Evangelical Christendom*, July 1874, p. 202.

[121]*Missionary Herald* (London), 1850, index.

1799, operated on an even more extensive scale: in West Africa (Sierra Leone), Yorubaland, Syria, Smyrna and Cairo, East Africa, Bombay and western India, Calcutta and northern India, Madras and southern India, Ceylon, China, New Zealand, the West Indies and northwestern America (the Canadian plains).[122] "The missionary age of the church," concluded an American commentator in 1851, "has indubitably appeared."[123]

Home support for this vast venture was drummed up in various ways. Church work in aid of missions, the New York Methodist weekly explained in 1883, could include study of the different mission fields, personal sympathy for the missionaries, active canvassing of interest by the pastor and missionary committee, a monthly missionary Sunday at Sunday school, liberality in giving, definite prayer for various fields, a monthly meeting at church (the American term was "Missionary Concert") and special district meetings.[124] An Anglican recommended English churches to hold missionary meetings quarterly, biquarterly or monthly.[125] Missionaries themselves, at home on furlough and telling entrancing tales of faraway places, were usually the best advertisements for the cause. By no means had every evangelical congregation, however, backed the missions. In 1850-1851 only 44 percent of Particular Baptist churches in England and 46 percent of Independent churches made contributions to their denominational societies.[126] Yet churches could be generous to the enterprise. Allen Street Congregational Church, Kensington, raised £32,821 in the twenty-five years down to 1868. A high proportion went toward the maintenance of the ministry, but around £5,500 was spent each on education and poor relief while as much as nearly £9,000 was given to missionary work.[127] Between 1860 and 1884 some 12 percent of total spending by Anglicans of all church parties was on foreign missions: the proportion among Evangelicals was undoubtedly

---

[122]*Proceedings of the Church Missionary Society for Africa and the East, 1849-50* (n. p., n. d.), p. iii.

[123]Charles Adams, *Evangelism in the Middle of the Nineteenth Century* (Boston: Gould and Lincoln, 1851), p. 30.

[124]*Christian Advocate*, January 18, 1883, p. 43.

[125]Kemble, *Parochial Machinery*, p. 18.

[126]Brian Stanley, "Home Support for Overseas Missions in Early Victorian England, c. 1838-1873" (Ph.D. diss., Cambridge University, 1979), p. 194.

[127]John Stoughton, *Congregationalism in the Court Suburb* (London: Hodder & Stoughton, 1883), p. 90.

far higher.[128] Even the Civil War did not deflect Methodists in the American North from their overseas responsibilities. "We do not intend," declared a minister of the East Baltimore conference, "to let the missionary cause fall behind. We are determined to carry on the war against rebels and the devil at the same time, and freely give our money to both."[129] Toward the end of the period, a significant proportion of missionary giving came from collecting boxes, often placed on parlor mantelpieces as symbols of household allegiance. In 1895 21 percent of donations to local associations of the Church Missionary Society came from that source.[130] The cause commanded widespread popular support.

Already in the middle years of the century missionary work, even though it was conceived as the occupation of a lifetime, attracted significant numbers of volunteers. In 1857 it was estimated that America had sent out 450 preaching missionaries together with 570 helpers, male and female.[131] Even a small denomination, the Free Will Baptists of New England, maintained a missionary society, proudly announcing in 1851 that it had sent its third agent to Orissa in India.[132] Many of the personnel, at least in England, were drawn from the lower middle and artisan classes, and specialist training colleges sprang up to meet their needs. Thus Harley House in London prepared more than 900 men and women for the missionary field in the twenty-four years down to 1896.[133] There was a surge of interest in overseas work from the mid-1880s, much of it in response to the stirring news that a group of gifted young university men, the "Cambridge Seven," had undertaken service with the China Inland Mission. Now it became much more common for men of higher social rank to join foreign missions. At the same time the societies began to accept single women, a policy they had normally avoided in the past. Consequently the Church Missionary Society could report in 1897 that, whereas in the first fifty years of the

---

[128]Steven Maughan, " 'Mighty England do Good': The Major English Denominations and Organisation for the Support of Foreign Missions in the Nineteenth Century," in *Missionary Encounters: Sources and Issues*, ed. R. A. Bickers and Rosemary Seton (Richmond, U.K.: Curzon Press, 1996), p. 15.

[129]J. A. Coleman in *Christian Advocate and Journal*, January 2, 1862.

[130]Maughan, "Mighty England do Good," p. 23.

[131]*American Missionary*, March 1857, p. 59.

[132]*Free-Will Baptist Register* (Dover, N.H.), 1851, p. 81.

[133]*Christian*, July 2, 1896, p. 12.

reign of Queen Victoria it had sent out nine hundred missionaries, in only ten years since 1887 it had commissioned seven hundred.[134] Fresh societies operating on the faith principle that will call for examination in chapter six, of which the China Inland Mission was the first and largest, were becoming specially attractive.[135] By the opening of the twentieth century England and Wales had a total of 8,197 missionaries on the field, Scotland 666, Ireland 27 and the United States 4,159. America was ahead of Britain in the number of societies (fifty-two as against forty-five), but the traditional lead of Britain in missionary personnel was still being maintained.[136] Together the British missionaries, it has been pointed out, were as numerous as the members of a small profession such as accountants or architects.[137]

The archetypal missionary of the period was also the most exceptional. David Livingstone had been born in Blantyre, a village in the industrial west of Scotland, in 1813. By the age of ten he had joined the workforce at a cotton mill, and his story is a classic instance of a Scot overcoming his early disadvantages by dint of hard work. Eventually armed with a medical degree, as an Independent he joined the London Missionary Society and went out to southern Africa in 1841. He served with the veteran missionary Robert Moffat in the interior among the Tswana people, but eager to find fresh regions to evangelize, he made a series of exploratory probes to the north. In 1852 he undertook an immense four-year journey from Cape Town to the Makololo people of central Africa, turning west to the Atlantic coast at Luanda before returning east across the whole continent to the Indian Ocean. His achievement, recorded in his *Missionary Travels and Researches in South Africa* (1857), brought him personal fame and a wide hearing for his views. In a celebrated speech at Cambridge in 1857 he argued that, for the sake of the peoples of region whom he wanted to evangelize, the slave trade must be put down; that the best way was to promote legitimate commerce; and that a limited number of Europeans should enter Africa to teach technological skills. Above all, though, his call

---

[134]*Record* (London), May 7, 1897, p. 465.

[135]See chap. 6, pp. 188-89.

[136]James S. Dennis, *Centennial Survey of Foreign Missions* (New York: Fleming H. Revell Co., 1902), p. 257.

[137]Andrew Porter, "Religion and Empire: British Expansion in the Long Nineteenth Century, 1780-1914," *Journal of Imperial and Commonwealth History* 20 (1992): 372.

was for more missionaries, and many, including the High-Church founders of the Universities Mission to Central Africa, responded to the summons. From 1858 to 1864 he led an expedition up the Zambesi River that was much plagued by difficulties, some of his own making, and in 1862 his wife, Mary, who was accompanying him on his travels, died; nevertheless from 1866, supported by the Royal Geographical Society, he returned to Africa in order to discover the source of the Nile. In the later phase of his career, although no longer supported by the London Missionary Society, Livingstone still regarded himself as a "missionary-explorer" and would habitually preach at the villages he visited. When he died in 1873, his body was carried by devoted followers to the coast and brought back for burial in Westminster Abbey. This strong-willed man became embalmed in myths that associated him with different attitudes prevailing in succeeding generations. Yet the establishment in his memory of Church of Scotland and Free Church missions in what was to become Malawi ensured that his supreme ambition, the evangelization of Africa, remained a major portion of his enduring legacy.[138]

One of the misrepresentations of Livingstone in later legend was that he was an advocate of the type of empire that emerged in the last third of the nineteenth century. The belief is a part of a broader association of the missionary enterprise with the spread of the British Empire that has become commonplace. It is held that missions were the ideological arm of territorial expansion in the period. Certainly evangelicals saw imperial advance as an opportunity for the gospel. British Wesleyans, for instance, applauded their Australian coreligionists in 1860 for "laying the foundations of a great Protestant empire."[139] Furthermore the protection of indigenous peoples from the slave trade and other forms of oppression could seem a worthy humanitarian motive for annexation. Yet there was no simple correlation between missions and empire. Sometimes, as in northern Nigeria at the end of the century, the British authorities discouraged evangelistic effort since it might cause public disorder. Missionaries themselves were often wary of the colonial authorities because they might do as much to corrupt the peoples under their care as to protect them. Within British territory, the advance of evangelical bodies usually owed little or

---

[138]On Livingstone, see Tim Jeal, *Livingstone* (London: Heinemann, 1973) and Andrew C. Ross, *Livingstone: Mission and Empire* (London: Hambledon and London Books, 2002).

[139]*Minutes of the Methodist Conferences* (London: John Mason, 1862), 14:536.

nothing to government patronage, which in a formal sense had all but disappeared by the middle of the century. There are instances, conversely, where British Christians established flourishing missions outside British territory and
even outside a British sphere of influence. The Baptist mission in the Congo,
which became the personal appanage of the King of the Belgians, is a case in
point. There was a marked difference between Anglicans, who rarely saw draw-
backs to the expansion of empire, and Nonconformists, who leaned toward a
pacific policy abroad and so commonly opposed imperial wars. Thus slaughter
on the northwest frontier of India was denounced by the Nonconformist newspaper the *Christian World* in 1897 as "A National Crime."[140] Although the distinction between the two parties within evangelicalism was eroded in the last
few years of the century, when many Nonconformists were caught up in the
popular imperialism of the times, there remained among them vestiges of resistance to the growth of empire. Consequently the relationship between missions
and empire is much more ambiguous than it is usually supposed to be. Evangelicals were by no means consistent apologists for painting the map red.[141]

The overriding result of global missions was not the growth of empire but
the implanting of Christian faith in fresh lands. It is true that the bulk of evangelization was performed not by agents who had been sent out but by local people. At midcentury the West Africa operations of the Church Missionary Society employed only nineteen European staff but as many as fifty-nine African
missionaries, catechists and teachers.[142] The entrusting of the work to indigenous Christians, however, was long the aim of most missions.[143] Nevertheless
the consequence was commonly the creation of a religious culture virtually indistinguishable except in language from what the missionaries had known at
home. In 1857 an American visitor to Siam felt himself at home on Sunday
despite the worship being conducted in Siamese. "I observe," he reported, "the
same order in these services that is usually observed in Sabbath day preaching

---

[140] *Christian World* (London), November 25, 1897, pp. 10-11.

[141] On missions and empire, see Brian Stanley, *The Bible and the Flag: Protestant Missions and British
Imperialism in the Nineteenth and Twentieth Centuries* (Leicester: Apollos, 1990); Andrew Porter,
"Religion and Empire," in *The Imperial Horizons of British Protestant Missions, 1880-1914*, ed.
Andrew Porter (Grand Rapids: Eerdmans, 2003); and David W. Bebbington, "Atone-
ment, Sin and Empire," in Porter, *Imperial Horizons*.

[142] *Proceedings of the Church Missionary Society, 1849-50*, p. lii.

[143] On missionary strategy, see chap. 4, pp. 141-44, and chap. 6, pp. 188-90.

in the United States."[144] Likewise the 1876 Sunday school anniversary at the Wesleyan chapel in Annshaw in the Eastern Cape was identical to what might have taken place in England. The local minister presided over a Saturday celebration; there were two Sunday services with a visiting preacher from the local town; in between the children were questioned about their Scripture knowledge; and at all three sessions there were exuberant hymns by the children, the reporter cryptically remarking that "Most of the singing was in good taste." On Monday, which was kept as a holiday, ten different Sunday schools marched past in the open air, "singing with flags and banners flying." An eminent Wesleyan layman delivered a suitable address to the children, which was followed by cheers for the speaker and his mother; a local magistrate "spoke to them kind and encouraging words"; there were three cheers for the queen, for the magistrate, for their ministers, "&c." Next came playtime with bats and balls, and a "bun was given to each child." In the evening there was a final climax when there were addresses, songs and recitations in the chapel. Apart from the Wesleyan layman being described as a chief, the children singing in Xhosa and the weather being fine in November, the whole description would have fitted an anniversary in Lancashire.[145] Even if there is room for doubt about how appropriate some of the details of the proceedings were to the cultural setting, it is evident that one brand of English evangelicalism had been successfully exported to another hemisphere.

Support for missionary effort, it was generally agreed, did not dissipate the energy of the churches for work at home but rather reinforced their vigor. Interest in foreign missions, according to an English parson in 1890, "stimulates, encourages, directs Christian life by calling attention to the example of converts from heathendom."[146] This reflex effect of missions was but one of the factors that explains the sustained vitality of evangelical congregations in the later nineteenth century. The centrality of prayer, whether for individuals, homes or churches, ensured the priority of the spiritual quest. The struggle with sin, doubt and anxiety gave meaning to the human condition, even in the face of death, when the promise of heaven could become an immense comfort. Worship, though varying between the denominations, had in almost all of them a

---

[144]Dr. Bradley in *American Missionary*, December 1857, p. 268.

[145]*Christian Express* (Lovedale, South Africa), December 1, 1876, pp. 7-8.

[146]Herbert James, *The Country Clergyman and his Work* (London: Macmillan 1890), p. 156.

focal place for the sermon. For many the style of music underwent revolutionary change, with the introduction of hymns, gospel songs and organs, each catering in a different way for the taste of the times. The evangelism of individual congregations was supplemented by the outreach of myriad organizations and complemented by a social concern that was embodied most strikingly in Lord Shaftesbury. Literature, youth organizations and particularly Sunday schools were additional agencies for transmitting the faith in the period. Revivals, especially in the years 1858-1860, played a major part in raising the spiritual temperature and bringing people to the point of conversion. And overseas missions provided an occupation for missionary collectors at home and an outlet for the adventurous spirit of a David Livingstone in Africa. Apart from their effect in the sending countries, the missionary efforts carried the Christian culture of the English-speaking world to new lands. Here was an elaborate pattern of devotion and mission that ensured the continuing vibrancy of the churches. A robust spirituality, together with adaptable styles of worship, gave a powerful dynamic to evangelicalism, turning it increasingly into a movement that covered the globe.

4

THE LEGACY OF THE ENLIGHTENMENT

The ideas of the evangelicals of the later nineteenth century were deeply molded by the assumptions of the earlier phase of Western thought known as the Enlightenment. The progressive thinkers of the eighteenth century had so admired the powers of the human intellect that the period has been dubbed the "age of reason." By casting off the prejudices of the past, it was held, it would be possible for humanity to advance into a better future. The powers of the mind could be applied successfully to the problems of the day, banishing ignorance, eliminating misery and purifying government. The high culture of the era was inclined to oppose anything that stood in the way of progress for humanity, whether obscurantism, oppression or corruption. The goal was greater happiness, entailing a diminution of pain and an increase in pleasure. The characteristic method was a single-minded quest for knowledge of how the world really operated. There must be an end to useless metaphysical debates, and instead a concentration on empirical techniques. Facts must be established by free enquiry; the universe would yield up its secrets; and humanity would gain from the fresh understanding. There was a premium on science, on exploration, on wisdom from new sources. At first only the educated elite might possess a grasp of the way of improving the lot of the human race, but eventually, as the brighter ideals percolated down to the masses, enlightenment would become general. This movement of thought, associated above all with the *philosophes* of France, is often depicted as the dawn of modernity.

AN AFFINITY FOR ENLIGHTENMENT IDEALS

The evangelicals are commonly supposed to have been resolutely hostile to the

Enlightenment. Its intellectual posture seemed to encourage disbelief or at best a form of religion that had broken with biblical faith. The luminaries of the French Enlightenment, Voltaire, Diderot and their fellows in the Paris salons, despised organized religion. David Hume in Scotland and in England men such as Edward Gibbon lampooned Christian belief. Latitudinarians in the Church of England and Arians in Dissent abandoned orthodoxy in order to uphold what they believed to be a more rational form of Christianity. The eighteenth-century revival, on the other hand, is often seen as a protest against the intellectual restrictions of the age. People fired by emotion went into rebellion against the notion that religion must be circumscribed by the bounds of rationality. John Wesley and George Whitefield are seen as preachers to the heart and not to the head. Deeper historical probing, however, shows that the antagonism between evangelicalism and the Enlightenment has been overdrawn.[1] Although eighteenth-century evangelicals did denounce the irreligious conclusions of Hume and Gibbon and did oppose both latitudinarianism and Arianism, they were not opponents of the whole age of reason. Wesley, for instance, disliked the metaphysical speculations of the past and encouraged his followers to adopt the latest techniques of electrotherapy. He and his fellow leaders of the revival wanted to promote learning and to spread civilized values to the multitudes. Wesley commended what he called "a religion founded upon reason, and every way agreeable thereto."[2] There was in reality an affinity between many of the ideals of the Enlightenment and the attitudes of the leaders of the evangelical revival.

The bond between the two movements became, if anything, tighter during subsequent years. As both slowly grew in popularity over time, they interacted and in many ways fused together. The most influential of early nineteenth-century evangelical thinkers, Thomas Chalmers, married evangelical and Enlightenment themes in his social theory as much as in his theology. New causes among the people such as the burgeoning temperance campaign and the inter-

---

[1] Bruce Hindmarsh, *John Newton and the English Evangelical Tradition between the Conversions of Wesley and Wilberforce* (Oxford: Clarendon Press, 1996), p. 330. G. M. Ditchfield, *The Evangelical Revival* (London: UCL Press, 1998), pp. 31-32. David W. Bebbington, "Revival and Enlightenment in Eighteenth-Century England," in *On Revival: A Critical Examination*, ed. Andrew Walker and Kristin Aune (Carlisle: Paternoster Press, 2003).
[2] G. R. Cragg, ed., *The Works of John Wesley*, vol. 11 (Oxford: Clarendon Press, 1975), p. 55.

national peace movement blended the fervor of the one with the rational calculation of the other. In America the values of the youthful republic, framed by Enlightenment theorists, readily meshed with those of the advancing evangelicals. Thomas Dick, a member of one of the Scottish Secession Churches, argued in his work *The Christian Philosopher* (1823), which enjoyed enormous popularity on both sides of the Atlantic, that it is "a most dangerous and delusive error to imagine that reason . . . ought to be discarded from the science of religion." The light of nature, he recognized, was a totally inadequate guide: unassisted reason was helpless without revelation. Yet the Christian must use reason to investigate the material world so as to understand its Creator. Dick could write unselfconsciously of "the enlightened Christian."[3] By the middle of the nineteenth century it was normal for evangelicals to assume that the values of the Christian faith were equally those of progressive thinking. There were, it is true, exceptions, those who felt that the cause of the gospel had been betrayed by a capitulation to modern thought. The views of some of these traditionalists are noted in this chapter and the ideas of others will be discussed in chapter six. Nevertheless the predominant school of thought within evangelicalism around 1850 maintained that the advance of knowledge that had marked recent times was in entire harmony with Christian truth. There was no possibility of a divorce between faith and reason.

The affinity of the thought of the evangelicals for the legacy of the Enlightenment in the later nineteenth century has often been obscured by their sustained polemic against what they saw as a formidable intellectual foe. A willingness, especially on the part of higher critics, to modify the teaching of the Bible rather than humbly submit to it was the leading characteristic of the phenomenon they called "rationalism." The advance of this force, according to Lord Shaftesbury in 1856, was "rapid, fearful, resistless."[4] It was constantly denounced by evangelical theologians between the 1850s and the 1870s. "Rationalism," declared T. R. Birks, a Cambridge professor of moral philosophy and a leading evangelical, in 1879, "may be defined as the abuse and perversion of human reason, in dealing with the claims of Divine Revelation." The barrage of

---

[3]Thomas Dick, *The Christian Philosopher*, 2nd ed., 2 vols. (Glasgow: William Collins, 1846) 1:19, 24.

[4]Lord Shaftesbury's Diary, May 28, 1856, quoted by Geoffrey B. A. M. Finlayson, *The Seventh Earl of Shaftesbury, 1801-1885* (London: Eyre Methuen, 1981), p. 378.

censure directed against rationalism has given the impression that evangelicals were hostile to the affairs of the mind in general and any critical use of the intellect derived from the age of reason in particular. Birks, however, was objecting not to the use of reason, but to its abuse. The first step toward the cure of rationalism, he went on to say, is the recognition of the real dignity of reason. Nobody in any theological camp was more eager in the period than Birks to urge that, in theology as in other fields, the right approach should be adopted. The correct method was what he termed "Baconian inductivism," the technique of open-ended enquiry commended by Francis Bacon that had achieved such strides in the physical sciences. Birks was approving nothing other than the Enlightenment ideal of intellectual method.[5] The denunciation mounted by evangelicals, fierce and sustained though it was, concentrated on speculation that ignored or explained away scriptural teaching. What they opposed was not reason in itself, but any intrusion of reason into the proper sphere of revelation.

A COMMON INTELLECTUAL PERSPECTIVE

Consequently preoccupations characteristic of the Enlightenment of a hundred years before were still very apparent in the writings of late nineteenth-century evangelicals. There was in the first place an explicit appeal to reason. William Cunningham, a leading theologian of the Free Church of Scotland, saw it as an impartial arbiter between those who accepted revelation and those who did not. If, he contended, we are discussing positions in natural religion with those who do not admit the authority of Scripture, "we must prove them from the principles of reason, which they admit."[6] Rationality, it was universally held, was what separated humanity from the animal kingdom. There must be no toying with limiting the powers of reason in the name of exalting faith. Thus the teaching of H. L. Mansel in the Bampton Lectures of 1858, that the absolute God is beyond the capacity of the human mind to grasp, had no appeal for evangelicals even though it was mounted in defense of orthodoxy.[7] Reason must not be trammeled by restrictions of any kind. Evangelicals commonly professed a

---

[5]T. R. Birks, *Supernatural Revelation: Or First Principles of Moral Theology* (London: Macmillan, 1879), pp. 214, 237, 203.

[6]William Cunningham, *Theological Lectures on Subjects connected with Natural Theology, Evidences of Christianity, the Canon and Inspiration of Scripture* (London: James Nisbet & Co., 1878), p. 111.

[7]Birks, *Supernatural Revelation*, p. 2.

belief in the ideal of free enquiry, the unhampered search for truth. Thus when Charles Finney, the American revivalist, codified his theological lectures from Oberlin College, he rejoiced in the "spirit of inquiry" into the truths of religion.[8] Likewise in 1879 Alexander Raleigh, a senior Congregational minister in London, argued that the principle of authority had rightly been replaced in religion by free inquiry.[9] Raleigh was one of the more advanced within the range of evangelical thinkers, and many others would have maintained the enduring authority of the Bible against him. Nevertheless Raleigh's contention was symptomatic of a powerful current of thought within the movement. The Enlightenment had bequeathed to evangelicals the conviction that reason should be deployed to roll back the borders of ignorance.

The principle on which enquiry should proceed, as the Enlightenment had taught, was investigation of how things actually were. As a general rule, evangelicals believed in hard facts as the remedy for the vagaries of their more liberal theological opponents. "We deal with facts," declared a leading article in the *Record*, the Evangelical Anglican newspaper in 1863, "not with first principles":

> It is really high time that the good sense of England should no longer be deluded by the vain speculations of romancing rationalists. So long as we stand on the *terra firma* of facts, we can keep our ballast; but as soon as we enter into the ideal world, unless we adhere to FACTS, we are at the mercy of the winds, without rudder or compass.[10]

Likewise Sir Emilius Bayley, a clergyman who was one of the regular speakers at the annual Islington conference of Evangelicals, appealed nineteen years later to "facts—well-attested facts."[11] The Scottish Free Church theologian James Denney drew a parallel between the "facts with which the physicist deals" and the "facts with which the theologian deals," claiming that "a scientific *method* is demanded in both cases."[12] The scientific technique of induction from the facts

---

[8]Charles Finney, *Lectures on Systematic Theology*, ed. George Redford (London: William Tegg & Co., 1851), p. viii.

[9]Mary Raleigh, ed., *Alexander Raleigh: Records of his Life* (Edinburgh: Adam and Charles Black, 1881), p. 282.

[10]*Record* (London), January 2, 1863.

[11]*Record*, January 18, 1882.

[12]James Denney, "A Brother of the Natural Man," in *On "Natural Law in the Spiritual World"* (Paisley: Alexander Gardner, 1885), p. 17.

was recognized as the standard way in which fresh knowledge was acquired. The natural theologian, according to James McCosh, a Scotsman who served as president of Princeton College in New Jersey from 1868 to 1888, proceeds as in any other investigation. "He sets out in search of facts; he arranges and co-ordinates them, and rising from the phenomena which present themselves to their cause, he discovers, by the ordinary laws of evidence, a cause of all subordinate causes."[13] Even in the theological realm, that is to say, evangelicals were as committed to empirical method as any *philosophe* of the eighteenth century.

By using this technique, they believed, they could discover fresh knowledge. The Bible was the supreme source of information about ultimate issues, but it could never contradict new information about the natural world. A fuller understanding of the universe would therefore assist the appreciation of the message of Scriptures. Furthermore, as T. R. Birks explained, the Bible itself could be expected to yield more truth over time:

> No bound is set to the growing light and increasing knowledge of the Name and Character of God . . . which the Christian may gain by the persevering study of those Divine oracles, which are the most precious gift of God the Holy Ghost to successive generations of mankind.[14]

Hence advances in theology were to be expected. Theologians, according to Finney, must be willing to change their minds, or else "all improvements would be precluded." Knowledge of divine as well as human things could be expected to make forward strides. The chief obstacle, in the opinion of some evangelicals, was the obscurantism of the past. The truths of the gospel, Finney believed, had been "hidden under a false philosophy."[15] Technical terms from earlier doctrinal systems might prevent a simple understanding of the words of the Bible. Even Spurgeon, who did not share Finney's aversion to the Puritan legacy, held that Christian thinking must avoid "the cloudland of METAPHYSICS."[16] There was a powerful sense that there could be progress in religious knowledge if it was not retarded by the deadweight of

---

[13]James McCosh, *The Method of the Divine Government Physical and Moral*, 11th ed. (London: Macmillan and Co., 1878), p. 17.

[14]Birks, *Supernatural Revelation*, p. 36.

[15]Finney, *Systematic Theology*, pp. x, vii.

[16]*Annual Paper concerning the Lord's Work in connection with the Pastors' College, Newington, London, 1886-87* (London: Alabaster, Passmore and Sons, 1887), p. 7.

the past. The attitudes would have been familiar to Enlightenment thinkers of a century before.

A specific inheritance from the Enlightenment was commonsense philosophy. The debt here was to a school of Scottish thinkers of whom the most eminent was Thomas Reid, Professor of Moral Philosophy at Glasgow from 1764 to 1796, and the most influential Dugald Stewart, Reid's counterpart at Edinburgh from 1785 to 1820. Reid had taught that there are intuitive beliefs (common sense) possessed by all human beings that cannot be denied without absurdity. They include acceptance of the existence of the external world and, crucially, belief in God. This position, which was particularly attractive because it provided a philosophical answer to the scepticism of David Hume, was widely endorsed by evangelicals in the subsequent century. Naturally Presbyterians from Scotland carried these views with them abroad. Thus Robert Burns, a professor at Knox College in Toronto at midcentury, praised Reid and his school for refuting Hume and appealing successfully to "primary principles of human belief, as ultimate facts in the arrangements of God."[17] These views, however, spread to virtually all the evangelical denominations of America, including, by the later nineteenth century, Methodists as well as those in Reformed traditions.[18] It has hardly been noticed, however, that they were barely less pervasive among English evangelicals. The *Record*, for Anglicans, applauded "the 'Common Sense' of REID" as a preservative against German rationalism.[19] W. B. Pope, the leading Methodist theologian of the age, taught that the idea of God was innate.[20] At the Pastors' College founded by Spurgeon, David Gracey contended that "those self-evident truths which arise, not from experience, but from the constitution of our nature, are first principles that must be assumed."[21] The rest of the English-speaking world followed suit. Thus in South Africa James McCosh's edition of the more popular version of Scottish commonsense philosophy propounded by Dugald Stewart was prescribed for

---

[17]Richard W. Vaudry, *The Free Church in Victorian Canada, 1844-1861* (Waterloo, Ontario: Wilfrid Laurier University Press, 1989), p. 51.

[18]Mark A. Noll, *America's God: From Jonathan Edwards to Abraham Lincoln* (New York: Oxford University Press, 2002).

[19]*Record*, January 2, 1863.

[20]W. B. Pope, *A Compendium of Christian Theology*, 2nd ed., 3 vols. (London: Wesleyan Methodist Book Room, 1880), 1:234.

[21]David Gracey, *Sin and the Unfolding of Salvation* (London: Passmore and Alabaster, 1894), p. 16.

Wesleyan ministerial candidates in 1887-1888.[22] The commonsense position remained particularly useful as a defense against the current philosophical view, unfriendly to theism, expounded by John Stuart Mill. Although a few sophisticated thinkers, chiefly (ironically) in Scotland, turned before the end of the century to an idealist stance, especially of the Kantian variety, common sense was still a foundation of much evangelical thinking down to 1900 and beyond.

Another eighteenth-century author who remained in high favor was Joseph Butler, bishop of Durham. His sermons were valued for their moral theology, but the work to which evangelicals—and not evangelicals only—repeatedly turned was *The Analogy of Religion* (1736). Bishop Butler argued against the deists that the difficulties in accepting full-blooded Christian faith were no greater than those involved in their bare belief in a God who created the world but did not sustain it by providential oversight. Butler, according to the *Record* in 1863, appealed to our natural convictions without attempting to analyze them in the manner of Kant and his successors. That was the method of the Bible.[23] The apologetic of the bishop may have been less popular in America, where at least one Methodist circuit rider found its rather dry pages unpalatable.[24] Nevertheless Butler's influence was widespread. He was commended at the Islington conference in 1882 for upholding the principle of the moral government of God.[25] The *Analogy* was a part of the curriculum at the Pastors' College from 1873 onward.[26] At the North Wales Baptist College in Llangollen the examiner reported in 1866 that the students could discuss the output of Butler as though "it were a favourite study."[27] Butler's *Analogy* was a textbook for Presbyterian Free Churchmen at Knox College, Toronto, in 1856-1857.[28] In the last decades of the century the bishop was as fixed a feature of the Wesleyan curriculum in

---

[22]*Minutes of the Fifth Conference of the Wesleyan Methodist Church of South Africa* (Cape Town: W. A. Richards and Sons, 1887).

[23]*Record*, January 2, 1863.

[24]S. P. Richardson, *The Lights and Shadows of Itinerant Life* (Nashville: Publishing House of the Methodist Episcopal Church South, 1900), p. xviii.

[25]H. W. Dearden in *Record*, January 18, 1882.

[26]*Annual Paper descriptive of the Lord's Work connected with the Pastors' College, 1873-1874* (London: Passmore & Alabaster, 1874), p. 11.

[27]*Report of the North Wales Baptist College instituted at Llangollen in 1862 for the Year 1866* (Llangollen: printed by W. Williams, 1866), p. 9.

[28]Vaudry, *Free Church*, p. 52.

South Africa as John Wesley himself.[29] Bishop Butler provided an apologetic that seemed to possess enduring value because evangelicals retained a worldview whose main outlines had been drawn in the previous century.

Their broader apologetic, at least in the earlier decades of the period, had a similar coloring. Evangelicals relied on what were known as "Christian evidences," arguments forged in the eighteenth century and subsequently refined by thinkers such as Thomas Chalmers. In a substantially rational spirit, apologists would meet freethinkers on their own ground, confident that they could gain the victory in the intellectual debate. They would contend, for example, that miracles were to be expected and that the Bible showed signs of divine origin. That was the burden of the latter part of *Bases of Belief*, a substantial treatise by Edward Miall, an English Congregational preacher-politician.[30] Equally it was what a coreligionist, S. A. Dwinnell, sent as a missionary to the frontier state of Wisconsin, was preaching in the same decade. Believing that infidelity was stalking the land, Dwinnell delivered a series of seven or eight sermons on "the Divine authority of the Scriptures," dwelling on "the *evidences*."[31] A course at Knox College, Toronto, a few years later covered sketches of various theories of infidelity ancient and modern, the existence, attributes and government of God and evidences of revelation.[32] Frequently in the 1850s the central case was the argument from design, the contention that, because the universe showed signs of having been designed, there must have been a Designer. It was often inculcated through the study of William Paley's *Evidences of Christianity* (1794), a lucid compendium of the standard apologetic of the eighteenth century. Paley was on the curriculum at Cambridge, but also in the Pastors' College. He was highly regarded in America, Canada and elsewhere. The argument from design, as we shall see, was to receive a shock from the writings of Charles Darwin, but for a long time after the publication of his *Origin of Species* in 1859 the substance of the same apologetic case was repeated. Evangelicals supposed that, though peo-

---

[29]*Minutes of the Second Conference of the Wesleyan Methodist Church of South Africa* (Grahamstown: Richards, Slater & Co., 1884), and subsequent issues to 1900.

[30]Edward Miall, *Bases of Belief: An Examination of Christianity as a Divine Revelation by the Light of Recognised Facts and Principles* (London: Arthur Hall, Virtue and Co., 1853), parts III and IV.

[31]*American Missionary* (New York), May 1857, p. 114.

[32]Vaudry, *Free Church*, p. 52.

ple might not be argued into the kingdom of God, at least they might be persuaded of the truth of Christian claims by means of rational discussion.

CONSEQUENCES OF AN ENLIGHTENED APPROACH

The respect for empirical method, the appeal to evidences in the natural world and especially the popularity of the argument from design made evangelicals the firm friends of scientific endeavor in the years around the middle of the century. They habitually praised Francis Bacon and Sir Isaac Newton, the patron saints of scientific method. They numbered in their ranks scientific writers of distinction such as the self-taught Scottish geological specialist Hugh Miller, the author of *The Testimony of the Rocks* (1857), and his compatriot Sir David Brewster, a prolific inventor and eventually principal of the University of Edinburgh. Their apologists insisted, as John Pratt, Archdeacon of Calcutta, explained, that science was not the foe of religion:

> The progress of Science is the setting forth of the greatness and wisdom of the Creator in His works: and to desire to check it, or to fear its results, is to betray our narrow prejudices, and to refuse to recognise the hand of God in His own world.[33]

Geology, it is true, was thought to challenge the biblical account of creation by demonstrating the vast epochs of time through which the world had passed. Evangelicals devised schemes to reconcile the text of Genesis with discoveries from the rocks. According to the gap theory espoused by Thomas Chalmers, there was an interval of time, perhaps immense, between the initial creation recorded in the first verse of Genesis and the ordering of the world described in subsequent verses. According to the alternative "day-age" interpretation popularized by Hugh Miller, however, the days of creation were in reality ages of enormous extent. Each method of harmonization long had its proponents. The day-age view, for example, was still being taught in the official American Methodist Sunday school lesson book for 1887.[34] There was an underlying confidence that, since the Bible and the natural world had the same author, they could not be at variance: "to assert," wrote Archdeacon Pratt, "that Scripture and Science are opposed to each other is UNPHILO-

---

[33] J. H. Pratt, *Scripture and Science not at Variance*, 3rd ed. (London: Thomas Hatchard, 1859), pp. 106-7.

[34] *Christian Advocate* (New York), January 6, 1887, p. 1.

SOPHICAL." [35] The predominant philosophy of the age, the legacy of the Enlightenment, provided a medium in which evangelical faith and scientific enquiry could be synthesized.

The Enlightenment tone of evangelical thinking extended to issues in the spiritual life. It colored opinion, for example, over whether individuals could be certain that they were true Christians. Although the Reformed churches had always entertained the belief that assurance of salvation might be given to believers, in the seventeenth century the normal conviction was that the experience rarely came until late in the spiritual pilgrimage. The eighteenth century had introduced a stronger form of the doctrine, reflecting the confidence of the age in the attainability of reliable knowledge. Many leaders of the evangelical revival, though by no means all, held that assurance was essential to authentic faith. That was certainly the general view in Methodism, where in the later nineteenth century it remained the overwhelming stance of the denomination. A woman from New York state who died in 1852 was believed to have enjoyed "the witness of her acceptance" for over sixty-nine years.[36] The American roving evangelist William Taylor spent time in the Eastern Cape during 1866 trying to ensure that a man obtained "the witness of pardon."[37] "The joyful assurance of the favour of God," it was insisted as late as 1903, "is one of the chief marks of a Methodist."[38] In the Refomed traditions, however, the question was less clear-cut. The older spirituality that expected alternating states of confidence and anxiety about salvation lived on in the Presbyterian Highlands of Scotland and among conservative Particular Baptists in many parts of the world. "Successive gloom and comfort" marked the experience of a Virginia young woman who died in 1857—until, in her case, baptism by immersion.[39] Nevertheless the mainstream evangelical view was that assurance is normal for the believer. Obituaries in the period tended to ignore the question since it was so generally assumed that the converted would know that they were saved. Even the conservative Irish Presbyterian Robert Watts, who recognized that there was

---

[35]Pratt, *Scripture and Science*, p. 66.

[36]Rebecca Foote in *Christian Advocate and Journal* (New York), January 13, 1853, p. 8.

[37]William Taylor, *Christian Adventures in South Africa* (London: Jackson, Walford and Hodder, 1867), p. 78.

[38]George Jackson, *The Old Methodism and the New* (London: Hodder & Stoughton, 1903), p. 43.

[39]*Religious Herald* (Richmond, Va.), January 14, 1858.

an issue to be addressed, pointed out that Calvin himself encouraged assurance.[40] The confidence of the Enlightenment in being able to obtain firm knowledge had become pervasive in the evangelical movement.

Another characteristic feature of eighteenth-century progressive thought, its eagerness to see the masses improve their attainments, was also near the heart of the churches. A thirst for knowledge, secular as well as spiritual, was regarded as a mark of the serious believer. At Wake Forest College, North Carolina, the young A. C. Dixon, who was to go on to a notable career as a Baptist preacher, loved the Euzelian Debating Society.[41] In the same way Spurgeon had the students in his college participate in a weekly discussion class that during 1867-1868 considered such questions as "Does morality increase with civilization?" "Has love a greater power in the world than fear?" and "Ought we as Dissenters to support Universal State Education?" The motto of the classes was "Excelsior."[42] The most widespread expression of this spirit, however, was the mutual improvement society attached to an individual place of worship. In any urban area, and in some rural ones too, a larger church would possess one of these agencies. In the Moruya Circuit in New South Wales, for example, there was in 1867 a Young Men's Wesleyan Mutual Improvement Society. In a single half-year it organized two lectures, on elocution and English history, one address on the mind of man, three debates, three original essays "and a great number of instructive readings and recitations." The climax of the half-year came when there was a soiree in a room decorated by the lady friends of the members and four young ladies sat at the head of each of the two meal tables.[43] But it would be a mistake to see the female presence on one evening as the *raison d'être* of the whole organization. Although the average attendance was only fourteen, the society clearly met the aspirations of the attenders for a higher culture. The Young Men's Christian Association, which specialized in its early years in organizing lectures, fulfilled the same role for many of its adherents. These bodies, by yoking self-improvement to religion, symbolized the absorption by evangelicalism of enlightened secular ideals.

---

[40]*Evangelical Witness and Presbyterian Review* (Dublin), November 1865, pp. 283-87.

[41]Helen C. A. Dixon, *A. C. Dixon: A Romance of Preaching* (New York: G. P. Putnam's Sons, 1931), p. 35.

[42]"Discussion Classes Pastor's College Metropolitan Tabernacle Minutes commencing September 12th 1867," Spurgeon's College Heritage Room, London.

[43]*Christian Advocate and Wesleyan Record* (Sydney), November 23, 1867, p. 115.

The same matrix produced capable scholarship during the period. It is often supposed that evangelicals, perhaps because of their preoccupation with doing rather than with thinking, were deficient in learning. It is true that relative to the High and Broad Church parties within the Church of England, the Evangelicals were, on the whole, less notable for their intellectual attainments. The stereotype of mindless religious enthusiasts, however, does no justice to the range of individuals who, with a high respect for knowledge, were diligent in the pursuit of learning. At the start of the twentieth century, Handley Moule, shortly to become bishop of Durham and himself no mean biblical scholar, identified a short list of theologians during the previous century of whom the Evangelical school in the Church of England could be particularly proud. He singled out for preeminence William Goode, Dean of Ripon from 1860, whose book *The Divine Rule of Faith and Practice* (1842; republished 1903) provided an authoritative answer to Tractarianism. He also listed Alexander McCaul, Professor of Hebrew (from 1841) and Divinity (from 1846) at King's College, London; E. A. Litton, the author of *The Church of Christ* (1851; republished 1898) and of *Introduction to Dogmatic Theology* (1882-1892); R. Payne Smith, a Syriac scholar who became Regius Professor of Divinity at Oxford and then dean of Canterbury; Nathaniel Dimock, the author of *The Doctrine of the Sacraments* (1871); and Henry Wace, a Luther expert who as principal of King's College, London (1883-1897), gravitated into the Evangelical party and who was subsequently, as Dean of Canterbury, to be its doughty champion.[44] Scotland supplied a procession of distinguished theologians, of whom William Cunningham, Principal of the Free Church's New College from 1847, was outstanding at the start of the period and James Orr, Professor of Church History at the United Presbyterian College from 1891, justly enjoyed an international reputation at its end. America could boast able men in each of the denominations. They included Edwards A. Park for the Congregationalists, Francis Wayland for the Baptists and John Miley for the Methodists. But the most monumental achievement in the new world was that of the Old School Presbyterian Charles Hodge, whose *Systematic Theology* (1872-1873) was to exercise an enduring influence during the twentieth century. Not all of these men remained stalwarts of the intellectual approach inherited from the eighteenth century, but it

---

[44] *Record*, January 4, 1901, pp. 38-40; January 18, 1901, p. 79.

was crucial to their formation. Hodge's declaration at the opening of his work that, since the Bible contains all the necessary facts, the "true method of theology is . . . the inductive" was a symptom of the debt of these men to the Enlightenment.[45]

EVANGELICAL DOCTRINE

The theologians of the evangelical movement were still divided between Calvinists, upholding the election of a limited number to salvation, and the Arminians, believing that all might in principle belong to the saved. Even when revival tended to bring the two parties together, there were devotees of doctrine who insisted that the other side was in the wrong. Thus in Ireland in the wake of the 1859 revival, the Wesleyan William Arthur issued a tract contending unequivocally that Christ died for all. A contributor to the journal of the Belfast Presbyterian Young Men's Association, while eager to claim that (in harmony with Scripture) he held *in some sense* that Christ gave himself as a ransom for all, also wanted to lay down that he died only for those who will be saved, that is, the elect.[46] Irish, as much as Scottish, Presbyterians were committed to the Westminster Confession, the litmus test of Reformed orthodoxy. In Scotland around 1850 the Baptists polarized into separate denominational bodies because of disagreement over the scope of the atonement.[47] The leading Scottish Congregationalist theologian Ralph Wardlaw, who died in 1853, was insistent on Reformed orthodoxy. "Ours is a Calvinistic body," he wrote, "and therefore those who stand forth as its teachers must be Calvinists."[48] The generality of Wardlaw's coreligionists in England tended to be less exclusive, but even south of the border there were ministers such as John Kelly of Crescent Chapel, Liverpool, who was well versed in Calvin's *Institutes*.[49] Among the Baptists, it was not just Spurgeon who remained staunchly Reformed. The college formed at

---

[45]Mark A. Noll, *Charles Hodge: The Way of Life* (New York: Paulist Press, 1987), p. 279.

[46]*Presbyterian Magazine in Connection with the Belfast Presbyterian Young Men's Association* (Belfast), October 1859, pp. 224-26.

[47]Brian R. Talbot, *The Search for a Common Identity: The Origins of the Baptist Union of Scotland, 1800-1870* (Carlisle: Paternoster Press, 2003), pp. 259-62.

[48]W. L. Alexander, *Memoirs of the Life and Writings of Ralph Wardlaw, D.D.* (Edinburgh: Adam and Charles Black, 1856), p. 425.

[49]Anne J. Davidson, ed., *The Autobiography and Diary of Samuel Davidson, D.D., Ll.D.* (Edinburgh: T & T Clark, 1899), pp. 45-46.

Bury in 1866, for example, was committed to the Calvinist doctrines of the 1689 Confession of Faith.[50] On the other side of the Atlantic, there were many similar doctrinal conservatives among the Congregationalists, the Baptists and especially the Presbyterians. When a Presbyterian preacher arrived in a part of the Rocky Mountains, he could attract "all the Calvinistic element in the community."[51] There was still vitality in the Reformed tradition.

The Calvinists of the period, however, were not, on the whole, the polar opposite of Arminians. An Islington speaker in 1880 declared that a feature of Evangelical Churchmanship was "Moderate Calvinism," which he equated with Augustinianism.[52] Its moderation consisted primarily in its refusal to accept "double predestination," the belief that the Almighty selected souls for damnation as well as choosing others for salvation. Moderate Calvinists held, on the contrary, that unsaved sinners were responsible for their own perdition. This theological opinion usually rested on a distinction drawn by Jonathan Edwards, the New England theologian of the earlier eighteenth century, between natural and moral inability. Sinners possessed a natural ability to respond to the gospel, according to Edwards, but if they failed to repent and believe they were showing a moral inability that rendered them guilty before God. Edwards was still held in high esteem by many evangelicals of the middle nineteenth century. His reputation in America as the thinker who had successfully combined the essentials of Puritan theology with a wise endorsement of revival was secure. John Pye Smith, the leading English Congregational divine until his death in 1851, repeatedly cited Edwards with approval.[53] William Cunningham, for the Free Church of Scotland, was also, despite detailed reservations, a devotee.[54] In 1864 the contention that "Natural men" were "accountable for not believing" was asserted by an Irish Presbyterian divine on the basis of Edwards's distinction between different forms of human ability.[55] It was broadly the position of Ed-

---

[50]Charles Rignal, *Manchester Baptist College, 1866-1916* (Bradford: William Byles and Sons, 1916), p. 36.

[51]*Rocky Mountain Presbyterian* (Denver, Colo.), August 1873.

[52]F. F. Goe in *Record*, January 16, 1880.

[53]John Pye Smith, *First Lines of Christian Theology*, ed. William Farrer (London: Jackson and Walford, 1854), esp. pp. 5, 155, 354, 389, 409, 571, 583.

[54]William Cunningham, *The Reformers and the Theology of the Reformation* (Edinburgh: T & T Clark, 1862), pp. 483, 508, 512, 515, 520.

[55]Dr. Niblock in *Evangelical Witness and Presbyterian Review*, August 1864, pp. 208-10.

wards rather than any more rigid form of doctrine that prevailed among Calvinists around the middle of the nineteenth century.

It was not just Edwards who had taught it. The moderate Calvinism of the time was called by Americans "the New England Theology," which was defined in 1852 by Edwards A. Park of Andover Seminary as "the formal creed which a majority of the most eminent theologians in New England have explicitly or implicitly sanctioned, during and since the time of Edwards." This enduring tradition held, according to Park, that sin consists in choice and that our natural power equals, but also limits, our duty.[56] These "three radical principles," as he termed them, constituted a species of Calvinism that was willing to accept that freedom of choice is a reality and that there is no ought without can, both classic contentions of the broader Enlightenment. It was a school of Reformed teaching that had made its peace with the progressive thought of the age. Edwards's position had been amplified, and subtly altered, by Joseph Bellamy and by Samuel Hopkins, each of whom found enthusiastic readers on the other side of the Atlantic. Thus John Duncan, professor of Hebrew at New College, Edinburgh, considered Bellamy the best of the New Englanders; and the English Congregationalist Edward Miall echoed Hopkins on "the principle of active benevolence in God."[57] But the most influential expositor of the system of thought had been the English Baptist, Andrew Fuller. Although Fuller died in 1815, his standing remained high long into the century. Edward Steane, joint secretary of the Evangelical Alliance in the United Kingdom, estimated in 1872 that Fuller's writings had exerted the greatest influence in shaping the characteristics of modern Calvinism.[58] Fuller was also widely known in America. The theological paradigm he upheld, a recasting of Calvinism in the idioms of enlightened thought, was normal in the denominations with a Reformed inheritance.

The distinctive cast of mind of this body of opinion was apparent in the treatment of the doctrine of the atonement. The Almighty was conceived essen-

---

[56]E. A. Park, "The New England Theology," *Bibliotheca Sacra*, January 1852, pp. 174, 175.

[57]David Brown, *Life of the Late John Duncan, Ll. D.* (Edinburgh: Edmonston and Douglas, 1872), p. 193n. Edward Miall, *The British Churches in Relation to the British People* (London: Arthur Hall, Virtue and Co., 1849), p. 149.

[58]Edward Steane, *The Doctrine of Christ developed by the Apostles* (Edinburgh: Edmonston and Douglas, 1872), p. ix.

tially, in the words of an American New School Presbyterian, as "a moral governor, . . . a lawgiver, a judge, a dispenser of rewards and penalties."[59] Justice was the essential attribute of God. Far from being a hoary notion inherited from the remote past, this conception was a progressive view popularized only in the previous century. The Enlightenment had enthroned the ideal of public justice as a yardstick for the reform of criminal law and systems of administration, and so it was natural to see the divine government as operating on the same principle. Sinners were understood as rebels against the edicts of the Almighty and their redemption had to be achieved in accordance with immutable standards of equity. Thus Fuller taught that, although Jesus suffered the punishment due to human sins, he was not actively punished for them by his Father because guilt was not transferable.[60] The atonement was still a matter of substitution, but, though Fuller insisted that it was in some way penal, it was not penal in the traditional sense. The cross was a display of the eternal principles of justice enforced by the all-wise ruler of the world and willingly accepted by an obedient Son. "The sufferings of the Son of Man," according to Edward Miall in 1849, "were the costly testimony he offered to the propriety and the necessity of preserving unimpaired the authority of his Father's moral government in this world."[61] Edwards A. Park expounded such a view at length in *The Atonement* (1859), a classic statement of what has been called the governmental theory of the work of Christ.[62] It seemed the soundest way of explaining what happened at the cross in accordance with the assumptions of the Enlightenment.

THE DECAY AND DEFENSE OF CALVINISM

Those assumptions, however, had already begun, well before the middle of the nineteenth century, to modify Calvinism far more drastically. The New Haven theology of Nathaniel W. Taylor, though starting from the premises of the received New England view, estimated the capacity of human beings to exercise

---

[59]Robert Baird, *Religion in the United States of America* (Glasgow: Blackie and Son, 1844), pp. 662-63, quoted in Noll, *America's God*, p. 442.

[60]John McLeod Campbell, introduction to *The Nature of the Atonement*, by E. P. Dickie (London: James Clarke and Co., 1959), p. 82.

[61]Miall, *British Churches*, p. 82.

[62]Joseph A. Conforti, *Jonathan Edwards, Religious Tradition & American Culture* (Chapel Hill: University of North Carolina Press, 1995), p. 124.

freewill much more highly than his predecessors. The revivalist Charles Finney, with legal precision, formulated a similar position. Finney argued that the Holy Spirit, far from being the irresistible agent of regeneration, merely offers persuasive evidence of the truth of Christianity that each human being is then free to assess. A person is not passive in the process. "Neither God," he declared boldly, "nor any other being, can regenerate him, if he will not turn." Although Finney honored Jonathan Edwards as an innovative revivalist, he repudiated the explicit theology of his predecessor, dismissing the distinction between natural and moral inability as "nonsensical." [63] Those who in Scotland were bold enough to throw off Calvinism altogether similarly directed criticism against Bellamy and Fuller.[64] There was a growing inclination to see the New England tradition as insular and so defective. It had suffered, wrote an American Congregationalist in 1864, from neglecting the history of doctrine and biblical philology. Its adherents acted as though they believed that "God had come down into some New England village not a great while ago and told off the words of the English Bible, giving them as the whole of his revelation to mankind."[65] The inherited style of Calvinist teaching was losing its sway.

The erosion of Calvinism proceeded apace in the middle years of the century. The principle of free enquiry increasingly seemed to require the elimination of the assumed premises of any doctrinal scheme. The characteristic evangelical insistence on the uniqueness of the Scriptures, far from reinforcing dogmatism, had a similar effect. The result was clearly apparent, for example, in this description of James Acworth, president until 1863 of Rawdon College, the Baptist theological institution in Yorkshire:

> He was impatient of system and formulas. "Make your own system" was his unvarying counsel to his men. He seldom or never gave Theological Lectures. His one aim and desire was that his pupils should read and understand "the Word", or, as he loved to say, "the Words of God."[66]

[63]Finney, *Systematic Theology*, pp. 413, 491-92.

[64]James Morison, *Saving Faith: Or, the Simple Belief of the Gospel* (Kilmarnock: J. Davie, 1842), pp. 50-51.

[65]C. E. Stowe, "Sketches and Recollections of Dr. Lyman Beecher," *Bibliotheca Sacra*, July 1864, pp. 228-29.

[66]William Medley, *Rawdon Baptist College: Centenary Memorial* (London: Kingsgate Press, 1904), p. 26.

The Bible, on this understanding, could speak for itself without the assistance of any external doctrinal framework. Older ministers around midcentury might remain self-conscious Calvinists, but newly trained men often broke with the confessional legacy. The ministerial succession at Carr's Lane Congregational Church, Birmingham, is illuminating here. From 1805 down to his death in 1859 the minister was John Angell James, one of the most effective evangelistic preachers of his day; from 1853 he had a junior assistant, R. W. Dale, who took over as minister on James's death, remaining at Carr's Lane until his own in 1895. James rarely preached on the distinctive points of the Reformed scheme of thought, yet nevertheless counted himself their adherent. "I hold," he once told Dale, "the doctrines of Calvinism with a firm grasp!" Dale, by contrast, quietly broke with Calvinism soon after entering the ministry.[67] Rubbing shoulders with non-Calvinists in pan-evangelical activities reinforced the tendency to play down what separated the parties. Thus in 1872 it was difficult to tell at a New York meeting to promote holiness who belonged to which denomination because all used the language of the Bible.[68] Even Spurgeon participated in this process. "If I were asked my creed," he remarked at a meeting of the interdenominational Y.M.C.A. in 1868, "I should go in for the Calvinistic, but I should be very sorry to say that all the truth was there; I believe a great deal of what Arminians believe."[69] When the doughtiest English champion of Reformed teaching took that line, it is hardly surprising that Calvinist doctrine steadily decayed.

The decline of Calvinism, however, did not proceed without resistance. Perhaps its chief bastion was the Highlands of Scotland. In the 1880s the Free Church of Scotland held the allegiance of an absolute majority of the population in nearly the whole of the Highlands.[70] There was a continuing heartfelt attachment to the doctrines of the Westminster Confession, whose shorter catechism most people had learned in their youth. John Kennedy, Free Church minister at

---

[67] Dale A. Johnson, *The Changing Shape of English Nonconformity, 1825-1925* (New York: Oxford University Press, 1999), pp. 134, 93 n. 61.

[68] *Christian Advocate*, August 15, 1872, p. 262.

[69] *Revival* (London), May 7, 1868, p. 253.

[70] A. I. Macinnes, "Evangelical Protestantism in the Nineteenth-Century Highlands," in *Sermons and Battle Hymns: Protestant Popular Culture in Scotland*, ed. Graham Walker and Tom Gallagher (Edinburgh: Edinburgh University Press, 1990), p. 62.

Dingwall in Ross and Cromarty, was a stern critic of any defections from the faith of the fathers, denouncing, for example, Moody and Sankey for what he called "hyper-evangelism."[71] Nowhere else in Britain was there such strong communal commitment to doctrinal rectitude. Nevertheless there were pockets of Calvinism in many other parts of the land. The *Gospel Magazine,* founded in 1796, linked many of the individuals who, in Church and Dissent alike, maintained their testimony to "the doctrines of grace." George Cowell, one of its contributors, lamented the teaching, which he classified as Arminian, that was common among Congregationalists. Many, he believed, would appreciate something better. "They loathe the swine's food of free-will, and long to be led into the green pastures of free-grace."[72] The Strict and Particular Baptists, although riven by internal controversy, constituted the English grouping most committed to maintaining Calvinism. John Hazelton, a minister in their ranks in London, was typical in his continuing devotion to seventeenth-century exponents of the faith. "His divinity," it was said in an obituary, "was Puritanic, and he loved the truths to which John Owen, Thomas Manton, and Thomas Goodwin gave such prominence with the utmost affection and ardour."[73] Although their numbers as a proportion of the British evangelical community dwindled over time, those who retained their Calvinism knew what they believed.

In America, Presbyterians were again the most salient defenders of the Reformed position. The *raison d'être* of the Old School Presbyterians was adherence to traditional doctrine and polity without compromise with the novelties of the age. The *North Carolina Presbyterian,* which was aligned with the Old School, declared that its adherents entered 1858 "guiding our course not by the uncertain lights of modern theories and 'isms'; but, seeking out the 'good old paths,' direct[ing] our goings according to the ancient 'land marks' of the 'Confession of Faith' and the catechism of the 'Westminster Assembly'."[74] Learning was very much in evidence among them. When, in the same year, R. J. Breckinridge, professor of theology at Danville Seminary, Kentucky, issued a volume of systematic theology, "A North Carolina pastor" assailed the book, with copious cita-

---

[71] John Kennedy, *Hyper-Evangelism "Another Gospel" Though a Mighty Power* (Edinburgh, 1874).

[72] Ruth Cowell, *Memorials of a Gracious Life with the Diary and Letters of George Cowell* (London: W., H. & L. Collingridge, 1895), p. 88.

[73] *Freeman* (London), January 13, 1888, p. 21.

[74] *North Carolina Presbyterian* (Fayetteville, N.C.), January 1, 1858.

tions, for plagiarizing a work of 1743 published in Zurich.[75] A large part of the explanation for the persistence of scholarly Calvinism among Presbyterians was the existence of an institution, Princeton Seminary, committed to that position. There, between 1822 and 1878, Charles Hodge trained more than two thousand students. Hodge, although best known for his three volumes of systematic theology, was no exclusive intellectual, always insisting that life should be in harmony with mind. The influence of Princeton was widespread. Many professors at Canadian Presbyterian seminaries propagated the views of Charles Hodge; a Nova Scotia Baptist reviewed his *Systematic Theology*, praising its Calvinism; and Spurgeon's college used the *Outlines of Theology* written by Charles's son Archibald.[76] In Belfast, a Princeton graduate, Robert Watts, who considered Hodge's *Systematic Theology* "without a peer in the whole history of theological exposition," stiffened the backbone of Irish Presbyterians.[77] He also made "an occasional raid into Scotland to utter his noble testimony in favour of Princeton theology."[78] Scottish Presbyterian theologians might be losing their Calvinistic bearings, but there were those who were not following their lead.

ARMINIANISM

The other main theological party within the evangelical movement, the Arminians, did not suffer from a comparable division. The chief advocates of the Arminian position, the Methodists, were substantially at one in the fundamentals of the faith, partly because they majored on experience rather than thought. An analysis of recent developments in Methodism just after the turn of the twentieth century admitted that its members had continued their neglect of theology.[79] In general they felt that matters of doctrine had been successfully codified by their founder, John Wesley, and so did not need further debate. Wesley still exercised a remarkable intellectual hegemony over the movement.

---

[75] *North Carolina Presbyterian*, February 12, 1858.

[76] Barry Mack, "Of Canadian Presbyterians and Guardian Angels," in *Amazing Grace: Evangelicalism in Australia, Britain, Canada and the United States*, ed. George A. Rawlyk and Mark A. Noll (Montreal & Kingston: McGill-Queen's University Press, 1994), p. 273. *Christian Messenger* (Halifax, Nova Scotia), March 13, 1872, p. 81. *Annual Paper* (1886-1887), p. 19.

[77] Robert Allen, *The Presbyterian College, Belfast, 1853-1953* (Belfast: William Mullan & Son, 1954), p. 179.

[78] *Presbyterian Churchman* (Dublin), February 1878, p. 26.

[79] Jackson, *Old Methodism and the New*, p. 56.

His word on controverted issues was decisive and his sermons formed the core of the knowledge on which candidates for the ministry were examined. The priorities of some Methodists can be illustrated by the obituary of Letitia Williams, who died at Montoursville, Pennsylvania, in 1862. She was praised for having acquired "a thorough knowledge of the writings of Wesley and the Holy Scriptures."[80] The reproach of not offering fresh statements of Christian teaching, however, was largely wiped away by W. B. Pope, originally from Prince Edward Island in Canada, who served at Didsbury Wesleyan College, Manchester, from 1867 to 1885. His three-volume *Compendium of Christian Theology* (1880) was a masterly exposition of Arminian teaching, a work worthy of comparison with Hodge's *summa* of less than a decade before. It exercised a powerful influence, with Samuel Chadwick, for instance, preaching steadily through it from the platform of Oxford Place, Leeds.[81] Pope's book showed that Wesley's teaching could be formulated as a body of systematic theology.

The central distinctive doctrine of Arminianism was the contention that the atonement was universal, rather than, as Calvinists believed, limited to the elect. The confidence that everybody could be saved, the fruit of Wesley's optimism about human potential, can itself be seen as connected to the spirit of the Enlightenment.[82] The belief was undoubtedly making strides by the middle of the century. In 1850 the *Wesleyan Methodist Magazine* was asserting that the theological battle over the scope of redemption had been won. "That Christ died for all," it claimed, "is on all hands admitted."[83] It was alluding primarily to the fact that moderate Calvinists (though not the higher variety) generally conceded that, at least hypothetically, the benefits of the cross embraced the whole of humanity. Methodists seemed to be on the victory side. They had allies, furthermore, beyond their own ranks. The English General Baptists, according to their journal in 1854, "hold firmly the cardinal doctrine that the death of Christ was an atonement offered for the sins of all mankind."[84] Some General Baptists might approach moderate Calvinism more closely than others, the journal suggested, but there was unanimity on the main point. Arminianism was also reinforced from another quarter during the

---

[80] *Christian Advocate and Journal*, September 4, 1862, p. 286.
[81] N. G. Dunning, *Samuel Chadwick* (London: Hodder & Stoughton, 1933), p. 81.
[82] Bernard Semmel, *The Methodist Revolution* (London: Heinemann, 1974).
[83] *Wesleyan Methodist Magazine*, July 1840, p. 741.
[84] *General Baptist Magazine* (London), January 1854, p. 13.

middle years of the century. In Scotland James Morison, inspired largely by the teaching of Charles Finney, became an outspoken advocate of universal redemption. Leaving the United Secession Church, in 1843 he had set up a fresh denomination, the Evangelical Union, to propagate his new views. A scholarly man, he was able to sustain his position against the combined denunciations of the Presbyterian bodies of Scotland and lived to see many of their ministers accept views similar to his own.[85] Comparable events took place elsewhere in the world. In Canada Robert Peden of Amherstburg published a denial of the doctrine of particular redemption. Brought before the synod of the Free Church in 1850, Peden was condemned and deposed from the ministry. He duly established a congregation of the Evangelical Union.[86] The episode was an indication of the way in which the theological tide seemed to be flowing in favor of Arminianism.

POSTMILLENNIALISM

Another legacy of Enlightenment optimism was the belief that the world was steadily advancing toward a future millennium. "The ancient prophecies," declared an American commentator in 1851, "do certainly point to an era of righteousness, peace, and happiness, such as has never yet been witnessed in the earth."[87] This was a version of the postmillennial doctrine that there would be a thousand-year period when, according to the book of Revelation, Satan would be bound. The second coming would take place only after ("post-") this time of blessing. Held by Jonathan Edwards and many other leaders of the eighteenth-century revival, this view had become the normal way of looking at the future among evangelicals. Patrick Fairbairn, principal of the Free Church College at Glasgow, published an authoritative statement of this outlook in his book *The Interpretation of Prophecy* (1865). The millennium, explained Fairbairn, would be the time when gospel principles had spread across all lands; only afterward would the open and visible advent of Christ take place.[88] Alice Baptist

---

[85]William Adamson, *The Life of the Rev. James Morison, D. D.* (London: Hodder & Stoughton, 1898).

[86]Vaudry, *Free Church in Victorian Canada*, pp. 56-59.

[87]Charles Adams, *Evangelism in Middle of the Nineteenth Century* (Boston: Gould and Lincoln, 1851), p. 17.

[88]Patrick Fairbairn, *The Interpretation of Prophecy* (1865; London: Banner of Truth Trust, 1964), pp. 477, 479.

Church in the Eastern Cape echoed this sentiment when, at its foundation in 1874, it defined its purpose as embracing "the conversion of the world."[89] The conviction that the gospel would gradually conquer the globe had to be defended against the alternative premillennial view, to be discussed in chapter six, which expected, on the contrary, that the second coming was imminent.[90] In this perspective the return of Christ to the earth was an essential event before ("pre-") his millennial reign. A Canadian Methodist argued in 1880, however, that the theory of a premillennial advent was disproved by the account in Matthew 25 of the last judgment, leading directly to punishment or eternal life. The millennium could not follow that judgment, and so could not follow the second coming either.[91] The postmillennial stance was very general in the middle years of the century. An American Congregational home missionary in Illinois was clearly animated in 1857 by the "glorious prospect of the church"; in the eyes of a British Wesleyan the 1858-1860 spate of revivals seemed to be inaugurating the millennium; and a *Sacred Cantata on the Millennial Glory* was published in 1853.[92] Hope for the future seemed to have a solid theological grounding.

The postmillennial vision of the prospects for the church, however, gradually faded as the century wore on. Partly this ebbing was a consequence of the rise of the rival premillennial view. By 1893 Robert Rainy, the highly circumspect leader of the Free Church of Scotland, was opining in a commentary on Philippians that the thought of the Lord's imminent return was as valid as the expectation of steady progress in the reign of goodness.[93] At the same time advancing liberal views were undermining altogether the belief that prophetic passages in the Bible referred to times to come. Thus Daniel Curry, the editor in America of the scholarly *Methodist Review*, declared that the word *parousia* in the New Testament is not a description of a future coming of Christ but instead an affirmation of his abiding presence with his people.[94] The content of post-

---

[89]Sydney Hudson-Reed, *By Taking Heed: The History of Baptists in Southern Africa, 1820-1977* (Roodepoort: Baptist Publishing House, 1983), p. 56.

[90]See chap. 6, pp. 190-96.

[91]T. L. Wilkinson in *Christian Guardian* (Toronto), April 28, 1880, p. 134.

[92]*American Missionary*, December 1857, p. 282. *Wesleyan Methodist Magazine*, January 1860, p. 65. *Baptist Magazine* (London), October 1853, p. 628.

[93]*Christian* (London), March 2, 1890, p. 10.

[94]*Christian Advocate*, March 10, 1887, p. 151.

millennialism, furthermore, rendered it particularly liable to erosion. It was formulated in terms that embraced extraordinarily this-worldly hopes. In 1854 the English *General Baptist Magazine* expected the millennium to achieve not only the universal triumph of the gospel but also the ending of war, famine and "the oppressive weight of taxes that grind nations to the dust." Crime, drunkenness, "lewdness," slavery and all oppression would disappear. There would be family happiness in the place of a mixture of scandal, loose talk, false teaching, idols and "the damnable superstitions of popery and paganism." The author of the article calculated that this program of reform was so vast that it could not be achieved before the year 2016.[95] Likewise in America the holiness teacher W. E. Boardman contended in 1869 that the beginning of millennial triumph would be achieved by the elimination of "corrupt and selfish practices" from business.[96] Temporal aims such as these, however ambitious they might be, could readily become secularized. In many cases that is exactly what took place. It was easy for the postmillennial hope to be elided with the Victorian idea of progress, itself a legacy of the Enlightenment. Trust in divine leading into an age of blessedness turned into applause for new books on human progression. By the end of the century the articulation of postmillennialism, even by preachers, was often becoming non-theological. The English Methodist Mark Guy Pearse, according to his biographer, merely "had a firm belief that the world was getting better."[97] The doctrinal formulation of Christian optimism had been reduced to a secular confidence in human improvement.

MISSIOLOGY

The same intertwining of spiritual and material interests was evident in the theory of missions. Evangelicals were vigorous participants in the debates of the Enlightenment era over whether pagans could receive the Christian faith without first being civilized. They were generally of the view that human beings were capable of responding to the gospel without previous expansion of their intel-

---

[95] *General Baptist Magazine*, July 1854, pp. 303-11, quoted in pp. 308-310.

[96] W. E. Boardman, *He that Overcometh* . . . (Boston, 1869), pp. 208-9, quoted in T. L. Smith, *Revivalism and Social Reform: American Protestantism on the Eve of the Civil War* (New York: Harper & Row, 1965), p. 234.

[97] Mrs. George Unwin and John Telford, *Mark Guy Pearse: Preacher, Author, Artist* (London: Epworth Press, 1930), p. 233.

lectual horizons.[98] Nevertheless it was also a widespread opinion that civilization must follow hard on the heels of conversion. John Mackenzie, a pioneer missionary to the Tswana people of southern Africa, put the point like this at his ordination in Edinburgh in 1858:

> As to the civilization and temporal interests of the people, I conceive that I am furthering both when I preach the Gospel. . . . In order to complete the work of elevating the people, we must teach them the arts of civilized life. . . . We must teach them to till their own land, sow and reap their own crops, build their own barns.[99]

The arrival of the faith would bring secular benefits. David Livingstone, furthermore, is celebrated for his yoking of commerce with Christianity and civilization. The gospel would promote legitimate trade, which in turn, in the missionary's view, would extinguish the traffic in slaves. Livingstone was by no means the first to think in these terms, but his advocacy of the triad made it commonplace. The spread of Christian settlers across the globe, according to an interdenominational New Zealand newspaper in 1870, was part of the providential design "that Christianity might go hand in hand with commerce."[100] The association of the spread of the faith with economic development was yet another indication of the way in which evangelical thought operated within an Enlightenment paradigm.

Some evangelicals were actually of the opinion, in the manner of the French *philosophes*, that the best method of advancing their beliefs was initially to gain the allegiance of an intellectual elite. Alexander Duff, a Presbyterian whose formation was deeply molded by the Scottish Enlightenment, adopted a missionary strategy in India of giving high-caste students an education through the medium of English in a full range of modern knowledge. The rational force of the arguments for Christianity, he believed, would convince the pupils, who would

---

[98]Brian Stanley, "Christianity and Civilization in English Evangelical Mission Thought," in *Christian Missions and the Enlightenment*, ed. Brian Stanley (Grand Rapids: Eerdmans, 2001).

[99]A. J. Dachs, ed., *Papers of John Mackenzie* (Johannesburg: Witwatersrand University Press, 1975), p. 72, quoted in John L. Comaroff and Jean Comaroff, "Cultivation, Christianity & Colonialism: Towards a New African Genesis," in *The London Missionary Society in Southern Africa: Historical Essays in Celebration of the Bicentenary of the LMS in Southern Africa, 1799-1999*, ed. John de Gruchy (Cape Town: David Philip, 1999), p. 56.

[100]*Christian Observer* (Christchurch), January 1870, p. 7.

in due course influence the lower orders to follow their example of embracing the new faith.[101] This "trickle-down" theory was widely adopted in the subcontinent. Christian schools and higher education became the generally accepted medium by which India was to be evangelized. The results, however, were far behind expectations. In the "Native English School at Masulipatam for the Education of the Upper Classes," run by the Church Missionary Society, for example, two baptisms of pupils in 1852 caused a riot. Thereafter there was only a trickle of baptisms: three in 1855, four in 1860 and two in 1864.[102] The unfruitfulness of the policy inevitably led to a reaction in missionary thinking. Rufus Anderson, the foreign secretary of the American Board of Commissioners for Foreign Missions, argued persuasively during and after a visit to India in 1855 in favor of giving priority to preaching rather than schools, of using local languages extensively rather than concentrating on English and of employing indigenous ministry even though that would mean infringing the traditions of caste.[103] Missions were to encourage evangelistic efforts by newly Christianized peoples rather than see their own role as the propagation of Western learning. Henry Venn, the clerical secretary of the Church Missionary Society, joined Anderson in advocating the ideal of the so-called three-self principles of self-government, self-propagation and self-support. Since indigenous peoples should assume responsibility for the spread of the gospel, it became the settled policy of the missionary movement for much of the later nineteenth century to work toward its own elimination.

Underneath the overarching desire to propagate the gospel there was room for a variety of missionary strategies. That flexibility was a consequence of the pragmatic temper that marked the missionary movement and, to a large extent, the whole of evangelicalism in this era. Missionaries on the field were prepared to learn new techniques from their experience and so to change their ways, sometimes drastically. This paradoxical capacity of service in foreign lands to convert the missionaries is vividly illustrated in the case of Timothy Richard, a Welsh agent of the Baptist Missionary Society in China from 1870 onward.

---

[101]I. D. Maxwell, "Civilization or Christianity? The Scottish Debate on Mission Methods, 1750-1835," in *Christian Missions and the Enlightenment*, ed. Stanley.

[102]"Robert Turlington Noble, B. A.," in *Brief Sketches: C. M. S. Workers* (n.p., n.d.), 2:9-10.

[103]Paul W. Harris, *Nothing but Christ: Rufus Anderson and the Ideology of Protestant Foreign Missions* (New York: Oxford University Press, 1999), chap. 9.

Richard began by engaging in indiscriminate street preaching and Bible distribution; he turned to concentrate on particular groups, those who were already seriously dedicated to the religious quest; then, in 1876-1879, an immense famine made him take up relief work; next he determined to spread useful knowledge that would encourage the people to think well of the gospel, and so ran a newspaper; and gradually there dawned on him an appreciation of the religious culture of Buddhism, which he increasingly viewed as a preparation for the reception of Christianity.[104] The most common adaptation of missionary methods in the period, however, was the incorporation of medical care in the program. By the end of the century alongside 1,365 ordained American missionaries there were as many as 273 physicians in the field.[105] Methods could vary because missionaries were willing to learn. They took with them a mindset that was shaped by the pragmatic approach of the Enlightenment.

A Pragmatic Temper

The same flexible approach was evident in evangelical attitudes to church order. The movement as a whole, as R. W. Dale, the Birmingham Congregationalist, observed in a classic analysis of 1889, had not cared much for church polity. "It emphasized" according to Dale, "the vital importance of the Evangelical creed, but it regarded almost with indifference all forms of Church polity that were not in apparent and irreconcilable antagonism to that creed."[106] It promoted an nondenominational spirit that downgraded the earlier Puritan preoccupation with biblical warrant for correct ecclesiastical structures. Evangelicals looked at church organizations as instrumental agencies, and so there was a willingness to adapt them according to the needs of the times. Those who worshiped in the Church of England were in some measure exceptions because they thought of the traditional structures of their church as bastions of Protestantism inherited from the Reformation era. Even they, however, tended to justify

---

[104]Andrew Walls, "The Multiple Conversions of Timothy Richard: A Paradigm of Missionary Experience," in *The Gospel in the World: International Baptist Studies,* ed. David W. Bebbington (Carlisle: Paternoster Press, 2002).

[105]James S. Dennis, *Centennial Survey of Foreign Missions* (New York: Fleming H. Revell Co., 1902), p. 257.

[106]Robert W. Dale, *The Old Evangelicalism and the New* (London: Hodder & Stoughton, 1889), p. 17.

the establishment of religion in England and Wales, and in Ireland down to 1870, in terms of its usefulness to the cause of the gospel rather than on more principled grounds; and some of them supported the Prayer Book Revision Society, founded in 1854 to secure an alteration of the rubrics in a Protestant direction. Methodism offered nothing but a pragmatic explanation of its structures. J. H. Rigg, a leading Wesleyan, argued that "need and aptitude were the two factors which, from time to time, governed the steps of development" of Methodism.[107] The strength and number of parachurch organizations—at the time called benevolent associations in America—is a sign of the same spirit of adapting church life to contemporary requirements. The range of miscellaneous but vigorous groups was immense—including in England the Army Scripture Readers' Society, the Christian Vernacular Society for India, the Working Men's Lord's Day Rest Association and the Society for the Relief of Persecuted Jews. Evangelicalism characteristically spawned organizations beyond the control of strictly ecclesiastical bodies.

The way in which the pragmatic spirit made great advances is particularly evident among the Baptists. Their adherence to a distinctive viewpoint on the subjects and mode of baptism was originally a corollary of a willingness to break with the rest of Christendom for the sake of principle. By the late nineteenth century, however, they were as affected by the temper of the age as any. Spurgeon, for instance, declared that he would be willing to extend, change or abolish the college he founded as circumstances dictated.[108] Although Spurgeon was a convinced Baptist, his attitude to ecclesiology was distinctly low. "The church," he contended, "is only the aggregation of individuals, and if any good is to be done it must be performed by individuals."[109] Spurgeon's younger contemporary John Clifford was even more dismissive of institutional forms, being happy to contemplate denominational union with the Congregationalists. The extent of Baptist retreat from denominational exclusiveness is well illustrated by their changing stance on who might receive the bread and wine at the Lord's Supper. Originally only those baptized as believers were admitted,

---

[107]J. H. Rigg, *A Comparative View of Church Organisations, Primitive and Protestant*, 3rd ed. (London: Wesleyan Conference Office, 1897), p. 223.

[108]*Annual Paper* (1871-1872), p. 6.

[109]Charles H. Spurgeon, *The Messiah: Sermons on our Lord's Names, Titles and Attributes* (London: Passmore & Alabaster, 1898), p. 338.

but early in the nineteenth century Robert Hall had advocated the welcoming of all sincere Christians to the Lord's Table. That policy, which was termed "open Communion," continued to be seen in America as a "heresy."[110] In Britain, however, and in lands influenced by Britain, this more liberal policy gradually prevailed. A celebrated legal battle in 1857-1860 over whether or not St. Mary's Baptist Church, Norwich, was entitled to alter its Communion practice gave victory to the open communionists.[111] The newer policy appealed to the values of freedom and tolerance, inherited from the eighteenth century, which were so much a part of the Victorian ethos. The consequence was that a restrictive attitude to requirements for Communion seemed increasingly a badge of sectarian marginality. Opening the Communion table to fellow believers was a sign of an open mind as much as of a warm heart. Baptists, like other evangelicals, were prepared to adopt a pragmatic program, in their case even at the expense of their foundation principles.

This survey of some of the main contours of evangelical thinking illustrates the extent to which the ideas of the movement were at one with the dominant intellectual patterns of the age. Attitudes derived from the Enlightenment, especially in a moderate form that was compatible with religious faith, had made steady advances by the mid-nineteenth century so that their influence was widespread among aspiring artisans as much as among settled businessmen. Evangelicals in general shared the confidence of progressive thought in reason, a sifting of the facts and fresh achievements in science. The same set of premises that underlay expectations of the advance of human knowledge apparently provided a strong foundation for Christian belief. Paley, Butler and the evidences seemed to explode infidel objections to Christianity. The commonsense philosophy of Scotland appeared to vindicate the existence of the Almighty and the doctrine of assurance provided a rationale for personal knowledge of God. At the same time the self-improvement that the Enlightenment endorsed provided a stimulus to scholarship in which evangelicals fully participated. Theology was tinged with the hue of enlightened thought, whether Calvinist or Arminian. Calvinism was generally moderate, holding a view of the atonement that showed the universe to be governed by the canons of justice. So committed to free enquiry

---

[110]*Examiner and Chronicle* (New York), January 1, 1874, p. 1.

[111]E. A. Payne, *The Baptist Union: A Short History* (London: Carey Kingsgate Press, 1959), pp. 88-89.

were many theologians in the Reformed tradition their Calvinist distinctives were subject to erosion, though others put up a stout resistance. The Arminian message, stressing freedom and universality, needed no similar adaptation to harmonize with the spirit of the age. The wide diffusion of postmillennialism revealed an affinity for the optimism of progressive thought, as did the expected role of missions in promoting civilization and commerce. The pragmatic temper shown by evangelicals, whether abroad or at home, was a further indication of their characteristic mindset. Not all evangelicals possessed the worldview outlined in this chapter, as the next will make plain. Yet the great majority did share the prevailing assumptions of the age. That goes a long way to explaining why evangelicalism was so influential in the middle years of the nineteenth century. Gospel and culture were in a remarkable degree of harmony.

5

THE PERMEATION OF
ROMANTICISM

The nineteenth century witnessed the steady spread of new ways of thinking that gradually modified the inheritance from the Enlightenment. The eighteenth-century legacy was never wholly replaced and in many spheres of life remained dominant. There was a general trend, however, for a fresh cultural mood to supplant the older attitudes. The new way of looking at the world is usually called Romanticism. It was a diverse and evolving phenomenon, but its essential temper can be identified by contrast with the Enlightenment. Instead of exalting reason, those touched by the new spirit of the times placed their emphasis on will, spirit and emotion. They wanted to escape the tight framework of thinking imposed by the older rational approach in order to breathe a freeer air. Romantics saw untamed nature, growing spontaneously and luxuriantly, as expressing the values they admired. Trees and flowers absorbed their attention, leading them to marvel at the intricacy as much as the beauty of natural growth. They gloried in landscapes of mountain, waterfall and tempest, seeing them as embodiments of the sublime or even of the numinous. Typically Romantics showed a tendency toward pantheism, discerning God in nature if not equating him with the natural world. Such attitudes had their heartland in Germany, where the poet Johann Wolfgang von Goethe was their apostle. The fresh temper made its appearance in the English-speaking world around the beginning of the nineteenth century, especially in the works of the Lake Poets. William Wordsworth, with his sense of the divine presence in the hills of the Lake District, and Samuel Taylor Coleridge, with his adoption of German literary and philosophical idioms, brought the novel sensibility to public attention. A new cultural age had dawned.

Literary historians commonly confine the Romantic period to the end of the eighteenth century and the first three decades of the next, but it is important to insist that what was novel at that time gathered increasing popularity throughout the Victorian era. Those who formed the vanguard of Romanticism in America, the Transcendentalists, did not make their initial impact until the later 1830s. In England Thomas Carlyle transposed history into a Romantic key from the same decade and John Ruskin performed a similar service for art criticism from the 1840s onward. Victorian preferences differed from the taste of the early years of the century, evolving into fresh forms more attuned to a wider public, but a large part of the process consisted of the popularization of the new cultural attitudes. There was, for example, a stronger fascination with the past. The novels of Sir Walter Scott conveyed to his vast readership a delight in the otherness of past ages with all their vibrancy, their mannerisms and their archaic usage. There grew up a much stronger appreciation of traditions inherited from long ago. Instead of the best form of society being located in the future, as it had been by eighteenth-century theorists of progress, it was often seen as having been realized already in the past. The peasantry of previous generations, who had been despised by the *philosophes* for their ignorance, were now idealized for their closeness to nature. Admiration for the spirit of the folk, often a particular nation, became a common theme. Those affected by the Romantic temper commonly insisted on the importance of corporate identities. There was a strong awareness of the solidarity of the group, a sense (against the Enlightenment) that individuals could not flourish outside their social context. At the same time there was a willingness, as in Carlyle's *Heroes, Hero-Worship and the Heroic in History* (1841), to respect the great men who bent circumstances to their wills. Human beings were conceived as having immense potential, not because they shared a common rationality but because they each possessed distinct characteristics. They could be creative through the exercise of their imagination, their capacity to acquire knowledge by a leap of intuition that could not be reduced to the categories of scientific investigation. Such values, constituting a reaction against the ideals of the Enlightenment, slowly spread from high cultural circles to permeate society at large.

ROMANTICISM AND RELIGION

It has often been recognized that the Romantic spirit affected religion. In the

Roman Catholic Church, many of the trends of the time had Romantic affinities.[1] The growth of Ultramontanism meant that the pope was treated with the awe due to a sublime figure, worship became more dramatic and teaching paid more respect to what had been transmitted from the Middle Ages. In the Church of England the Oxford movement of the 1830s is generally recognized as having possessed a Romantic coloring.[2] Its leading figure, John Henry Newman, who acknowledged his intellectual debt to Sir Walter Scott, was one of the greatest of Romantic prose writers. The Tractarian doctrine of the movement, which gave rise to Anglo-Catholicism, dwelt on the traditional and the corporate, the ancient lineage of the Church of England and its claims as a Christian community. The Tractarians suspected scientific enterprise of being an attempt to undermine the principles of the faith; and they abominated what they called rationalism. Likewise the Broad-Church tendency within the Anglican communion was related to Romantic innovations. Frederick Denison Maurice, though never professing to be a Broad Churchman, was in many ways their epitome. His theology was marked by the influence of Coleridge and others swayed by German opinion; he wrote of the importance of feeling and saw lessons in flowers.[3] Equally the predominant school of Unitarian thought from midcentury onward, in Britain and America alike, was largely Romantic in inspiration. The writings of the greatest British Unitarian, James Martineau, were associated with the new sensibility in tone and content; in America Transcendentalism was originally rooted in Unitarianism.[4] It is clear that during the later nineteenth century there was a pervasive Romantic influence behind tendencies toward higher churchmanship and equally behind many of those toward broader churchmanship and unorthodoxy.

It is far less widely appreciated that Romantic traits deeply affected the evan-

---

[1] Mary Heimann, *Catholic Devotion in Victorian England* (Oxford: Clarendon Press, 1995), p. 142. Heimann nevertheless minimizes the ultramontane impact on Catholic devotion.

[2] Bernard M. G. Reardon, *Religious Thought in the Victorian Age: A Study from Coleridge to Gore* (London: Longman, 1980), pp. 92-93. Geoffrey Rowell, *The Vision Glorious: Themes and Personalities of the Catholic Revival in Anglicanism* (Oxford: Oxford University Press, 1983), pp. 10, 26-27. David Bebbington, *Holiness in Nineteenth-Century England* (Carlisle: Paternoster Press, 2000), chap. 1.

[3] Reardon, *Religious Thought*, chaps. 5-6.

[4] Ibid., pp. 312-15. Perry Miller, ed., *The American Transcendentalists: Their Prose and Poetry* (Baltimore: Johns Hopkins University Press, 1957).

gelical movement. The enduring debt of the movement to aspects of the Enlightenment did not prevent some of its leaders from reshaping their ideas in the new cultural fashion during the earlier years of the nineteenth century. Preeminent among them was Edward Irving, a minister of the Church of Scotland who served in London. Irving knew Coleridge personally, absorbed his way of looking at the world and applied it to evangelical teaching during the 1820s. At the same time in Ireland John Nelson Darby was beginning to approach doctrine under Romantic influence. Irving was to adhere to the Catholic Apostolic Church, a body that combined elaborate liturgy with prophetic speculation, and Darby was to become the leading intellectual in the Brethren, dividing the movement in the 1840s by the strength of his opinions. A larger number of those who were swayed by the newer intellectual currents of the day, however, were Anglicans. The members of the Church of England were more likely to be people of wealth, status and learning than Dissenters and so to be more open to fresh intellectual perspectives. By the middle of the century there were significant numbers of Evangelicals who professed ideas with a distinctively Romantic provenance. At the same time, however, the trends of thought associated with Romanticism were alarming to the great bulk of evangelicals, whether inside or outside the Church of England. The Tractarian heightening of churchmanship seemed a dangerous threat to vital Christianity, and the initial symptoms of liberal theology appeared to evacuate the gospel of its power. Evangelicals were therefore ambiguous in their response to the Romantic intellectual influences. Some, though still relatively few at midcentury, refashioned their thinking under the sway of the new cultural mood; but others found its chief expressions a challenge to combat.

A development in evangelical taste can be traced over the years. At midcentury the initiators of the Romantic literary revolution were still suspect, with commentary tending to concentrate on their theological errors. In 1850 a review of a new edition of Coleridge's *Confessions of an Inquiring Spirit* in the *Christian Observer*, the Evangelical Anglican magazine, expressed regret that Coleridge failed to accept the Bible as the Word of God, preferring to see the Bible as merely containing the religion revealed by God.[5] Similarly an article of the same year on Wordsworth in the *Wesleyan Methodist Magazine*, while approving his "no-

---

[5] *Christian Observer* (London), April 1850, pp. 246-47.

ble sentiments" and admiring "language so chaste and felicitous," condemned his trespassing on the territory of religion. He was led "by an ambitious desire of working some great moral effect, vaguely intimated rather than defined, to overstep the legitimate boundaries of his art."[6] He should not set up as an instructor. The author of the article, however, was not moved merely by concern for the welfare of souls, for he expressed disgust with some of Wordsworth's poems for "the meanness of their subject, or the unconquerable vulgarity of their associations."[7] The critic was aligning himself with the classical canons of verse enjoining dignified topics that Wordsworth had explicitly challenged. The Wesleyan commentator retained the taste of a previous age that had undergone no Romantic reconstruction. Before long, however, others were taking a different line. The Old School Presbyterian William G. T. Shedd, who in 1874 was to be appointed professor of systematic theology at Union Theological Seminary, New York, became an enthusiast for the Romantics without abating one jot of his commitment to Westminster orthodoxy, editing in 1853 the complete works of Coleridge.[8] Similarly David Thomas, a Congregational minister at Bristol from 1844 to 1875, had what his biographer described as "almost . . . a passion" for Wordsworth. Thomas was alive to the poet's ideological defect of seeking in nature what could be found only in God himself, but a volume of Wordsworth's verse was always at the side of the minister's desk, he packed it in his portmanteau when he was away from home and he found it the best medicine when he was vexed. Thomas knew every part of *The Excursion*, Wordsworth's long autobiographical poem, pronouncing it "delicious," and visited the Lake District to identify spots connected with the poet.[9] A feeling for the spirit of the Romantic movement was beginning to grip certain cultivated evangelicals as much as their contemporaries.

The same transformation of aesthetic preferences was evident in church architecture. Associated with the Romantic love of the past was a vogue for the Gothic style that favored pointed windows in imitation of the middle ages. Dur-

---

[6] *Wesleyan Methodist Magazine* (London), October 1850, p. 1075.
[7] *Wesleyan Methodist Magazine*, December 1850, p. 1308.
[8] W. G. T. Shedd, *The Complete Works of Samuel Taylor Coleridge*, 7 vols. (New York: Harper & Brothers, 1853).
[9] H. A. Thomas, *Memorials of the Rev. David Thomas, B. A., of Bristol* (London: Hodder & Stoughton, 1876), pp. 49-50.

ing the 1840s the fashion was closely bound up with the rise of Anglo-Catholicism, but it soon became popular with church builders serving evangelical bodies. Its chief initial impact was on Anglicans, but soon Scottish Presbyterians and
English Nonconformists who wanted striking new buildings turned to Dissenting Gothic instead of to classical architecture. The battle of the styles that
marked public patronage in the high Victorian years affected Nonconformity
too. Philip Sambell, a Falmouth architect practicing largely in Cornwall who was
also a Baptist church member, wrote to the denominational magazine in 1867
to denounce the imitation of traditional Anglican architecture by Dissenters:

> Pointed architecture [he thundered] is, *par excellence,* from its origin, the Romish-
> Priest-architecture, and was designed to thoroughly subserve their superstition.
> . . . It cuts up and wastes valuable accommodation-space, and costs far more than
> a chaste and simple classical edifice.[10]

Such protests, however, failed to stem the trend away from the classical and
toward the Gothic. Prosperous industrialists in particular wanted to mark their
social standing by choosing designs in keeping with the rising conventions of the
age. Thus in 1863 at Huddersfield, in the West Riding of Yorkshire, a building
committee for a Congregational church in a new suburb presided over by William Willans, a successful woolstapler, required its architect to plan a Gothic
chapel complete with a spire.[11] The taste for Gothic became widespread. Thus
Dowling Street Wesleyan Chapel in Wooloomooloo, New South Wales, erected
in 1859, was designed in the early English style of Gothic. "This building,"
opined the denominational press, "is a proof that the Gothic style of Architecture is far more suitable for Churches and Chapels than any other style that can
be named."[12] In Ontario a form of Gothic adapted to Protestant needs became
popular.[13] Although America remained more attached to the classical idiom of
the "colonial style" that seemed to embody the spirit of the nation, even there
the Gothic made inroads into the great cities. The physical plant of the denominations showed signs of expressing the altered taste of the times.

---

[10] *Baptist Magazine* (London), March 1867, pp. 171-72.
[11] Clyde Binfield, "Dissenting Gothic," in *So Down to Prayers: Studies in English Nonconformity, 1780-1920* (London: J. M. Dent & Sons, 1977), pp. 151-53.
[12] *Christian Advocate and Wesleyan Record* (Sydney), June 9, 1859, p. 229.
[13] William Westfall, *Two Worlds: The Protestant Culture of Nineteenth-Century Ontario* (Montreal & Kingston: McGill-Queen's University Press, 1989), p. 156.

THE REACTION AGAINST HIGH CHURCHMANSHIP

More ominously for the evangelicals, the liturgical practice within the buildings was also drastically affected. The ritualist heirs of the Oxford movement wanted to introduce a whole range of innovations into churches of the Anglican communion. Their aim was to reproduce the patterns of worship of the Catholic past, as perceived through Romantic eyes, replete with color, mystery and elaborate ceremony. The Eucharist, understood as the chief channel of grace, became more frequent, more dignified and more dramatic. The priest, consciously acting as an intermediary between the people and the Almighty, adopted the eastward position, which meant that he faced the altar while consecrating the elements. He placed lit candles on the Communion table, intoned part of the service and recruited a surpliced choir. He might wear medieval vestments, use unleavened or wafer bread and mix water in the wine so as to represent more precisely the outflow from the body of the dying Christ.[14] Initially all of this alteration of practice was anathema to Evangelicals. It was condemned, as by Edward Garbett at the Islington Clerical conference in 1868, as "a growing tendency to assimilate our worship to that of Rome."[15] William Pennefather, vicar of St. Jude's, Mildmay Park, warned that if in a congregation the bread and wine were elevated by the priest, it meant that the people were supposed to offer worship to the presence of Christ in the elements and so Evangelicals should not partake there of an idolatrous Communion.[16] Charles Bury, an unbeneficed Evangelical clergyman living in the Isle of Wight, expressed contempt for "this playing at religion," but thought matters became really serious when a priest encouraged his flock to confess their sins to him in private so that he could offer sacramental absolution. "Let fathers, husbands, brothers look to this," he exclaimed, "if they would preserve the sacredness and purity of English homes!"[17] The ritualist reintroduction of disused Catholic customs stirred deep Evangelical passions.

Accordingly in 1865 an organization, the Church Association, was

---

[14]Nigel Yates, *Anglican Ritualism in Victorian Britain, 1830-1910* (Oxford: Oxford University Press, 1999).

[15]*Record* (London), January 17, 1868.

[16]Robert Braithwaite, *The Life and Letters of the Rev. William Pennefather, B. A.* (London: John F. Shaw & Co., 1878), p. 454.

[17]C. A. Bury, *The Church Association* (London: William Macintosh, 1873), p. 32.

launched to resist the incoming tide of ritualism. Priests were prosecuted for failure to observe the provisions of the *Book of Common Prayer*. "The Protestant-ism of our Church," according to an apologist, "was at stake." Within four years the Association had gathered over 7,000 members and in the early years there were some successes. In the case of John Purchas, vicar of St. James's, Brighton, for example, it was established that certain points of ceremony were illegal: they included vestments, the eastward position and such curiosities as a "Stuffed Dove over the Holy Table on Whitsun-Day." When the ecclesiasti-cal authorities failed to enforce the court decisions, parliament passed the Public Worship Regulation Act (1874) to supply a procedure for disciplining errant clergymen. The problem now, however, was that ritualists were willing to go to prison for their beliefs and so acquired an aura of martyrdom. The Church Association earned the nickname "The Persecution Society, Ltd."[18] From the start certain Evangelicals were unwilling to join in imposing civil penalties for religious offenses, believing that the process would turn public sympathy in favor of their opponents. When, in 1887, the Association mounted a case against the elaborate ritual observed on a particular occasion by the patently saintly Edward King, bishop of Lincoln, and judgment was eventually given almost entirely on the side of the bishop, the appetite for prosecution faded away.[19] Yet the intense hostility of Evangelicals to Anglo-Catholic ceremony remained. There were reproductions of the English strug-gles elsewhere in the Anglican world. In America the leading Evangelical, Bishop C. P. McIlvaine, joined in 1867 with traditional High-Church col-leagues to condemn ritualist innovations, but many in his ecclesiastical party wanted to go further by revising the Prayer Book so as to exclude any pretext for advanced ceremonies.[20] In Canada the introduction of early morning Communion, Lenten observance and choral services at Trinity Church, Tor-onto, aroused firm Evangelical opposition that became organized in 1869 as the Evangelical Society.[21] In Australia the proposal to erect in St. Andrew's Ca-

---

[18]Ibid., pp. 9, 24, 11.

[19]James C. Whisenant, *A Fragile Unity: Anti-Ritualism and the Division of Anglican Evangelicalism in the Nineteenth Century* (Carlisle: Paternoster Press, 2003).

[20]Diana H. Butler, *Standing against the Whirlwind: Evangelical Episcopalians in Nineteenth-Century America* (New York: Oxford University Press, 1995), p. 198.

[21]Philip Carrington, *The Anglican Church in Canada* (Toronto: Collins, 1963), p.144.

thedral, Sydney, an alabaster reredos that seemed to display a crucifix provoked stout and successful resistance, leading to the formation of the Church
of England Association (1886).[22] Throughout the English-speaking world
Evangelicals felt themselves to be confronting an immense conspiracy to reverse the Reformation. What in reality they were facing was a blending of doctrinal conviction with one of the most powerful cultural currents of the age.

The effect of the Anglo-Catholic exaltation of the sacraments was a corresponding diminution of their significance among evangelicals. A contributor to
the *Christian Observer* in 1852, it is true, defended Evangelicals against the charge
of undervaluing the sacraments. It pointed out that Evangelicals had encouraged attendance at Holy Communion, having been the first to introduce its
monthly observance. Against the Tractarians, however, they had to contend that
there must be no enthroning of the sacraments.[23] In the case of baptism there
was little public controversy within the Church of England after the Gorham
Judgement of 1850 settled that Evangelical clergy were at liberty to reject the
belief that baptism is the agent of regeneration. In America, however, the language of the Prayer Book, which declared at the end of the order for the baptism of infants that the child was now regenerate, continued to be a rock of offense. "Extravagant churchmanship," according to Bishop McIlvaine in 1869,
"has created in brethren to whom the Gospel in its simplicity is dearer than life,
an extreme dissatisfaction" with the language of the Prayer Book.[24] So strong
was the feeling that it helped precipitate the secession of the Reformed Episcopal Church in 1873.[25] Beyond the bonds of the Anglican communion there
was a similar effect. Baptism, where it was conferred on infants, was not entirely
minimized. The newspaper of the South African Methodists declared in 1885
that, "We are not believers in the dogma of 'Baptismal Regeneration,' but nor
are we believers in a *Baptismal nothing*."[26] Even among Baptists, however, for
whom the rite was a defining principle, there was a tendency to downgrade its

---

[22] William J. Lawton, *The Better Times to Be: Utopian Attitudes to Society among Sydney Anglicans, 1885
to 1914* (Kensington, U.K.: New South Wales University Press, 1990), p. 16.

[23] "Are the Evangelical Body justly chargeable with a want of due regard to the sacraments?"
Christian Observer (London), February 1852, pp. 82-86.

[24] Butler, *Standing against the Whirlwind*, p. 204.

[25] Allen C. Guelzo, *For the Union of Evangelical Christendom: The Irony of the Reformed Episcopalians*
(University Park: Pennsylvania State University Press, 1994).

[26] *South African Methodist* (Grahamstown), December 2, 1882, p. 543.

importance.[27] By 1888 John Clifford, the most prominent Baptist leader around the end of the century, commended "a religion wholly independent of ritual."[28] In 1893 the widely read British nondenominational newspaper the *Christian* took its criticism of High-Church innovations so far as to question the very notion of a sacrament. It was possible, confessed the editor, that it might become best to drop the two Christian ordinances altogether. After all, Hezekiah had broken up the brazen serpent because the Israelites burned incense to it. It would be better to end the observance of the ordinances than that they should take the place of the realities of which they were shadows.[29] The reaction against the legacy of the Oxford movement pushed many evangelicals into a denigration of the sacramental principle altogether.

In the case of the Communion service, however, there was some effort to wrestle with its theological significance. Anglican Evangelicals in particular tried to articulate a theory of the Lord's Supper that would do justice to the place of the Eucharist in the church's worship without conceding Anglo-Catholic claims. In 1856 William Goode published *The Nature of Christ's Presence in the Eucharist*, a substantial work that repudiated any doctrine locating the activity of God in the material elements rather than in the experience of the believer. Later in the century Nathaniel Dimock composed a series of books challenging the novel position of the advanced High Churchmen. Their version of Eucharistic theology, discerning a sacrifice in the action of the priest, he argued, supplanted the uniqueness of the sacrifice of Christ on the cross: but "with this as the object of our remembrance, we want nothing more."[30] Evangelicals were generally memorialists, believing with Zwingli that the purpose of the Lord's Supper was to remember Christ's work on the cross rather than to receive any spiritual benefit peculiar to the sacrament. That was the position of the influential Bishop J. C. Ryle, though others, such as A. W. Thorold, also a bishop from 1877, urged that there should be acceptance in the Evangelical ranks of those with sacra-

---

[27] Michael Walker, *Baptists at the Table: The Theology of the Lord's Supper amongst English Baptists in the Nineteenth Century* (London: Baptist Historical Society, 1992), chap. 3.

[28] *Freeman* (London), January 6, 1888, p. 5.

[29] *Christian* (London), February 9, 1893, p. 8. A week later, however, the editor retracted.

[30] Nathaniel Dimock, *The Doctrine of the Lord's Supper* (London: Longmans, Green, 1910), p. 51, quoted by Christopher J. Cocksworth, *Evangelical Eucharistic Thought in the Church of England* (Cambridge: Cambridge University Press, 1993), p. 83.

mental views that placed them closer to High Churchmen.[31] Some Evangelicals did venture to hold very much higher opinions, one speaker at Islington in 1883 repudiating "the erroneous idea of Zwingle [sic]" and another admitting there in 1900 that there was an element of sacrifice in the Eucharist.[32] If such ideas could be tolerated amongst Anglican Evangelicals, there was much less breadth of opinion in other circles. Spurgeon was one of the few Baptists who in this era adhered to Calvin's teaching that Holy Communion is a unique means of grace.[33] In Congregationalism C. A. Berry was virtually alone in falling under the influence of higher Anglican doctrine. At the Congregational Union Assembly in 1897, there was reportedly a "dead silence" when Berry referred to the real presence in Communion.[34] The Brethren movement was exceptional among evangelicals in placing "the breaking of bread" at the center of Sunday worship.[35] There was a widespread tendency during this period, through reaction against sacramentalist claims, to maintain a low estimate of the place of the Lord's Supper in Christian discipleship.

HIGHER CHURCHMANSHIP AMONG EVANGELICALS

Nevertheless there was a countervailing trend among Evangelicals in the Anglican communion to adopt higher forms of liturgical practice. The first bishop of Goulbourn in New South Wales, Mesac Thomas, noticed on returning to England in 1874 that there had been a general change over the previous eleven years in a ritualist direction, what he called a "universal elevation." Vestments and decorations had multiplied; the eastward position was widely adopted.[36] Evangelicals were by no means immune to the new developments. "Churches now deemed decidedly Evangelical," according to an Islington speaker in 1883, "would, thirty years ago, have been regarded as High Church."[37] Traditionalists

---

[31] Record, January 21, 1870.

[32] P. F. Eliot in Record, January 19, 1883, p. 56; Chancellor Bernard in Record, January 12, 1900, p. 40.

[33] Walker, Baptists at the Table, chap. 5.

[34] Christian World (London), May 13, 1897, p. 15.

[35] Neil Dickson, " 'Shut in with thee': The Morning Meeting among Scottish Open Brethren, 1830s-1960s," in Continuity and Change in Christian Worship, Studies in Church History, 35, ed. R. N. Swanson (Woodbridge, U.K.: Boydell Press, 1999).

[36] Record, January 22, 1875.

[37] Record, January 19, 1883, p. 59.

sympathizing with the Church Association roundly denounced the trend, rejecting even harvest festivals and flower services as symptoms of declension. The innovations seemed a consequence of too much contact with clergy of a higher persuasion, especially at the Church Congresses that were highly suspect to the more conservative Evangelicals. The attenders, according to the heightened rhetoric of Church Association zealots, were "Neo-Evangelicals" who often went to the Congresses as ministers but returned as priests.[38] High-Church ideas also rubbed off on Evangelicals in diocesan events and during the joint missions that became common from the 1870s. Many Evangelicals, particularly in the more fashionable churches in the south of England, began to compromise. William Cadman introduced daily prayer and weekly Communion, both at the time considered High-Church customs, to Holy Trinity, Marylebone, from his arrival there in 1859.[39] At Tunbridge Wells in 1886 Canon Hoare allowed choral singing, though no surpliced choristers or intoning of prayers.[40] E. H. Bickersteth, shortly to be elevated to the episcopal bench, argued at Islington in 1880 that even choirs wearing surplices could be tolerated.[41] Evangelicals could hardly avoid being influenced by what contemporary critics called "the spirit of the age" or "the prevailing taste of the day."[42]

There was a significant breakthrough for the more progressive spirits at the Islington conference of 1883. This gathering, which partly set and partly reflected the tone of Anglican Evangelicalism, displayed in that year a marked divergence of opinion between traditionalists and the broader-minded. F. F. Goe, who three years later was to become bishop of Melbourne, urged that aesthetic taste had grown and that young people liked innocent ceremony possessing no doctrinal significance. Likewise J. F. Kitto contended that they should not deny liberty to those who chose to adopt surplices, choral services and decorations. Even Canon Lefroy, one of the more conservative speakers, conceded that they were narrow if they failed to bring services into harmony with the ideas of the

---

[38]James Bateman, *The Church Association*, 2nd ed. (London: William Ridgeway, 1880), pp. 6-7 85n.

[39]L. E. Shelford, *A Memorial of the Rev. William Cadman, M. A.* (London: Wells, Gardner, Darton & Co., 1899), p. 61.

[40]*Christian*, August 5, 1886, p. 2.

[41]*Record*, January 16, 1880.

[42]G. T. Fox in *Record*, January 18, 1878; Daniel Wilson in *Record*, January 14, 1881.

age by improving the music, observing saint's days and holding a daily or at least weekly Holy Communion: "surely" he concluded, "a man is not less Evangelical because he is in favour of these."[43] The conference seemed to give a green light for the raising of the liturgical level by the more progressive section of the Evangelical party. By 1900 it was common to see advertisements for "Liberal Evangelical" curates, meaning at this time those who enjoyed a measure of ceremony rather than those of broader theological views. Nevertheless the stricter party maintained certain distinctive marks of their lower churchmanship. One was the wearing of the black gown rather than the surplice for preaching. On this question it was traditionally minded Evangelicals, not ritualists, who were the lawbreakers, for the Purchas Judgement had settled in 1871 that the correct dress for preaching was the surplice. But conservative Evangelicals, seeing the surplice as tainted with ecclesiasticism, refused to comply. Another distinctive was holding Holy Communion in the evening. Ritualists objected to evening celebrations because that prevented their practice of fasting before receiving the elements, whereas many Evangelicals preferred the evening because it was the time of the biblical Last Supper. The rise of Anglo-Catholicism was setting the pace in Anglican practice, and Evangelicals were divided in how far they were willing to be carried along in its train.

Happenings in the Church of England, the undoubted epicenter of liturgical change, were reflected elsewhere. Although evangelicals in other parts of the world were frequently fierce opponents of ritualism, they also accommodated themselves to the novelties of the times. Thus in New Zealand an interdenominational newspaper voiced the opinion in 1870 that evangelical churches had too much neglected tasteful music. "To grace the brow of Truth," it recommended, "let us seize the flowers—Beauty and Music—with which the Romanists and Ritualists have sought to adorn a falsehood."[44] By the first decade of the twentieth century the Evangelical congregations of the Church of England in Adelaide, South Australia, all had surpliced choirs and Holy Communion every Sunday.[45] What is more, members of other denominations were also feeling the same impulse that was raising the liturgical levels

---

[43] *Record*, January 19, 1883, pp. 57, 59, 55.

[44] *Christian Observer* (Christchurch), March 1, 1870, p. 35.

[45] David Hilliard, *Godliness and God Order: A History of the Anglican Church in South Australia* (Netley, South Australia: Wakefield Press, 1986), p. 65.

within the Anglican communion. Despite their traditional adherence to austere worship, Presbyterians began to include fresh features derived chiefly from the Anglican example during the later nineteenth century. Services to mark the church year, hitherto objectionable in principle, began to creep in. From the 1870s there were Christmas services in many congregations, from the 1880s Holy Week services and by 1896, at least at Central Presbyterian Church in Rochester, New York, Lenten services.[46] Similarly Congregationalists, who had been committed almost exclusively to extemporary prayer, began in this period to use set forms. At the 1872 autumn meetings of the Congregational Union of England and Wales the gathered delegates of the churches for the first time recited the Lord's Prayer.[47] A decade later John Hunter, Congregational minister at Hull, published *Devotional Services for Use in Nonconformist Chapels*, which pioneered the introduction of a variety of liturgical elements into worship. Meanwhile at Clinton Avenue Congregational Church, Brooklyn, New York, there were already unison prayers, doxologies, the Gloria Patri, responsive readings, chanted psalms and kneeling for prayer.[48] The cultural revolution leading to a desire for greater beauty and dignity was spreading across the world and across the denominations.

THE LANGUAGE OF RELIGION

The same transformation inevitably affected the language used in preaching and other forms of religious discourse. The result was to encourage an exuberant grandiloquence that, in its ablest exponents, overwhelmed awed congregations. The addresses of William Morley Punshon, the greatest pulpit orator of Victorian Methodism, were praised for "the beauty of finish, the gorgeous vocabulary, the pungent aphorism, the rainbow-tinted play of fancy" that they displayed.[49] Crowds thronged to hear him and they were frequently powerfully affected. Once, merely because he placed emphasis on the word *man* while read-

---

[46]Charles D. Cashdollar, *A Spiritual Home: Life in British and American Reformed Congregations, 1830-1915* (University Park: Pennsylvania State University Press, 2000), p. 42 and n.

[47]John W. Grant, *Free Churchmanship in England, 1870-1940* (London: Independent Press, 1955), p. 36.

[48]Cashdollar, *Spiritual Home*, p. 43.

[49]F. W. MacDonald, *The Life of William Morley Punshon, Ll. D.* (London: Hodder & Stoughton, 1887), p. 452.

ing John 9:32, "Since the world began was it not heard that any *man* opened the eyes of one that was born blind," a listening Unitarian was said to have been won over to orthodoxy.[50] The inflated style of oratory, however, could pass over at times into exaggerated bombast. Thus a preacher in Albany, New York, could describe the assassination of Abraham Lincoln at the end of the struggle with the Confederacy in strongly overdrawn imagery: "As the contest culminates, a murderer mutilates the heroic brain, but under that firm foot of his the hundred-headed Moloch lay dead."[51] A similar, though quieter, attempt to evoke feeling by piling words on words is evident in a British obituary of 1882:

> For two years our friend has lived in the valley of the shadow of death, and often have its cold chilling mists pierced his frail frame. The angel of death, which has so long hovered round his dwelling, has at last delivered his message, and our friend, not as an unwilling captive, but in glad submission to the call of his Master, has gone forth to a better and nobler world.[52]

The phraseology was entirely congruent with evangelical teaching, and indeed drew on the language of the Bible, but there was a striving for effect that, for the modern reader, obscures what is being said. The same may have been true for contemporaries who were less familiar with the conventions than others. The aesthetics of the age were sometimes being exalted to the extent of imperiling content.

Among some of the most admired writers of the era a certain imprecision of expression was considered a strength. Partly because of its love for poetry, Romantic taste expected ideas to be conveyed in a way that evoked powerful emotion rather than with an overriding concern for accuracy. Inevitably theology fell under the influence of this novel preference for thought with blurred edges. The initial response of evangelicals, who cherished exact doctrine, was overwhelmingly unfavorable. In 1850 there were complaints in the *Record*, the Evangelical Anglican periodical, that "the Anglo-American sentimentalists," numbering Carlyle and Emerson in their ranks, were etherealising evangelical phraseology. Broader theologians such as F. D. Maurice and A. P. Stanley were

---

[50] Thomas M'Cullagh, *The Rev. William Morley Punshon, Ll. D.: A Memorial Sermon* (London: Wesleyan Conference Office, 1881), p. 22.

[51] Dr. Magoon in *Examiner and Chronicle* (New York), April 27, 1865.

[52] *Baptist Magazine*, December 1882, p. 532.

following in their wake. All, concluded the *Record*, had fallen under the sway of the "German Neology and Mysticism" that they had learned from Coleridge.[53] Maurice in particular became something of a *bête noire*. The author of *The Kingdom of Christ* (1838), Maurice taught that all human life was founded in Christ. There was no need, as evangelicals universally maintained, for people to be converted before they could be accounted Christians. When, in 1853, Maurice published a volume of *Theological Essays* urging that eternal punishment need not be endless in duration, evangelicals applauded the pressure that led to his resignation as professor of theology at King's College, London. But what they most disliked about his thought was its vagueness, a refusal to stand by the received truths of Scripture and an unwillingness to erect barriers against the erosion of doctrine. "The Maurician theory," declared the *Record* in 1856, "is traceable to Gnosticism, graduating through various strata of free-thinking, scepticism, and sophistical philosophy, principally of the German school, and its *ultima Thule* is Infidelity."[54] Evangelicals were normally hostile to what Edward Garbett condemned in 1877 as the "tendency to resolve dogma into sentiment."[55]

THE BEGINNINGS OF LIBERAL TENDENCIES

A few, however, began to be attracted by the new style of thinking. The pioneer of importing Romantic idiom into the theology of evangelicalism itself was Horace Bushnell, Congregational minister at Hartford, Connecticut. Bushnell had already marked out a distinctive personal path by arguing, in *Christian Nurture* (1847), that children should be treated as Christians from their youngest days, not needing to pass through the wicket gate of conversion. He had clearly fallen under the influence of the strands in Romantic thought which maintained that children are naturally innocent creatures and that human beings, like trees, develop through steady growth. The starting point for his reconstruction of theology, as he readily avowed, was Coleridge's *Aids to Reflection*, providing him with a new vocabulary of faith. In 1849 Bushnell issued a collection of addresses, *God in Christ*, prefaced by a dissertation on language that set out its lim-

---

[53] *Record*, November 4, 1850, p. 8.

[54] *Record*, January 2, 1856.

[55] Edward Garbett, *Religious Thought in the Nineteenth Century: A Paper read at the Southport Evangelical Conference, May 29, 1877* (Southport: Robert Johnson, 1877), p. 8.

itations as a medium of precise communication. Phraseology, he contended, was so full of connotations that it could not convey exact meanings. "Considering the infirmities of language," he wrote, "all formulas of doctrine should be held in a certain spirit of accommodation. They cannot be pressed to the letter for the very sufficient reason that the letter is never true." Using a Coleridgean distinction, Bushnell argued that Christian truth should appeal to "feeling and imaginative reason," not to "the natural understanding."[56] The evangelical community did not quite know what to make of the new teaching. Bushnell evidently wanted to vindicate the Trinity and the atonement, but his unfamiliar and loose phraseology opened the doctrines to question. Edwards A. Park of Andover tried to steady nerves by contending in the following year that the theology of the intellect, precise in its formulations, was as valid as the theology of the feelings that Bushnell had commended, but suitable for different purposes. Charles Hodge of Princeton replied with a stern rejection of any confusing of the one with the other.[57] At Bushnell's death he was condemned by the leading Methodist newspaper for "his aberrations from the old and long-accepted standards of orthodoxy,"[58] but many Congregationalists, in particular, had been won over to his way of thinking. Henry Trumbull, the influential editor of the *Sunday School Times*, for instance, hailed Bushnell for having shown him that the Bible "suggests to us far more than it can define."[59] That essentially literary perception was the germ of the theological liberalism that began to make its way into the evangelical movement.

The man who did most to develop Bushnell's perspective was Henry Ward Beecher. The son of Lyman Beecher, a leading Connecticut Congregationalist, and the brother of Harriet Beecher Stowe, the author of *Uncle Tom's Cabin* (1852), Henry possessed preaching and literary gifts in abundance. For forty years from 1847 he served as minister of Plymouth Church, Brooklyn Heights, a genteel congregation in the prosperous suburbs of New York. Beecher was im-

[56]Horace Bushnell, *God in Christ: Three Discourses delivered at New Haven, Cambridge and Andover* (Hartford: Brown & Parsons, 1849), pp. 81, 111.

[57]D. G. Hart, "Divided between Heart and Mind: The Critical Period for Protestant Thought in America," *Journal of Ecclesiastical History* 38 (1987).

[58]*Christian Advocate* (New York), February 24, 1876, p. 60.

[59]P. E. Howard, *The Life Story of Henry Clay Trumbull* (Philadelphia: Sunday School Times Co., 1905), p. 256.

bued with the characteristic Romantic love of the natural world, which he de-lighted to recollect in tranquility. "I do not seem to think," he wrote, "I *see*. If I speak in images it is because they glow, I see landscapes or cliffs—or forests, or prairies and the *impression* is as minute and vivid as if it were really before my eyes."[60] Like Bushnell, Beecher did not strain for theological precision. On one occasion, when it was pointed out to him that a sermon contradicted what he had said the previous Sunday, he was entirely untroubled. "Oh yes," he re-marked, "Well, that was last week!"[61] Beecher, however, wished to advance be-yond Bushnell to apply the diffuse teaching they shared to the issues of life. Beecher's reputation soared because he acted as an eloquent champion of the abolition of slavery. His earlier ministry was applauded even by those of much more conservative convictions in theology. Thus, when in England in 1863, he was the chief guest at the opening of a new chapel erected for Charles Spur-geon's brother, James.[62] In 1870 New Zealanders saw Beecher as the American equivalent of Charles Spurgeon himself.[63] But Beecher's views were causing se-rious unease. When, two years later, he deprecated theology in favor of com-mon sense, a Methodist censured him for creating confusion. He was too vague, too indefinite, positing only "images of fog."[64] Likewise when Beecher was honored in London shortly before his retirement, Henry Allon, the grand old man of English Congregationalism, was careful to distance himself from the American preacher, insisting that it was a mistake to "disparage dogmatic opinions."[65] Beecher retained a place within the evangelical community of his day, but he was decidedly on the radical fringe.

The equivalent evolution of opinion in Britain first became apparent in a controversy that racked Congregationalism. In 1855 Thomas Toke Lynch, a London minister, published a collection of verse called *Hymns for Heart and Voice:*

---

[60] Henry W. Beecher to unknown correspondent, November 29, 1851, in *Henry Ward Beecher: Spokesman for a Middle-Class America*, ed. Clifford E. Clark, Jr. (Urbana: University of Illinois Press, 1978), p. 85.

[61] Gary Dorrien, *The Making of American Liberal Theology: Imagining Progressive Religion, 1805-1900* (Louisville, Ky.: Westminster John Knox Press, 2001), p. 193.

[62] G. H. Pike, *James Archer Spurgeon, D. D., Ll. D.* (London: Alexander & Shepheard, 1894), p. 77.

[63] *Christian Observer* (Christchurch), March 1, 1870, p. 36.

[64] *Christian Advocate*, August 1, 1872, p. 244.

[65] *Henry Ward Beecher in England, 1886* (London: James Clarke & Co., 1886), p. 29.

The Rivulet. The book, as the subtitle implied, showed a high regard for the place of nature in fostering Christian devotion, but neglected familiar evangelical themes such as the atonement. It was roundly condemned in a press review for being "pervaded throughout by the Rationalist Theology of Germany,"[66] but fifteen well known ministers defended its conformity with orthodoxy. However, John Campbell, the pugnacious editor of the *British Banner,* disagreed vehemently, and stirred up alarm about the *Rivulet* in his newspaper. The affair, which was complicated by many side issues, was laid to rest only by a special session of the Congregational Union assembly in 1857, when a resolution of the previous year recording unabated attachment to evangelical principles was reaffirmed. It was during the controversy that James Baldwin Brown, another London minister, wrote *The Divine Life in Man,* a book that he published in 1859. It argued for a break with the doctrinal inheritance of moderate Calvinism. Instead Baldwin Brown expounded ideas that reflected those of Alexander Scott, once Edward Irving's assistant and deeply molded by his brand of Romantic spirituality. The themes of the Fatherhood of God, the freedom of man and the responsibility to pursue righteousness loomed large.[67] The book, according to the senior Baptist minister John Howard Hinton, was "the first open inroad into English Evangelical Nonconformist churches of a theology fatally deficient in the truth and power of the gospel."[68] It certainly represented a shift from the Enlightenment paradigm to a theological system expressed in Romantic categories of thought.

DOCTRINAL CHANGE

Certain key themes in evangelical thought were subsequently affected by the alteration in the theological climate. A central one was the idea of God, who had been conceived within the Enlightenment framework as essentially a law-giver administering public justice in the universe. It is true that evangelicals

---

[66] James Grant, review of *Hymns for Heart and Voice: The Rivulet,* by Thomas Toke Lynch, *Morning Advertiser* quoted in Albert Peel, *These Hundred Years: A History of the Congregational Union of England and Wales, 1831-1931* (London: Congregational Union of England and Wales, 1931), p. 222.

[67] Mark Hopkins, *Nonconformity's Romantic Generation: Evangelical and Liberal Theologies in Victorian England* (Carlisle: Paternoster Press, 2004), chap. 2.

[68] *Baptist Magazine,* March 1860, p. 226.

were used to speaking of the Almighty as Father too. A keen American Congregational home missionary in 1857 described the ability to call him Father as the greatest privilege of the Christian.[69] But that comment entailed a limitation: only believers could claim God as their Father, whereas for other human beings he was essentially a judge. Even believers were primarily those whom the judge had acquitted. It was the complaint of the two pacesetting theologians in this field, the Scots John McLeod Campbell and Thomas Erskine, that moderate Calvinists were guilty, as McLeod Campbell put it, of talking about God in legal rather than family terms.[70] On the newer view, however, God was the common Father of all, even, as Erskine emphasized, of the prodigals.[71] Progressive leaders of Congregational thought such as Henry Ward Beecher and Baldwin Brown were persuaded of the universal Fatherhood of God. J. C. Ryle, however, rallied Anglican Evangelicals to the conviction that the God was Father only to those who believed in God's Son.[72] Likewise John Kennedy, the conservative minister of the Free Church of Scotland, resisted the notion that God was Father of every human being. "The relation of fatherhood," he wrote, "would impose conditions which cannot consist with the free exercise of God's sovereignty."[73] If God were automatically Father of every human being, he could not forbear to love each one of them and so would not be in a position to deal severely with their guilt. It is clear that Kennedy felt the force of the cultural trend toward reformulating the conception of deity in terms of fatherhood, but was steeling himself to resist it. Perhaps it is not surprising, therefore, that by the end of the century the newer view, though still rejected by traditional Calvinists, had triumphed in evangelicalism at large. The catechism of the Evangelical Free Churches, drawn up in 1898 to represent the common faith of the Nonconformists of England and Wales, emphasized that God was "Our Father in Heaven."[74] And the journal

---

[69]*American Missionary* (New York), July 1857, p. 157.

[70]John McLeod Campbell, *The Nature of the Atonement*, ed. E. P. Dickie (1856; reprint, London: James Clarke and Co., 1959), p. 69.

[71]Thomas Erskine, *The Doctrine of Election*, 2nd ed. (1837; reprint, Edinburgh: David Douglas, 1878), p. 347.

[72]*Record*, January 16, 1860, p. 3.

[73]John Kennedy, *Man's Relations to God* (Edinburgh: John Maclaren, 1869), p. 25.

[74]*An Evangelical Free Church Catechism for Use in Home and School* (London: National Council of the Evangelical Free Churches, 1899), p. 7.

of the main American female missionary organization drew the corollary: "O Christian women, let us teach the world that all are brothers because all are children of one Father!"[75] The prevailing way of understanding the identity of God was being transformed.

There was a corresponding change in the doctrine of the atonement. The cross remained a central theme in evangelical theology, but its formulation underwent modification. The change sprang primarily, as Kennedy discerned, from the prior set of assumptions surrounding the Fatherhood of God. Thus according to McLeod Campbell, who published his book on *The Nature of the Atonement* in 1856, the Father did not need to have his attitude to humanity altered by the sacrifice of Christ from wrath to mercy because, despite his anguish over sin, from eternity he had been full of paternal pity. The cross was therefore not a matter of retributive justice but an expression of the permanent kindly disposition of God toward the men and women he had created. Likewise Bushnell, in his *Vicarious Sacrifice* (1866), taught that the Father had always agonized over the ways of his children. "There is a cross in God," he declared, "before the wood is seen on Calvary."[76] Such views were initially resisted by the bulk of evangelical commentators. McLeod Campbell, suggested an American Congregationalist in 1878, did not insist adequately on the divine government.[77] Bushnell was generally censured, in Australia and Canada as well as America and Britain, for dropping essential features of the evangelical understanding of the atonement.[78] Others, however, felt the need to come to terms with the trends of thought that were generating the new interpretations of the cross. In particular the English Congregationalist R. W. Dale, who had been strongly swayed by the ideas of Carlyle and Maurice, wrestled with blending Romantic assumptions into received evangelical opinion. In *The Atonement* (1875), Dale argued, on the basis of extensive New Testament exegesis, that the cross was an objective expression of the supreme

---

[75]Mrs. C. M. Lamson in *Life and Light* (Boston, Mass.), October 1900, p. 462.

[76]Horace Bushnell, *The Vicarious Sacrifice grounded in Principles of Universal Obligation* (New York: Charles Scribner and Co., 1866), p. 73.

[77]John Morgan, "Atonement" II , *Bibliotheca Sacra* (New York), January 1878, p. 136.

[78]*Australian Evangelist* (Melbourne), August 3, 1866, p. 238. H. F. Bland in *Christian Guardian* (Toronto), March 10, 1880. Morgan, "Atonement," p. 142. *Religious Herald* (Richmond, Va.), February 21, 1878. *Baptist Magazine*, June 1866, pp. 362-69.

moral law of the universe. His synthesis became the standard work on the subject for more than a generation. The change in attitudes relating to the atonement went less far than the revolution over the Fatherhood of God, but it is significant that, around the end of the century, even conservative theologians such as the Scottish Presbyterian James Orr, later a contributor to *The Fundamentals*, could cite McLeod Campbell with approval.[79] The consequence was that evangelicals in general held a much less mechanistic understanding of the cross in 1900 than in 1850.

There was a cognate tendency to rate the doctrine of the incarnation higher than in the past. A stress on the taking of flesh by the Son of God was characteristic both of High-Church theology stemming from the Oxford movement and of Broad-Church teaching associated with Maurice and his disciples, but those who were trying to reconstruct evangelical thinking on a wider basis took a similar line. Bushnell and Baldwin Brown both placed much emphasis on the incarnation. So did John Young, a United Presbyterian minister serving in London, who in 1866 published *The Life and Light of Men*. Excerpts appearing in the *Australian Evangelist* in the same year spoke of the incarnation as "this central truth," showing that human nature must be very dear to God. "We may not have made too much of the cross," said Young; "but there is ground to think that we have made too little of the earlier fact, which invests the cross with all its mysterious significance."[80] Anglican Evangelicals, always alive to the risk of defections from their ranks to higher or broader churchmanship, regularly insisted that the cross must never take second place. At Islington in 1896 T. W. Drury repudiated the view that the death of Christ was only an accident of the incarnation, and three years later W. H. Griffith Thomas contrasted evangelical Protestantism's religion of the atonement with the religion of the incarnation that he attributed to "Romanism and its Anglican counterpart."[81] Dale, however, while believing that the power of the gospel lay in the atonement, also held that the primacy belonged to the doctrine of the incarnation.[82] Orr was ready

---

[79] James Orr, *God's Image in Man and its Defacement in the Light of Modern Denials* (London: Hodder & Stoughton, 1905), pp. 277-78.

[80] *Australian Evangelist*, August 18, 1866, p. 251.

[81] *Record*, January 17, 1896, p. 71; January 13, 1899, p. 69.

[82] Robert W. Dale, *The Old Evangelicalism and the New* (London: Hodder & Stoughton, 1889), pp. 48-51.

to give greater space to the implications of Christ becoming man than to those of his sacrifice.[83] "The great central mystery of the Christian faith," he wrote, "is undeniably the doctrine of the *incarnation*."[84] The most intellectual evangelicals, though not occupants of the pews in general, were likely to be drawn by the temper of the age to elevate the incarnation to a place of unprecedented prominence.

A more widespread shift took place in the attitude toward hell. The Evangelical Alliance basis of faith, drawn up in 1846, avowed the eternal punishment of the wicked, and, especially in the earlier years of the period, the doctrine was sometimes vividly deployed in preaching. The English revivalist Richard Weaver robustly defended the practice in 1860. "If," he declared, "you had stood by the death-beds I have stood by, and heard the dying shrieks of lost souls going down to the fiery lake of hell, you'd say, 'Richard, talk about it, they want to be warned'."[85] Perhaps the melodramatic expression owed something to Romantic conventions, which for a time reinforced literalist ways of thinking about the doom of the impenitent. As late as 1880 a Methodist layman from Tennessee commented in the denominational newspaper that it was easy to go to hell: the current of this world would readily carry us to the lake burning with everlasting fire.[86] There was nevertheless a common feeling among evangelicals that everlasting punishment was not to be given undue weight. The preacher, contended an article in the Evangelical Anglican magazine in 1852, has to remember that he is to proclaim the gospel of the grace of God rather than announce death and ruin. The biblical pictures of chains, prison, fire and so on, though representing realities, were merely "images and figures of speech." Only Catholics and sectarians, the article concluded, resorted to moving the heart by "strong and coarse excitement."[87] The Methodist William Arthur, however, reported that even in the unrestrained atmosphere of the Ulster Revival of 1859 the themes associated with damnation were less prominent than on the lips of

---

[83]James Orr, *The Christian View of God and the World as centring in the Incarnation*, 2nd ed. (Edinburgh: Andrew Elliot, 1893), pp. 38-39.

[84]Orr, *God's Image in Man*, p. 267.

[85]*Revival* (London), June 23, 1860, p. 198.

[86]D. R. Britton in *Christian Advocate*, January 15, 1880, p. 38.

[87]T. D. B[ernard?], "On the Method of Preaching the Doctrine of Eternal Death," *Christian Observer* (London), January 1852, pp. 5-6.

Jesus himself.[88] Moody referred occasionally to hell, but the subject was deliberately downplayed in order to give prominence to the love of God.[89] In the private notes of Handley Moule for 1897 there are some remarks on the doctrine of future punishment. "We are *not* pledged," he wrote, "to the literality of all the imagery. . . . Nor pledged to the same degree of doom. Nor to a precise theory for those who have never heard the Gospel." It was a gross injustice, he concluded, to attribute pleasure to the preachers of the doctrine.[90] Even Spurgeon, with all his zeal for orthodoxy, was prepared to quote Henry Ward Beecher in support of the view that the future state of the impenitent, though a reality, was accepted only with a sense of dismay.[91] So the general evangelical attitude was to endorse the reality of hell, but not to dwell on the prospect or its attendant details and certainly not to do so with relish.

The mood of the times, however, induced many individuals to turn away from the received doctrine of everlasting punishment. The warm humanitarianism associated with Romantic thought often recoiled from the stark contours of traditional belief. Maurice and many Broad Churchmen led the way in modifying the view of future judgment and significant numbers of evangelicals were drawn in their wake. T. R. Birks, the honorary secretary of the British organization of the Evangelical Alliance, published in 1867 *The Victory of Divine Goodness*, which proposed the bold hypothesis that the lost would be able to enjoy a passive contemplation of blessedness at the same time as enduring their punishment. Although there was a campaign to remove Birks from his post, the Alliance accepted that he did uphold its doctrinal statement and allowed him to continue in office. A few took the far more drastic course of adopting universalism, the belief that all will in the end be saved. In 1877 Samuel Cox, an English Baptist minister and editor of the *Expositor*, argued for a universalist position in a book called *Salvator Mundi* while retaining the confidence of his

---

[88]William Arthur, *The Revival in Ballymena and Coleraine* (London: Hamilton, Adams and Co., 1859), p. 5.

[89]Stanley N. Gundry, *Love Them In: The Life and Theology of D. L. Moody* (Chicago: Moody Press, 1999), pp. 97-100.

[90]Handley C. G. Moule, "Detached remarks on the Doctr[ine] of Future Punishment," Lecture Notebook, Handley Moule Papers, Ridley Hall, Cambridge.

[91]Charles H. Spurgeon, "Preface," to *The Duration of Future Punishments*, by William Barker (London: Passmore & Alabaster, 1865), p. v. Cited by Hopkins, *Nonconformity's Romantic Generation*, p. 151.

Nottingham congregation.[92] Far more took the view that there would be a further opportunity for repentance and so of salvation beyond the grave, a position called at the time "future probation." At Andover Theological Seminary in Massachusetts the adoption of this conviction by five of the academic staff was the chief charge in an attempt to remove them in 1887. Egbert Smyth, one of the five, was dismissed, but subsequently reinstated by the supreme court of the state.[93] Perhaps the most popular alternative to the inherited doctrine, however, was belief in conditional immortality, the view that only those who trusted in Christ would be granted everlasting life. Those who had not turned from their sins would simply be extinguished. The English Congregationalist Edward White offered the first exposition of this stance to attract widespread notice as early as 1846, but it gathered far more adherents from the 1870s.[94] In 1883, when the Church Missionary Society dismissed one of its agents for embracing conditional immortality, Hay Aitken, an Evangelical missioner, provoked a storm by writing a tentative defense of the position.[95] Thus by the 1880s there was a great deal of unsettlement in this area. Milder opinions about human destiny were becoming common.

NEW VIEWS OF THE BIBLE

Attitudes to the Bible underwent a transformation too. At the start of the period older evangelicals were generally satisfied with the theory of inspiration propounded by Philip Doddridge in the early eighteenth century. It held that the authors of the biblical books were all inspired, but to different degrees.[96] Romantic notions about poetic inspiration, however, posed a challenge to the belief that there were different levels of divine influence in various parts of the Bible. How far did the lower levels of perception in the Scriptures differ from the spiritual vision of the greater poets? Transcendentalists claimed that there was no distinction at all, but evangelicals could not embrace a view that ruled out the uniqueness of divine revelation. They began to draw back from positing

---

[92]Geoffrey Rowell, *Hell and the Victorians* (Oxford: Clarendon Press, 1974), pp. 124-33.

[93]Dorrien, *Making of American Liberal Theology*, pp. 290-93.

[94]Rowell, *Hell and the Victorians*, chap. 9.

[95]Charlotte E. Woods, *Memoir and Letters of Canon Hay Aitken* (London: C. W. Daniel Co., 1928), pp. 174-81.

[96]*Christian Observer* (London), September 1854, p. 587.

varying degrees of inspiration. Thus J. M. Cramp, the Baptist president of Acadia College in Nova Scotia, declined to speculate about the nature, degree and method of inspiration. It might, he admitted, be different at different times, but it was dangerous to dogmatize.[97] Others were attracted to the theory propounded in *Theopneustia* (1841) by Louis Gaussen, a Geneva theologian. Again it offered no opinion on how the Bible had been given, but asserted the "plenary" inspiration of the whole biblical text, down to every word. Many echoed Gaussen in claiming that the result was a Bible that could be guaranteed free from error. Even many people of a pre-Romantic frame of mind were swayed by Gaussen's case. Thus John Pratt, archdeacon of Calcutta, contended in 1856 that "the Scriptures were written under the guidance of the Holy Spirit, who communicated to the writers facts before unknown, directed them in the selection of other facts already known, and preserved them from error of every kind in the records they made."[98] Such unqualified declarations of biblical inerrancy, however, were far from universal. T. R. Birks, for example, commented in 1853, when his soundness was still unchallenged, that there could be no doctrinal objection to the idea that there had been flaws in the original writings of the prophets and apostles. "God," he wrote, "is the God of truth. But when He condescends to the use of human instruments . . . it is not easy to say beforehand how far this accommodation to our weakness may extend."[99] There was entire confidence in the reliability of the substance of revelation, but no consensus about the definition of inspiration.

Evangelicals were thrown on to the defensive when, in 1860, *Essays and Reviews* was published. This collection of articles set out, with varying degrees of radicalism, the views of seven Anglican theologians who had been influenced by the school of biblical criticism that flourished in Germany. Evangelicals reacted sharply against opinions that seemed to undermine the authority of Scripture. Edward Garbett condemned the German speculation, "a dreamy world of empty abstractions," that underlay the volume; and Bishop Robert Bickersteth insisted that the inspiration of the Bible was different in kind from

---

[97] *Baptist Magazine*, January 1866, p. 25.

[98] J. H. Pratt, *Scripture and Science not at Variance*, 3rd ed. (1856; London: Thomas Hatchard, 1859), p. 69.

[99] T. R. Birks, *Modern Rationalism and the Inspiration of the Scriptures: Two Lectures* (London: Seeleys, 1853), p. 111.

that of Homer or Milton.[100] It was quite inadmissible, agreed an article in the *Christian Observer*, to suppose that divine inspiration was the same as the poetic variety. However, it explained, there were two views of the subject current among evangelicals. On the one hand, some held, like Gaussen, that the Holy Spirit had directed the authors so that their writings were infallible; on the other, some believed that the Spirit had superintended the religious content but that in other matters inaccuracies were possible. The author preferred the former theory, but admitted that, at a recent meeting of clergy, the majority had favored the latter opinion.[101] Nevertheless the stronger view gained ground among Anglican Evangelicals in the wake of *Essays and Reviews*. By 1862 Birks, who had previously avoided Gaussen's position, endorsed the conviction that the Scriptures were "free from all error."[102] At the Islington conference of that year Garbett expounded this position and by 1870 A. W. Thorold had to warn the assembled Evangelicals that dissenters from verbal inspiration should not be excluded from their ranks.[103] Those outside the established church, much less directly affected by the stir over *Essays and Reviews*, tended to take a more broad-minded view. From the chair of the Congregational Union in 1864 Henry Allon declared verbal inspiration untenable and in the same office four years later Alexander Raleigh admitted that there were "errors and mistakes" in Scripture.[104] There were already the beginnings of a tendency to divide into conservative and liberal camps over the nature of inspiration.

Controversies within evangelical denominations over Scripture on both sides of the Atlantic were signs of the same process. The first took place in the Lancashire Independent College in 1856-1857. Samuel Davidson, a tutor at the college, published a revision of one of the volumes of T. H. Horne's

---

[100]Edward Garbett, *The Bible and its Critics: An Enquiry into the Objective Reality of Revealed Truths* (London: Seeley and Griffiths, 1861), p. 90. M. C. Bickersteth, *A Sketch of the Life and Episcopate of the Right Reverend Robert Bickersteth, D. D., Bishop of Ripon, 1857-1884* (London: Rivingtons, 1887), p. 197.

[101]*Christian Observer* (London), April 1861, pp. 254-56.

[102]T. R. Birks, *The Bible and Modern Thought*, new ed. (London: Religious Tract Society, 1862), p. 33.

[103]*Record*, January 13, 1862, p. 3; January 21, 1870.

[104]W. H. Harwood, *Henry Allon, D. D.: Pastor and Teacher* (London: Cassell and Co., 1894), p. 42. Mary Raleigh, ed., *Alexander Raleigh: Records of his Life* (Edinburgh: A. and C. Black, 1881), p. 142.

standard work of 1818 on biblical criticism. Taking account of the general drift of German scholarship on the Old Testament, Davidson was prepared to say that Moses was not the author of the first five books of the Bible. Despite being willing to acknowledge Scripture "as an unerring rule of faith and practice," Davidson lost the confidence of the college committee and eventually resigned.[105] In 1874 David Swing, professor at the Presbyterian Seminary in Chicago, was arraigned for heresy. His chief offense, according to contemporaries, was to teach in effect that the Bible was only as inspired as other great books. An imitator in the same city compared the Old Testament, in the manner of the Germans, to mythology.[106] Swing left the denomination, but continued to preach popular poetic sermons in Chicago. There was soon a similar episode among Southern Baptists. Crawford Toy, who had studied for two years in Berlin before taking up a post at Southern Baptist Seminary, Louisville, was criticised for drawing on the theories associated with the leading German biblical critic Julius Wellhausen. Toy resigned in 1879, pursuing his subsequent career at Harvard.[107] The most celebrated debate, however, took place during the same decade in the Free Church of Scotland. An encyclopedia article on the Bible by William Robertson Smith, the brilliant young professor of Hebrew in the church's Aberdeen college, was attacked for following the Wellhausen approach by taking Deuteronomy not as contemporary history but as a subsequent construct. Robertson Smith defended himself as merely suggesting that Scripture adopts "certain forms of literary presentation which have always been thought legitimate in ordinary composition, but which were not always understood to be used in the Bible."[108] There was prolonged skirmishing; Robertson Smith was virtually acquitted; but then a further article reiterating his views sealed his fate. He was dismissed in 1881 and moved to Cambridge. The litigation over Robertson Smith case drew much wider attention to the so-called higher criticism, that

---

[105] J. A. Picton in *The Autobiography and Diary of Samuel Davidson, D. D., Ll. D.*, ed. Anne J. Davidson (Edinburgh: T & T Clark, 1899), p. 44.

[106] *Examiner and Chronicle*, February 12, 1874.

[107] L. Russ Bush and Tom J. Nettles, *Baptists and the Bible*, rev. ed. (Nashville: Broadman & Holman, 1999), pp. 208-20.

[108] *Free Church of Scotland Special Report of the College Committee on Professor Smith's Article Bible* (Edinburgh: Thomas and Archibald Constable, 1877), p. 20.

is, biblical scholarship founded on German principles. Many trembled for the defensibility of inspiration, but others concluded that this "scientific" style of criticism was compatible with evangelical faith.

The novel attitudes made rapid progress during the latter part of the century. In 1878 during discussion at the Islington conference Edward Batty, a London clergyman, urged that they ought "to admit that certain historical parts of the Bible were allegorical or open to different interpretations, and to show that they were fully alive to the importance of the claims of just, honest, reverential, and scholarly criticism."[109] By 1893, even the conservative Scottish Presbyterian James Orr was prepared to describe the third chapter of Genesis as probably "old tradition clothed in oriental allegorical dress."[110] English Nonconformity revolutionized the teaching in its colleges during the decade from 1885 by the general acceptance of the higher criticism.[111] In 1894 the *Christian Advocate*, the American Methodist newspaper, wishing to be even-handed, published a series of three papers setting out the case in favor of advanced higher criticism, the argument against it and a mediating position. Although the *Advocate's* editorial position remained resolutely hostile to denials of the supernatural in the Bible, a more academic journal, the *Methodist Review*, printed an article in 1896 musing about whether traditional beliefs might soon be called into question by critical research.[112] Scholarly works by evangelicals embracing the new methods began to appear, though they tended to reach conclusions little different from received opinion. Thus *The Foundations of the Bible* (1890), studies in the Old Testament by the Anglican R. B. Girdlestone, admitted that Genesis was a compilation, but claimed that it was mainly as Moses and his circle left it.[113] At Cambridge, however, H. E. Ryle, Hulsean Professor of Divinity from 1888 and a son of Bishop Ryle, published works of Old Testament criticism showing much less attempt at compromise with traditional views, being denounced for his pains (by a ritualist) as "one of the most noto-

---

[109] *Record*, January 18, 1878.

[110] Orr, *Christian View*, p. 217.

[111] Willis B. Glover, *Evangelical Nonconformists and Higher Criticism in the Nineteenth Century* (London: Independent Press, 1954).

[112] *Christian Advocate*, February 1, 1897, p. 105. H. A. Butz, "Conditions of Authentic Biblical Criticism," *Methodist Review* (New York), March 1896, p. 203.

[113] R. B. Girdlestone, *The Foundations of the Bible: Studies in Old Testament Criticism* (London: Eyre and Spottiswoode, 1890).

rious of the destructive school."[114] In America the conservative Presbyterians A. A. Hodge and B. B. Warfield produced a reasoned critique of the critical enterprise.[115] There was also great deal of grassroots uneasiness within the evangelical movement about the trend of opinion, and the some of the resistance will be noted later on.[116] There can be no doubt, however, that, as the century drew to a close, the broader school of thought was gathering strength.

EVOLUTIONARY THINKING

Science was a further area in which there was major change of mind during the period. The existing Enlightenment paradigm was confronted in 1859 by the challenge of Charles Darwin's theory of evolution. Hitherto evangelicals, like most other Christians, had placed a great deal of weight on the apologetic case provided by natural theology. The evidence of design in nature, they held, implied that there must have been a Creator.[117] Each species was carefully adapted for its distinctive role in life. Then Darwin showed in *The Origin of Species* that, on the contrary, there were indications that the adaptation could be sufficiently explained by the response of plants and animals to their environment. The most successful adapters, by means of natural selection, were the ones to survive. Consequently the phenomena of nature needed no theistic interpretation. The initial evangelical reaction was one of dismay and disbelief. In 1860 the *Christian Observer* dismissed the whole of Darwin's findings as conjecture.[118] T. R. Birks, who launched a personal crusade against Darwin's theory for defying the principles of sound induction, censured it a few years later as a "wholesale substitution of ingenious guesswork for the evidence of facts."[119] In 1863 the Congregationalist Edward Hitchcock, a capable geologist at Amherst College, Massachusetts, treated the Darwinian hypothesis as a comprehensive assault on Christianity, tending to atheism and materialism, destroying immortality and responsibility and undermining the doctrines of

---

[114]M. H. Fitzgerald, *A Memoir of Herbert Edward Ryle* (London: Macmillan and Co., 1928), chap. 6, p. 100.

[115]Mark A. Noll, *Between Faith and Criticism: Evangelicals, Scholarship and the Bible* (Leicester, U.K.: Inter-Varsity Press, 1991), pp. 18-27.

[116]See chap. 8, p. 258-62.

[117]See chap. 4, p. 125.

[118]*Christian Observer* (London), August 1860, p. 565.

[119]T. R. Birks, *The Scripture Doctrine of Creation* (London: SPCK, 1872), p. 253.

sin and salvation.[120] There were continuing echoes of the initial outright opposition to evolution in subsequent years. During the 1870s evangelical newspapers in America and Australia denounced Thomas Huxley and John Tyn-
dall, the popularizers of Darwin's theories who gave them an explicit
antireligious thrust.[121] In 1882 a tutor at Spurgeon's college was still using his
philosophy lectures to maintain a protest "against being considered a blood
relation of the ape or the oyster."[122] Even later a Welsh correspondent of the
nondenominational *Christian* sustained a one-man campaign against Darwin's
influence as a reproach to the age.[123] So there were many evangelicals, including
prominent spokesmen, who rejected evolution immediately after Darwin's
publication of the theory, and some, though usually more obscure figures, who
retained their skepticism much longer.

The general drift of opinion, however, was definitely in favor of the new science inaugurated by Darwin. It has been shown that many Presbyterian intel-
lectuals of conservative views took evolution in their stride. Although Charles
Hodge equated Darwinism with atheism, he did so only because Darwin's particular formulation of evolution was subversive of design in nature. It was per-
fectly possible, Hodge held, for evolution to be expounded in a way that was
compatible with design, and his successor at Princeton, B. B. Warfield, endorsed
a Christian understanding of Darwin's version of the teaching.[124] James Iverach,
a professor at the Free Church College in Aberdeen, explained in his *Christianity
and Evolution* (1894) that evolution was simply God's method of creation. "But
creation by evolution," he wrote, "is still evolution."[125] Others gradually came

---

[120]Edward Hitchcock, "The Law of Nature's Constancy subordinate to the Higher Law of
Change," *Bibliotheca Sacra*, July 1863, pp. 522-23.

[121]*Examiner and Chronicle*, January 12, 1871. R. W. Campbell in *Methodist Journal* (Adelaide),
June 4, 1875, p. 1.

[122]*Annual Paper concerning the Lord's Work in connection with the Pastors' College, Newington, London,
1881-1882* (London: Alabaster, Passmore and Sons, 1882), p. 17.

[123]*Christian*, September 23, 1887, p. 16; H. Heber Evans in *Christian*, May 2, 1895, p. 22.

[124]David N. Livingstone, *Darwin's Forgotten Defenders: The Encounter between Evangelical Theology and
Evolutionary Thought* (Grand Rapids: Eerdmans, 1987), pp. 100-5, 115-22. Cf. James R.
Moore, *The Post-Darwinian Controversies: A Study of the Protestant Struggle to come to Terms with
Darwin in Britain and America, 1870-1900* (Cambridge: Cambridge University Press,
1979).

[125]James Iverach, *Christianity and Evolution*, 3rd ed. (London: Hodder & Stoughton, 1900), p.
107.

to terms with the novel teaching. Whereas in 1872 the premier American theological journal *Bibliotheca Sacra* had carried an article by Frederic Gardiner of Berkeley Divinity School criticizing Darwin's theories as baseless, only six years later a fresh contribution by the same author contended that the issue of material evolution could safely be left to scientists to resolve, that it had no bearing on doctrine "except as it gives us higher and nobler views of the Creator" and that even if it was found that life could spring from nonliving things there would be no threat to theology.[126] There was a similar accommodation in the southern hemisphere. The editor of the Sydney Wesleyan newspaper, George Martin, remained convinced in 1876 that it was impossible to accept both evolution and the Bible, but his brother minister A. R. Fitchett of Dunedin, New Zealand, published a lecture in which he insisted that "evolution is essentially theistic." The lecture was designed to reclaim what was true in evolutionary thought from the infidels.[127] Likewise in Canada by 1880 the chief Methodist newspaper distinguished carefully between materialistic and theistic forms of evolutionary theory. Whereas the materialist mistakenly saw evolution as the sufficient explanation of all things, the theist rightly regarded it as "a method which God uses in the accomplishment of his wise purposes."[128] By the last two decades of the century evangelicals in general had come to accept that Darwin's discoveries could be interpreted within a Christian framework.

The extent of the reconciliation of evangelical theology with evolutionary thought is illustrated by the career of Henry Drummond, the lecturer in natural science at Glasgow's Free Church College. In 1883 he published a book that enjoyed enormous popularity, *Natural Law in the Spiritual World.* By Drummond's death in 1897 the work had gone through twenty-nine editions in Britain and fourteen in the United States. Its author had found his calling as an evangelist when he served as a lieutenant of Moody during his 1873-1874 campaign in Scotland. Drummond was known as an expert counselor, a specialist in preaching to students and subsequently, from 1883, one of the most prominent ad-

---

[126]Frederic Gardiner, "Darwinism," *Bibliotheca Sacra*, April 1872, esp. p. 288; Gardiner, "The Bearing of Recent Scientific Thought upon Theology," *Bibliotheca Sacra*, January 1878, pp. 65-69.

[127]*Christian Advocate and Wesleyan Review*, September 1, 1876, pp. 84-87; A. R. Fitchett in November 1, 1876, p. 125; December 1, 1876, p. 135.

[128]*Christian Guardian*, January 21, 1880, p. 20.

vocates of the Boys' Brigade, a uniformed evangelistic movement. He was also
respected for being well versed in science. Coming from a family of seedsmen,
he was particularly knowledgeable in biology, but, though little more than a
gentleman amateur in other fields, he enjoyed the confidence of many of the
leading practitioners and traveled the world on scientific expeditions. Consequently he seemed well placed to bring together Christian teaching and the latest discoveries of science. *Natural Law*, which began as lectures to working people at a Glasgow mission, was not a sophisticated work, but it was beautifully
written and expounded what evangelicals yearned to hear—that their own distinctive teachings, and particularly conversion, were in harmony with scientific
thinking. Drummond argued for the "law of biogenesis," the principle that
only life gives birth to life. Hence spiritual life must be received from Christ,
its author. A later work, *The Ascent of Man* (1894), tried to embrace Darwin's legacy and press it further by contending that the selfish struggle for life was accompanied by an altruistic struggle for the life of others that formed an expression of love. But already in the earlier work, Drummond was frankly accepting
the evolutionary worldview. He drew on Herbert Spencer, the contemporary
social philosopher whose theories seemed a counterpart to Darwin's writings.
Drummond appeared to offer a satisfying blend of evangelical religion and
contemporary science to replace the old natural theology.[129]

The effect of the rise of evolutionary thinking was to reinforce many of the
Romantic themes that were already gaining currency. The two shared common
ground in the idea of development. For the evolutionist, all nature adapted
gradually to its surroundings; for the Romantic, growth was as normal for human beings as for plants. Drummond, who was deeply influenced by authors
such as Carlyle, Ruskin and the Transcendentalists, dwelt on how Jesus' lesson
about the lilies of the field was designed to "teach us how to live a free and natural life, a life which God will unfold for us, without our anxiety, as he unfolds
the flower."[130] An age used to Romantic literature appreciated the metaphor of
growth. It was characteristic of those who wished to be up to date in their
thinking to dwell on the same motif. Thus Egbert Smyth, one of the advocates

---

[129]David W. Bebbington, "Henry Drummond, Evangelicalism and Science," in *Henry Drummond: A Perpetual Benediction*, ed. T. E. Corts (Edinburgh: T & T Clark, 1999).

[130]Henry Drummond, *Natural Law in the Spiritual World*, 19th ed. (London: Hodder &
Stoughton, 1887), p. 123.

of "progressive orthodoxy" at Andover Seminary, wrote in 1874 that "theology is a growth, and should be studied as a growth."[131] A drastic step was taken when it began to be asserted that the whole of religion fell into the same category. In 1897 Milton S. Terry, a Methodist theologian at Garrett Biblical Institute, Evanston, Illinois, expounded what he called the "new theological standpoint." "In matters of religious life and thought," Terry wrote, "as in all other human interests, there has been advancement from lower forms to higher."[132] Christianity was the highest form that had hitherto appeared, but the thought that, on his premises, something higher was bound to supersede his own faith does not seem to have occurred to him. This approach to world religions was to give rise in the early years of the twentieth century to such works as J. N. Farquhar's *The Crown of Hinduism* (1913), which contended that Christianity was in continuity with other types of spiritual quest. Already before the end of the nineteenth century there were indications that evangelical denominations had produced a style of theology that made the gospel a transient factor in world history.

This way of thinking was associated with another fruit of the synthesis of Romantic and evolutionary ideas, the fresh prominence given to the doctrine of immanence, the pervasive presence of God in his creation. The theory of evolution, according to the progressive theologian Frank H. Foster in 1893, had served theology well by leading to a stress on the immanence of God.[133] If nature evolved, then God as Creator was intimately involved in the processes of the universe in a way hitherto unconceived. James Iverach declared that "we have not a God who is absent from His creation, or who interferes now and then with its working, but a present living God."[134] The implication was often, as here, to discard the traditional notion of providence as the intervention of the hand of God in the world from the outside. Appealing to the greatest teachers of the nineteenth century such as Wordsworth and Emerson, the English Congregational theologian W. F. Adeney rejected the distinction between

---

[131]Egbert Smyth, *The Value of the Study of Church History in Ministerial Education* (Andover, Mass.: Andover Seminary, 1874), p. 14. I am grateful for this reference to Charlie Phillips.

[132]*Christian Advocate*, March 25, 1897, p. 187.

[133]F. H. Foster, "Evolution and the Evangelical System of Doctrine," *Bibliotheca Sacra*, July 1893, p. 413.

[134]Iverach, *Christianity and Evolution*, p. 206.

special and general providence, between divine action at particular junctures and his perennial concern for the world. "The great Gardener," he wrote in 1901, "is always moving about among His plants, fostering and tending them."[135] Such thinking, as Adeney was aware, was not far from pantheism. A further implication, in the eyes of some, was to downplay the miraculous. There was no need for supernatural events in human history if God was fully involved in every event in the first place. God, according to J. F. Chaffee, a leading Methodist minister at Minneapolis, is the only true locus of the supernatural, "and between him and nature there can be no conflict, for in the last analysis they are one."[136] The entire elimination of the supernatural as a separate category was too revolutionary for many to follow, but a larger number of thinkers entertained a novel sympathy for magnifying the omnipresence of God in his world. The seed was being sown for the liberal evangelicalism of the early twentieth century.

The prevailing pattern of theological change during the later nineteenth century was therefore a trend toward a more liberal stance. The main agent of change was the spread of the cultural mood associated with Romanticism as it evolved into a more popular phase. The Enlightenment principle of free enquiry, together with the associated suspicion of miracle, played a part in encouraging new modes of thought, but the novel content was largely shaped by the growing preference in the public at large for the natural, the traditional and the imaginative. The aesthetic impact, evidenced in a growing taste for poetry, transformed the church buildings erected in many parts of the world. The Romantic species of High Churchmanship generated by Tractarianism initially induced a reaction amongst evangelicals, who mounted an onslaught on what they regarded as a reinvigorated expression of popery, and often, in order to avoid Anglo-Catholic error, they took a decidedly low estimate of the sacraments. Soon, however, evangelicals, swayed by the same changes in taste as their opponents, began to adopt a higher liturgical practice as well as a more elaborate style of preaching. At first they were alarmed by the sentimental theology of the Broad Churchmen, but gradually the same intellectual influences

---

[135] W. F. Adeney, *A Century's Progress in Religious Life and Thought* (London: James Clarke & Co., 1901), p. 102.

[136] J. F. Chaffee, "The Significance of Current Religious Unrest," *Methodist Review*, July 1898, p. 565.

affected their thinking. Horace Bushnell and Henry Ward Beecher led the way in America while Thomas Toke Lynch and James Baldwin Brown did the same in Britain. The predominant idea of God changed from judge to Father; the atonement was subject to reinterpretation; the incarnation came into greater prominence; and hell lost much of its power. The formulation of biblical inspiration, too, was transposed into modes that appealed to the age, though some were firmer rather than weaker. The irruption into England of biblical criticism founded chiefly on Romantic axioms prevalent in Germany roused Anglican Evangelicals to resistance, and then controversies racked several denominations as the new techniques were applied, at first tentatively but then more confidently, within evangelical bodies. Likewise evolutionary thinking was initially resisted but then gradually assimilated. The motifs of growth and immanence bore witness to the intellectual currents that had been flowing into evangelicalism. Henry Drummond on one occasion insisted that the leading human faculty was not reason, as had been supposed in the past, but imagination.[137] The era when evangelicals generally thought within a framework inherited from the age of reason was passing, being gradually replaced by a Romantic age of imagination.

---

[137]Henry Drummond, *The New Evangelism and Other Papers*, 2nd ed. (London: Hodder & Stoughton, 1899), p. 28.

6

CONSERVATIVE
THEOLOGICAL TRENDS

Although the predominant tendency in the later nineteenth century was for evangelical theology to become broader in tone and content, there existed a simultaneous trend toward stiffer doctrinal convictions. The liberal movement of ideas was in part counteracted by currents that flowed into conservative theological channels. The cultural setting, which was so influential in fostering the broadening process, also nurtured many of the developments that pointed in the reverse direction. Features of the developing Romantic mood in particular helped to shape ways of thinking about mission, prophecy and sanctification that were to become associated with conservative groupings. The Evangelical section of the Church of England, still at the center of the wider global movement, was deeply swayed by changes of conviction in all three areas, so that its members entered the twentieth century with very different attitudes from those their fathers had entertained in the middle years of the nineteenth. Many in the American circles around Dwight L. Moody also adopted the novel but firmer theological views. The alteration of stance by Anglicans and Moody influenced many others in different parts of the world. It was in and around these groupings that anxieties about broader doctrinal ideas, and especially about biblical criticism, began to crystallize into stern resistance. A grassroots movement, especially in America, started to take shape opposing theological laxity and the erosion of evangelical norms in society at large. As George Marsden has shown in his classic *Fundamentalism and American Culture*, tendencies that were to emerge in the early years of the twentieth century were already at work in a more subterranean way before 1900.[1] So the later nineteenth century was marked by several theological movements that were decidedly conservative in their outcome.

THE FAITH PRINCIPLE

One of the major developments emerged in the context of the philosophy of missions. The foreign missionary enterprise, already considered in chapter three,[2] was originally based on what the era considered sound business practice. The early missionary societies were modeled on joint stock companies, with shares, boards of directors and annual accounts. The conception of mission, molded by Enlightenment maxims, was pragmatic and flexible.[3] That whole understanding of missionary activity had been challenged in 1824 by Edward Irving, a quixotic minister of the Church of Scotland serving in London. In a sermon preached before the London Missionary Society he had set out a vision of the missionary task that he explicitly related to the thought of Samuel Taylor Coleridge. Taking the Romantic poet's view that the expediency of the age had banished ideal methods from all spheres of life, Irving called for those spreading the gospel to reintroduce them. Missionaries were to take Christ at his word and so go to their fields relying on the Almighty alone for their support. The apostles had been sent forth "destitute of all visible sustenance, and of all human help." Consequently the missionaries should dispense with the elaborate business structures of the sending societies and should trust that God would provide for their needs. Knowing that "faith and prudence are opposite poles in the soul," they should opt for faith and reject prudence.[4] This was the faith principle, a species of heightened supernaturalism. Although at the time the idea seemed outrageous to most of Irving's hearers, the new technique was well calculated to exert a growing appeal to younger generations increasingly affected by Romantic sensibilities. As the century wore on, the method Irving recommended was to fascinate more and more minds.

Its most celebrated exponent was not an overseas missionary but a preacher/

---

[1]George M. Marsden, *Fundamentalism and American Culture: The Shaping of Twentieth-Century Evangelicalism, 1870-1925* (New York: Oxford University Press, 1980).

[2]See chap. 3, pp. 109-16.

[3]See chap. 4, pp. 141-44.

[4]Edward Irving, *For Missionaries after the Apostolical School: A Series of Orations* (London: Hamilton, Adams & Co., 1825), pp. 18, xv.

philanthropist. George Müller, born in Prussia in 1805, was converted in 1825 at Halle University and moved four years later to England intending to become a missionary to the Jews. Instead he became minister of a chapel at Teignmouth in Devon and then, from 1832, co-minister of Bethesda Chapel in Bristol, which evolved into one of the earliest and strongest Brethren assemblies. Müller married the sister of A. N. Groves, an early Brethren missionary who put Irving's principles into practice. From the start of Müller's ministry he took no stipend and from 1841 the two regular preachers removed the offering boxes where the members of the congregation had placed donations for their support, preferring to trust that the Lord would provide in other ways through his people. Müller's constant way of life is illustrated by his diary entry for August 7 that year:

> To-day we had one sixpence left for our own personal necessities. We needed some money to buy eggs and cocoa for a brother who is come to stay with us, when this brother gave me four shillings, which he had brought for me from the place whence he comes. Thus we are helped for the present.[5]

In 1835 Müller began setting up an orphanage, a home for girls who had lost their parents being opened in the following year. By 1870 there were five large buildings housing orphans at Ashley Down on the edge of Bristol. This massive operation, catering for some two thousand children at a time, was famous for being run on the faith principle. The needs were publicized, but no other effort was made to collect funds. The primary purpose of the whole institution, which was modeled on the orphan home that Müller had known at Halle, was to demonstrate that the Almighty was "as willing as ever to *prove* Himself to be the LIVING GOD, in our day as formerly, *to all who put their trust in Him*."[6] By the time of Müller's death in 1898, his approach had become a celebrated method of organizing Christian ventures.

The *Narrative of the Lord's Dealings with George Müller*, an autobiography first written in 1837 and extended in successive editions, did much to propagate his ideals. So did Müller's public addresses, delivered and reported in many parts of the world during his later years. Thus a lecture he gave on "The Power of Prayer" at Dundee in Scotland was highlighted in the first issue of

---

[5]G. F. Bergin, ed., *Autobiography of George Müller* (London: J. Nisbet and Co., 1905), p. 158.
[6]Ibid., p. 80.

an interdenominational monthly newspaper published in southern Africa.[7] The notion of radical discipleship entailing reliance on God alone appealed strongly to Müller's fellow members of the Brethren, whose influence was much greater than their relatively small numbers might suggest. Donald Munro and Donald Ross, for example, were two Scottish evangelists associated with the movement who traveled to North America in the 1870s. Instead of planning their campaigns in advance, according to the biographer of Munro, it was their custom "to seek their orders direct from the Master, sometimes only getting directions for a day at a time."[8] The more dedicated revivalists of the period were often drawn to aspects of this style of life. Thus Philip Bliss, the pioneer of solos as a means of evangelism in the United States, decided in 1874 to surrender everything, including attending music conventions and writing secular music, for the sake of spreading the gospel. The decision entailed giving up his income and so trusting God for his means of support.[9] Spurgeon originally adopted a version of the faith principle for the finances of the college he founded, relying in part on income from his sermons. The funds usually ran low in the summer and autumn, and when sales of the sermons collapsed in the American South because of the preacher's denunciation of slavery, the whole enterprise was threatened until a lady unexpectedly supplied £200 for training ministers. The college had no paid collectors, no subscribers and "nothing to rely on but the hand of the Lord."[10] Many in Moody's network connected with the Northfield conferences likewise adopted the same way of thinking. Thus Arthur T. Pierson, an independent-minded Presbyterian minister who participated in Northfield, wrote a booklet titled *George Müller of Bristol and his Witness to a Prayer-Hearing God* (1899) and testified that his own temporal needs, like Müller's, had frequently been met in answer to prayer. Pierson, who habitually refused accident insurance when traveling, was a leading advocate of applying Müller's principle to overseas

---

[7] *Christian Express* (Lovedale, South Africa), January 1, 1876, pp. 3-4.

[8] John Ritchie, *Donald Munro, 1839-1908: A Servant of Jesus Christ* (Glasgow: Gospel Tract Publications, 1987), p. 98.

[9] D. W. Whittle, ed., *Memoir of Philip P. Bliss* (London: F. E. Longley, 1877), pp. 46-47.

[10] *Outline of the Lord's Work by the Pastor's College and its Kindred Organisations at the Metropolitan Tabernacle* (London: Passmore & Alabaster, 1867), pp. iv, iii. *Outline of the Lord's Work by the Pastor's College during the Year 1869* (London: Passmore & Alabaster, 1870), p. 5.

missions.[11] The ideal of living by faith proved to have great appeal.

The axiom that God makes provision for believers increasingly led some evangelicals to draw drastic inferences. For one thing, they began to distance themselves from traditional methods of fundraising. The usual church techniques of pew rents, collections, anniversaries, tea meetings, lectures, concerts, bazaars, raffles and lotteries were condemned by the more radical spirits as "human devices." It was far better, according to a writer in the British *Revival* in 1868, for Christian organizations to rely on "love-prompted gifts" since "a spontaneous gift has a higher worth than that which is solicited."[12] Likewise Pierson censured any giving that was not done in response to a divine stimulus. "To ask unbelievers for gifts to carry on God's work," he wrote in 1900, "or even to urge believers to give, is not God's way, and neither will be done by a church that is devout and truly consecrated."[13] It was a call for a drastic overhaul of ecclesiastical finances that was to be widely heeded among conservative evangelicals during the twentieth century. Again, certain bold individuals started to apply the same fundamental principle to matters of health. The American evangelist and holiness advocate W. E. Boardman, who in 1870 gave up all his possessions to enter on a life of trust for all his temporal needs, subsequently became convinced that healing should also come by faith. The atonement had been designed, he believed, to remedy the physical as well as the spiritual deficiencies of humanity. So in 1882 he established in London a house of rest, Bethshan, where invalids could go in quest of supernatural therapy.[14] Others such as A. B. Simpson, the founder of the Christian and Missionary Alliance, and J. A. Dowie, a Scot who discovered divine healing in Australia before propagating it in America and (through his followers) in South Africa, held similar views. The faith principle could lead to radical initiatives.

In missions the most influential figure to adopt living by faith was James Hudson Taylor. A Yorkshireman born into a Methodist family in 1832, Taylor

---

[11]Dana L. Robert, *Occupy until I Come: A. T. Pierson and the Evangelization of the World* (Grand Rapids: Eerdmans, 2003), pp. 258-59. D. L. Pierson, *Arthur T. Pierson: A Biography* (London: James Nisbet, 1912), pp. 279, 300.

[12]*Revival* (London), February 27, 1868, p. 113.

[13]Arthur T. Pierson, *Forward Movements of the Last Half Century* (New York: Funk & Wagnalls Co., 1900), p. 118.

[14]Mrs. Boardman, *Life and Labours of the Rev. W. E. Boardman* (London: Bemrose and Sons, 1886), pp. 142, 234.

was converted in 1849 and started medical training in London three years later. By that point he had joined the Brethren and been inspired by Müller's *Narrative*. Cutting short his medical studies, he went out in 1853 as an agent of the newly formed Chinese Evangelization Society. Settling in Shanghai, he traveled on preaching tours into the interior and soon decided that, in order to minimize cultural obstacles to the transmission of the gospel, he would adopt Chinese customs including the wearing of the pigtail. He returned to England for further medical training in 1860. His thoughts about a new style of evangelistic enterprise in the east crystallized five years later in the foundation of the China Inland Mission (CIM). Its basic premise was the faith principle: there were no appeals for funds and its members went out with no assured salary. It was directed not by a committee in London, but by Taylor himself in the field so that there could be a rapid response to providential openings. The CIM was prepared to take fresh initiatives such as accepting the minimally educated for missionary service, sending out young unmarried women and pushing into fresh fields on the edge of China such as Manchuria and Tibet. The first party of sixteen CIM missionaries sailed in 1866; by 1885 there were two hundred in the field. In that year, their ranks were augmented by the celebrated "Cambridge Seven," a set of privileged young graduates including the Cambridge and England cricketer C. T. Studd. Taylor visited the United States in 1888, speaking at the Northfield conference and securing his first North American volunteers. The result, often through the dedicated efforts of Chinese evangelists converted under the auspices of the CIM, was the planting of Christianity in many regions of the Far East. Taylor, who died in 1905, had set an example of a thriving faith mission.[15]

He was copied by many others. In 1872 Henry Grattan Guinness, an evangelist from the Dublin brewing family who for a while was identified with the Brethren, established the interdenominational East London Training Institute, soon moved to Harley House, with the aim of preparing missionaries for such ventures as the CIM. The institute operated on the same principles as the CIM and many of the people it trained joined Grattan Guinness's own Regions Beyond Missionary Union. A cluster of smaller missionary bodies was also

---

[15]A. J. Broomhall, *Hudson Taylor and China's Open Century*, 7 vols. (London: Hodder & Stoughton, 1981-1989).

founded by those associated with the institute. Two of them, the Livingstone Inland Mission (1878) and the Congo Balolo Mission (1889), were run directly by Guinness and his wife Fanny.[16] In America the same impulse, strongly influenced by Hudson Taylor and Grattan Guinness, resulted in the creation of a sequence of major agencies. The Evangelical Missionary Alliance (1887) was united ten years later by its founder, A. B. Simpson, a Canadian Presbyterian who had become pastor of the independent New York Gospel Tabernacle, with a network of American fellowships to form the Christian and Missionary Alliance, in which there was an unusually close bond between home and overseas mission. The Sudan Interior Mission (1893) and the Africa Inland Mission (1895) soon followed. So popular was the notion of spontaneous giving that the older societies began to imitate the methods of the faith missions. In 1887, faced by a wave of earnest potential recruits, the committee of the Church Missionary Society (CMS) had to decide whether to let the extent of the work be determined by the available funds or to accept all the volunteers in the hope that money to support them would be forthcoming. After considerable debate, it was determined to refuse no candidate on financial grounds. Although this "policy of faith," as it was called, wavered in 1894 in the face of a deficit, it was subsequently reaffirmed as settled CMS policy.[17] The ideal was one of the most potent bequests of nineteenth-century evangelicalism to the succeeding century, when it would become a watchword for conservatives and fundamentalists.

PREMILLENNIAL DOCTRINE

A second broad area in which there was major change was in beliefs about the future. Although some important evangelicals shared Augustine's belief that there was no millennium to come, the predominant conviction, as chapter four has shown, was that the gospel would advance through the world until the establishment of the millennium. Only after that period of peace and prosperity would the second coming of Christ take place.[18] In the intellectual ferment surrounding the rise of Romantic feeling in the early nineteenth century, however, an entirely different approach to the future had been broached. Again the key

---

[16]Klaus Fiedler, *The Story of Faith Missions* (Oxford: Regnum, 1994), pp. 37-38.

[17]Eugene Stock, *The History of the Church Missionary Society*, 3 vols (London: Church Missionary Society, 1900), 3:333, 677-79.

[18]See chap. 4, pp. 139-41.

initial figure was Edward Irving. In 1827 he published a translation of a treatise in Spanish, purportedly written by a converted Jew but in reality by a Chilean Jesuit, entitled *The Coming of Messiah in Glory and Majesty.* The book, according to Irving, showed "the erroneousness of the opinion, almost universally entertained amongst us, that [Christ] is not to come till the end of the millennium."[19] Instead the present age was to come to a close with the second advent, which would therefore precede the millennium. Hence this school of thought, which had antecedents in early church history, is usually called premillennialism. Initially most evangelicals were skeptical about Irving's latest aberration, but the idea that the second coming was imminent rather than far ahead gradually made headway. It made sense in the light of the biblical injunctions to watch out for the signs of the return of Christ. How was that possible if the millennium was to precede it? The novel teaching also had the great attraction that, unlike much previous belief, it held that the return of Christ would be in person. New Testament passages about the coming of the Lord had often been interpreted in a spiritual sense either as predicting a great display of his power or as referring to his coming to fetch believers at death. The strongest insistence of the premillennialists, however, was that Christ would himself return, literally, to earth. Believers could therefore soon expect the arrival of the Lord to put right all the ills of the world. For many it proved an animating hope.

The expectation of an imminent second coming was not merely a doctrinal detail, an addendum to the central body of beliefs. On the contrary, as David Brown, a theologian of the Free Church of Scotland explained, premillennialism "stops not till it has pervaded with its own genius the entire system of one's theology, and the whole tone of his [*sic*] spiritual character, constructing, I had almost said, a world of its own."[20] Brown knew, for, as a one-time assistant to Irving, he had been an early convert to the scheme but had turned back to the postmillennial position. The adventist "world of its own" transformed the whole outlook of its adherents. The effect on the personal experience of Philip Bliss, the American gospel singer, was described by his minister:

---

[19]Juan Josafat Ben-Ezra [M. de Lacunza y Diaz], *The Coming of Messiah in Glory and Majesty,* trans. Edward Irving (London: L. B. Seeley and Son, 1827), p. i.

[20]David Brown, *Christ's Second Coming: Will it be Premillennial?* 3rd ed. (Edinburgh: Johnstone & Hunter, 1853), p. 8.

With him the "coming of the Lord" was a Scripture truth, so real and vivid, that his life felt the inspiration of it in everything he said or did. He felt profoundly that the Bridegroom might come at any moment, and hence it was his intense desire to have his work done, his lamp trimmed, and to be ready to enter in to the marriage.[21]

The shortness of time before the end of the age gave a heightened significance to everyday life and an added urgency to evangelism. Souls needed to turn to the Savior now because they might not have a second chance. There was no hope elsewhere. Far from making progress under gospel influences, the present age was degenerating. "A favorite notion of all pre-Millenarians," complained a Canadian Methodist opponent in 1880, "is that the world is growing worse."[22] Whereas postmillennialists were habitually optimistic about the course of events, believing that the Almighty was overruling human affairs to establish his kingdom on earth, premillennialists were characteristically pessimistic, supposing that the only remedy for the evils of the day was the return of the king. Despite their confidence in the power of the gospel to save souls, they put no faith in the secular world around them. The newer school of opinion dropped the earlier evangelical confidence in the steady advance of civilization, replacing it with a belief that the present was bad and the future was worse.

In America the most extreme expression of the new millenarian spirit had been the prediction of William Miller, a Vermont farmer and Baptist lay preacher, that the second advent would take place in 1843-1844. Thousands of humble followers prepared for the event, only to be disappointed on successive days during the two years. A section of them, however, retained the belief that the second coming could not be long delayed, evolving into two new denominations, the Seventh-day Adventists and the Adventist Christians.[23] In Britain, by contrast, the initial appeal of premillennialism was chiefly to the well-to-do. Its adherents, according to an opponent writing in 1865, "are not mere ignorant enthusiasts, but belong in considerable numbers to the respect-

---

[21]Dr. Goodwin in *P. P. Bliss, Joint Author of "Sacred Songs and Solos": His Life and Life Work*, ed. D. W. Whittle and William Guest (London: Morgan and Scott, 1877), p. 36.

[22]*Christian Guardian* (Toronto), February 11, 1880, p. 44.

[23]Gary Land, ed., *Adventism in America: A History* (Berrien Springs, Mich.: Andrews University Press, 1986).

able and educated classes."[24] They worshiped chiefly in the denominations most attractive to the higher social echelons. The Brethren, who, especially in their early days, drew disproportionately on the upper middle classes, were almost solidly behind the teaching, and the Evangelicals of the English established church were increasingly persuaded by the new prophetic views. A Prophecy Investigation Society consisting largely of Anglican clergymen met twice annually to hear scholarly papers on the subject; the leading Evangelical spokesman in the Church of England J. C. Ryle published a collection of sermons on premillennial themes in 1867; and, even as bishop of Exeter in 1888, E. H. Bickersteth devoted a whole primary charge to itemizing twenty-four events connected with the second advent.[25] In a review of the Victorian era at the 1897 Church Congress, Samuel Garratt identified as an Evangelical achievement, alongside the abolition of slavery and the maintenance of the inspiration of Scripture, the assertion of the second coming of Christ.[26] Evangelical Anglicans in other lands also became identified with prophetic doctrine. Thus, for example, Nathaniel Jones, principal of Moore College, Sydney, from 1897, was an earnest advocate of the teaching, exerting a powerful sway over the future course of the diocese he served.[27] By the end of the century premillennialism was part of Evangelical Anglican orthodoxy.

Presbyterians were rather less affected, but the newer point of view about prophetic themes nevertheless had its champions among them. Horatius Bonar, one of the most influential ministers of the Free Church of Scotland, had as a student imbibed his convictions about the second coming from the lips of Irving himself.[28] Between 1849 and 1873 Bonar edited a quarterly *Journal of Prophecy*, which carried weighty articles discussing the variety of possible interpreta-

---

[24] Patrick Fairbairn, *The Interpretation of Prophecy* (1865; reprint, London: Banner of Truth Trust, 1964), p. vii.

[25] Robert Braithwaite, *The Life and Letters of Rev. William Pennefather, B.A.* (London: John F. Shaw & Co., 1878), p. 253. J. C. Ryle, *Coming Events and Present Duties* (London: n.p., 1867). E. H. Bickersteth, *Some Words of Counsel* (Exeter: H. Besley and Son, 1888), pp. 118-54.

[26] E. R. Garratt, *Life and Personal Recollections of Samuel Garratt* (London: James Nisbet and Co., 1908), p. 108.

[27] William J. Lawton, *The Better Times to Be: Utopian Attitudes to Society Among Sydney Anglicans, 1885 to 1914* (Kensington, U.K.: New South Wales University Press, 1990), pp. 67-75.

[28] *Christian* (London), January 12, 1893, p. 12.

tions of future events within a premillennialist paradigm.[29] Methodist advocates of an imminent second coming, however, were rare. When Dr. Slade Robinson of Toronto sent a letter to the Canadian Methodist newspaper making a point in favor of the millennium falling after the advent, the editor published it, but with a weary note saying that he was allowing their venerable brother to express his personal view.[30] Clearly premillennialism seemed no more than a pardonable eccentricity. Likewise the standard Methodist view in England remained postmillennialist to the end of the century. Almost the only place where adventist teaching could be heard was on the platform of the Southport Convention, a gathering of holiness enthusiasts, and even there it was no more than a small minority position.[31] Congregationalists were almost immune to prophetic speculations, though Baptists were rather more open. Spurgeon adopted a premillennial position early in his ministry, though rarely mentioning the topic; F. B. Meyer, a leading Baptist who consorted with Evangelical Anglicans at Keswick conferences, became a strong proponent; and William Edwards, principal of the South Wales Baptist College from 1880, confessed in private his conversion to the premillennial standpoint.[32] Yet it remains true that Scottish Presbyterians, members of the Nonconformist denominations of England and Wales and their equivalents elsewhere were far less likely to embrace the novel prophetic teaching than their Evangelical Anglican contemporaries.

The reception of the newer views in the United States, not as a species of Millerite populism but as a matter of theological choice, came in the later years of the century. A decisive event was the encounter on a train journey in 1878 between Arthur T. Pierson, a Presbyterian product of the 1858 Businessmen's

---

[29]Ernest R. Sandeen, *The Roots of Fundamentalism: British and American Millenarianism, 1800-1930* (Chicago: University of Chicago Press, 1970), pp. 84-87.

[30]*Christian Guardian*, March 10, 1880, p. 78.

[31]Eliza A. Wood, *Memorials of James Wood, Ll. D., J. P., of Grove House, Southport* (London: Charles H. Kelly, 1902), p. 276. I. E. Page, ed., *John Brash: Memorials and Correspondence* (London: Charles H. Kelly, 1912), pp. 175-87.

[32]Mark Hopkins, *Nonconformity's Romantic Generation: Evangelical and Liberal Theologies in Victorian England* (Carlisle: Paternoster Press, 2004), p. 150. Ian M. Randall, *Spirituality and Social Change: The Contribution of F. B. Meyer (1847-1929)* (Carlisle: Paternoster Press, 2003). Henry Pickering, *Chief Men among the Brethren*, 2nd ed. (London: Pickering & Inglis, 1931), p. 105.

Revival, and George Müller, who, as one of the Brethren, was a keen student of prophecy. Pierson had lectured in favor of the postmillennial scheme, but found Müller so persuasive that he invited the visitor to his home in Detroit for ten days of private Bible study. There he was convinced. "Ever since that time," Pierson wrote, "I have been looking for the Lord's personal return. . . . Two-thirds of the book which had been sealed to me were opened by this key."[33] Pierson became one of the main speakers at the series of conferences that acted as two of the chief media for the diffusion of premillennial teaching in America. One was held each summer at a variety of places before settling at Niagara in 1883. Its leading light, James H. Brookes, a Presbyterian minister from St. Louis, also edited *Truth*, a popular magazine that spread the message from 1875. The other sequence of gatherings was Moody's Northfield conferences, where the second coming regularly claimed prominence on the program. Although at the 1885 conference Moody conceded that equally good men upheld the premillennial and postmillennial views, he also declared that he had derived much personal comfort from the thought of Christ's premillennial return. The New Testament, he was reported as saying, "did not encourage the idea that the world was gradually to grow better and better during this Gospel dispensation. We are everywhere taught that in the last days there will come 'perilous times'."[34] Other speakers were brusquer with opposing views. At Northfield in the following year, a questioner asked, "If Christ were to come now, what would become of the post-millennialists?" "They would all," according to the reply from the platform, "become pre-millennialists."[35] By the late 1890s the newer understanding of the future had been widely adopted in the circles around Moody.

The convictions of the premillennialists rested on a distinct hermeneutic. Evangelicals in general believed in accepting as true whatever the Bible taught, but the issue of how far the text was to be understood metaphorically was not agreed. Those who looked for an early return of Christ, as was explained at a London conference on the second advent in 1886, wanted to limit the scope of metaphorical interpretation. "It is a principle of vital importance to the study of Scripture," declared Fuller Gooch, a Baptist minister of independent spirit, "that the literal signification of words should be accepted in all cases ex-

---

[33]Pierson, *Pierson*, p. 143.
[34]*Christian*, September 17, 1885, pp. 23-24.
[35]*Christian*, September 23, 1886, p. 8.

cept where the obvious nature of the language employed necessitates a figurative or symbolic sense." If passages were interpreted literally, there would be no room for spiritualizing away passages dear to students of prophecy. "Only by a continued violation of this principle," Gooch went on, "can the personal reign of Christ during the millennial era be eliminated from revelation."[36] The appeal to the literal sense became a watchword of the premillennial school. Their opponents, however, rejected it, arguing that a bald literalism could give rise to nonsensical views. Thus a Wesleyan critic poured scorn on the suggestion in a premillennial work that the Judaean landscape would in the future be changed in order to accommodate the huge size of Ezekiel's temple and the river flowing out from it to the sea. Such a wooden exposition of biblical passages, he argued, was possible only if they were wrested from their historical context by expositors who were "totally blind to their Oriental imagery."[37] Literal interpretation severed premillennialists from their fellow evangelicals.

HISTORICISTS AND FUTURISTS

Yet the principle did not yield unanimity among students of prophecy. On the contrary, there was a deep fissure among them over the proper method of understanding the book of Revelation. On the one hand, the so-called historicists tried to relate the various portions of the book to events that had already taken place in world history. Thus there was general agreement among historicists that the pouring out of the sixth vial on the Euphrates described in Revelation 16 was to be identified with the decay of the Ottoman Empire that was being witnessed in the nineteenth century. There was endless scope for debate about details of the scheme, which gained in fascination as they neared the present day. Thus the leading article in the Evangelical Anglican newspaper *The Record* at the opening of 1868 commented on the signs of the times:

> Some have calculated that we are just arriving at the end of the 1,335 years spoken of by DANIEL the Prophet; whilst others, more cautious or more accurate, have been led to suppose that we have only reached the close of the 1,260 Apocalyptic years, so that 75 years still separate us from the final termination of the prophetic times.

---

[36] *Christian*, March 11, 1886, p. 24.

[37] J. Robinson Gregory in *Wesleyan Methodist Magazine* (London), December 1885, pp. 931-32.

From this prophetic standpoint the iniquities of Roman Catholicism loomed large. The authoritarianism of the papacy, as the *Record*'s leading article explained, fitted readily into the vista of Revelation:

> It cannot be reasonably disputed that ROME is BABYLON of the Apocalypse, the seven-hilled city which St. JOHN beheld in visions, that reigned over the nations of the earth. No well-instructed Protestant can therefore doubt that the Romish apostasy is depicted in that Babylon which is foredoomed of GOD.[38]

The fall of Babylon predicted in Revelation 18 seemed to seal the fate of popery. The historicist understanding mingled with inherited Protestant convictions to constitute a powerful intellectual amalgam.

Yet on the other hand there was an entirely different way of interpreting prophecy. The futurists held that the predictions of the book of Revelation, far from having been fulfilled over past years, would not take place until the future. The looming figure of antichrist, they argued, was not to be equated with the Roman Catholic Church for he was evidently an individual. Only as the end of the present age approached would his identity become plain. The futurist scheme had first been elaborated at a series of conferences at Powerscourt in Ireland during the 1830s, when its most confident exponent was J. N. Darby, a member of the emerging Brethren who in general were to embrace his scheme.[39] Darby taught that world history could be divided into distinct eras called "dispensations," each characterized by a particular way in which God dealt with humanity, so that his standpoint was labeled dispensationalism. The crucial point for believers in the present was to grasp that the current church age was about to terminate in the catastrophes described by the apostle John, the "great tribulation." A serious issue for students of prophecy was whether the church was to pass through this harrowing time or whether, as Darby himself claimed, true Christians would all be called away from the earth to meet the Lord in the air before that time. "What think you of the coming future?" the Evangelical clergyman William Pennefather, whose thinking had been molded by Powerscourt, asked a cor-

---

[38] *Record* (London), January 1, 1868.

[39] Max S. Weremchuk, *John Nelson Darby: A Biography* (Neptune, N.Y.: Loizeaux Brothers, 1992).

respondent. "[S]hall the Church be caught up before the vials are poured out, or must she feel at least the first drops of the impending tempest?"[40] On Darby's interpretation, the church would escape, for there were no more events of prophecy to take place before it was caught away to the heavens. This so-called rapture could therefore happen at any time, leaving the world to its fate. Futurism, especially in its dispensationalist form, created a profoundly dramatic worldview.

The two ways of looking at prophetic subjects, the historicist and the futurist, vied for the ascendancy among premillennialists during the later years of the century. Several substantial books, and in particular the 615-page treatise on *The Approaching End of the Age* (1878) by Grattan Guinness, reinforced the historicist point of view.[41]

> I am now convinced [wrote a careful reader of Guinness's volume in 1880] that the historical scheme of interpretation is the key which will be found, if used with prayer and patience, to fit every ward in the Apocalyptic lock. I can say that this book has removed the last link of the chain of Futurism which has been galling my neck for more than thirty years.[42]

Guinness's efforts seem to have retarded, at least in Britain, a slow movement of minds in favor of the alternative position. In 1886 an Advent conference was held in London at which there was an uneasy truce between the rival camps. Some speakers cobbled together a blend of the two views. Thus Robert Anderson, the leading Scotland Yard detective of his day, contended that "it would not be easy to convince us that the history of Christendom is entirely ignored in the visions of the Apocalypse" but also that there would be "a more absolute and complete fulfillment in days that are to come."[43] In the following decade, however, the *Christian*, an influential nondenominational newspaper circulating widely among students of prophecy, declared for "Dispensational Truth,"[44] and in America the same scheme, fully espoused by Arthur T. Pierson, made even more headway. Nathaniel West, one of the

---

[40]Braithwaite, *Pennefather*, p. 277.

[41]H. Grattan Guinness, *The Approaching End of the Age viewed in the Light of History, Prophecy and Science* (London: Hodder & Stoughton, 1878).

[42]S. A. Blackwood in *Christian*, April 29, 1880, p. 5.

[43]*Christian*, March 11, 1886, pp. 11-28.

[44]*Christian*, July 21, 1892, p. 8.

founders of the Niagara conference, stoutly resisted Darby's theory of a secret rapture,[45] but the drift of opinion was toward a full-blooded dispensationalism. In 1898 C. I. Scofield, who eleven years later was to produce an immensely influential version of the Bible containing notes expounding Darby's scheme, was already, when discussing the work of the Holy Spirit, insisting on "the dispensational aspects of the question."[46] Dispensational teaching was well on the way to its eventual prominence in the teachings of the fundamentalist coalition of interwar America.

The implications of dispensationalism for attitudes toward other issues can hardly be overestimated. Historicist premillennialists might be pessimistic about the prospects of the world, but, as the instance of Lord Shaftesbury illustrates, they could be wholly committed to social improvement. Their fears of Rome also drove some of them into the political arena, where they saw resistance to papal claims as a priority to urge on statesmen. Futurists, and particularly dispensationalists, however, generally regarded politics as a perilous snare. A Baptist minister in Norwich named Govett who had embraced Darby's doctrines argued in 1868 from the premise that the believer was to avoid the world. "All entanglement in politics," he wrote, "is unnecessary, and so hinders spiritual life, and is unsuited to the Christian."[47] A bemused critic of his views could not comprehend what Govett meant by saying that Christians who become politicians "offend against their dispensation."[48] Political developments were often, to the student of prophecy, most important for presaging the time of the end. The trend toward democracy in Britain in particular seemed fraught with warning. "Household suffrage and lodgers' franchise," opined the *Christian* in 1880, "are fulfilling prophecy, and causing us to hear the chariot-wheels of the coming King."[49] Likewise in 1886 an American Baptist and colleague of Hudson Taylor, A. J. Frost, pointed to the "seething, surging, rioting masses of the dangerous classes" and the "armies marching and countermarching with banners on which are emblazoned dynamite, anarchism, communism, nihilism" as the political signs of the

---

[45] *Christian,* July 18, 1895, p. 16.
[46] *Evangelistic Record* (Chicago), July 1898, p. 345.
[47] *Baptist Magazine* (London), July 1868, pp. 461-64; December 1868, pp. 792-95.
[48] Samuel Green in *Baptist Magazine,* August 1868, pp. 528-30.
[49] *Christian,* April 22, 1880, p. 12.

times.[50] Single-minded concentration on the blessed hope of Christ's appearing was the only resort for the spiritually minded believer. Even social concern was treated with suspicion by the more extreme premillennialists. Human misery, according to G. H. Pember, a Brethren Bible teacher, would flow on till Christ's return. Although philanthropists were not to be disparaged, he declared in 1886, they would do no more than pluck brands from the burning. There was no point in trying to improve society at large, for it was soon destined to be destroyed in a "great conflagration."[51] Although many evangelicals entirely disregarded such opinions, the prophetic turn of mind left to the twentieth century a powerful persuasive toward withdrawal from the broader affairs of society.

HOLINESS TEACHING

A third dimension of conservative theological change, alongside the rise of the faith principle and of premillennial doctrine, was a growth of holiness teaching. During the last third of the century there was an upsurge of a distinctive understanding of sanctification, the way in which believers become holy. Before that time, however, special views on the subject were almost entirely confined to Methodism and, in America, to circles around the revivalist Charles Finney. The Methodist view of sanctification calls for initial attention. Whereas those in Calvinist traditions believed that Christian discipleship was a matter of steady combat against sin leading to gradual advance in holiness, a struggle never completed on earth, John Wesley had held that an individual could reach a state of entire sanctification before death. At a crisis point beyond conversion, according to Wesley, a believer, usually after a long quest, "experiences a total death to sin."[52] Like justification, this sanctification was gained entirely by faith, not by works. It meant that, although Christians might still commit errors of judgment, there was no motivating principle of sin in their lives. The state of "perfect love," as Wesley

---

[50] *Prophetic Studies of the International Prophetic Conference* (Chicago, [1887?]), p. 176, quoted by Marsden, *Fundamentalism and American Culture*, p. 66.

[51] *Christian*, March 11, 1886, p. 21.

[52] John Wesley, "A Plain Account of Christian Perfection," in *John and Charles Wesley: Selected Prayers, Hymns, Journal Notes, Sermons, Letters and Treatises*, ed. Frank Whaling (London: SPCK, 1981), p. 334.

preferred to call it, could be lost by the commission of any wrongdoing, but it could be regained by the repetition of the original act of surrender. This teaching, still drawn primarily from Wesley's own writings, remained in the mid-nineteenth century the official position of all branches of Methodism. In England, John Hannah, the theological tutor at the Didsbury branch of the Wesleyan Theological Institution from 1843 until his death in 1867, continued to expound Wesley's ideas on the subject.[53] In America, the veteran Methodist leader Nathan Bangs argued in 1853 that when we are delivered from the law, "sin is totally destroyed from the heart."[54] The experience was also known wherever Methodism had spread. At Port Macquarie in Australia, a visiting minister found in 1858 that several enjoyed the blessing; in 1866 William Taylor carried the message of full salvation around southern Africa; and in Ontario, a convert named William Ireland was urged in 1855 to press forward to entire sanctification and as a local preacher became its stalwart advocate.[55] Wesley's ideas were still very much current around the middle of the century.

Yet by that time entire sanctification was passing through vicissitudes. For one thing, it was undergoing adaptation. The Irish-American evangelist James Caughey, who wanted to make the experience available to the multitudes as he traveled around North America and the British Isles, taught that there was no need to engage in long searching, that it could be gained by an act of deliberate will and that confirmatory feeling was superfluous. These diversions from Wesley's pattern did permit thousands to claim full salvation, but made the requirements much more shallow.[56] Again, William Arthur, a secretary of the Wesleyan Methodist Missionary Society in London, published in 1856 a book entitled *The Tongue of Fire* designed to spread the teaching, but he was so concerned to commend his message in respectable circles that the distinctive contours of what Wesley describes were eroded. At the same time professions

---

[53]John Hannah, *Introductory Lectures on the Study of Christian Theology* (London: Wesleyan Conference Office, n.d.), chaps. 57-58.

[54]*Christian Advocate and Journal* (New York), January 13, 1853, p. 5.

[55]*Christian Advocate and Wesleyan Record* (Sydney), September 21, 1858, p. 54; William Taylor, *Christian Adventures in South Africa* (London: Jackson, Walford and Hodder, 1867), p. 102; *Christian Guardian*, March 24, 1880, p. 95.

[56]*Earnest Christianity Illustrated: Or, Selections from the Journal of the Rev. James Caughey* (London: Partridge and Co., 1857), p. 152.

of the experience were becoming rarer. We learn about it from the pulpit, wrote a correspondent of the *Wesleyan Methodist Magazine* in 1850, but "we hear little more about it."[57] Official descriptions became more circumspect. The editor of the Methodist *Christian Guardian* in Toronto, when asked about Christian perfection in 1880, replied that it was merely "maturity of character and experience which is through grace attainable in this life."[58] In 1892 an American Methodist divine, while insisting that entire sanctification was distinct from regeneration, was willing to deny that anybody "jumps into this state from a half-worldly and careless state by a single bound"—which was close to rejecting the immediacy of the experience, an essential point in Wesley's analysis.[59] In the 1870s a future president of the English Primitive Methodist conference went so far as to repudiate the doctrine altogether, and in 1888 a Southern Methodist, J. M. Boland, ignited controversy by doing the same.[60] So the inherited Wesleyan tradition fell into decay in mainstream Methodism during the second half of the century.

Fresh stirrings, however, were abroad even before midcentury. In 1836 Phoebe Palmer, the wife of a New York Methodist doctor, Walter C. Palmer, and her sister Sarah Lankford organized in their joint home a long-term series of Tuesday afternoon meetings for the promotion of holiness. These two-hour gatherings fostered a cultivated approach to the possibilities of the spiritual life well designed for the leisured folk of a prosperous city. The teaching fell primarily to Phoebe, who developed a personal terminology, tinctured by Transcendentalist sensibility, based on the idea of Christ as the altar of sacrifice. Rather than use the traditional language of entire sanctification, Phoebe Palmer urged believers to "lay all on the altar" immediately. This act was, in Romantic fashion, a matter of will rather than of experience. Like Caughey, she taught that there was no need to wait or to feel anything; full salvation was simply a

---

[57] *Wesleyan Methodist Magazine*, April 1850, p. 365. For the process of decline, see David W. Bebbington, "Holiness in Nineteenth-Century British Methodism," in *Crown and Mitre: Religion and Society in Northern Europe since the Reformation*, ed. W. M. Jacob and Nigel Yates (Woodbridge, U.K.: Boydell Press, 1993).

[58] *Christian Guardian*, March 10, 1880, p. 76.

[59] *Christian Advocate* (New York), January 14, 1892, p. 19.

[60] John Stephenson, *The Man of Faith and Fire: Or the Life and Work of the Rev. G. Warner* (London: Robert Bryant, 1902), p. 165; Timothy L. Smith, *Called unto Holiness: The Story of the Nazarenes: The Formative Years* (Kansas City, Mo.: Nazarene Publishing House, 1962), pp. 42-43.

matter of faith, taking God at his word; but it was imperative to confess what God had done.[61] Phoebe and Walter Palmer carried the message to the British Isles in the years 1859-1864, and from 1864 until her death in 1874 Phoebe edited the *Guide to Holiness,* which enjoyed a worldwide circulation. The impression made by her teaching on a more traditional Methodist can be illustrated by the estimate of her best known book, *The Way of Holiness* (1845), by George Rose, a future minister, when he read it in South Africa in 1859. Rose followed Phoebe Palmer's prescription, but was troubled by the discrepancy with Wesley's *Plain Account of Christian Perfection:* "My experience with reference to this blessing is this:—In approaching the throne of grace, I can believe for it, and come away in possession of it; but I have only the evidence of my own faith. I want, in addition, the *witness of the Spirit.*"[62] For Wesley the empiricist, evidence was needed in experience; for Phoebe Palmer, in keeping with Romantic currents of thought, bare faith was all that was required. A new era had dawned in holiness teaching.

The gathering at the Palmers's home in New York gradually took on a less particularly Methodist character. By 1872 a Presbyterian brother who attended was testifying to having "laid all on the altar" and so experiencing "peace and comfort."[63] A close associate of Phoebe Palmer, Professor Thomas C. Upham of Bowdoin College, Maine, was a Congregationalist who linked entire sanctification to Catholic mystical traditions. In parallel with the Palmers but by a different route, the evangelist Charles Finney and Asa Mahan of Oberlin College, Ohio, both with Congregational backgrounds, became champions of a form of Christian perfection.[64] Finney's *Views of Sanctification* (1840) and Mahan's *The Baptism of the Holy Spirit* (1870) did much to spread belief in full salvation outside the bounds of Methodism. "I humbly beg the prayers of all Christians," ran a letter from an ordinary Massachusetts church member reported in the *Oberlin Evangelist* in 1850, "that I may live entirely devoted to God, and have

---

[61] Thomas C. Oden, ed., *Phoebe Palmer: Selected Writings* (New York: Paulist, 1988). The Transcendentalist affinities are noted by Timothy L. Smith, *Revivalism and Social Reform: American Protestantism on the Eve of the Civil War* (1957; New York: Harper & Row, 1965), pp. 142-43.

[62] *South African Methodist* (Grahamstown), January 28, 1885, p. 20 (Rose's diary for August 19, 1859).

[63] *Christian Advocate,* August 15, 1872, p. 262.

[64] Smith, *Revivalism and Social Reform,* chap. 7.

such measures of grace as will keep me from all known sin."[65] Probably the most influential single text in propagating the ideal of Christian perfection was *The Higher Christian Life* (1858) by the New School Presbyterian minister W. E. Boardman. The title, chosen to avoid giving the impression of commending a merely Methodist notion, rapidly became a catch phrase. The book refreshed the spirit of the Congregational editor of an interdenominational church newspaper in Sydney when he read it in 1860: "all things are possible to faith," he concluded, and "all believers are invited without difference to press forward to that perfect exercise of faith which realises the highest blessings."[66] The message of holiness by faith was spreading beyond its original Methodist home.

Meanwhile, however, it was beginning once more to flourish within Methodism. The centenary of the American movement in 1866, falling immediately after the close of the Civil War, made some Methodists realize anew that holiness was the very purpose of Methodism. At the New Jersey Centenary Camp Meeting in that year, "the work of entire sanctification progressed finely."[67] J. S. Inskip, a minister who had recently received full salvation through the guidance of Phoebe Palmer, took the lead in organizing fresh camp meetings, particularly in the east, where they had previously been less common, but where they now drew on a feeling of rural nostalgia among city dwellers. From 1867 there was a National Camp Meeting Association for the Promotion of Holiness, sponsoring frequent gatherings and promoting Inskip's *Advocate of Christian Holiness*.[68] His meetings possessed a "free and easy tone" which proved popular, though, when in 1881 he carried the message to Australia, the style was judged "thoroughly American" and more fitted to the fireside than the church.[69] The renewed holiness impulse spread to Britain, where, although no organization was formed, in 1872 the *King's Highway* was launched and in 1885 an annual convention was founded at Southport in Lancashire. A Canada Association for the Promotion of Holiness was formed in 1879 and in Australia a convention was held in Sydney in 1886 leading to a series of camp meetings and the United

---

[65] *Oberlin Evangelist* (Oberlin, Ohio), October 9, 1850, p. 162.

[66] *Christian Pleader* (Sydney), January 21, 1860, p. 19; February 4, 1860, p. 36.

[67] G. Hughes in *Christian Advocate*, August 23, 1866, p. 266.

[68] Melvin E. Dieter, *The Holiness Revival of the Nineteenth Century* (Metuchen, N.J.: Scarecrow Press, 1980), chap. 3.

[69] *Southern Cross* quoted in *Primitive Methodist Record* (Adelaide), April 8, 1881, p. 5.

Methodist Holiness Association.[70] Sections of opinion within Methodism were reviving the testimony to entire sanctification.

As the National Camp Meeting Association of America grew in influence, it established state and local bodies to carry on its work. Gradually they developed a life of their own and tendencies toward separatism began to emerge, especially in the Midwest and Southwest. Already there existed a vigorously independent Free Methodist Church, founded in 1860, which maintained a firm adherence to the doctrine of a clean heart. Like the would-be separatists in the National Association, the Free Methodists kept up a steady critique of the worldliness of existing denominations. A Free Methodist group holding revival services in Algonquin, Illinois, was disgusted that members of a congregation in the town held a frivolous church fair. "The next morning," according to the revivalists, "they filled a basket with fragments and sent them to us, but we wrote them a kindly note and returned the same, as we did not care to eat the refuse of the sacrifice offered to Dagon."[71] Traditional churches tolerated fancy clothes and jewelery, erected ornate buildings and toyed with false doctrine. Above all they were torpid, looking askance, for example, on the prostrations that sometimes marked services among the extreme holiness people. J. P. Brooks, an Illinois Methodist preacher, decided to urge a break with all ecclesiastical corruptions and so developed the theory of "come-outism," a summons to form separate holiness bodies.[72] The first new holiness denomination, set up in 1881, was the Church of God (later "Anderson, Indiana"). In Britain similar tendencies generated a small Holiness Church that was begun in 1882; in Canada three leading holiness leaders were expelled from Methodism in 1894-1895, giving rise to separate organizations.[73] By 1907 there were some twenty-five bodies upholding entire sanctification in America alone,[74] but in the following year several merged to become the Church of the Nazarene, which

---

[70]David W. Bebbington, "The Holiness Movements in British and Canadian Methodism in the Late Nineteenth Century," *Proceedings of the Wesley Historical Society* 50 (1996); *Intercolonial Christian Messenger* (Brisbane), January 8, 1886, p. 649; W. G. Taylor, *Taylor of "Down Under": The Life-Story of an Australian Evangelist* (London: Epworth Press, 1920), p. 147.

[71]*Free Methodist* (Chicago), January 11, 1898, p. 4.

[72]Smith, *Called unto Holiness*, p. 29.

[73]Bebbington, "Holiness Movements," pp. 210, 224, 213-14.

[74]Robert M. Anderson, *Vision of the Disinherited: The Making of American Pentecostalism* (New York: Oxford University Press, 1979), p. 37.

was to remain by far the largest of them.[75] There had arisen a fresh sector of evangelical Christianity, the holiness denominations.

The most striking organization among them was the Salvation Army, the creation of William Booth. Born in England in 1829, Booth was a pawnbroker's assistant who became a powerful evangelist in the Methodist New Connection. Chafing under its restrictions on his freedom to rove as a preacher, in 1861 he left the denomination and soon began to concentrate on mission work in the East End of London. His organization, called the Christian Mission from 1869, was originally administered on the Methodist pattern in circuits and under a conference, but in 1878 it was turned into an autocracy directed by Booth. In the following year it adopted the title of the Salvation Army and rapidly adopted the paraphernalia of uniforms, flags and brass bands under its "General" that seemed appropriate to warfare against sin.[76] The novelty of its military style brought immense growth during the early 1880s among the poor both at home and abroad, but existing churches initially looked askance at its populism. "Of all the crude sensations passing current as religion," growled the *Presbyterian Churchman* in Ireland, "this seems to be the last and worst."[77] The extent to which the movement was motivated by commitment to full salvation is usually underestimated. The motto on the flag was "Blood and Fire," not just the redeeming blood of the atonement but also the sanctifying fire of the Holy Spirit. William Booth's capable wife Catherine, in many ways the brain behind the Army, had embraced Phoebe Palmer's form of holiness theology as well as following her example of female public speaking.[78] The Salvation Army in southern Africa, claimed (with some exaggeration) George Railton, one of Booth's most senior officers, contained "the only people who urgently teach holiness."[79] Although the emphasis on entire sanctification gradually faded, in America there was a stalwart champion of the doctrine in Samuel Logan Brengle. "The Salvation Army," he insisted in 1900, "believes in the baptism of the

---

[75]Smith, *Called unto Holiness*, n.p.

[76]Pamela J. Walker, *Pulling the Devil's Kingdom Down: The Salvation Army in Victorian Britain* (Berkeley: University of California Press, 2001).

[77]*Presbyterian Churchman* (Dublin), August 1884, p. 219.

[78]John Kent, *Holding the Fort: Studies in Victorian Revivalism* (London: Epworth Press, 1978), pp. 325-40.

[79]G. S. Railton, *The History of our South African War* (London: Salvation Army Book Department, 1901), pp. 108-9.

Holy Spirit and of fire . . . and at all costs this fire must be kept."[80] Although Catherine died in 1890, William lived on until 1912, presiding over a vigorously expanding worldwide organization.

THE KESWICK MOVEMENT

An even more influential global force proclaiming holiness was the Keswick movement, named after the town in the English Lake District where annual conventions were held from 1875 onward. The origins of this new development were in the network of keen evangelicals around William Pennefather, an Anglican clergyman of wide nondenominational sympathies. From 1856 in Barnet, and from 1864 in his new parish at Mildmay Park in north London, Pennefather held an annual conference that drew together Christian workers with a strong interest in evangelism and personal consecration. Among these people the message of the higher life found a natural home. From 1868 regular articles on the subject started to appear in the *Christian* from the pen of Robert Pearsall Smith, an American of Quaker background who had embraced entire sanctification at a Methodist camp meeting in the previous year. The secret of holiness, he claimed, lay "simply in ceasing from all efforts of our own, and trusting Jesus."[81] In 1873 he and his wife Hannah Pearsall Smith traveled to Britain, participating in an invited conference at Broadlands in Hampshire for those aspiring to a deeper spiritual experience. Hannah, simply dressed in traditional Quaker clothes, made a particular impact with her teaching, which was to be summarized in *The Christian's Secret of a Happy Life* (1875). Larger gatherings followed at Oxford in 1874 and Brighton in 1875, but there a catastrophe threatened the rising movement. Robert Pearsall Smith was accused of whispering improper endearments to a young woman, and was hastily dispatched back to the United States. Yet it was agreed to go ahead with a further convention already planned for Keswick in the same year at the invitation of a local vicar, T. D. Harford-Battersby. A tent holding one thousand was generally well filled for a week of meetings "for the promotion of practical holiness."[82] The event became

---

[80]*Evangelistic Record*, January 1900, p. 93. The American movement is discussed in Edward H. McKinley, *Marching to Glory: The History of the Salvation Army in the United States, 1880-1972*, 2nd ed. (Grand Rapids: Eerdmans, 1995).

[81]*Christian*, January 9, 1868, p. 17.

[82]*Christian*, July 15, 1875, p. 17.

annual, nondenominational but appealing particularly to well-to-do Anglicans. Keswick turned into the epicenter of a novel and potent style of spirituality.[83]

The adherents of Keswick upheld holiness by faith as their central conviction. "They believe," according to the convention's Australian journal, "there is an experience which it is the privilege of God's children to enter into where sin is vanquished, where the heart rests in God's peace, and where a joyous ability to do God's present will is realized."[84] Like the Methodist tradition from which it sprang, Keswick maintained that there should be a juncture of full consecration as well as subsequent steady progress in the Christian life. Handley Moule, a leading convention speaker and bishop of Durham from 1900, summarized Keswick teaching as "a crisis with a view to a process."[85] Traditional Calvinists, disliking the element of crisis, also condemned the core principle of sanctification by faith. J. C. Ryle, whose *Holiness* (1877) was the most trenchant rebuttal of the new movement, objected that "in following holiness the true Christian needs personal exertion and work as well as faith."[86] Traditionalists such as Ryle were alarmed lest followers of Keswick should delude themselves into supposing that an intense experience could be a guarantee of effortless spirituality. They flung at conventiongoers the charge of maintaining "sinless perfection." Some on the fringe of Keswick did indeed teach that sin could be entirely rooted out of believers, but the official line was very different. "Is it true," an enquirer asked at the 1880 convention, "that the old nature, with its tendencies to sin, can be wholly eradicated in this life?" The reply from Evan Hopkins, the theological guardian of the movement, was a definite no. "The tendency to sin is not eradicated," he explained, "but by the power of the Holy Ghost the flesh is kept under as we walk in the Spirit."[87] Sin was repressed, not removed. Hence the Reformation conviction that believers do not escape from their sinful state until death was sustained. Keswick made the idea of entire sanctification palatable to those in the Calvinist tradition.

This new expression of holiness teaching spread rapidly. Already in 1875

---

[83]Charles Price and Ian Randall, *Transforming Keswick* (Carlisle: OM Publishing, 2000).

[84]*Life & Light* (Melbourne), October 1, 1895, p. 6.

[85]H. C. Lees, "The Effect on Individual Ministry," in *The Keswick Convention: Its Message, its Method and its Men*, ed. Charles F. Harford (London: Marshall Brothers, 1907), p. 180.

[86]J. C. Ryle, *Holiness* (London: W. Hunt & Co., 1887), p. ii.

[87]*Christian*, August 12, 1880, p. 10.

it was stirring debate in Australia. One correspondent of the *Australian Church-man* complained that the "incipient poison of flesh-pleasing doctrine" called the higher life was gaining ground; another replied that he could personally profess to know the blessedness of the faith life.[88] Australia was to have its own equivalent of Keswick from 1891 at Geelong in Victoria, with other conventions following. By 1896 they were being held at Bowral, Warrnambool, Wangaratta, Richmond and Ballarat.[89] A regular annual convention was begun in Scotland at Bridge of Allan in 1892, the new teaching was introduced into Canada in 1893 and by 1900 Jamaica had its own convention at Mandeville.[90] Wales was to follow with its Llandrindod Wells Convention from 1903 and Ireland with the Portstewart Convention from 1914.[91] Keswick made a major impact in South Africa, where Andrew Murray, a veteran minister of the Dutch Reformed Church, was a leading exponent of its sanctification teaching. A convention at Wellington in the Cape was mother to others at Johannesburg, Cape Town, Port Elizabeth, Durban, Pietermaritzburg and Kroonstad. Murray's convention hymnbook, though circulating only in South Africa, nevertheless sold more than fifty thousand copies.[92] In West Africa the son of the founder of Keswick, C. F. Harford-Battersby, serving with the Church Missionary Society, led an assault on what he regarded as previous laxity in enforcing moral standards on converts.[93] In India there were similar events. Thomas Walker, another of the large crop of CMS missionaries inspired by the Keswick message, held a day of humiliation and prayer throughout the Tinnevelly district in 1893. Afterward there was a

---

[88]*Australian Churchman* (Sydney), September 11, 1875, p. 176; Robert Taylor in *Australian Churchman*, September 18, 1875, p. 186.

[89]*Life & Light*, March 2, 1896, pp. 6-7; May 1, 1896, p. 5; September 1, 1896, p. 7; November 2, 1896, p. 3.

[90]N. C. Macfarlane, *Scotland's Keswick* (London: Marshall Brothers, n.d.), p. 15; R. N. Burns in *Christian Guardian*, April 19, 1893, p. 244; *The Story of Mandeville Keswick Convention* (n.p., n.d.), p. 3.

[91]B. P. Jones, *The Spiritual History of Keswick in Wales, 1903-1983* (Cwmbran, Gwent: Christian Literature Press, n.d.), p. 7; J. T. Carson, *The River of God is Full: Portstewart Convention through Seventy Five Years, 1914-1988* (Londonderry, Ireland: Convention Committee, n.d.), p. 9.

[92]W. M. Douglas, *Andrew Murray and his Message* (London: Oliphants, n.d.), pp. 172-74.

[93]Andrew Porter, "Cambridge, Keswick and Late Nineteenth-Century Attitudes to Africa," *Journal of Imperial and Commonwealth History* 5 (1976): 25-28.

purging of the church, with solemn excommunications for observing caste, contracting irregular marriages, drunkenness and financial dishonesty.[94] In America, Keswick doctrine was heard at Northfield and equivalent conferences but rarely became the organizing principle for a whole gathering. Moody's teaching, without becoming identical to Keswick's, turned into something very similar.[95] The convention fostered a fresh approach to the Christian life in many parts of the world.

THE ROOTS OF PENTECOSTALISM

The holiness movements, whether Wesleyan or Keswick in inspiration, reinforced an existing emphasis among many late nineteenth-century evangelicals on the work of the Holy Spirit. The Spirit was often mentioned in connection with lively prayer meetings. Thus attenders at a cottage meeting in Devizes in England in 1860 were said to be "filled with the Holy Spirit"; and during a week of prayer in Meadville, Pennsylvania, in 1868, "The room was literally filled with Holy Spirit."[96] Times of revival, whether sought or experienced, could be described as "Pentecostal," whether in Nova Scotia or South Australia, Ireland or South Africa.[97] The Brighton holiness convention was called "our Pentecost" and at Keswick the Spirit was termed the "Pentecostal gift."[98] Arthur T. Pierson, in a book published in 1900, could say that the period had produced a "Pentecostal Movement." He did not mean what in the twentieth century was to receive that name, but rather the "new emphasis upon the work of the Spirit of God, in three aspects—*sanctifying, enduing, and filling.*"[99] The element of enduement had come to the fore, particularly among Moody's friends. "We need most of all an *evangelistic baptism,*" Pierson had written in the Chicago newspaper associated with Moody's work in 1882: "Pentecost endued [those

---

[94]Mildred E. Gibbs, *The Anglican Church in India, 1600-1970* (Delhi: Indian SPCK, 1972), p. 336.

[95]Marsden, *Fundamentalism and American Culture,* pp. 77-80.

[96]*Revival* (London), January 21, 1860, p. 22; *Examiner and Chronicle* (New York), January 23, 1868.

[97]*Christian Messenger* (Halifax, Nova Scotia), January 20, 1858, p. 21; *Methodist Journal* (Adelaide), July 11, 1874; *Irish Presbyterian* (Belfast), February 1853, p. 97; *Minutes of the Seventh Conference of the Wesleyan Methodist Church of South Africa* (Grahamstown: J. Slater, 1889), p. 104.

[98]J. B. Figgis in *Christian,* October 8, 1874, p. 13; August 4, 1892, p. 8.

[99]Pierson, *Forward Movements,* p. 137.

whom Christ sent out] with 'power' to witness."[100] R. A. Torrey, who was to become Moody's successor, wrote a book, *The Baptism with the Holy Spirit* (1895), urging the same case at length.[101] Part of Torrey's object was to counter those who were sharpening a conceptual division between inner and outer circles of Christians corresponding to their relationship to the Spirit. Asa Mahan, for example, had taught that there were two classes of believers, those who had and those who had not yet received the Holy Ghost.[102] The implication that ordinary Christians did not possess the Spirit might be repudiated by virtually all contemporary evangelical leaders, but on the ground similar thoughts seem to have become common. There were widespread stirrings around the doctrine of the Spirit.

By the last two decades of the century the belief was gaining currency among some of the more extreme American holiness teachers that beyond the second blessing of entire sanctification there was a third blessing. It was thought to be much like Pierson's gift of enduement with power, a "baptism of fire."[103] Perhaps there might soon be other extraordinary developments. Even Pierson mused that supernatural gifts, lost to the church as it went into decline from the age of Constantine, might be poured out once more. "If in these degenerate days," he wrote in 1900, "a new Pentecost should restore primitive faith, worship, unity and activity, new displays of divine power might surpass those of any previous period."[104] Might they include the gift of tongues? A Scottish critic of Keswick argued in 1892 that logically higher life movements might be expected to lead to an outbreak of speaking in tongues such as had once been associated with Edward Irving and which (he assumed) all would condemn.[105] R. C. Morgan, as editor of the *Christian* at the center of British revivalist-inclined evangelicals, held that tongues were needed to authenticate the original outpouring of the Holy Ghost, but were unnecessary in the present dispensation.[106] Some, on the other hand, were prepared to consider the possibility that tongues, "so

---

[100]*Evangelistic Record*, March 1882, p. 3.

[101]Anderson, *Vision of the Disinherited*, p. 42.

[102]*Christian*, December 23, 1875, p. 8.

[103]*Free Methodist*, January 4, 1898, p. 3.

[104]Pierson, *Forward Movements*, p. 401.

[105]Charles Jerdan in *United Presbyterian Magazine* (Edinburgh), January 1892, p. 5.

[106]*Christian*, December 23, 1875, p. 8.

much needed by our missionaries," might be restored to the church.[107] There
were already occasions when apparently inexplicable events took place. Simon
Richardson, a Florida Methodist circuit rider, was taking part in a protracted
meeting in 1855:

> I had during that meeting a strange, and to this day an unaccounted for, experi-
> ence in praying. I lost control of my tongue and utterances. I could not control
> either. The prayer was simply awful. Several women screamed out—not shout-
> ing, but alarmed. Finally, that mysterious influence subsided, and my tongue be-
> came natural.[108]

The experience, which sounds like a classic instance of glossolalia, the experience of speaking in an unknown tongue, was never repeated. When, around
January 1, 1901, something similar happened to Agnes Ozman at Topeka,
Kansas, the Pentecostal movement that was to become the largest sector of
twentieth-century evangelicalism was launched.[109] It was the fruit of tendencies
already developing in the previous century.

In the three areas reviewed in this chapter, the later nineteenth century witnessed the rise of drastically revised attitudes among evangelicals. Although
large numbers in the constituency remained untouched by these developments,
many of the most committed adopted fresh views about living by faith, expecting the second advent and attaining holiness. In each case the new convictions
were closely associated with the Romantic mood that was steadily permeating
English-speaking societies all over the world during the period. That was not
the sole intellectual inspiration of the new theological interpretations, for it is
true that many of the popular speculations of the time, especially in America,
were founded on a commonsense reliance on what was thought to be the Baconian ideal of scientific investigation.[110] These folk assumptions were deeply
indebted to the persistent legacy of the British and American Enlightenments.
Yet the main currents of thought behind the new understandings of mission,
the future and spirituality resonated far more with the succeeding Romantic

---

[107] *Life of Faith* (London), December 1881, p. 236.

[108] S. P. Richardson, *The Lights and Shadows of Itinerant Life* (Nashville, Tenn.: Publishing House
of the Methodist Episcopal Church South, 1900), p. 138.

[109] Anderson, *Vision of the Disinherited*, pp. 51-57.

[110] Marsden, *Fundamentalism and American Culture*, pp. 55-62.

age. The faith principle and premillennialism derived originally from Edward Irving, who in the earlier part of the century had transposed evangelical theology into a Romantic key. The holiness teaching of Phoebe Palmer, emerging in parallel with Transcendentalism, was discernibly Romantic. So was the temper of Keswick, which convened in the Lake District beloved by Wordsworth and Coleridge.[111] An enlarged conception of faith typical of the Romantic era bound together the three developments: it was the explicit basis for faith missions; it underlay the advent hope; and it was the means by which holiness was reached. These doctrines were therefore all radical, a consequence of the permeation of the evangelical movement by fresh cultural attitudes. That was why each of them was resisted in its day as a dangerous novelty. A common characteristic of all these positions was that they were new.

Yet these were the teachings that, by the end of the period, were turning into the rallying cries of the conservative resistance to theological change. Premillennialism in particular gave rise to shrill denunciation of contemporary trends in church and society. Horatius Bonar, long the chief Scottish champion of the advent hope, wrote to commend a London conference on the theme in 1886:

> Antichrist is rising rapidly and gathering strength. Multitudes are enlisting unconsciously under his banner, and adopting his watchword—LIBERALITY, reckoning it illiberal to believe in judgment to come, or in hell, or in the wrath of God, or in the sinner's eternal doom. To meet all this we look for the arrival of the Christ of God.[112]

The inherent pessimism of premillennial beliefs about the course of history magnified the significance of the symptoms of declension. Holiness teaching, by contrast, contained no inherent bias toward looking on the worst side, but from the very first convention at Keswick premillennial doctrine was heard on its platform. So Keswick too became aligned with the conservative tendency within evangelicalism. The movements reviewed in this chapter turned into the chief sources of strength for the cause of resisting liberalism. Those who supported faith missions were to become the backbone of interwar fundamentalism; the premillennial second coming was the ideological glue of most of the

---

[111]David W. Bebbington, *Holiness in Nineteenth-Century England* (Carlisle: Paternoster Press, 2000), chap. 4.

[112]*Christian*, March 11, 1886, p. 11.

fundamentalist coalition, and the holiness movements, together with the Pentecostalism to which they so largely contributed, were to provide the shock troops of conservative evangelicalism during the twentieth century. Fundamentalists often went into battle for beliefs which they perceived to be part of the ancient deposit of faith but which in reality went back for less than a hundred years. It was a number of novelties from the nineteenth century rather than traditional convictions that did most to stiffen theological conservatism in the next.

7

EVANGELICALS
AND SOCIETY

The late nineteenth century posed a variety of questions to evangelicals about their role in society. Industrialization—first in Britain, but then elsewhere in the English-speaking world—brought new wealth, with consequent problems about its use, but also new poverty, as cycles of unemployment afflicted the working people. The migration of population from countryside to city and from continent to continent created fresh opportunities but also caused dislocation to traditional ways. The improvement in the expectation of life began to affect how families organized their lives. The churches wrestled with how to respond to the questions of the age, with three subjects achieving particular salience. One was the relationship between the sexes. What was the proper role of women in the light of the gospel? Another was the relationship of the races. What, in particular, should be the dealings between black and white believers? And a third was the attitude of Christians to leisure. Should recreational activities be avoided as unspiritual or encouraged as healthy? Furthermore, a series of issues arose about how the churches should exert their corporate strength in the wider society. Many saw their task as opposition to the elements in contemporary life of which they disapproved. They launched campaigns against Sunday desecration, Roman Catholicism and sexual abuse. Above all, a high proportion of evangelicals mounted a powerful onslaught on strong drink, advocating total abstinence and trying to restrict the availability of alcohol. From their efforts to combat particular problems sprang the broader social gospel movement, dedicated to engaging with the needs of the body as well as those of the soul. In this phase, which continued into the twentieth century, many evangelicals aspired to transform the whole of society. Because evangelical Christians enjoyed such prominence during the period, they could exert a potent influence over the social and even the public life of their countries. In this era as much as in any other, their values helped to mold the broader history of the English-speaking world.

THE ROLE OF WOMEN

The centrality of their place in the wider society is evident, in the first place, in their influence over the role of women. Evangelicals have been identified as the group most responsible for the Victorian ideal of separate spheres, according to which men played their part in public life while women were confined to the private sphere of home.[1] It has more recently been appreciated that this "domestic ideology" has a much longer lineage, flourishing in its broad outlines over previous centuries.[2] Nevertheless evangelical spokespeople did a great deal to reinforce the notion that women should play a different and in many ways subordinate role. "With fierce warnings and denunciations from the pulpit, and false interpretations of Scripture," fulminated the American feminist Elizabeth Cady Stanton, "women have been intimidated and misled, and their religious feelings have been played upon for their more complete subjugation."[3] The judgment, though jaundiced, is not entirely without foundation. John Angell James, Congregational minister in Birmingham, published a book on *Female Piety* (1852) that was to prove extremely popular, being quoted in America as a standard work five years later[4] and reaching its seventeenth edition in 1881. James argued that Christianity had elevated the status of woman, but that man was the main subject of the Bible. "That woman is intended to occupy a position of subordination and dependence," he claimed, "is clear from every part of the word of God." Because her chief role was to cater to the comfort of man,

---

[1] Leonore Davidoff and Catherine Hall, *Family Fortunes: Men and Women of the English Middle Class, 1780-1850* (London: Hutchinson Education, 1987), chap. 2.

[2] Amanda Vickery, "Golden Age to Separate Spheres? A Review of the Categories and Chronology of English Women's History," *Historical Journal* 36 (1993).

[3] Elizabeth Cady Stanton, Susan B. Anthony and Matilda Joslyn Gage, eds., *History of Woman Suffrage* (New York: Fowler and Wells, 1881), 1:16-17.

[4] *American Missionary* (New York), February 1857, p. 29.

her proper sphere was the home. Taking her away into other trying worlds, whether academic, judicial or political, was advocated only by "a few wild visionaries, and rash speculators, and mistaken advocates of women's rights."[5] Baldwin Brown, a much more liberal theologian than James, was nevertheless equally willing to denounce the "foolish and frothy talk in these days of women's rights."[6] It was typical that the women's section of the February 1895 issue of the *Irish Presbyterian* contained a story about hospitality, three cookery recipes and advice to mistresses about how to treat maids.[7] The evangelical expectation was that women would stay at home.

The picture, however, can be painted in too monochrome a way. Another writer of guidance for young women, William Landels, a fashionable Baptist minister in London, actually issued two titles on the subject, one in 1859 and another just over a decade later. There was a definite change of mind in between. In 1859 Landels, like James, endorsed the domestic ideology, teaching that "woman's sphere is not the public arena, but the retirement of home."[8] He contended that women, though spiritually equal to men, were secondary and dependent. In the later work, however, he wholly rejected the notion that women were inferior to men, dropping his earlier judgment that men possessed uniformly superior reasoning powers. It was simply, he now held, that men were better at argumentation and women better at "intuitive perception and tact." Landels was not a feminist. "Man has no aptitude for domestic duties," he wrote, "and so long as they require to be done—that is, so long as the world lasts—women will be required to do them."[9] Yet he had been prepared to alter his view of the natural capacities of women. Elsewhere opinion could take a broader view of female potential. In the same year in New Zealand, it was argued on the basis of Proverbs 31 that, apart from looking after her husband

---

[5]John Angell James, *Female Piety or the Young Woman's Friend and Guide through Life to Immortality,* 17th ed. (London: Hamilton Adams and Co., 1881), pp. 60, 72.

[6]James Baldwin Brown, *The Home: In its Relation to Man and Society,* 2nd ed. (London: James Clarke and Co., 1883), in Dale A. Johnson, *Women in English Religion, 1700-1925* (New York: Edwin Mellen Press, 1983), p. 157.

[7]*Irish Presbyterian* (Dublin), February 1895, pp. 30-31.

[8]William Landels, *Woman's Sphere and Work, Considered in the Light of Scripture: A Book for Young Women* (London: James Nisbet and Co., 1859), p. 27.

[9]William Landels, *Woman: Her Position and Power* (London: Cassell, Petter and Galpin, 1870), pp. 26-28, 68-69, 97.

and children, a woman must be strong: "woman, as well as man, is sometimes called to meet the stern demands of an unsympathising world."[10] Perhaps a colonial context made it easier to envisage self-reliant women. In Canada by 1891 a correspondent of the Methodist newspaper argued that it was inconsistent to aim for the emancipation of Chinese women and yet use "our own mothers, sisters, and wives, as . . . domestic slaves."[11] Even in the British parliament the chief support for female enfranchisement in the 1880s came from a knot of Congregationalists.[12] So there were varying views among evangelicals on the extent to which women should be restricted to the private sphere.

The association of women, home and evangelical faith is a cornerstone of a number of perspectives on nineteenth-century history informed by feminism. Barbara Welter has contended that during the period 1800 to 1860 there was a feminization of American religion. Gradually, as the young republic was evangelized, there was growing scope for female activity within the churches, belief in infant damnation faded and the hymnody dwelt increasingly on the more feminine themes of love and mercy.[13] Likewise the stimulating interpretation of the British experience offered by Callum Brown in *The Death of Christian Britain* (2001) argues that from around the start of the nineteenth century down to the 1960s evangelical piety was identified with femininity. Women transmitted evangelical attitudes to their children in the home and so sustained the dominant self-image of virtuous behaviour. Men, however, possessed no automatic place within this construction of piety and so were understood, according to Brown, as being perennially exposed to worldly temptation. There was a gulf between female and male spirituality.[14] Yet more detailed work by Linda Wilson casts doubt on parts of this analysis. By examining a substantial number of obituaries of evangelical Nonconformists, male as well as female, Wilson confirms that spirituality was gendered in relation to the home. Female obituaries, unlike their male counterparts, often referred to the skills of their subjects in caring for children, manag-

---

[10] *Christian Observer* (Christchurch), January 1870, p. 3.

[11] *Christian Guardian* (Toronto), August 5, 1891, p. 483.

[12] Elizabeth Cady Stanton, Susan B. Anthony and Matilda Joslyn Gage, eds., *History of Woman Suffrage* (Rochester, N.Y.: Charles Mann, 1887), 3:872-78.

[13] Barbara Welter, "The Feminization of American Religion, 1800-1860," in Mary S. Hartman and Lois Baner, eds., *Clio's Consciousness Raised: New Perspectives on the History of Women* (New York: Harper and Row, 1974).

[14] Callum G. Brown, *The Death of Christian Britain* (London: Routledge, 2001), esp. chaps. 4-5.

ing servants and offering hospitality. Personal devotion, on the other hand, was largely undifferentiated by sex, with only Congregational women showing any significant difference from their male coreligionists through spending more time in reading and meditation. When it came to matters of belief, there was a measure of differentiation by denomination but none at all by sex.[15] Women might be expected by the conventions of the age to display their faith in the home, but they shared their religious convictions and in large measure their devotional style with the men of their families. There was no fundamental fissure along gender lines between those who professed a common evangelical faith.

It is nevertheless true that women and men were not found in the churches in equal proportions. In England attenders were more often women than men, and figures for membership, which entailed greater commitment, showed an even greater disparity. Although proportions varied from chapel to chapel, on average around two-thirds of those in Baptist and Congregational church membership in the period were female.[16] In the Church of England, Evangelicals sometimes claimed to create a manly ethos and so to attract men in larger numbers, but, at least in the Lambeth district of south London in 1902, the available figures show a lower proportion of men at Evangelical services than at their High-Church counterparts.[17] In America the ratio between the sexes differed between regions. Many of the churches of the most settled states on the eastern seaboard had more women than men, though, at least in 1850, the difference was less marked than in England. In that year Rhode Island, the state with fewest men, had ninety-five males for every hundred females. On the frontier, however, the ratio was very different. In Wisconsin, the state with the most men, there were one hundred and seventeen males for every hundred females.[18] Elsewhere in the world the pioneer-

---

[15]Linda Wilson, *Constrained by Zeal: Female Spirituality Among Nonconformists, 1825-1875* (Carlisle: Paternoster Press, 2000), chaps. 3-6. For America, see Candy Gunther Brown, *The Word in the World: Evangelical Writing, Publishing and Reading in America, 1789-1880* (Chapel Hill: University of North Carolina Press, 2004).

[16]Clive D. Field, "Adam and Eve: Gender in the English Free Church Constituency," *Journal of Ecclesiastical History* 44 (1993).

[17]Jeffrey Cox, *The English Churches in a Secular Society: Lambeth, 1870-1930* (New York: Oxford University Press, 1982), p. 283.

[18]Roger Finke and Rodney Stark, *The Churching of America, 1770-1990: Winners and Losers in Our Religious Economy* (New Brunswick, N.J.: Rutgers University Press, 1992), p. 67.

ing areas notoriously suffered from a scarcity of women, and the churches inevitably reflected their settings. But where patterns of life had become more
stable and respectability prevailed, women normally outnumbered men in
church. The reasons are many. Women of good reputation were excluded from
the main foci of male sociability among the working people, the public house
and (increasingly) the sports ground. Female sociability, by contrast, found a
natural outlet in a place of worship, often the only alternative gathering place
to the bar. And, because it was assumed even by the least committed that religion was good for children, mothers found their way to places of worship.
Churches were welcome meeting places for women.

Another reason for the large number of women in the churches was the avenue for service they offered. Linda Wilson has suggested that, alongside the
private and public spheres, the church provided a "third sphere," overlapping
the other two, in which women could flourish.[19] Certainly some church activities could be regarded as extensions of an archetypal female role. Thus when
women supplied the tea at a congregational function they were simply doing
on a larger scale what they would also do at home. Visiting those who were
ill was seen as a way in which women could carry their natural compassion
beyond the bounds of their families. Thus Mrs. J. C. White of Bathurst, New
South Wales, was praised on her death for being "delighted to visit the sick
room."[20] The visiting societies set up by many churches, especially in urban
areas, were staffed more by women than by men.[21] There was no bar to
women caring for those in need, even in a way that called for administrative
skill. Mrs. Pamela Clark Smith of Springfield, Massachusetts, who took the
lead in organizing the campaigns to set up a home for the friendless and a
children's home in the city, was hailed as one of its most active philanthropists.[22] Alongside volunteer charitable workers there were paid female employees in a range of evangelical agencies. In 1857, for example, Ellen Ran-
yard set up the London Bible and Domestic Mission for evangelistic work,
but its "Bible women" soon began to concentrate on nursing and turned into

---

[19] Wilson, *Constrained by Zeal*, p. 210.

[20] *Christian Advocate and Wesleyan Record* (Sydney), December 19, 1867, p. 123.

[21] Frank K. Prochaska, *Women and Philanthropy in Nineteenth-Century England* (Oxford: Clarendon
Press, 1980), p. 109.

[22] *Christian Advocate* (New York), January 7, 1897, p. 11.

the first paid cadre of social workers.[23] An Irish Presbyterian doctor who employed a nurse to visit the sick poor in his own town projected a much grander scheme for at least thirty-five of them to cover Catholic Ireland with a network of beacons of Protestant care. Each should be drawn from a humble home. "Taken from among the people," wrote the doctor, "she should dress as they do, and be distinguished from them only by cleanliness and tidiness."[24] These women, like their unpaid sisters, would embody feminine gospel values.

Women played an equally important part in the money-raising efforts of the churches. They were the usual collectors for home missions or for foreign missions, in the earlier part of the period normally going from door to door to receive subscriptions.[25] They could be responsible for large-scale enterprises. Cornelia Burling, a widow who worshiped at the 24th Street Methodist Episcopal Church in New York, raised the funds, with two or three friends, to launch a mission among the Flathead Indians of Oregon.[26] The proportion of subscribers to overseas missions and Bible societies who were themselves female increased over time until by the end of the century, in the case of four main British organizations, they formed between 40 and 50 percent.[27] Dorcas meetings, named after the character in Acts 9 who was "full of good works and almsdeeds," making "coats and garments," sometimes allowed (as at Donald Wesleyan Church, Victoria, Australia, in 1891) the women members to sell their products so as to pay off the church liabilities.[28] The most enjoyable means by which women raised money, however, was the bazaar. This type of event, part sale, part entertainment, was a popular feature of the program of a large number of churches during the period. Almost always controlled by women alone, the bazaar required thorough preparation over many months. Sewing circles made up clothes, promoters collected other goods for sale and organizers

---

[23]Kathleen Heasman, *Evangelicals in Action: An Appraisal of their Social Work in the Victorian Era* (London: Geoffrey Bles, 1962), pp. 36-37.

[24]*Evangelical Witness and Presbyterian Review* (Dublin), April 1864, pp. 109-10; October 1864, pp. 277-80.

[25]E.g., *Spectator and Methodist Chronicle* (Melbourne), May 5, 1877, p. 8; *Christian Advocate and Wesleyan Record*, June 9, 1859, p. 226.

[26]*Christian Advocate*, January 11, 1883, p. 27.

[27]Prochaska, *Women and Philanthropy*, p. 29.

[28]*Spectator and Methodist Chronicle*, January 23, 1891, p. 79.

planned refreshments. An element of competition was injected by seeing which stall could raise the most money for the cause. Initially bazaars attracted censure. "Is not," demanded the Australian editor of the *Church of England Chronicle* in 1857, "a certain air of frivolity and worldliness thrown over the whole affair?" He also felt "a strong repugnance" to ladies, "but especially young ladies," being expected to deploy feminine wiles to sell their goods and so wear at least "the appearance of evil."[29] The criticisms help account for the description of the Ladies' Bazaar at Helena, Montana, Presbyterian Church in 1873 as "the pleasantest and most honorable affair of the kind ever gotten up in the place."[30] It raised $800, and similar substantial sums could be drawn in by quite small congregations. Remarkably, women were the financial mainstay of many a missionary organization and many a church.

A further way in which women participated prominently in Christian work was through education. The Virginia Baptist newspaper, when in 1868 considering "The Sphere of Woman's Usefulness," listed, alongside praying, living good lives and giving, private teaching as a female speciality.[31] The role of women in bringing up children made them natural candidates for Sunday school teaching. Early in the century men had predominated, at least in England, but as the century wore on the proportion of women increased. Around three-quarters of teachers were female.[32] So great was the imbalance that congregations sometimes tried to recruit more men in order to provide role models for the boys.[33] Although according to one survey only about 4 percent of English Sunday school teachers received training, some women were extremely conscientious, one spending six or seven hours a week in preparation for teaching her classes.[34] Women were often harmonium players, song leaders, librarians and secretaries of Sunday schools, and could sometimes rise to become superintendent, especially of the infant department. Forceful women, such as Cor-

---

[29] *Church of England Chronicle* (Sydney), November 2, 1857, p. 292-93.

[30] *Rocky Mountain Presbyterian* (Denver, Colo.), February 1873.

[31] *Religious Herald* (Richmond, Va.), May 14, 1868.

[32] Callum G. Brown, *The Death of Christian Britain* (London: Routledge, 2001), pp. 96-97.

[33] Charles D. Cashdollar, *A Spiritual Home: Life in British and American Reformed Congregations, 1830-1915* (University Park: Pennsylvania University Press, 2000), p. 129.

[34] Philip B. Cliff, *The Rise and Development of the Sunday School Movement in England, 1780-1980* (Redhill, U.K.: National Christian Education Council, 1986), p. 182; Wilson, *Constrained by Zeal*, p. 191.

nelia Burling of New York, could occasionally assume the demanding but prestigious office of superintendent of a whole Sunday school.[35] Educational work could also take women beyond the Sunday school of their own congregation. Thus the Sussex Street Ragged and Industrial School in Sydney was staffed in the 1860s by an Irish schoolmaster and his daughter, Miss Danne, who visited the destitute children in their homes and conducted a Sunday evening meeting for adults.[36] The Lady Superintendent of the Girls' School in the Presbyterian mission at Lovedale, South Africa, from 1881 until her death ten years later, Mrs. Muirhead, was clearly a person who had discovered her *métier.* "Womanly wisdom," according to her obituary, "the loftiest moral tone, keen common sense, fine feeling, strength, sympathy, ripe experience, missionary zeal embracing both the outward and the inward life of the girls, all shone in her."[37] Education, though not an exclusively female province, was one in which women could find fulfillment.

Leadership in the church itself was a more problematic area. There was usually less difficulty with all-female auxiliaries, which multiplied during the period. Women took the lead in the Church of Scotland's Woman's Guild (1887), though even there the chair was occupied at the Central Council by a man until as late as 1935.[38] The Young Women's Band at Lydiard Street Methodist Church at Ballarat in Victoria, which received impetus from the minister's wife, Mrs. Nye, also gave scope for Mrs. Boswarrick to be the vice-chairman and Miss Cook to be the librarian, though again the chairman seems to have been the minister, E. W. Nye.[39] The women's missionary unions that sprang up in America were animated by a semifeminist consciousness, sending single women to the mission field and supporting them by exclusively female organizations. The Women's Union Missionary Society, founded in 1861 by Sarah Doremus, together with its denominational counterparts set up around a decade later and

---

[35] *Christian Advocate*, January 11, 1883, p. 27.

[36] Sophie McGrath, "Beyond Florence Nightingale and Caroline Chisholm: Women in Nineteenth Century History," in *Long, Patient Conflict: Essays on Women and Gender in Australian Christianity,* ed. Mark Hutchinson and Edmund Campion (Sydney: Center for the Study of Australian Christianity, 1994), p. 5.

[37] *Christian Express* (Lovedale, South Africa), May 1, 1891, p. 65.

[38] Mamie Magnusson, *Out of Silence: The Woman's Guild, 1887-1987* (Edinburgh: Saint Andrew Press, 1987), p. 104.

[39] *Spectator and Methodist Chronicle*, April 3, 1891, p. 318.

various imitative agencies, gave ample opportunity for women to exercise their organizational gifts.[40] By 1890 over 60 percent of the American overseas mission force was female.[41] In mixed gatherings at home, however, in the light of the apostle Paul's prohibition of women speaking in church, there was strong and widespread resistance to women being heard at all. Methodism was an exception, for women had the opportunity to lead society classes, and so, for example, Mary Boxsell, of Kiama in New South Wales, was highly regarded for her "practical teaching" as well as for her "wonderful gift in prayer."[42] In the Church of England, however, authority frowned on any female participation in acts of worship. When E. W. Moore, the incumbent of Brunswick Chapel in London, allowed women to pray aloud at a holiness meeting in his church during the 1870s, he was summoned by his bishop to receive a reprimand.[43] The position in the Church of England was particularly anomalous because women could act as patrons of livings, appointing clergy to their posts and, as churchwardens, organizing the life of the parish churches. The supreme governor of the church was even a woman, Queen Victoria. It was when, in 1897, parochial church councils were first set up but women were excluded from them that the initial wave of feminism began to affect Anglicanism.[44] The ability of women to provide leadership was often severely circumscribed.

The sharpest tensions were felt over whether women should be allowed to enter the preaching ministry. There was no problem for the Quakers, amongst whom a large majority of itinerant ministers were female.[45] The Primitive Methodists, like the Free Methodists in North America, upheld the opening of the pulpit to women, though one of their ministers named Smith, while advocating this position at Bloemfontein in the Orange Free State, revealed the practical limitations on this doctrine. "He maintained that while woman's chief and best influence was at home, still, when she had done her duty there, . . .

---

[40]R. Pierce Beaver, *American Protestant Women in World Mission: History of the First Feminist Movement in North America*, 2nd ed. (Grand Rapids: Eerdmans, 1980).

[41]Dana L. Robert, *American Women in Mission: A Social History of their Thought and Practice* (Macon, Ga.: Mercer University Press, 1997), p. 130.

[42]*Christian Advocate and Wesleyan Record*, August 2, 1876, p. 68.

[43]John B. Figgis, *Keswick from Within* (London: Marshall Brothers, 1914), pp. 79-80.

[44]Brian Heeney, "The Beginnings of Church Feminism," *Journal of Ecclesiastical History* 33 (1982).

[45]Elizabeth Isichei, *Victorian Quakers* (Oxford: Clarendon Press, 1970), pp. 94-95.

[s]he had the right, when she had the ability and time thereto, to preach."[46] In 1859 the holiness teacher Phoebe Palmer published *The Promise of the Father* vindicating the liberty of women to speak so long as they did not usurp authority over men. Female proclamation, she held, ought to be a feature of the last days in which they lived.[47] She was echoed by Catherine Booth, and the Salvation Army was to give equality to female officers.[48] Female preaching nevertheless remained unusual. In 1891 the novelty of a lady preacher at a Bacchus Marsh Methodist Church in Victoria still drew crowded congregations.[49] The prevailing opinion in most denominations was definitely against female ministry. Women speaking in public, according to a South Carolina Baptist in 1868, "seems to be plainly forbidden in Scripture, and we need not be surprised that it is, for such a practice ill accords with the modesty which is native to the sex."[50] Even when, in 1878, an American Congregationalist conceded that female silence was a matter of custom rather than principle in New Testament times, he was still unwilling to accept female ordination "unless under very rare circumstances."[51] In practice a female member of his own denomination, Antoinette Blackwell, had become a pastor in New Jersey in 1852, though she subsequently turned to Unitarianism.[52] But she was an exceptional figure. Outside a few Christian groups, the entry of women into ordained ministry was to be deferred until the twentieth century.

Yet women did reach other positions. A significant development of the period was the creation of orders of deaconesses. The enterprising Anglican clergyman William Pennefather founded a training home for female missionaries in 1860 that moved with him to Mildmay Park in north London four years later. Gradually it turned into a base for deaconesses modeled on the Lutheran community at Kaiserwerth in Germany. The sisters, wearing distinctive dress as a protection against molestation, were responsible for a range of church work that included nursing and social care as well as evangelism and general

---

[46] *Christian Express*, December 1, 1876, p. 6.
[47] Thomas C. Oden, ed., *Phoebe Palmer: Selected Writings* (New York: Paulist Press, 1988), p. 39.
[48] Pamela J. Walker, *Pulling the Devil's Kingdom Down: The Salvation Army in Victorian Britain* (Berkeley: University of California Press, 2001), pp. 109-19.
[49] *Spectator and Methodist Chronicle*, March 6, 1891, p. 223.
[50] *Religious Herald*, April 2, 1868.
[51] W. D. Love in *Bibliotheca Sacra* (New York), January 1878, p. 42.
[52] A. Maude Royden, *The Church and Woman* (London: James Clarke, 1925), p. 131.

visitation. By 1893, under the direction of Pennefather's widow Catherine, eighty of them staffed twenty Mildmay missions in the poorer parts of London.[53] By that date the success of the deaconesses had encouraged most other English denominations to copy them, overcoming initial suspicions that the sisters were altogether too like nuns, and there were also imitations in America and Australia. In the twentieth century the work of some of them, such as the English Baptist deaconesses, was to become virtually indistinguishable from that of ordained ministers.[54] Other women spearheaded causes that blended Christianity and feminism, bringing them prominently into the public eye not just in the church but also in society at large. In England Josephine Butler, the wife of an Anglican clergyman, led a long but ultimately successful campaign to remove the Anti-Contagious Diseases Acts from the statute book. The acts, passed in the 1860s, provided for the compulsory medical inspection of prostitutes in the vicinity of military and naval barracks. Driven by her evangelical faith, Butler denounced the implied toleration of sexual immorality and the unequal treatment of women.[55] In America Frances Willard, a Methodist ex-teacher and sometime colleague of Dwight L. Moody, became in 1879 president of the Women's Christian Temperance Union, waging war on drink. She turned the organization into a broad front campaigning for "home protection," deftly negotiating political alliances in order to advance the cause of women.[56] Willard, who claimed that she would have preferred a career in the ministry, published *Women in the Pulpit* (1888) to urge that gender should be no barrier to ordination.[57] For these women it was possible to break through contemporary convention to play a major part in life beyond the home. We can conclude that evangelical religion could enlarge as well as circumscribe the role of women in society.

---

[53]Hariette J. Cooke, *Mildmay: Or the Story of the First Deaconess Institution*, 2nd ed. (London: Elliott Stock, 1893), p. 86.

[54]Nicola Morris, *Sisters of the People: The Order of Baptist Deaconesses, 1890-1975* (Bristol: Center for Comparative Studies in Religion and Gender, 2002).

[55]Helen Mathers, "The Evangelical Spirituality of a Victorian Feminist: Josephine Butler, 1828-1906," *Journal of Ecclesiastical History*, 52 (2001).

[56]Ruth Bordin, *Woman and Temperance: The Quest for Power and Liberty, 1873-1900* (Philadelphia: Temple University Press, 1981).

[57]Royden, *Church and Woman*, p. 131. The standard is Ruth Bordin, *Frances Willard: A Biography* (Chapel Hill: University of North Carolina Press, 1986).

RACE RELATIONS

The issue of the relationship between the races, in the second place, was particularly fraught during this period. Evangelicals could boast a proud record of leading the successful campaigns for the abolition of the British slave trade (1807) and for the emancipation of slaves in British dominions (1833). At the start of the period, however, the institution of black slavery remained firmly entrenched in the American South, where most evangelicals maintained that it was divinely sanctioned. Several of the denominations of the North, on the other hand, fostered a fierce abolitionism, seeing slavery as "the most formidable obstacle to Christian missions."[58] At a gathering in Boston in 1857, the abolitionist leader Lewis Tappan called on his hearers "to come out distinctly and unequivocally on the Lord's side in behalf of the oppressed, and against the stupendous iniquity that threatens to bring upon this nation the wrath of God."[59] Antislavery sentiment continued to flourish in the British Isles. In 1853 the *Friend*, the evangelical Quaker newspaper, deplored the selling of three free black men into slavery at New Orleans; and a Belfast Presbyterian newspaper praised "the peerless work" of Harriet Beecher Stowe, meaning her abolitionist novel *Uncle Tom's Cabin.*[60] The General Baptists looked on in dismay during the 1850s as America admitted more slave states to the Union.[61] When, in 1861, Civil War broke out between the Southern Confederacy, upholding the institution of slavery, and the Federal government in the North, it was the "enormous guilt of holding our fellow-men in bondage" that swung most evangelical opinion in Britain against the South.[62] Even in the last decade of the century, the same cause rallied evangelical Nonconformists to take an interest in eliminating slavery from the island of Zanzibar that Britain had acquired in 1890.[63] A deep-seated aversion to slavery was a powerful influence on the public attitudes of many evangelicals.

The intellectual premises of this position were firmly laid in the worldview

---

[58]*American Missionary*, February 1857, p. 29.

[59]*American Missionary*, July 1857, p. 149.

[60]*Friend* (London), 1852, pp. 24-25; *Irish Presbyterian* (Belfast), January 1853, p. 25.

[61]*General Baptist Magazine* (London), April 1854, p. 187; February 1855, p. 88; December 1856, p. 472.

[62]N. Haycroft in *Baptist Magazine*, April 1863, pp. 205-11.

[63]*Christian World* (London), August 8, 1895, p. 606; Nottingham Free Church Council, January 30, 1896, p. 83.

that evangelicals shared with the Enlightenment. Around 1850, as the *Christian Messenger* of Halifax, Nova Scotia, declared in that year, it was generally agreed that there was no fundamental difference between the races:

> Modern writers have said much of the energies of the "Anglo-Saxon Race," but in this respect their views are futile, unmeaning and unphilosophical: for they have written as if there was some innate capacity in this branch of the human family, to which it is indebted for its superiority.[64]

The undoubted achievements of English-speaking peoples, it went on, must be put down not to inherent ethnic qualities but to the reverence for the Bible that they had acquired. In principle, therefore, any other body of people on earth, if molded by biblical values, could manage the same attainments. This conviction was held to be a scientific inference from the unity of the human race.[65] It was therefore the general opinion that, as the English Congregationalist Edward Miall declared in 1863, "Christianity nowhere gives countenance to the modern pretence that . . . white complexioned humanity [may] play havoc with black."[66] Hence British evangelicals, and especially Baptists, could be mobilized to demand the punishment of a Governor of Jamaica who suppressed black unrest with undue violence.[67] Hence, too, missionary agencies were willing to encourage black people to enter the ministry. There was no question of their being permanently incapable of gaining the necessary qualifications. On the contrary, the Fourah Bay Institution in Sierra Leone had existed under the auspices of the Church Missionary Society since 1827 to provide an advanced education for the peoples of west Africa. Its first student, Samuel Crowther, went on to become the first black Anglican bishop in 1864.[68] The evangelical assumption was that differences in individual capacity were chiefly determined by religion and learning, not by race.

There was, however, a darker side to the record of evangelical racial atti-

---

[64] *Christian Messenger* (Halifax, Nova Scotia), January 25, 1850, p. 25.

[65] John Duns, *Science and Christian Thought* (London: Religious Tract Society, 1866), chap. 13.

[66] Edward Miall, *The Politics of Christianity* (London: Arthur Miall, 1863), p. 147.

[67] Timothy Larsen, "English Baptists, Jamaican Affairs and the Nonconformist Conscience: The Campaign against Governor Eyre," in *The Gospel in the World: International Baptist Studies*, ed. David Bebbington (Carlisle: Paternoster Press, 2002).

[68] J. F. A. Ajayi, *Christian Missions in Nigeria, 1841-1891: The Making of a New Elite* (London: Longmans, 1965).

tudes. The irruption of Caucasian peoples into territories previously occupied by other ethnic groups led to mutual hostility and, at least on the white side, contempt for the indigenous tribes. In Australia it was confidently expected, for instance by Bishop Frederic Barker of Sydney, that the aborigines were doomed to rapid extinction.[69] Because it was supposed that there would soon be no aborigines to reach, a large gift to the Free Church in South Australia for their education and evangelization was diverted, despite protests by the donor in 1871, to other Christian work.[70] There existed an Aborigines Protection Society in New South Wales, but the attendance at its 1886 annual meeting was small. "The public," it was remarked, "are not much interested in blacks."[71] Support in England for the Aborigines Protection Society, largely an expression of the evangelical conscience, likewise languished.[72] In Canada, although there were effective missions to the native peoples to the west, they were also expected to wither away. "With the sad experience we have of the great evils brought upon weaker races by contact with a stronger one in New Zealand and in the United States," wrote a missionary in 1872, "we cannot but tremble for the future of the Red Indians in Manitoba and Rupert's Land."[73] The note of compassionate regret in this observation was soon to be muffled as social Darwinism spread, teaching that the triumph of the stronger race was inevitable and in some senses desirable. From the middle of the century, at first only in restricted circles but increasingly in society at large, the old belief in the homogeneity of humanity was supplanted by the suppositions that races were radically dissimilar, that they could be ranked in order of intellectual capacity and that race was the chief determinant of personal characteristics. Many evangelicals succumbed to this rising body of opinion. There was more than a hint of it in *Our Country: Its Possible Future and its Present Crisis* (1885), a celebration of Anglo-Saxon superiority by Josiah Strong, who in the following year became General Secretary of the Evangelical Alliance in America. In this perspective members of weaker races might deserve protection, but

---

[69] *Church of England Chronicle*, December 1, 1856, p. 45; December 1, 1857, p. 309.

[70] R. J. Scrimgeour, *Some Scots were Here: A History of the Presbyterian Church in South Australia* (Adelaide: Lutheran Publishing House, 1986), pp. 106-8.

[71] *Intercolonial Christian Messenger* (Brisbane), March 19, 1886, p. 803.

[72] *Christian World*, July 13, 1899, p. 7.

[73] *Church Missionary Society Record* (London), November 1872, p. 352.

should not attain leadership.[74] The prevalence of this point of view explains why no other black African Anglican bishops were appointed after Samuel Crowther until long into the twentieth century.

The American South did not need an intellectual revolution to mount a defense of the sharpness of racial divisions. In the years before the Civil War its theologians generated an elaborate vindication of slavery that was powerful enough to persuade some Northerners of their biblical case.[75] Belief in the legitimacy of "the peculiar institution" was nevertheless sufficiently divisive to cleave the Methodists and Baptists in two, so that by 1845 there were separate Southern denominations vigorously upholding slavery. Nor did the enforced emancipation of the slaves at the end of the war bring Southern whites to accept more generous attitudes. A veteran Methodist preacher of the North Georgia conference writing in 1900 still held that slavery "did wonders for the negro," raising him from the jungles of Africa to the highest level of civilization.[76] An editorial of 1883 in the Baptist newspaper of the same state repudiated (remarkably) the statement in the Declaration of Independence that "all men are created equal." "We believe," it continued, "that some of these various races are inferior to others in physical organization, in intellectual ability, and in capacity for development, political, social, moral, or religious, and that they will so remain until the end of time."[77] A. C. Dixon, the prominent American Baptist minister, had a father from the Carolinas, another Baptist minister, who took him into the Ku Klux Klan shortly after the Civil War. Although the father resigned rather than join in a lynching, he originally felt that a vigilante organization of this kind was the only way of keeping order. The son rejected social equality because it would mean intermarriage, which "would portend the extinction of the Anglo-Saxon race, and its transmutation into a race of mulat-

---

[74]Andrew Ross, "David Livingstone: The Man behind the Mask," in *The London Missionary Society in Southern Africa: Historical Essays in Celebration of the Bicentenary of the LMS in Southern Africa, 1799-1999*, ed. John de Gruchy (Cape Town: David Philip, 1999), pp. 39-41.

[75]Mark A. Noll, *America's God: From Jonathan Edwards to Abraham Lincoln* (New York: Oxford University Press, 2002), chap. 19.

[76]S. P. Richardson, *The Lights and Shadows of Itinerant Life* (Nashville: Publishing House of the Methodist Episcopal Church, South, 1900), p. 23.

[77]"Georgia Editorial on Race, 1883," in *A Sourcebook for Baptist Heritage*, ed. H. L. McBeth, (Nashville: Broadman Press, 1990), p. 286.

tos."[78] Even an official statement of the Southern Baptist Convention Home Mission Board issued in 1891 was convinced that "colored people" showed a "perfect willingness to accept a subordinate place" so long as they received justice and kindness.[79] The white churchgoers of the South remained deeply committed to the inequality of the races.

Consequently a marked feature of the period was an exodus of black Christians to form their own congregations. The first separate black denomination had been founded as long ago as 1816, when the African Methodist Episcopal Church had been established, but most congregations remained mixed. Yet worship was often segregated in practice. Thus at Tallahassee, Florida, in 1851 the black section of the Methodist population occupied the galleries for main services and held their own separate service on a Sunday afternoon.[80] Neo-African customs such as ecstatic singing and the energetic circle dance marked black religious practice outside the walls of the church, and features of voodoo were by no means unknown. But gradually the syncretist elements fell away, leading to black congregations upholding the evangelical faith while maintaining distinctive worship patterns. By 1865 between a quarter and one-sixth of the black population belonged to a church.[81] In that year emancipation was enforced throughout the United States. A black woman baptized as a Methodist at Huntsville, Alabama, emerged from the water shouting, "Freed from slavery, freed from sin; bless God and General Grant."[82] Over the next few years the great majority of African Americans withdrew to form their own churches. It was not so much that they were driven out but that they wanted to escape the tutelage of the whites in spiritual matters as much as in secular affairs. A similar motivation began to influence black Christians in South Africa before the end of the century. There the existence of separate mission congregations had maintained a higher degree of segregation and so what happened there was the creation of separate denominations. In 1884, Nehemiah Tile, a Methodist minis-

---

[78]Helen C. A. Dixon, *A. C. Dixon: A Romance of Preaching* (New York: G. P. Putnam's Sons, 1931), pp. 32, 151.

[79]"A Statement on Race Relations, Home Mission Board of SBC, 1891," in *Sourcebook*, ed. McBeth, pp. 286-87.

[80]Richardson, *Itinerant Life*, p. 109.

[81]Mechal Sobel, *Trabelin' On: The Slave Journey to an Afro-Baptist Faith* (Princeton: Princeton University Press, 1988).

[82]*Christian Advocate*, January 11, 1866, p. 11.

ter, left after a dispute with a missionary to form the Tembu Church that would be free from white interference.[83] Other separations followed, leading to the creation of a fresh sector of independent black Christianity that was destined to outstrip the traditional churches during the twentieth century.

The black churches in the American South rapidly came to play a central role in African American life. Since they were denied access to public space, black people turned their places of worship into clubs and schools, theaters and restaurants, publishing houses and venues for political rallies. The Christian press took the place of the secular variety, so that, by 1900, there were forty-three black Baptist newspapers in the United States.[84] Black churches, as other Baptists would occasionally concede, usually operated a more resolute system of discipline than their white counterparts, insisting on standards of behavior among church members that matched the professions of their lips.[85] African-American spirituality had its own emphases, the central preoccupations being the five books of Moses (dwelling on redemption, profane as well as sacred), the saving work of Jesus and the book of Revelation (promising compensation in heaven to the downtrodden). Millennial expectations fostered hopes for the secular future and pride in Africa gave black people a sense of their own dignity and potential. Africa, in fact, provided an alternative allegiance to some of those who believed that divine judgment would fall on "the Negro-hating white Christians."[86] In 1896 the African Methodist Episcopal Church launched a mission from America to South Africa, absorbing an indigenous "Ethiopian" church that had started four years earlier and so binding together the black Christian cause on the two continents.[87] In the previous year three bodies concerned with foreign mission, home mission and education came to-

---

[83]Daryl M. Balia, *Black Methodists and White Supremacy in South Africa* (Durban: Madiba Publishers, 1991), chap. 4.

[84]Evelyn Brooks Higginbotham, "The Black Church: A Gender Perspective," in *African-American Religion: Interpretive Essays in History and Culture*, ed. Timothy E. Fulop and Albert J. Raboteau (New York: Routledge, 1997), pp. 208-13.

[85]*Religious Herald*, January 24, 1878.

[86]Timothy E. Fulop, " 'The Future Golden Day of the Race': Millennialism and Black Americans in the Nadir, 1877-1901," in *African-American Religion*, ed. Fulop and Raboteau, p. 236.

[87]James T. Campbell, *Songs of Zion: The African Methodist Episcopal Church in the United States and South Africa* (Chapel Hill: North Carolina University Press, 1998).

gether to form the National Baptist Convention, the first African American Baptist denomination aspiring to cover the land.[88] By 1906 it enjoyed the support of 61 percent of black church members in the United States.[89] The "black church" had turned into what it would remain during the whole of the twentieth century, by far the most important agency for the improvement of the condition of those who had once been slaves.

RELIGION AND RECREATION

The attitude of the churches to recreation was a third controversial subject within the period. The issue often came down to the question of what the believer ought to avoid. At the start of the period there was no stronger taboo than that on the theater. Evangelical Anglicans were told by their magazine in 1851 that, since there was no prospect of improving the theater, Christians should stand aloof from it. "To act otherwise," it declared, "to sanction the representation of sin, is surely equivalent to mocking at it; to wink at the playing with iniquity, is as much as to allow that we account that which cost the Saviour's blood a thing of nought."[90] Six years later the Anglican newspaper in Australia was able, in three successive issues, to list thirteen reasons, including shameless profanity and the doubtful character of actresses, why Christians should not go to see plays.[91] A general aversion to the stage persisted long into the period. The theater could not be excused, remarked an English Methodist journal in 1882 without a trace of irony, "because *the whole audience do not*, on their dismissal from the play, immediately, unanimously, and violently proceed to the full degree of delinquency of which man is capable."[92] Nor did Christian content, such as in the passion play at Oberammergau in Germany, improve matters. One of the sterner opponents of ritualism in the Church of England noted in 1880, equally without irony, that Charles Lowder, an advanced Anglo-Catholic priest, "met his death shortly after witnessing the dreadful perfor-

---

[88] Owen D. Pelt and Ralph Lee Smith, *The Story of the National Baptists* (New York: Vantage Press, 1960).

[89] Higginbotham, "Black Church," p. 207.

[90] *Christian Observer* (London), May 1851, p. 300.

[91] *Church of England Chronicle*, September 1, 1857, pp. 241-42; September 15, 1857, pp. 253-54; October 1, 1857, pp. 265-66.

[92] *Experience* (London), January-March 1882, p. 16.

mances at Ober-Ammergau."[93] There was, however, a problem for lovers of good literature, since the greatest poetic artist in the English language was, by common consent, the dramatist William Shakespeare. The hymnwriter Frances Ridley Havergal turned, despite some misgivings, to the bard for intellectual inspiration.[94] Likewise, when asked in 1887 whether it was right to perform any part of Shakespeare in a Methodist Episcopal Church, the official respondent for the denominational newspaper gave a firm negative but added the rider that it was acceptable to read extracts as part of a young people's entertainment.[95] Henry Allon, among the most cultured of English Congregational ministers, sat on the Shakespeare Tercentenary Committee, and yet, though he allowed liberty of judgment to others, he would never go to the theater himself.[96] Genius must be honored, but the glamorous representation of wrongdoing must be shunned.[97]

Other forms of entertainment also fell under the evangelical ban. Horse racing was prominent among them. The Evangelical Anglican *Record* was resolute that the turf could not be reformed and so must be abolished. "Racing," declared a leading article in 1862, "is the hotbed of vices, which oppose honorable exertion, and the temple of illicit barter."[98] The newspaper was pointing to the gambling that was the kernel of the objection to the sport. It was equally condemned on that ground in America, where it was suggested by the New York Baptist newspaper in 1865 that there was nothing manly about horse racing. Organized pickpockets had just caused havoc at a Brooklyn racecourse, and so it was easy to draw attention to "the passions and crimes that gambling begets."[99] Trying to achieve financial gain by appealing to chance was widely seen as not just unwise but immoral. The British *Baptist Magazine* carried a long

---

[93]James Bateman, *The Church Association: Its Policy and Prospects considered in a Letter to the Chairman* (London: William Ridgeway, 1880), p. 5n.

[94]Maria V. G. Havergal, *Memorials of Frances Ridley Havergal* (London: James Nisbet, 1880), p. 194.

[95]*Christian Advocate*, January 6, 1887, p. 4.

[96]W. H. Harwood, *Henry Allon, D. D.: Pastor and Teacher* (London: Cassell and Co., 1894), pp. 40-41.

[97]On the preceding period, see Doreen M. Rosman, *Evangelicals and Culture* (London: Croom Helm, 1984), pp. 75-79.

[98]*Record* (London), January 3, 1862, p. 2.

[99]*Examiner and Chronicle* (New York), July 6, 1865.

article in 1868 demonstrating that gambling was a sin against God, self and society.[100] Hence any trace of the gambling spirit must be banished from church and home. When a bazaar at one of the Wesleyan circuits in Victoria, Australia, advertised a lottery, the president of conference intervened and the money taken for tickets was returned.[101] Games of chance that involved wagers were frowned on in Christian households, and stricter souls condemned any use of playing cards at all.[102] If anything, anxieties about gambling strengthened rather than fading over time. By 1885 the *South African Methodist*, troubled by the rise of professional gambling in the diamond fields of Kimberley, spoke out against it; and four years later evangelical opinion was roused against gaming clubs in England.[103] Opposition to gambling was a persistent feature of the evangelical conscience.

There were nevertheless areas in which attitudes mellowed. At the beginning of the period there was strong condemnation of dancing, with an obituary of a Virginia young woman in 1858 stressing her total avoidance of "the giddy dance."[104] Some associated with revivalism or holiness maintained their disapproval of all dancing, recommending Christian parents to shun schools where it was taught and rejoicing when a successful mission caused the closure of a dancing school in a Scottish town.[105] Others, however, began to be more discriminating, even in this sensitive activity that brought the two sexes together. An American Baptist newspaper drew a distinction in 1871 between, on the one hand, balls and dancing parties, which were still considered "inconsistent with a Christian profession" and "injurious to health and morals," and, on the other, square or plain dances, which, "when *limited to seasonable hours* and *private parlors*," were altogether more innocent diversions.[106] By 1880 an American Methodist bishop recommended that, when invited to a ball, a Christian should pray for the blessing of the heavenly Father upon the event and so would

---

[100]W. Walters in *Baptist Magazine*, July 1868, pp. 438-43.

[101]*Methodist Journal* (Adelaide), November 14, 1874.

[102]George Dixon in *Christian* (London), October 21, 1875, p. 8.

[103]*South African Methodist* (Grahamstown), September 23, 1885, p. 430; *Christian World*, May 23, 1889, p. 426.

[104]*Religious Herald*, February 11, 1858.

[105]*Christian*, November 5, 1874, p. 13; Isobel R. Govan, *Spirit of Revival: The Story of J. G. Govan and the Faith Mission*, 4th ed. (Edinburgh: Faith Mission, 1978), p. 34.

[106]*Examiner and Chronicle*, February 2, 1871.

discover anything hurtful about it.[107] Even attitudes to the stage relaxed in the last decades of the century, with the bishop saying the same about the theater as about the ball. Joseph Parker, the flamboyant Congregational minister of the City Temple in London, announced, to the dismay of Spurgeon, that he could accept theater-going.[108] Likewise in Sydney two clergy disagreed in public about the legitimacy of the stage.[109] The theater had done much to improve its image, but at least as important an explanation of the more relaxed attitude was that many evangelicals wanted to match their social calendar to their advancing respectability. In some respects evangelicals were becoming broader-minded.

Christian sponsorship of entertainment was a further development of the period. The first stage was the provision of reading rooms, a way of taking men, especially in such places as mining towns, away from "the billiard-hall, dance-house or liquor-saloon."[110] Grander counter-attractions could follow, such as the coffeehouses organized in Toronto from 1881 by an association under the patronage of the rich Polish engineer Sir Casimir Gzowski, remarkably an Evangelical.[111] At Christchurch in New Zealand, popular entertainments began on winter evenings in 1868 and in the next season the churches followed suit.[112] Music was commonly the staple of activities on church premises. Welsh chapels held their own eisteddfods, with Nebo Baptist Chapel in Ebbw Vale in 1888 hosting three juvenile choirs that competed in singing a piece from Sankey's hymnbook.[113] Manchester Methodist Mission, started in 1885, soon had a regular Saturday night concert complete with paid artistes.[114] Sunday school activities, especially at Christmas, were an avenue whereby traditional reservations about amusements were overcome. In New York by 1868 several churches already had a live Santa Claus, and some arranged practical jokes when making

---

[107]Bishop Bowman in *Christian Advocate*, August 19, 1880, p. 535.

[108]Patricia S. Kruppa, *Charles Haddon Spurgeon: A Preacher's Progress* (New York: Garland Publishing, 1982), p. 449.

[109]*Intercolonial Christian Messenger*, March 5, 1886, p. 776.

[110]*Rocky Mountain Presbyterian*, October 1873.

[111]D. C. Masters, "The Anglican Evangelicals in Toronto, 1870-1900," *Journal of the Canadian Church Historical Society* 20 (1978): 55, 61.

[112]*Christian Observer* (Christchurch), January 1, 1870, p. 8.

[113]*Freeman* (London), January 13, 1888, p. 29.

[114]George Jackson, *Collier of Manchester: A Friend's Tribute* (London: Hodder & Stoughton, 1923), pp. 133-35.

the annual gift to the minister. In that year at one church "a trained turkey walked up the aisle, loaded with greenbacks [dollars]."[115] Such developments caused alarm among those whose piety was more single-minded. "One of the principal churches here," wrote a holiness supporter in Dunfermline, "has a weekly concert instead of a prayer-meeting, and occasional comic readings, and the people are drifting down to doom!"[116] But in most circles the trend continued unabated down to the end of the century and beyond. By the 1890s the Melbourne *Spectator and Methodist Chronicle* ran part of a column headed "Fun" and the Dublin *Irish Presbyterian*, though supplying Scripture warrant with a verse from Proverbs about a merry heart being good medicine, offered a set of jokes under the heading "Smiles and Laughter."[117] The churches were trying to take popular entertainment under their wing.

In a similar way they aspired to ally themselves with sport. A prominent feature of the last third of the nineteenth century was the rise of organized sport marked by standardized rules and national coordination. With increasing leisure time at their disposal, men flocked to matches as spectators as well as joining in sporting activities themselves. Much of this seemed in direct competition with the churches, which, where sterner views prevailed, often reacted with hostility. The breaking up of cricket clubs was reckoned one of the blessed results of revival in the mining towns of South Australia in 1875.[118] "If we get saved," said a young footballer at Bathgate near Edinburgh, "we canna' go on playing."[119] Yet the predominant attitude in the churches was that recreation could be annexed to religion, encouraging a legitimate celebration of masculine prowess. In America the Young Men's Christian Association led the way, providing facilities for sports and actually inventing basketball and volleyball.[120] When bicycling became the rage, A. C. Dixon provided a service especially for cyclists at his church in Baltimore.[121] In England doubts were stilled for many by the prestige of the Cambridge and England cricketer C. T. Studd, the best known

---

[115]*Examiner and Chronicle*, January 16, 1868.

[116]Govan, *Govan*, p. 36.

[117]*Spectator and Methodist Chronicle*, January 2, 1891, p. 20; *Irish Presbyterian*, January 1895, p. 15.

[118]J. G. Wright in *Primitive Methodist Record* (Adelaide), July 1875, p. 280.

[119]Govan, *Govan*, p. 80.

[120]Daniel G. Reid, Robert D. Linder, Bruce L. Shelley and Harry S. Stout, eds., *Dictionary of Christianity in America* (Downers Grove, Ill.: InterVarsity Press, 1990), p. 1299.

[121]Dixon, *Dixon*, p. 101.

of the Cambridge Seven who volunteered for missionary service in China.[122] In the early 1890s while at Cambridge it was natural for Stuart Holden, a leading Evangelical Anglican of a later period, to play cricket and teach the game to boys in his Bible class.[123] Cycling and cricket were equally the chief sporting activities sponsored by Nonconformist chapels during the 1890s and long into the twentieth century. "In these days of broader conceptions of religion," announced the annual report of the Young Men's Society at College Street Baptist Church, Northampton, in 1890, "not only is stress laid on man's spiritual nature, but the church is waking up to the fact that man has a body to be cared for."[124] Many evangelicals, like Broad Churchmen of an earlier generation, were becoming convinced of the value of promoting physical health. Sport was more than a technique for attracting young men to church, though it was that. For many it also became an essential part of the life abundant that religion was expected to provide.

Fiction was a further field that became yoked to an evangelical purpose. There were, once more, those who rejected light reading as a snare to the soul. An article entitled "Novels, the Alcohol of Literature" in a British Methodist home mission journal for 1882 concluded with an exhortation to total abstinence, as from other deadly intoxicants.[125] The South African Dutch Reformed leader and Keswick speaker Andrew Murray, according to his daughter, "could not and would not" read novels.[126] In a way the reaction was not surprising, since so many writers of fiction were, in varying degrees, avowedly hostile to evangelical religion.[127] Others, however, recognized the power of some of the great novelists of the age. The London Congregational minister Alexander Raleigh most admired George Eliot's *Middlemarch*, which in 1876 was also a book

---

[122]Norman P. Grubb, *C. T. Studd: Cricketer and Pioneer* (London: Religious Tract Society, 1933).

[123]*John Stuart Holden: A Book of Remembrance* (London: Hodder & Stoughton, 1935), p. 42.

[124]Quoted by Hugh McLeod, " 'Thews and Sinews': Nonconformity and Sport," in *Modern Christianity and Cultural Aspirations*, ed. David Bebbington and Timothy Larsen (London: Sheffield Academic Press, 2003), p. 37.

[125]*Experience*, January-March 1882, pp. 96-101.

[126]Johannes du Plessis, *The Life of Andrew Murray of South Africa* (London: Marshall Brothers, 1919), p. 479.

[127]Valentine Cunningham, *Everywhere Spoken Against: Dissent in the Victorian Novel* (Oxford: Clarendon Press, 1975).

that the South African evangelical newspaper expected many of its readers to know.[128] Sir Walter Scott, in the opinion of the Sydney *Christian Pleader* in 1859, had greatly improved the genre, though it was hard to discern a specific moral purpose in his works. "Fictitious narrative, to be justified," it argued, "must have some positively beneficial aim."[129] Because of such views, explicitly religious novels, such as those by the prolific Mary Sherwood, were extremely popular, and in the second half of the century ministers often turned their hand to them. The boundary between entertainment and edification was hard to draw in such works as *Daniel Quorm and his Religious Notions* (1875) by the Wesleyan Mark Guy Pearse. Two Cornish United Methodist ministers and their sister, Silas, Joseph and Salome Hocking, were together responsible for over two hundred novels between 1878 and the 1930s.[130] Equally an evangelical tone was often evident in the Scottish "Kailyard school" of literature sponsored by the journalist and ex-Free Church minister William Robertson Nicoll and in the equivalent Canadian novels of the Presbyterian minister Charles Gordon, writing as Ralph Connor. Rooted in particular localities, the Kailyard was typified in the collection of short stories *Beside the Bonnie Brier Bush* (1894) by another Presbyterian minister, John Watson, using the pseudonym Ian Maclaren.[131] Although customarily criticized as amateurish and overly sentimental, these works reveal a sustained attempt to blend faith and fiction. Judged on the basis of sales figures, they were remarkably successful.

CRUSADING ISSUES

If evangelicals did much to Christianize entertainment, sport and fiction, they also spent a great deal of energy in resisting the forces that in their view tended to debase society. The second half of the nineteenth century witnessed a long series of campaigns against particular targets. One concern was about the desecration of the Lord's Day. Although a small band of Seventh-Day

---

[128]Mary Raleigh, ed., *Alexander Raleigh: Records of his Life* (Edinburgh: Adam and Charles Black, 1881), p. 12; *Christian Express*, August 1, 1876, p. 1.

[129]*Christian Pleader* (Sydney), July 9, 1859, p. 107.

[130]Alan M. Kent, *Pulp Methodism: The Lives & Literature of Silas, Joseph and Salome Hocking, Three Cornish Novelists* (St. Austell, U.K.: Cornish Hillside Publications, 2002).

[131]T. H. Darlow, *William Robertson Nicoll: Life and Letters* (London: Hodder & Stoughton, 1925), p. 115.

Baptists observing Saturday as the sabbath had survived in America from the seventeenth century, the great mass of evangelicals believed that Sunday was to be free of work or play. Some thought the Christian Sunday milder than the Jewish sabbath,[132] but it was more common to identify the two. Accordingly in Britain there was a Lord's Day Observance Society that agitated in the 1850s against railway trains running, post offices carrying mail, military bands playing or the Crystal Palace opening.[133] When, in 1855, a New South Wales counterpart was established at a public meeting presided over by the Bishop of Sydney, it was claimed that "the Sabbath is a Divine Institution and of perpetual obligation."[134] After all, as a Free Church pastoral address in Canada had put it three years before, the Sabbath was "enshrined in the very heart of the decalogue, and is surrounded by commands which are looked upon as universally binding."[135] Some evangelicals nevertheless had reservations about imposing Christian standards on society at large. Thus Alexander Thomson, a Congregational minister at an Edinburgh public meeting protesting in 1850 against Sunday labor in the post office, claimed not to be requesting government to compel the keeping of the sabbath, but merely to be asking government not to compel people to break it.[136] Anglicans, Presbyterians and Methodists rarely suffered from such scruples. Even American Baptists, who might have been expected to reveal qualms about calling for state enforcement of church principles, normally joined heartily in the general demand for strict sabbatarianism. "To save our Sabbaths," said their main organ at the end of the Civil War in 1865, "is to preserve the force of a living, permeating and controlling Christianity."[137] Evangelical preoccupation with this question tended to decline over time as attention turned to other issues, so that by 1897 the English Baptist leader John Clifford was

---

[132] *Baptist Magazine*, October 1855, pp. 620-25; *Religious Herald*, April 9, 1868.

[133] John Wigley, *The Rise and Fall of the Victorian Sunday* (Manchester: Manchester University Press, 1980), chap. 4.

[134] *Church of England Chronicle*, October 1, 1856, p. 5.

[135] Richard W. Vaudry, *The Free Church in Victorian Canada, 1844-1861* (Waterloo, Ontario: Wilfrid Laurier University Press, 1989), p. 70.

[136] *Witness* (Edinburgh), February 20, 1850; cf. Timothy Larsen, *Friends of Religious Equality: Nonconformist Politics in Mid-Victorian England* (Woodbridge, U.K.: Boydell Press, 1999), pp. 189-206.

[137] *Examiner and Chronicle*, April 6, 1865.

happy to attend a political rally on a Sunday,[138] but it could outcrop whenever there were local challenges to the sanctity of the Lord's Day. The defense of the Christian sabbath was a crusading question.

A second issue that stirred even more visceral feeling was anti-Catholicism. For evangelicals, as the evidence of resistance to ritualism and the association of Rome with antichrist has already suggested,[139] the Catholic Church seemed a sinister and dangerous force. Memories of Reformation struggles remained fresh, with the English Nonconformist historian John Stoughton imagining on his deathbed in 1897 that he was being persecuted by Roman Catholics.[140] When, in 1850, the Catholic hierarchy was restored in England and Wales for the first time since the sixteenth century, evangelicals participated fully in an outburst of strident opposition, fueled by traditional prejudice and political exploitation of the issue. The London Board of Baptist Ministers protested against "the efforts which are made by the Roman pontiff to regain his former ascendancy in this Kingdom, since of all intolerant and persecuting powers popery has ever shown itself the most despotic and cruel."[141] Rivalry for souls led to continuing confrontations such as when, in 1858, Catholics threw stones at an Anglican clergyman preaching in the open air in Manchester or when, in the early 1870s, priests in Las Vegas issued threats in order to deter their flock from attending a Presbyterian school just opened in the town.[142] The sense of competition was particularly acute in Ireland, where Catholic dominance over vast tracts of the island seemed almost impervious to evangelism. The people of the province of Connaught, according to the *Irish Presbyterian* in 1853, were "the poorest, the most ignorant, the most servile and degraded in Europe. They are what Rome has made them."[143] Wherever Irish Protestants immigrated, whether to Ontario, the Cape or New South Wales, they reinforced anti-Catholicism; and wherever the diaspora of Irish Catholics was to be found, its members provoked Protestant alarm. The New York Methodist newspaper recognized with dismay "the power of Irish Papists" in the state's Democratic

---

[138] *Christian World*, March 25, 1897, p. 10.

[139] See chap. 5, pp. 154-58, and chap. 6, p. 197.

[140] *Christian World*, November 4, 1897, p. 14.

[141] *Baptist Magazine*, February 1851, p. 108.

[142] *Occasional Paper*, 53 (London: Church Pastoral Aid Society, April 1858), p. 7.

[143] *Irish Presbyterian* (Belfast), March 1853, p. 82.

Party in 1876 and four years later highlighted the extent of criminality among immigrant Catholics.[144] So the era was prolific in Protestant organizations dedicated to bringing the gospel to Catholics, resisting their political claims or some mixture of the two.[145] Anti-Catholicism may have been at its peak around the middle of the century, but it retained much of its powerful appeal throughout the period.

A further cause that aroused militancy was the sexual exploitation of women and children. Evangelicals tried to rescue prostitutes from their trade and set up homes for their rehabilitation such as the Sydney Female Refuge. There was a need, said an evangelical newspaper in the city, for "a secure public virtue" on this subject.[146] Josephine Butler's Anti-Contagious Diseases Acts Movement aimed to create exactly that in Britain, demanding that prostitutes should not be treated like cattle while their male customers were excused. This was not a subject, Butler's supporters argued, that could be ignored through a delicate reticence on sexual matters. "There is no public sin," according to Robertson Nicoll while still a Free Church minister, "of which a Christian man can lawfully say, 'What is that to me'?"[147] In 1885 there was an electrifying campaign to call for the raising of the legal age of consent to sexual relations from its low level of thirteen. W. T. Stead, a brilliant journalist and a Congregationalist, ran a series of articles on "The Maiden Tribute of Modern Babylon," went in disguise to show how easy it was to procure a young girl for immoral purposes and, attended by huge publicity, found himself imprisoned for his pains. Parliament duly passed a measure raising the age of consent to sixteen. Although some thought Stead's methods outrageous, evangelicals were in the vanguard of those who demanded action on what was called "social purity." A National Vigilance Committee and a Gospel Purity Association were established to sustain public pressure on questions of sexual morality. The private lives of politicians were exposed to fresh scrutiny for signs of personal lapse.[148] In America similar ac-

---

[144] *Christian Advocate*, September 7, 1876, p. 284; January 22, 1880, p. 57.

[145] Ray Allen Billington, *The Protestant Crusade* (New York: Macmillan, 1938); John Wolffe, *The Protestant Crusade in Great Britain, 1829-1860* (Oxford: Clarendon Press, 1988).

[146] *Christian Advocate and Wesleyan Record*, March 31, 1859, p. 162.

[147] *Christian*, March 25, 1880, p. 5.

[148] David W. Bebbington, *The Nonconformist Conscience: Chapel and Politics, 1870-1914* (London: George Allen & Unwin, 1982), pp. 44-45.

tivities fell under the aegis of the Women's Christian Temperance Union, which was largely responsible for the raising of the age of consent in several states to sixteen.[149] One of a pair of WCTU emissaries to South Africa in 1891 lectured on "the difficult and delicate department of Social Purity." It was shameful, declared the local *Christian Express,* "that the man who sins . . . is received in society and allowed, or invited, to associate with the innocent and the unclean."[150] The message, though sometimes distasteful to the fastidious, could stir people to the defense of the Christian home.

THE TEMPERANCE MOVEMENT

The strongest of the sustained agitations of the period, however, was on the drink question. The temperance movement had originated in the 1820s, initially attracting greater support in the United States than in Britain. In its early years it concentrated more on opposing distilled spirits than on condemning beer or wine, but by midcentury most of its supporters were total abstainers. Gradually teetotalism gained ground among evangelicals, but not without resistance. Many feared it was another gospel, offering a path to self-improvement independent of personal faith. Sometimes abstinence meetings were held at the same time as worship, so that teetotallers were accused of "doing much to frustrate and hinder the progress of vital godliness."[151] There was often heavy lay involvement in the liquor trade. A Belfast Presbytery report in 1853 found that 210 public houses in the city were kept by seat-holders in Presbyterian churches (and of those, seventy-eight sold spirits on the Lord's Day).[152] Ministers also enjoyed a drink, with the London Baptist Association declining to abandon wine for its dinners as late as 1880.[153] Although most Anglicans of higher social status and many Presbyterians in America continued to resist total abstinence, by the later years of the century there was strong church endorsement of the temperance movement. A Congregationalist preached in Auckland in 1870 on "Drunkenness, the sin of the colonies"; four years earlier the main Methodist newspaper in the United States had recommended abstinence as

---

[149]Bordin, *Woman and Temperance,* pp. 110-11.

[150]*Christian Express,* October 1, 1891, p. 154.

[151]*Occasional Paper,* 77 (Church Pastoral Aid Society, April 1866), p. 6.

[152]*Irish Presbyterian* (Belfast), June 1854, p. 161.

[153]*Christian,* February 26, 1880, p. 13. "Union" must be an error for "Association."

probably the best course; and in 1871 a review in its Baptist counterpart contended that "appeals for moderate drinking, as a remedy or preventive against intemperance, are a waste of breath."[154] Young people were particularly targeted for antialcohol propaganda. In answer to the question of whether parents should encourage their children to become members of juvenile abstinence societies, the Nova Scotia Baptist newspaper, citing a Scottish source, replied in 1850 with a definite yes: "as *abstainers,* your children will not only be safer, *but . . . they are likely to be more successful in the world.*"[155] As a result of instilling the message into the young, the Christian temperance movement steadily gathered force as the century wore on.

The aim of putting away drink became, for many evangelicals, a cause second only to that of preaching the gospel itself. "As a moral evil," thundered a Free Church of Scotland report on drunkenness in 1869, "being a sin against God, it differs from every other sin, and exceeds them all in its direful effects, for it is the only sin which is the direct voluntary extinction of reason. . . . It is the main cause of poverty, crime, insanity, ignorance, and numerous other evils."[156] Yet those who agreed that drunkenness was so high on the scale of iniquities did not necessarily hold that total abstinence was to be enforced within the churches. In India in 1850, a Methodist minister working among soldiers stationed at Bangalore found that zealous teetotallers tried to impose their practice on candidates for society tickets and had to be told that, though there must be no overindulgence in strong drink, members need not pledge themselves to abstinence.[157] The question of whether moderate drinkers could remain in communion came to trouble many denominations. The Dutch Reformed Church in the Cape, where many church members cultivated the vine, was riven by a dispute on the subject in 1877 and again at intervals afterward.[158] The further question of whether wine should continue to be used at Communion also agitated a large number of the churches. Jesus had commanded his followers to

---

[154] *Christian Observer* (Christchurch), February 1, 1870, p. 30; *Christian Advocate,* January 25, 1866, p. 28; *Examiner and Chronicle,* January 5, 1871.

[155] *Christian Messenger,* January 4, 1850, p. 1.

[156] *Free Church of Scotland Report of the Committee on Temperance, May 1869* (Edinburgh: Free Church of Scotland, 1869), p. 1.

[157] Thomas Cryer in *Wesleyan Methodist Magazine* (London), September 1850, p. 994.

[158] du Plessis, *Andrew Murray,* 360-64; *Christian Express,* October 1, 1877, pp. 5-6.

drink wine, urged traditionalists; not so, said reformers, he had merely directed them to drink the "fruit of the vine," which could be unfermented.[159] In 1872 the Alleghany Christian Temperance Alliance was urging that alcohol was unnecessary for the rite and exposed participants to undue temptation.[160] By eight years later the General Conference of the Methodist Episcopal Church had determined that unfermented wine should be used at its services.[161] Before the end of the century the practice became almost universal outside Anglicanism and a few sets of traditionalists. The culture of temperance found a home within the churches.

The primary aim of the movement was always to persuade the population to abandon strong drink voluntarily. That was equally the aim of Bands of Hope for the young and the Blue Ribbon Gospel Union for adults. Nearly all the immigrants disembarking from a ship arriving in Queensland in 1886 were sporting the blue ribbons of this organization to show that they had chosen to be Christian teetotallers.[162] Yet most temperance advocates were by no means content with moral suasion alone, wanting to add the force of law to their struggle. In 1851 the state of Maine enacted the prohibition of alcohol, providing a model for other states and countries to imitate. The measure received widespread evangelical endorsement. The Methodist Episcopal Church, for example, issued official tracts called *Six Reasons for the Maine-Law* and *The Maine-Law: A Christian Law.*[163] Pressure from the Women's Christian Temperance Union, the Prohibition Party (from 1869) and the Anti-Saloon League (from 1895), all led and supported chiefly by members of evangelical denominations, swayed states and counties to limit or abolish the drink trade. It could be a risky business, since so much profit came from manufacturing and selling liquor. Thus a Methodist minister in Iowa was shot down while trying to enforce the state's prohibition law, and the reported aftermath is revealing: when his assassin was tried and acquitted, the jury was feasted by local brewers.[164] There were equivalent prohibitionist efforts elsewhere. In England the United Kingdom Alli-

---

[159] *Christian,* April 8, 1880, p. 12.

[160] *Rocky Mountain Presbyterian,* December 1872.

[161] *Christian Advocate,* August 19, 1880, p. 537.

[162] *Intercolonial Christian Messenger,* March 26, 1886, p. 823.

[163] *Christian Advocate and Journal* (New York), January 27, 1853, p. 14.

[164] *Freeman,* January 20, 1888, p. 39.

ance tried without success to induce parliament to allow localities a vote on whether to go dry; in New Zealand there was a similar Permissive Bill; and in West Africa Bishop Tugwell demanded official limits on the import of spirits for the sake of Africans and Europeans alike.[165] But it was in America that the agitation became most powerful, eventually resulting, in the aftermath of the First World War, in the passing of the Eighteenth Amendment to the constitution that, until its repeal in 1933, imposed prohibition on the whole of the United States. Already before the end of the nineteenth century it was the legislative goal dearest to many evangelical hearts.

THE SOCIAL GOSPEL

The temperance campaign did a great deal to prepare for the social gospel movement that blossomed toward the end of the century. Previously, it is often supposed, the churches had been silent on most social questions, acquiescing in the undisturbed reign of political economy and the malign consequences of industrialization. It is true that in earlier years mainstream evangelicals had believed that economic laws meshed closely into the tenets of natural theology.[166] Consequently their organs, such as the New York Baptist *Examiner and Chronicle* in 1871, sometimes defended the law of supply and demand against the claims of working men for higher wages.[167] But it has been pointed out that between the 1850s and the 1870s there was a great deal of debate about the application of Christian thought to economic questions, with many commentators questioning received maxims.[168] Thus the English Congregational editor and politician Edward Miall urged the future organization of trade on "the highest and most unselfish principles endorsed by Christianity."[169] Despite his pietistic ten-

---

[165]Brian Harrison, *Drink and the Victorians: The Temperance Question in England, 1815-1872* (London: Faber & Faber, 1971), chaps. 9-10; *Christian Observer* (Christchurch), January 1, 1870, p. 8; *Record*, March 30, 1899, p. 336.

[166]Boyd Hilton, *The Age of Atonement: The Influence of Evangelicalism on Social and Economic Thought, 1785-1865* (Oxford: Clarendon Press, 1988), chaps. 2-5.

[167]*Examiner and Chronicle*, February 9, 1871.

[168]Jane Garnett, "The Gospel of Work and the Virgin Mary: Catholics, Protestants and Work in the Nineteenth Century," in *The Use and Abuse of Time in Christian History*, ed. R. N. Swanson (Woodbridge, U.K.: Boydell Press, 2002).

[169]Edward Miall, *An Editor off the Line: Or Wayside Musings and Reminiscences* (London: Arthur Miall, 1865), p. 100.

dencies, the Evangelical Anglican William Pennefather was willing to denounce money hoarding and spending on personal indulgences, often giving serious offense.[170] In 1865 the *Examiner and Chronicle*, notwithstanding its later backing for economic principle, argued in the manner of later social gospelers that Christianity must influence the sanitary arrangements of great cities since, in the light of the incarnation, God puts a high estimate on the worth of the body.[171] "Neither Jesus nor his apostles," concurred the *Christian* in 1880, "ever separated the physical from the spiritual well-being of men."[172] Even before the emergence of the social gospel, evangelical voices were raised in criticism of existing economic practice and in favor of improved welfare measures.

The accumulating ills of urban-industrial society, however, led to a quickening of the pace of Christian social critique during the 1880s. Much of it came from figures outside the evangelical movement. In England the major force was the Christian Social Union (1889) led by the High-Church Bishop B. F. Westcott, and in America the Episcopal economist Richard T. Ely was in the vanguard. The most characteristic doctrine of the social gospelers, that the kingdom of God was to be realized by social improvement, was derived primarily from the German liberal theologian Albrecht Ritschl. There were anxieties among more conservative evangelicals that truth was being compromised. "The humanitarian or 'social gospel'," warned the *Christian* in 1892, "is by itself not a gospel. The Gospel has always antagonised social evils by regenerating the hearts and minds of individual men. But its social aspects are not primary, but secondary. Its first appeal to man is as a sinner needing redemption."[173] Yet a great deal of the impetus for the social gospel movement came from evangelicals. T. B. Stephenson, a Wesleyan minister who pioneered welfare services for children, as president of the conference in 1892 urged Methodist voters to support progressive change. "Social improvement," he declared, "could never be substituted for the Gospel, but reforms that made life possible must prepare the way for Christ."[174] Hugh Price Hughes, a Wesleyan colleague of Stephen-

---

[170]Robert Braithwaite, *The Life and Letters of the Rev. William Pennefather, B. A.* (London: John F. Shaw & Co., 1878), p. 426.

[171]*Examiner and Chronicle*, March 23, 1865.

[172]*Christian*, January 8, 1880, p. 13.

[173]*Christian*, June 9, 1892, p. 8.

[174]*British Weekly* (London), February 4, 1892, p. 244.

son's and the most flamboyant of British social gospelers, insisted that, whatever
social themes were taken up on other occasions at his West London Mission,
the evening services were strictly evangelistic. His admirers in Canada wanted
to copy his combination of social engagement with evangelism.[175] There was
much agreement in America that the gospel was primarily a matter of spiritual
salvation, but that under modern conditions it was also necessary to strive for
social reform.[176] In its origins the social gospel movement was in large part a
broadening expression of evangelicalism.

A prominent feature of the social gospel was its eagerness to address the issues of contemporary society, and especially those concerning the poor. In
1895 the American *Methodist Review* carried "A Study in Sociology," and four
years later John Clifford, the leading British Baptist social gospeler, wrote that
"sociological questions are Divine questions."[177] The remedy for social problems was often seen, especially in Britain and her colonies, as greater state action. The English Congregationalist R. W. Dale had embraced a much higher
doctrine of the state than most of his contemporaries and the many whom he
influenced were less reluctant to witness a growth of collectivism.[178] Another
facet was an assault on received beliefs about political economy, which, it was
now claimed on both sides of the Atlantic, did not have universal validity.[179]
New economic views allowing greater flexibility in meeting the demands of
working men were required. Counsels, however, were divided. At the 1893 autumn assembly of the Congregational Union of England and Wales, in the wake
of a period of strikes, R. F. Horton proposed a resolution urging mutual for-
bearance between capital and labor. He argued that the premises of political
economy could not be granted by Christians, but that instead the law of Christ

---

[175]Phyllis D. Airhart, *Serving the Present Age: Revivalism, Progressivism and the Methodist Tradition in Canada* (Montreal & Kingston: McGill-Queen's University Press, 1992), p. 75.

[176]David Kinley, "The Relation of the Church to Social Reform," *Bibliotheca Sacra* (July 1893), p. 392.

[177]E. D. McCreary in *Methodist Review* (New York), November 1895, pp. 861-76; John Clifford, *God's Greater Britain* (London: James Clarke & Co., 1899), p. 136.

[178]David M. Thompson, "The Emergence of the Nonconformist Social Gospel in England," in *Protestant Evangelicalism: Britain, Ireland, Germany and America, c. 1750-c. 1950*, ed.
Keith Robbins (Oxford: Basil Blackwell, 1990), pp. 276-77.

[179]*Congregationalist* (London), November 1884, pp. 920-25; A. G. Fradenburgh in *Methodist Review*, May 1895, pp. 423-29.

should govern industrial questions. An amendment was put forward by the leading denominational firebrand, Fleming Williams, that "the rights of humanity must always take precedence over those of property." Inadequate wages, he insisted, were inconsistent with the principle of righteousness. But then a London merchant called O'Neill rose to object that many employers were Christian men who were anxious to pay whatever they could afford. Despite O'Neill's intervention, the amendment was carried and the amended resolution passed unanimously.[180] The victory of the radical prescription on this occasion says nothing about the relative strength of opinion, but the episode sheds light on a three-way split among those sympathetic to the social gospel. There was the progressive middle way, represented by Horton, that deeply wished to conciliate labor; there existed a much smaller radical group, represented by Fleming Williams, that wanted economic reconstruction on something like socialist principles; and there were conservative figures like O'Neill who, though sometimes willing to engage with social problems, were not prepared to challenge existing economic practice. The division among American social gospelers followed much the same lines.[181]

The practical outworking of the social gospel took many forms. The settlement movement, begun in Chicago in 1889 by the Presbyterian ex-Quaker Jane Addams, erected centers where well-to-do philanthropists could live in the midst of urban squalor.[182] The Salvation Army was captured for social reform when, in 1890, the newspaperman W. T. Stead ghostwrote *In Darkest England and the Way Out* for General Booth. The Army remained ever afterward a champion of Christian social service.[183] During the 1890s Walter Rauschenbusch, later the leading theologian of the social gospel movement, threw himself into efforts to better the conditions of the poor in New York City at the same time as developing his theoretical perspectives.[184] Hugh Price Hughes launched the Wesleyan West London Mission in 1887 as a showpiece of social Christianity.

---

[180] *Christian World*, October 19, 1893, pp. 807-8.

[181] Robert T. Handy, ed., *The Social Gospel in America, 1870-1920* (New York: Oxford University Press, 1966), pp. 3-16.

[182] Jane Addams, *Twenty Years at Hull-House with Autobiographical Notes* (New York: Macmillan, 1910).

[183] Walker, *Pulling the Devil's Kingdom Down*, pp. 236-41.

[184] W. S. Hudson, "Walter Rauschenbusch and the New Evangelism," *Religion in Life* 30 (1961).

At its opening he declared that he agreed with George Eliot's charge that evangelicals were guilty of otherworldliness. "The salvation of the individual soul was not sufficient. Society must be saved as well as Christians."[185] Hughes's efforts were replicated in Sydney, where the Centenary Hall was opened in the following year. There were eleven open-air services a week, visits to hospitals and a Deaf, Dumb and Blind Asylum, three cottage prayer meetings, eight large classes, a mothers' meeting, a working man's meeting, a workers' conference, a seaman's institute, a working man's club, a boys' club, a musical department, a seamen's mission, an evangelists' home, a sisters' home, a religious bookstall and an employment agency. Centenary Hall aimed at "caring for the bodies as for the souls of men."[186] And John Clifford pursued his vision of a better society into advanced political circles. By 1898 he was recommending socialism unequivocally. "Only," he wrote, "when the people own or control the necessary instruments of production in the large industries will the formal be translated into substantial freedom."[187] Just as the American social gospel provided inspiration for Progressivism in politics, so Clifford laid some of the intellectual foundations for the Labour Party in Britain during subsequent years.

During the second half of the nineteenth century, evangelicals did a great deal to shape their societies. Since they were so numerous and active, they could often sway the direction of change in the English-speaking world. In various respects their influence was exerted in a restrictive way. Women were expected to find fulfillment in the home rather than in a wider setting; in many places the gospel came to be associated with white domination; and evangelicals put the theater and gambling under the ban. Work and pleasure on Sunday were alike condemned; Roman Catholicism was sternly opposed; sexual wrongdoing was denounced; and drink was increasingly attacked as the root of all evil. Yet that negative program by no means represents the whole of the evangelical impact on society. Women found an outlet for their energies in the life of the churches, whether as carers, moneyraisers or teachers, and some of them were propelled into prominence by their Christian activities. White evangelicals continued to

---

[185] *Christian World*, October 27, 1887, p. 810; cf. Christopher Oldstone-Moore, *Hugh Price Hughes: Founder of a New Methodism, Conscience of a New Nonconformity* (Cardiff: University of Wales Press, 1999).

[186] James Caldwell in *Spectator and Methodist Chronicle*, January 23, 1891, p. 88.

[187] *Christian World*, January 20, 1898, p. 9.

defend oppressed people of other races while black evangelicals established flourishing churches as bastions of their culture. Evangelicals created entertainment, sports and literature of their own that would conform to gospel standards. Economic life was always subjected to critical scrutiny and, at the end of the period, the social gospel set up a new wave of agencies for welfare work and made an idealistic contribution to politics. The social gospelers were trying to do no less than Christianize society as a whole. If evangelicals were hostile to whatever they judged to be wrong, they also threw themselves into efforts to advance the causes they endorsed. Many of their ventures proved formative not only at the time but also long into the succeeding century.

8

THE DOMINANCE OF EVANGELICALISM

This exploration of the life and thought of evangelicals during the later nineteenth century has suggested that they continued to display much of the vigor they had inherited from the evangelical revival. They were still concerned above all with the cultivation of vital Christianity. Their spirituality, as chapter three illustrated, was centered on Christ as Savior. They made much of prayer, not just as individuals but also in corporate gatherings. Family prayers almost constituted a badge of the movement. Evangelicals taught that life was a sustained conflict with sin, but that beyond death beckoned the consolations of heaven. All this gave their religion a depth, a seriousness and a dynamic. Their worship showed enormous variety, but in this heterogeneity lay one of their strengths. There was a style of service for every taste, whether the preference was for the structured liturgy of the *Book of Common Prayer*, the quiet reflection of a Quaker meeting or the impromptu choruses of African American communities. Somewhere in between lay the most common pattern, with its hymns, prayers and substantial sermon. Variety was also a feature of their missionary methods. Much evangelism must have been of an informal kind, but a great deal was carefully planned through district visitors, paid agents and elaborate organizations, all equipped with abundant literature. Social work demonstrated that concern for others was genuine, while Sunday school and other youth organizations ensured that the rising generation heard the gospel. Revivals supplemented regular church methods and overseas missions set an example of sustained outreach. The whole spirit of the movement was expansive. Wherever settlers moved, evangelists followed, often hard on their heels. Thus a Congregational home missionary in Minnesota could report in 1857 that three-quarters of the houses in his vicinity had been erected only in the last three months. There could be no schools or meeting houses until there were saw mills, but already worship was held in private homes. The aim was "the salvation of many sinners in this 'Far West'."[1] The evangelical movement maintained much of its earlier vitality.

DOMINANCE IN CHURCH AND CULTURE

Continuing evangelistic energy enabled the churches to grow between the middle and the end of the nineteenth century. The Free Churches of England and Wales, which were overwhelmingly evangelical, increased from roughly 1,021,000 members in 1850 to 1,803,000 in 1900. Although the Free Churches grew less than the population from the 1880s onward, this degree of expansion represents no mean achievement. Similarly the Scottish Presbyterian denominations almost doubled from 603,000 members in 1850 to 1,164,000 in 1900.[2] In the United States the figures are even more impressive, though they need to be qualified by the recollection that the American population was mushrooming from 23 million in 1850 to 76 million in 1900. Methodists increased from rather over 1,250,000 to about 5,500,000 members over the second half of the nineteenth century. Baptists rose from about 750,000 to about 4,500,000.[3] Canadian statistics, available for the whole nation only from 1871, show growth from 578,000 Methodist adherents in that year to 917,000 in 1901, a pace of increase closer to the slower British rate.[4] Statistics from the southern hemisphere, starting from a low base, are the most striking of all. Presbyterians in New South Wales, according to census self-identification, went from 18,000 in 1851 to 133,000 half a century later; and Methodists in the same colony rose from 10,000 to

---

[1] *American Missionary* (New York), January 1857, pp. 6-7.
[2] Robert Currie, Alan Gilbert and Lee Horsley, *Churches and Churchgoers: Patterns of Church Growth in the British Isles since 1700* (Oxford: Clarendon Press, 1977), p. 25.
[3] E. S. Gaustad and P. L. Barlow, *New Historical Atlas of Religion in America* (New York: Oxford University Press, 2001), p. 374.
[4] M. C. Urquhart and K. A. H. Buckley, eds., *Historical Statistics of Canada* (Cambridge: University Press, 1965), p. 18.

138,000.[5] In New Zealand numbers of professing Methodists increased from 3,000 to 84,000 between 1851 and 1901.[6] What is clear is that, even setting aside the emergence of new Christian communities on the mission field, the period represented a time of sustained expansion for the global evangelical movement.

The evangelical faith naturally occupied a strong position within the ecclesiastical world. The salience of evangelicalism in England is often obscured by its relative weakness in the established church. The Evangelical party in the Church of England was no longer, as in the first half of the century, advancing relative to other types of churchmanship. Historians of the period tend to stress the growth of Broad-Church opinion and the progress of High-Church practices, especially among the advanced ritualists. It is certainly the case that after a brief spell in the 1850s when Evangelicals were favored for appointment as bishops, they ceased to be represented strongly on the episcopal bench.[7] Likewise in America the central theme in the church history of the later nineteenth century is normally the supplanting of evangelicalism by more liberal theological views. The replacement at Andover Seminary, the largest institution training Congregational ministers, of an evangelical regime by the "Andover liberals" between 1863 and 1881 is sometimes taken as a symbol of a change in the theological temper of America at large.[8] Both these images, however, represent a distortion of the overall picture. In England the Broad and High Churchmen, together with non-Anglicans holding broader theologies, and the liberals in the United States were to hold the ascendancy in the future, but that was not until after the beginning of the twentieth century. At the time the global position was that, except in the Church of England and a few other Anglican bodies such as the Church of

---

[5] Wray Vamplew, ed., *Australians: Historical Statistics* (Broadway, U.K.: Fairfax, Syme & Weldon Associates, 1987), p. 421. As with the other statistics in this paragraph, the figures are rounded to the nearest thousand. Figures for South Africa, where the first overall census took place in 1904, are not readily available.

[6] *Statistics of New Zealand for the Crown Colony Period; 1840-1852* (Auckland: Department of Economics, Auckland University College, 1954); *Census of Population and Dwellings* (Wellington: Government Printer, 1903).

[7] Nigel Scotland, *"Good and Proper Men": Lord Palmerston and the Bench of Bishops* (Cambridge: James Clarke 2000), pp. 180-81.

[8] Daniel Day Williams, *The Andover Liberals: A Study in American Theology* (New York: King's Crown Press, 1941).

the Province of South Africa, the evangelicals were the party in possession of the field. Their numbers outstripped those of their rivals within the churches. Methodists, Baptists and Presbyterians, all overwhelmingly evangelical at the grassroots, rather than the much more theologically mixed Anglicans, showed the great advances of the period. It was evangelicalism that was the cutting edge of Christian numerical progress during the late nineteenth century.

There were other signs of vitality besides growth. New bodies within the evangelical sector bore witness to its continuing vibrancy. The recently formed Brethren played a part among evangelicals out of all proportion to their still relatively low numbers, setting the trend in revivalist evangelism and dispensational thought alike. The Churches of Christ, another creation of the earlier nineteenth century, increasingly functioned within rather than on the edge of the evangelical world. Black churches in the American South turned during the later 1860s from a small number of congregations into dynamic bodies strongly representing the identity of their members, and by the 1890s the same process was beginning in South Africa. Methodist fragmentation continued in the Old World with the withdrawal of the United Methodist Free Churches and Wesleyan Reform Union. In America a similar process led, in 1860, to the creation of the Free Methodists and, from the 1880s, to the emergence of several energetic new holiness bodies. The Salvation Army, with its remarkable worldwide spread, was a result of the same impetus. What is more, even the High-Church tendency within Anglicanism could not avoid being tarred with the evangelical brush during these years. Several High Churchmen such as Bishop George Howard Wilkinson deliberately tried to integrate evangelical priorities with their elevated sense of the dignity of the visible church; other Anglo-Catholics took up revivalist missions on the evangelical model, except that they called for frequent Communion rather than immediate conversion.[9] So powerful were evangelical currents that they spilled over into other brands of churchmanship.

Another symptom of evangelical dominance can be seen in the relationship between the gospel and the secular culture, especially in the earlier years of the period. The legacy of the Enlightenment was pervasive in society at large, and evangelicalism, as chapter four revealed, shared much common ground with it.

---

[9]Dieter Voll, *Catholic Evangelicalism: The Acceptance of Evangelical Traditions by the Oxford Movement during the Second Half of the Nineteenth Century* (London: Faith Press, 1963), pp. 53-74; John Kent, *Holding the Fort: Studies in Victorian Revivalism* (London: Epworth Press, 1978), chap. 7.

Although midcentury evangelicals resisted the onslaught of rationalism, they stoutly championed the values associated with the use of reason. They believed in empiricism and scientific endeavour, common sense and Christian evidences. They aspired to self-improvement and commonly respected scholarship. The prevailing form of Calvinism professed in the churches, with its heavy debt to the eighteenth-century theologians of New England, had undergone modifications during the Enlightenment era. The principle of free enquiry persuaded many to discard the Calvinist system altogether. Meanwhile the rival Arminian creed showed distinct affinities with the spirit of the Enlightenment in its optimistic belief that all might be saved. Optimism was equally apparent in the postmillennial view of the future generally espoused by evangelicals and in standard missionary theory, which, though concentrating on the evangelistic imperative, held that commerce would help the spread of the gospel and that civilization would follow in its train. A pragmatic approach to issues, embracing a willingness to adapt inherited ways and ecclesiastical principles, also evinced a mindset deriving from the Enlightenment. Not all Christian bodies were willing to abandon their traditional convictions, and significant numbers of Presbyterians and Baptists in particular clung to older ways of formulating doctrine. In general, however, evangelicals had espoused a modern worldview that closely reflected the prevailing attitudes of the age. The harmony of gospel and culture meant that evangelicalism shared in the persisting intellectual sway of Enlightenment patterns of thought.

Evangelical influence over social life, furthermore, was profound. During the period, as chapter seven showed, evangelical assumptions molded many of the most characteristic features of the age. The role of women as homemakers, though by no means an evangelical invention, was endorsed by the literature of the movement. Conversely, women were encouraged to find fulfillment in the work of the churches through caring ministries, fundraising and educational work. A few such as Frances Willard could even rise to international prominence through their championship of causes defending the home. The opposition of evangelicals to gambling helped limit the cases of family destitution, their sabbatarianism normally ensured a day off for workers and their protests over sexual issues led to greater protection for the vulnerable. Their anti-Catholicism, while sometimes displaying inveterate prejudice and restricting the liberties of their opponents, was an inevitable consequence of the rivalry of vigorous creeds. The efforts of many evangelicals to advance the cause of total abstinence, though leading to further restrictive measures, prevented some of the damage that strong drink might otherwise have wrought. Although many of these efforts were essentially negative, protesting against what was considered wrong, evangelicals also created opportunities for leisure activities such as reading newspapers, drinking coffee and playing sports. They even fostered schools of literature displaying their values. By the end of the century many were venturing into the social gospel, and some of their political prescriptions were taken into subsequent party programs. Throughout the period, furthermore, the language and issues of politics had been shaped by evangelicalism. In the United States, it has been shown, the clash between Northern postmillennial nationalism and Southern theological apologias gave a strongly ideological dimension to the rift that led to Civil War.[10] In Britain the agricultural trade unionists of the 1870s, led by Primitive Methodists, thought of their campaign in biblical terms as a struggle to cast off bondage.[11] Public as well as private life was conditioned by evangelical concerns.

CHANGE AND RESISTANCE

There were nevertheless signs that evangelical hegemony was insecure. The problems of urbanism posed fresh difficulties for the churches. In 1845 Friedrich Engels had given a classic analysis of *The Condition of the Working Class in England*, arguing that cities created a physical separation between classes, so that bourgeois entrepreneurs living in the suburbs could ignore the plight of their workers in the inner cities.[12] In Manchester, the city where Engels formed his views, incumbents of evangelical parishes were finding by 1858 that the more respectable inhabitants were moving to the outskirts.[13] By the 1890s, as the *Irish Presbyterian* explained, people at a lower social level were following the example of the upper middle classes:

---

[10]Richard J. Carwardine, *Evangelicals and Politics in Antebellum America* (New Haven: Yale University Press, 1993).

[11]Nigel Scotland, *Methodism and the Revolt of the Field: A Study of the Methodist Contribution to Agricultural Trade Unionism in East Anglia, 1872-96* (Gloucester: Alan Sutton, 1981).

[12]Friedrich Engels, *The Condition of the Working Class in England*, ed. W. O. Henderson and W. H. Chaloner (Oxford: Blackwell, 1958).

[13]*Occasional Paper*, 53 (London: Church Pastoral Aid Society, April 1858), p. 6.

as soon as a family is "lifted" by means of the Gospel into a better position, owing to new habits of sobriety and thrift, its members naturally desire more wholesome surroundings, both physically and morally. Soon there is a "house to let," and a pew vacant in the neighboring church.[14]

Except in denominations that provided a place of worship in every parish, there was a resulting tendency for churches to follow their affluent attenders to the suburbs, abandoning the inner cities to the slum dwellers. Thus in the north end of Boston, Massachusetts, in 1895 it was noted that two former Methodist churches had been abandoned by their fleeing congregations to immigrant Catholics.[15] Whole sections of cities were deserted by the evangelical denominations. Meanwhile the prosperous citizens on the outskirts might maintain their church allegiance, often lavishing their resources on fine buildings and elaborate facilities, but commonly their attachment was lukewarm. Their churches were of the type denounced by Free Methodists as "cold and formal."[16] It was in such circles as these that inhibitions about dancing and the theater disappeared most rapidly. There might still be evangelical belief, but far less energy was channeled into evangelistic activity. The advance of respectability was responsible for weakening the ability of the movement to recruit.

It was among the respectable that there was the greatest willingness to move on to fresh doctrinal views. The central theme of the intellectual history of the evangelical movement during the period is the growing reception of ideas colored by the Romantic spirit of the times. Part of the process, as chapter five demonstrated, was a gradual shift in evangelical thinking toward higher and broader theological opinions. It is true that Romanticism was closely associated with the rise of ritualism in the Anglican communion that Evangelicals solidly resisted. Yet it is also true that Romantic taste exercised a growing fascination over the evangelicals of the later nineteenth century, especially those who were younger and better educated. They listened to sermons quoting the Lake Poets; they built their churches, if they could afford it, in the Gothic style; and Evangelicals copied Anglo-Catholic innovations such as surpliced choirs. Ideas with a Romantic lineage induced some of them, with Horace Bushnell in the lead,

---

[14]*Irish Presbyterian* (Dublin), February 1895, p. 37.

[15]H. G. Mitchell in *Methodist Review* (New York), March 1895, p. 263.

[16]A. P. Goode in *Free Methodist* (Chicago), January 9, 1884, p. 4.

to broaden their doctrinal position. The Fatherhood of God, a milder view of the atonement and the centrality of the incarnation came into vogue. Eternal punishment faded away, the Bible was studied critically, and evolutionary thought led to a stress on immanence. The net effect of all these trends was to promote a more liberal brand of theology. At first the newer views were stated in ways that normally seemed compatible with evangelical convictions, and in the short run they undoubtedly appealed to many in the growingly prosperous congregations. Gospel and culture were remaining in step. But in the longer term the newer stance was to develop into a version of liberalism that self-consciously diverged from the evangelical faith. The seeds of the modernism of the twentieth century had been sown.

These developments, however, were in some measure balanced by a counter-vailing movement of opinion that was equally affected by the Romantic temper of the times. Fresh modes of stating and practicing the faith, as chapter six argued, fostered a more conservative expression of evangelicalism. One dimension was associated with the faith principle. Embodied in the practice of George Müller, the idea of undertaking some venture in entire dependence on divine provision gathered support as the century wore on. It was applied to finance, to healing and above all to missions. A second aspect was the growth of premillennial teaching. Based on a more literal reading of Scripture, it held that the future was gloomy until the return of Christ should set all to rights. In one form, it fused with anti-Catholicism to create an influential amalgam; in another, it generated the dispensationalism that was to exert a powerful sway over the imagination of many twentieth-century evangelicals. A third current of thought that was to lead primarily in a more conservative direction was the holiness impulse. Drawing on the Methodist tradition of entire sanctification, holiness doctrines were popularized in the period. They generated the Keswick style of teaching, acceptable to those in Reformed traditions, that became the message of a worldwide movement. They also pointed toward the emergence of Pentecostalism. Each of these features, though possessing longer-term antecedents, was stated in a novel form suited to the nineteenth century. Yet each tended to stiffen the theological views of those who embraced them, and they often formed a package that was adopted as a whole. By 1900 Anglican Evangelicals were predominantly Keswick in their spirituality, premillennial in their view of the future and at least respectful toward the faith principle. Theological conservatism was therefore reinforced by the trends of the times almost as much as liberalism. The new doctrines were to be rallying cries within the fundamentalist coalition of the early twentieth century.

The greatest champion of the conservative standpoint during the later nineteenth century was Spurgeon. He had adopted both premillennialism and the faith principle, though his chief allegiance was always to Reformed theology. Already in 1861, in the wake of Baldwin Brown's manifesto for a break with Calvinism,[17] Spurgeon was provoked into action. "Sound an Alarm!" he wrote in the *Baptist Magazine*, rejecting the notion that the gospel could legitimately be altered by Romantic reformulation.[18] "From our inmost souls," he declared six years later, "we loathe all mystic and rationalistic obscurations of the plain and full-orbed doctrines of grace."[19] His detestation of the newfangled teaching extended to the teachers who affected fine ways for the sake of impressing fashionable congregations. " 'Thinking men' of this superfine order," he complained sarcastically in 1871, "consider anything orthodox quite beneath them."[20] Knowing that Congregationalism was more affected by the new opinions than the Baptists, Spurgeon did not bring matters to a head until 1887. In that year, however, one of his students described in Spurgeon's church magazine the "Down Grade" of Dissenting theology during the eighteenth century, and Spurgeon added an article pointing out the similar risks in their own day. When no action was taken at the autumn assembly of the Baptist Union to deal with creeping heresy in its ranks, Spurgeon resigned his membership. Since he was by far its most outstanding personality, the move created consternation. Repeated efforts were made to regain his allegiance and the spring assembly passed a brief declaration of doctrines commonly believed in the affiliated churches. Yet Spurgeon did not return, creating great resentment by declining to name anybody whose views he was censuring. He carried very few members of the Union with him into independency.[21] This "Downgrade Controversy"

---

[17] See chap. 5, p. 166.

[18] *Baptist Magazine* (London), January 1861, pp. 6-11; February 1861, pp. 71-77.

[19] *Outline of the Lord's Work by the Pastor's College and its Kindred Organisations at the Metropolitan Tabernacle* (London: Passmore & Alabaster, 1867), p. 14.

[20] *Annual Paper descriptive of the Lord's Work connected with the Pastors' College during the Year 1870* (London: Passmore & Alabaster, 1871), p. 7.

[21] Mark Hopkins, *Nonconformity's Romantic Generation: Evangelical and Liberal Theologies in Victorian England* (London: Paternoster Press, 2004), chap. 7.

was a shot across the bow of the liberal tendencies of the times, an indication of the serious disquiet felt in some quarters over the moving of the historic landmarks of the faith.

Many of the anxieties of the more conservative began to focus on attitudes to the Bible. The advances of higher criticism among Christian scholars, particularly rapid during the decade from 1885, provoked growing alarm. The dyke erected by the condemnation of Robertson Smith in 1881 seemed to have been breached.[22] Some worries were voiced in relatively restrained terms. Thus in 1891 the editor of the Canadian Methodist newspaper set out a reasoned account of why he was concerned that "some of the 'results' of the higher criticism" tended to undermine the authority of the Bible.[23] Others, such as a New Hampshire Methodist writing in 1897, were more outspoken:

> The battle of the ages is raging. Satanic forces concentrate their attack against Christ, the incarnated word, and the Bible, the written word of God. . . . In this crisis the critics offer a Bible which is only literature, only the word and work of man.[24]

Here was a shrill form of protofundamentalism. In England books written by members of evangelical denominations about the Bible that seemed unsound were held up to similar censure. In 1892 the international evangelist Henry Varley denounced them in *The Infallible Word*, which even a sympathetic reviewer had to admit was marked by "heat of spirit and use of expletives."[25] A Bible League was organized in the same year, supported by a knot of people associated with the Mildmay holiness convention and Spurgeon's side in the Downgrade affair. The revivalist weekly the *Christian* might comment that the Bible needed no defense, but some were beginning to think otherwise.[26] A Bible League of North America was to be set up in 1903 and *The Fundamentals*, the joint American-British series of pamphlets setting out the basics of evangelical faith that was to give its name to fundamentalism, were to appear between 1910 and 1915.[27] Organized fundamentalism was making its first appearance around

---

[22]See chap. 5, pp. 175-76.

[23]*Christian Guardian* (Toronto), August 5, 1891, p. 488.

[24]C. Munger in *Christian Advocate* (New York), February 25, 1897, p. 132.

[25]James Douglas in *Christian* (London), July 14, 1892, p. 8.

[26]*Christian*, May 12, 1892, p. 7; February 13, 1896, p. 26.

[27]George M. Marsden, *Fundamentalism and American Culture: The Shaping of Twentieth-Century Evangelicalism, 1870-1925* (New York: Oxford University Press, 1980), p. 118.

the end of the nineteenth century, but it made very little impact until well into the twentieth.

UNITY ACROSS THE WORLD

It remained true at the end of the period, as at its beginning, that the main body of the evangelical movement possessed a self-conscious unity. Although conservative and liberal trends were very apparent, actual polarization along fundamentalist-modernist lines lay in the future. The evangelical denominational groups were but regiments in a single army. Anglicans might be more churchy, Presbyterians more intellectual, Methodists more exuberant, Baptists more rigid and Congregationalists more open, but they knew that they shared the same gospel. *The Evangelical Free Church Catechism*, issued in 1899 by a representative National Council for England and Wales, was able to state "the Christian doctrines held in common by all Evangelical Free Churches."[28] By the last years of the century, it is true, there was some weakening of the earlier insistence on conversion among the more liberal, but there was no actual tendency to schism over the issue. In America, Moody, whose death did not take place until 1898, devoted considerable energy to keeping together the evangelical coalition that supported his missions. His prophetic views placed him firmly in the conservative camp, and yet he stoutly defended the right of his broad-minded Scottish friend Henry Drummond to speak at the Northfield conference.[29] While personally disagreeing with higher criticism, Moody deplored the "bad temper and personal recriminations" of some of those who denounced the enterprise.[30] Similarly, in the 1890s and even beyond there was little or no divergence over the desirability of social work among evangelicals. F. B. Meyer, a leading English Baptist, regularly spoke at Keswick and yet also coordinated the social witness of the National Free Church Council in the years before the First World War.[31] His conservative American coreligionist A. C. Dixon, serving from

---

[28] *An Evangelical Free Church Catechism for Use in Home and School* (London: National Council of the Evangelical Free Churches, 1899), p. 6.

[29] G. A. Smith, *The Life of Henry Drummond*, 2nd ed. (London: Hodder & Stoughton, 1899), p. 421.

[30] G. A. Smith in *Dwight L. Moody: Impressions and Facts*, ed. Henry Drummond (New York: McClure, Philips, 1900), p. 28.

[31] Ian Randall, *Spirituality and Social Change: The Contribution of F. B. Meyer (1847-1929)* (Carlisle: Paternoster Press, 2003).

1901 as minister of Ruggles Street Baptist Church in Boston, Massachusetts, launched a campaign to reach the poor through social work. It was only while there that he began to look askance at the Boston Baptist Social Union on account of its neglect of the spiritual. After three years Dixon decided to abandon social work entirely.[32] The typical disparagement by fundamentalists of concern for physical welfare was only just beginning as the twentieth century opened. Down to 1900 what would later be called holistic mission was part of the agreed program of evangelicalism.

The unity of the evangelical movement was not just within particular lands but a global phenomenon. In the introduction to the *Evangelical Free Church Catechism*, Hugh Price Hughes claimed that its contents represented the beliefs of "not less, and probably many more, than sixty millions of avowed Christians in all parts of the world."[33] Including the converts of the missionary movement, his estimate was probably not far wrong. The evangelicals were often aware of forming a single movement that spanned the world. In 1870, for instance, the first issue of the New Zealand *Christian Observer* included news (in this order) from Australia, England, Scotland, Ireland, America and what was called "General," covering, on this occasion, Spain, Paris and Bombay.[34] It is true that, as chapter two has shown, there was a great deal of diversity within the global movement, for national variations were marked. Yet the growing web of international communications bound the various countries together. The flow of families, individuals and ideas kept up links between places on opposite sides of the world, so that, for example, when, in 1892, the Methodists of Canada began to recognize the gravity of their urban problems, they turned to British Methodists "to profit by your experience and example."[35] Denominational connections, as in this case, tended to reduce the force of national distinctiveness. There was still, too, a degree of colonial dependency at work. "We are much influenced in our church life in these colonies," remarked the *Methodist Journal* of South Australia in 1874, "by the example set us by the churches of the Father-

---

[32]Helen C. A. Dixon, *A. C. Dixon: A Romance of Preaching* (New York: G. P. Putnam's Sons, 1931), pp. 154-56.

[33]*Evangelical Free Church Catechism*, p. 6.

[34]*Christian Observer* (Christchurch), January 1, 1870, p. 15.

[35]*Minutes of Several Conversations . . . of the People called Methodists . . . 1892* (London: Wesleyan Methodist Book Room, 1890), p. 394.

land in spiritual advancement and Christian enterprise."[36] But even where there was no denominational or colonial bond, evangelicals of different lands drew on the common fund of literature circulating around the world. That is why parallel developments, as this book has documented, could take place so often in different parts of the English-speaking world. Despite the real contrasts between expressions of evangelicalism in the various lands, it is the unity of the movement that is most striking.

Furthermore, fissures within countries could sometimes be as sharp as—or sharper than—those between them. Social contrasts loomed large in the period, marking off classes from one another in terms of wealth, status and education. Those who aspired to an urbane respectability differed markedly from those who did not. The elite of New York had similar attitudes to those of the elite of London, as the comparable grandeur of their church buildings and refinement of their liturgical arrangements illustrate; while the excitements of popular revivalism were equally rooted in the fishing communities of Cornwall and those of Nova Scotia. National boundaries made no difference here. In England and Wales the gulf between church and chapel, going back to the seventeenth century, deeply divided the evangelical movement and generally ruled out cooperation. The evangelistic projects sponsored by the English Wesleyan Thomas Champness often seemed as much designed to rescue the villages from the power of the Church of England ("the tyranny of a clerical Trade Union") as to bring their inhabitants to heaven.[37] In the United States there were even more acute rifts, those between North and South and between black and white. The two geographical sections of America actually went to war against each other with the blessing of their evangelical communities. And, although they lived together in the South, the races worshiped apart. A black leader of the African Methodist Episcopal Church urged in 1888 a policy of "expunging from African Christianity all idolatrous imitations, which we have acquired from the white man."[38] Fellowship was usually as unthinkable

---

[36] *Methodist Journal* (Adelaide), July 11, 1874.

[37] Eliza M. Champness, *The Life-Story of Thomas Champness* (London: Charles H. Kelly, 1907), p. 230.

[38] J. A. Cole, "The Negro at Home and Abroad: Their Origin, Progress and Destiny," *African Methodist Episcopal Church Review* 4 (April 1888): 402, quoted by Timothy E. Fulop, " 'The Future Golden Day of the Race': Millennialism and Black Americans in the Nadir, 1877-1901," in *African-American Religion: Interpretive Essays in History and Culture*, ed. Timothy E. Fulop and Albert J. Raboteau (New York: Routledge, 1997), p. 238.

across the racial divide as across the sectional divide. So the deepest splits within the evangelical movement followed lines of social and political demarcation rather than international boundaries.

Consequently the most obvious features of evangelical experience were by no means necessarily determined chiefly by their national context. That, however, is not the impression that would be gathered from the existing historical accounts. Most secondary literature assumes that the nation, or a segment of it, possessed an evangelical movement of its own, largely divorced from other lands, with a role specific to its setting. The books on Australia and New Zealand are probably least affected by this tendency, for they commonly appreciate the close bonds between evangelical groupings within the colonies and between them and Britain.[39] There has been a leaning, however, toward seeing Irish evangelicalism as primarily a seedbed for later loyalty to the British connection that influences even the best work on the Ulster movement.[40] The literature on British evangelicalism commonly recognizes the impact of American revivalists, but does little else to show the way in which the churches of England, Scotland and Wales were part of a self-conscious global force.[41] Works on South Africa also tend to neglect the interdenominational and international linkages created by the common evangelicalism of the late nineteenth-century churches.[42] The treatment of South African religion often (understandably) dwells on the theme of race to the extent of underplaying other aspects of the Christian experience. Yet the reality was that the evangelicals of South Africa combined for common purposes and copied their coreligionists elsewhere. Even the Dutch Reformed Church, while retaining some Dutch links, was drawn into the inter-

---

[39]E.g., Stuart Piggin, *Evangelical Christianity in Australia: Spirit, Word and World* (Melbourne: Oxford University Press, 1996); Ian Breward, *A History of the Churches in Australasia* (Oxford: Oxford University Press, 2001); Allen K. Davidson and Peter J. Lineham, *Transplanted Christianity: Documents illustrating Aspects of New Zealand Church History*, 3rd ed. (Palmerston North: Massey University Department of History, 1995).

[40]David Hempton and Myrtle Hill, *Evangelical Protestantism in Ulster Society, 1740-1890* (London: Routledge, 1992).

[41]E.g., David W. Bebbington, *Evangelicalism in Modern Britain: A History from the 1730s to the 1980s* (London: Unwin Hyman, 1989).

[42]Richard Elphick and Rodney Davenport, eds., *Christianity in South Africa: A Political, Social & Cultural History* (Oxford: James Currey, 1997), is a book that recognizes the links (p. 3) but does not pursue them.

national web of English-speaking evangelical exchange. Andrew Murray, its most towering figure during the period, introduced Christian secondary education for girls from America, contributed to the *British Weekly* edited by Robertson Nicoll and spoke at the Keswick Convention.[43] Evangelicals in different lands were much more similar and connected to each other than many existing historical works suggest.

The same is true of North America. When, in 1858, news arrived in Boston, Massachusetts, of the death of the British Baptist hero of the Indian Mutiny, Major-General Sir Henry Havelock, several of the oldest citizens, remembering the war of 1812, were unmoved by the passing of a senior military officer of the enemy they still hated. The bulk of the ships in the harbor, however, lowered their flags to half-mast in honor of a fallen God-fearing celebrity.[44] A sense of evangelical solidarity prevailed over long-held animosities. The extent of that feeling has been too little appreciated in the secondary literature.[45] The United States is usually depicted as having broken with the ways of the old world, tossing British religious practice into the dustbin of history along with the principle of established churches. But in reality Americans thirsted for news of evangelical happenings in Britain, developing, especially among Congregationalists, a strong sense of their rootedness in the past of the British Isles. In 1856 the foundation stone of a church in London "holding the principle of our puritan forefathers" was laid by an American missionary and the English minister described his plans to visit the towns in England from which New England settlers came and then to travel to their New England equivalents to forge enduring links.[46] In the light of episodes such as this, it is not surprising that in so many respects the evangelical communities of America and Britain developed on parallel lines. Books on Canada are often more aware of the international affinities, frequently seeing dynamic religious influences from America warring

---

[43]Johannes du Plessis, *The Life of Andrew Murray of South Africa* (London: Marshall Brothers, 1919), pp. 274-89, 471, 448.

[44]*Christian Advocate and Journal* (New York), March 4, 1858, p. 35.

[45]Exceptions are Mark A. Noll, David W. Bebbington and George A. Rawlyk, eds., *Evangelicalism: Comparative Studies of Popular Protestantism in North America, the British Isles and Beyond, 1700-1990* (New York: Oxford University Press, 1994), and Charles D. Cashdollar, *A Spiritual Home: Life in British and American Reformed Congregations, 1830-1915* (University Park: Pennsylvania State University Press, 2000).

[46]*American Missionary*, January 1857, p. 18.

on Canadian soil with more restrained expressions of the faith derived from the United Kingdom. That portrayal oversimplifies the relationship, for evangelical exports from Britain could be as populist as those from America.[47] It is also true that works about Canada tend to antedate the emergence of Canadian national self-consciousness in the religious sphere, so that the enduring strength of the British connection is underestimated. So there is scope for a much fuller literature on transatlantic links in the evangelical world. While giving due weight to the contrasts in practice that did develop, it is likely to confirm the verdict of this book that the commonalties far outweighed the differences.

In the wilds of Newfoundland at the opening of the twentieth century, Methodist lay readers, lacking the education to qualify as lay preachers, conducted many of the services. Needing sermons to read, they habitually drew on two preachers: Spurgeon and Moody.[48] These two figures, as chapter one illustrated, embodied the essence of late nineteenth-century evangelicalism. Spurgeon was the greatest preacher of his age; Moody was the most famous evangelist. The East Anglian and the New Englander were alike superb speakers with an immense appeal to a worldwide audience. The burden of their sermons was the common testimony of the movement. They expounded the Bible, cherishing its good news of salvation. They proclaimed the power of the cross of Christ to turn people from darkness to light. They taught conversion as the way in which individuals could enter the Christian life. And they urged that true believers should be active in witness and service. Bible, cross, conversion and activism were the characteristic themes of the evangelical movement. By the second half of the nineteenth century its adherents had carried this message across the globe. It was found wherever Anglo-Saxon settlers had penetrated. But evangelicalism was not just a widespread phenomenon. It had penetrated deep into society, meshing with the assumptions of the age and forming the behavior of successive generations. Between 1850 and 1900 the evangelical movement was a dominant force in the English-speaking world.

---

[47]David Bebbington, "Canadian Evangelicalism: A View from Britain," in *Aspects of the Canadian Evangelical Experience*, ed. George A. Rawlyk (Montreal & Kingston: McGill-Queen's University Press, 1997).

[48]James Lumsden, *The Skipper Parson* (London: Charles H. Kelly, 1905), p. 109.

SELECT BIBLIOGRAPHY

Apart from periodicals, this bibliography is almost entirely confined to secondary works and, though it adds a number of extra publications, it does not include even all the books and articles cited in the notes. While the list is far from comprehensive, it contains many of the most useful items for the study of the evangelical movement in the later nineteenth century. The reference works listed toward the beginning have proved invaluable in the preparation of this book.

PRIMARY PERIODICALS

American Missionary (New York)

Annual Paper descriptive of the Lord's Work connected with the Pastors' College [and similar titles] (London)

Australian Churchman (Sydney)

Australian Evangelist (Melbourne)

Baptist Magazine (London)

Bibliotheca Sacra (New York)

British Weekly (London)

Christian (London)

Christian Advocate (New York)

Christian Advocate and Journal (New York)

Christian Advocate and Wesleyan Record (Sydney)

Christian Express (Lovedale, South Africa)

Christian Guardian (Toronto)

Christian Messenger (Halifax, Nova Scotia)

Christian Observer (Christchurch)

Christian Observer (London)

Christian Pleader (Sydney)

Christian Witness (London)

Christian World (London)

Church of England Chronicle (Sydney)

Church Missionary Society Record (London)

Congregationalist (London)

Evangelical Christendom (London)

Evangelical Witness and Presbyterian Review (Dublin)

Evangelistic Record (Chicago)

Examiner and Chronicle (New York)

Experience (London)

Freeman (London)

Free Methodist (Chicago)

Free-Will Baptist Register (Dover, N. H.)

Friend (London)

General Baptist Magazine (London)

Intercolonial Christian Messenger (Brisbane)

Irish Presbyterian (Belfast)

Irish Presbyterian (Dublin)

Life and Light (Boston, Mass.)

Life & Light (Melbourne)

Life of Faith (London)

Methodist Journal (Adelaide)

Methodist Review (New York)

Minutes of the Conference of the Wes-

leyan Methodist Church of South Africa (Cape Town and Grahamstown)
Minutes of the Methodist Conference (London)
Missionary Herald (London)
North Carolina Presbyterian (Fayetteville, N.C., and, subsequently, Charlotte, N.C.)
Oberlin Evangelist (Oberlin, Ohio)
Presbyterian Churchman (Dublin)
Presbyterian Magazine in connection with the Belfast Presbyterian Young Men's Association (Belfast)

Primitive Methodist Record (Adelaide)
Proceedings of the Church Missionary Society for Africa and the East (London)
Record (London)
Religious Herald (Richmond, Va.)
Revival (London)
Rocky Mountain Presbyterian (Denver, Colo.)
South African Methodist (Grahamstown)
Spectator and Methodist Chronicle (Melbourne)
United Presbyterian Magazine (Edinburgh)
Wesleyan Methodist Magazine (London)
Witness (Edinburgh)

REFERENCE WORKS

Cameron, Nigel M. de S., et al., eds. *Dictionary of Scottish Church History and Theology*. Edinburgh: T & T Clark; Downers Grove, Ill.: InterVarsity Press, 1993.

Cross, F. L., and E. A. Livingstone, eds. *The Oxford Dictionary of the Christian Church*, 3rd ed. Oxford: Oxford University Press, 1997.

Dickey, Brian, ed. *The Australian Dictionary of Evangelical Biography*. Sydney: Evangelical History Association, 1994.

Gaustad, Edwin Scott, and Philip L. Barlow, eds. *New Historical Atlas of Religion in America*. New York: Oxford University Press, 2001.

Hill, Samuel S., ed. *Encyclopedia of Religion in the South*. Macon, Ga.: Mercer University Press, 1984.

Larsen, Timothy, ed. *Biographical Dictionary of Evangelicals*. Leicester: Inter-Varsity Press, 2003.

Lewis, Donald M., ed. *The Blackwell Dictionary of Evangelical Biography, 1730-1860*. 2 vols. Oxford: Blackwell, 1995.

Reid, Daniel G., Robert D. Linder, Bruce L. Shelley and Harry S. Stout, eds. *Dictionary of Christianity in America*, Downers Grove, Ill.: InterVarsity Press, 1990.

OTHER WORKS

Acheson, Alan. *A History of the Church of Ireland, 1691-1996*. Dublin, Ireland: Columba Press, 1997.

Airhart, Phyllis D. *Serving the Present Age: Revivalism, Progressivism and the Methodist Tradition in Canada*. Montreal & Kingston: McGill-Queen's University Press, 1992.

Anderson, Robert M. *Vision of the Disinherited: The Making of American Pentecostalism*. New York: Oxford University Press, 1979.

Ansdell, Douglas. *The People of the Great Faith: The Highland Church, 1690-1900.* Stornoway: Acair, 1988.

Bacon, Margaret H. *The Quiet Rebels: The Story of the Quakers in America.* Philadelphia: New Society Publishers, 1988.

Bagwell, Philip S. *Outcast London: A Christian Response: The West London Mission of the Methodist Church, 1887-1987.* London: Epworth Press, 1987.

Balia, Daryl M. *Black Methodists and White Supremacy in South Africa.* Durban: Madiba Publishers, 1991.

Beaver, R. Pierce. *American Protestant Women in World Mission: History of the First Feminist Movement in America.* 2nd ed. Grand Rapids: Eerdmans, 1980.

Bebbington, David W. *Evangelicalism in Modern Britain: A History from the 1730s to the 1980s.* London: Unwin Hyman, 1989.

———. "Henry Drummond, Evangelicalism and Science." In *Henry Drummond: A Perpetual Benediction,* edited by Thomas E. Corts. Edinburgh: T & T Clark, 1999.

———. "Holiness in Nineteenth-Century British Methodism." In *Crown and Mitre: Religion and Society in Northern Europe since the Reformation,* edited by William M. Jacob and Nigel Yates. Woodbridge, U.K.: Boydell Press, 1993.

———. *Holiness in Nineteenth-Century England.* Carlisle: Paternoster Press, 2000.

———. "The Holiness Movements in British and Canadian Methodism in the Late Nineteenth Century." *Proceedings of the Wesley Historical Society,* 50, 1996.

———. *The Nonconformist Conscience: Chapel and Politics, 1870-1914.* London: Allen & Unwin, 1982.

Bebbington, David W., and Timothy Larsen, eds. *Modern Christianity and Cultural Aspirations.* London: Sheffield Academic Press, 2003.

Bentley, Anne. "The Transformation of the Evangelical Party in the Church of England in the Later Nineteenth Century." Ph.D. diss., Durham, 1971.

Billington, Ray Allen. *The Protestant Crusade.* New York: Macmillan, 1938.

Binfield, Clyde. *George Williams and the Y.M.C.A.: A Study in Victorian Social Attitudes.* London: Heinemann, 1973.

———. *So Down to Prayers: Studies in English Nonconformity, 1780-1920.* London: J. M. Dent & Sons, 1977.

Bordin, Ruth. *Frances Willard: A Biography.* Chapel Hill: University of North Carolina Press, 1986.

———. *Woman and Temperance: The Quest for Power and Liberty, 1873-1900.* Philadelphia: Temple University Press, 1981.

Boylan, Anne M. *Sunday School: The Formation of an American Institution.* New Haven: Yale University Press, 1982.

Breward, Ian. *A History of the Churches in Australasia.* Oxford: Oxford University Press, 2001.

Briggs, John H. Y. *The English Baptists of the Nineteenth Century.* Didcot: Baptist Historical Society, 1994.

Broomhall, A. J. *Hudson Taylor and China's Open Century.* 7 vols. London: Hodder & Stoughton, 1981-89.

Brown, Callum G. *The Death of Christian Britain.* London: Routledge, 2001.

————. *Religion and Society in Scotland since 1707.* Edinburgh: Edinburgh University Press, 1997.

————. *The Social History of Religion in Scotland since 1730.* London: Methuen, 1987.

Brown, Kenneth D. *A Social History of the Nonconformist Ministry in England and Wales, 1800-1930.* Oxford: Clarendon Press, 1988.

Brown, Roger L. *The Welsh Evangelicals.* Tongwynlais, U.K.: Tair Eglwys Press, 1986.

Bush, L. Russ, and Tom J. Nettles. *Baptists and the Bible.* rev. ed. Nashville: Broadman & Holman, 1999.

Butler, Diana H. *Standing against the Whirlwind: Evangelical Episcopalians in Nineteenth-Century America.* New York: Oxford University Press, 1995.

Butler, Jon. *Awash in a Sea of Faith: Christianizing the American People.* Cambridge, Mass.: Harvard University Press, 1990.

Campbell, James T. *Songs of Zion: The African Methodist Episcopal Church in the United States and South Africa.* Chapel Hill: University of North Carolina Press, 1998.

Carrington, Philip. *The Anglican Church in Canada.* Toronto: Collins, 1963.

Carter, Paul. *The Spiritual Crisis of the Gilded Age.* DeKalb: Northern Illinois University Press, 1971.

Carwardine, Richard J. *Evangelicals and Politics in Antebellum America.* New Haven: Yale University Press, 1993.

Casey, Michael W., and Douglas A. Foster, eds. *The Stone-Campbell Movement: An International Religious Tradition.* Knoxville: University of Tennessee Press, 2002.

Cashdollar, Charles D. *A Spiritual Home: Life in British and American Reformed Congregations, 1830-1915.* University Park: Pennsylvania State University Press, 2000.

Chadwick, W. Owen. *The Victorian Church.* 2 vols. London: Adam and Charles Black, 1966-70.

Cheyne, A. C. *The Transforming of the Kirk: Victorian Scotland's Religious Revolution.* Edinburgh: Saint Andrew Press, 1983.

Clark, Clifford E., Jr. *Henry Ward Beecher: Spokesman for a Middle-Class America.* Urbana: University of Illinois Press, 1978.

Cliff, Philip B. *The Rise and Development of the Sunday School Movement in England, 1780-1980.* Nutfield, Redhill, U.K.: National Christian Education Council, 1986.

Coad, F. Roy. *A History of the Brethren Movement.* Exeter: Paternoster Press, 1968.

Cocksworth, Christopher J. *Evangelical Eucharistic Thought in the Church of England.* Cambridge: Cambridge University Press, 1993.

Coffey, John. "Democracy and Popular Religion: Moody and Sankey's Mission to Britain, 1873-1875." In *Citizenship and Community: Liberals, Radicals and Collective Identities in the British Isles, 1865-1931,* edited by Eugenio F. Biagini. Cambridge: Cambridge University Press, 1996.

Coleman, Bruce I. *The Church of England in the Mid-Nineteenth Century: A Social Geography.* London: Historical Association, 1980.

Conforti, Joseph A. *Jonathan Edwards, Religious Tradition & American Culture.* Chapel Hill: University of North Carolina Press, 1995.

Cooke, Harriette J. *Mildmay: Or the Story of the First Deaconess Institution.* 2nd ed. London: Elliott Stock, 1893.

Cox, Jeffrey. *The English Churches in a Secular Society: Lambeth, 1870-1930.* New York: Oxford University Press, 1982.

Crowley, John G. *Primitive Baptists of the Wiregrass South: 1815 to the Present.* Gainesville: University Press of Florida, 1998.

Cunningham, Valentine. *Everywhere Spoken Against: Dissent in the Victorian Novel.* Oxford: Clarendon Press, 1975.

Currie, Robert, Allan Gilbert and Lee Horsley, eds. *Churches and Churchgoers: Patterns of Church Growth in the British Isles since 1700.* Oxford: Clarendon Press, 1977.

Dale, A. W. W. *The Life of R. W. Dale of Birmingham.* London: Hodder & Stoughton, 1898.

Dale, Robert W. *The Old Evangelicalism and the New.* London: Hodder & Stoughton, 1889.

Davidoff, Leonore, and Catherine Hall. *Family Fortunes: Men and Women of the English Middle Class, 1780-1850.* London: Hutchinson Education, 1987.

Davidson, Allan K., and Peter J. Lineham, eds. *Transplanted Christianity: Documents Illustrating Aspects of New Zealand Church History.* 3rd ed. Palmerston North: Massey University Department of History, 1995.

Davies, E. T. *Religion and Society in the Nineteenth Century: A New History of Wales.* Llandybie, Dyfed: Christopher Davies, 1981.

Davies, Rupert, A. Raymond George and Gordon Rupp, eds. *A History of the Methodist Church in Great Britain.* Vol. 3. London: Epworth Press, 1983.

de Gruchy, John, ed. *The London Missionary Society in Southern Africa: Historical Essays in Celebration of the Bicentenary of the LMS in Southern Africa, 1799-1999.* Cape Town: David Philip, 1999.

Dennis, James S. *Centennial Survey of Foreign Missions.* New York: Fleming H. Revell Co., 1902.

Dickson, J. N. Ian. "More than Discourse: The Sermons of Evangelical Protestants in Nineteenth Century Ulster." Ph.D. diss., Queen's University, Belfast, 2000.

Dickson, Neil W. *Brethren in Scotland: A Social Study of an Evangelical Movement.* Carlisle: Paternoster Press, 2003.

———. " 'Shut in with thee': The Morning Meeting among Scottish Open Brethren, 1830s–1960s." In *Continuity and Change in Christian Worship, Studies in Church History,* 35, edited by R. N. Swanson. Woodbridge, U.K.: Boydell Press, 1999.

Dieter, Melvin E. *The Holiness Revival of the Nineteenth Century.* Metuchen, N.Y.: Scarecrow Press, 1980.

Dorrien, Gary. *The Making of American Liberal Theology: Imagining Progressive Religion, 1805-1900.* Louisville, Ky.: Westminster John Knox Press, 2001.

du Plessis, Johannes. *The Life of Andrew Murray of South Africa.* London: Marshall Brothers, 1919.

Elphick, Richard, and Rodney Davenport, eds. *Christianity in South Africa: A Political, Social & Cultural History.* Oxford: James Currey, 1997.

Epstein, Barbara L. *The Politics of Domesticity: Women, Evangelicalism and Temperance.* Middletown, Conn.: Wesleyan University Press, 1981.

Fiedler, Klaus. *The Story of Faith Missions.* Oxford: Regnum, 1994.

Field, Clive D. "Adam and Eve: Gender in the English Free Church Constituency." *Journal of Ecclesiastical History* 44.

———. "The Social Structure of English Methodism: Eighteenth Twentieth Centuries." *British Journal of Sociology* 28 (1977).

Figgis, John B. *Keswick from Within.* London: Marshall Brothers, 1914.

Findlay, James F., Jr. *Dwight L. Moody: American Evangelist, 1837-1899.* Chicago: University of Chicago Press, 1969.

Finke, Roger, and Rodney Stark. *The Churching of America, 1776-1990: Winners and Losers in our Religious Economy.* New Brunswick, N.J.: Rutgers University Press, 1992.

Finlayson, Geoffrey B. A. M. *The Seventh Earl of Shaftesbury, 1801-1885.* London: Eyre Methuen, 1981.

Frank, Douglas W. *Less than Conquerors: How Evangelicals Entered the Twentieth Century.* Grand Rapids: Eerdmans, 1986.

Fulop, Timothy E., and Albert J. Raboteau. *African-American Religion: Interpretive Essays in History and Culture.* New York: Routledge, 1997.

Garnett, Jane. "The Gospel of Work and the Virgin Mary: Catholics, Protestants and Work in the Nineteenth Century." In *The Use and Abuse of Time in Christian History, Studies in Church History,* 37, edited by Robert N. Swanson. Woodbridge, U.K.: Boydell Press, 2002.

Gauvreau, Michael. *The Evangelical Century: College and Creed in English Canada from the Great Revival to the Great Depression.* Montreal & Kingston: McGill-Queen's University Press, 1991.

Genovese, Eugene D. *A Consuming Fire: The Fall of the Confederacy in the Mind of the White Christian South.* Athens: University of Georgia Press, 1999.

Gibbs, Mildred E. *The Anglican Church in India, 1600-1970.* Delhi: Indian SPCK, 1972.

Glover, Willis B. *Evangelical Nonconformists and Higher Criticism in the Nineteenth Century.* London: Independent Press, 1954.

Goen, C. C. *Broken Churches, Broken Nation: Denominational Schisms and the Coming of the American Civil War.* Macon, Ga.: Mercer University Press, 1985.

Gordon, James M. *Evangelical Spirituality.* London: SPCK, 1991.

Govan, Isobel R. *The Spirit of Revival: The Story of J. G. Govan and the Faith Mission.* 4th ed. Edinburgh: Faith Mission, 1978.

Grant, John W. *Free Churchmanship in England, 1870-1940.* London: Independent Press, 1955.

————. *A Profusion of Spires: Religion in Nineteenth-Century Ontario.* Toronto: University of Toronto Press, 1988.

Green, S. J. D. *Religion in the Age of Decline: Organisation and Experience in Industrial Yorkshire, 1870-1920.* Cambridge: Cambridge University Press, 1996.

Grubb, Norman P. *C. T. Studd: Cricketer and Pioneer.* London: Religious Tract Society, 1933.

Guelzo, Allen C. *For the Union of Evangelical Christendom: The Irony of the Reformed Episcopalians.* University Park: Pennsylvania State University Press, 1994.

Gundry, Stanley L. *Love Them In: The Life and Theology of D. L. Moody.* Chicago: Moody Press, 1999.

Gutjahr, Paul C. *An American Bible: A History of the Good Book in the United States.* Stanford, Calif.: Stanford University Press, 1999.

Hames, E. W. *Out of the Common Way: The European Church in the Colonial Era, 1840-1913.* Auckland: Wesley Historical Society of New Zealand, 1972.

Hamilton, J. Taylor, and Kenneth G. Hamilton. *History of the Moravian Church: The Renewed Unitas Fratrum, 1722-1957.* 2nd ed. Bethlehem, Penn.: Interprovincial Board of Christian Education, 1983.

Handy, Robert T. *A History of the Churches in the United States and Canada.* Oxford: Clarendon Press, 1976.

————, ed. *The Social Gospel in America, 1870-1920.* New York: Oxford University Press, 1966.

Harford, Charles F., ed. *The Keswick Convention: Its Message, its Method and its Men.* London: Marshall Brothers, 1907.

Harris, Paul W. *Nothing but Christ: Rufus Anderson and the Ideology of Protestant Foreign Missions.* New York: Oxford University Press, 1999.

Harrison, Brian. *Drink and the Victorians: The Temperance Question in England, 1815-1872.* London: Faber & Faber, 1971.

Hart, D. G. "Divided Between Heart and Mind: The Critical Period for Protestant Thought in America." *Journal of Ecclesiastical History* 38 (1987).

Harvey, Paul. *Redeeming the South: Religions, Cultures and Racial Identities Among Southern Baptists, 1865-1925.* Chapel Hill: University of North Carolina Press, 1997.

Heasman, Kathleen. *Evangelicals in Action: An Appraisal of Their Social Work in the Victorian Era.* London: Geoffrey Bles, 1962.

Heeney, Brian. "The Beginnings of Church Feminism." *Journal of Ecclesiastical History* 33 (1982).

Hempton, David, and Myrtle Hill. *Evangelical Protestantism in Ulster Society, 1740-1890.* London: Routledge, 1992.

Hill, Patricia. *The World their Household: The American Women's Foreign Mission Movement and Cultural Transformation, 1870-1922.* Ann Arbor: University of Michigan Press, 1985.

Hill, Samuel S., ed. *Religion in the Southern United States: A Historical Study.* Macon, Ga.: Mercer University Press, 1983.

Hilliard, David. *Godliness and Good Order: A History of the Anglican Church in South Australia.* Netley, South Australia: Wakefield Press, 1986.

Hilton, Boyd. *The Age of Atonement: The Influence of Evangelicalism on Social and Economic Thought, 1785-1865.* Oxford: Clarendon Press, 1988.

Hoeveler, J. David, Jr. *James McCosh and the Scottish Intellectual Tradition from Glasgow to Princeton.* Princeton: Princeton University Press, 1981.

Hofmeyr, J. W., and Gerald J. Pillay, eds. *A History of Christianity in South Africa.* Vol. I. Pretoria: HAUM Tertiary, 1994.

Holifield, E. Brooks. *The Gentleman Theologians: American Theology in Southern Culture, 1795-1860.* Durham, N.C.: Duke University Press, 1978.

Holmes, Janice. *Religious Revivals in Britain and Ireland, 1859-1905.* Dublin: Irish Academic Press, 2000.

Holmes, R. Finlay G., and R. Buick Knox, eds. *The General Assembly of the Presbyterian Church in Ireland, 1840-1990.* Belfast: Presbyterian Historical Society of Ireland, n.d.

Hopkins, Mark. *Nonconformity's Romantic Generation: Evangelical and Liberal Theologies in Victorian England.* Carlisle: Paternoster Press, 2004.

Howsam, Leslie. *Cheap Bibles: Nineteenth-Century Publishing and the British and Foreign Bible Society.* Cambridge: Cambridge University Press, 1991.

Hudson-Reed, Sydney. *By Taking Heed . . . The History of the Baptists in Southern Africa, 1820-1977.* Roodepoort: Baptist Publishing House, 1983.

Hughes, Richard T. *Reviving the Ancient Faith: The Story of Churches of Christ in America.* Grand Rapids: Eerdmans, 1996.

Hunt, Arnold D. *This Side of Heaven: A History of Methodism in South Australia* Adelaide: Lutheran Publishing House, 1985.

Hylson-Smith, Kenneth. *Evangelicals in the Church of England, 1734-1984.* Edinburgh: T & T Clark, 1988.

Inglis, K. S. *Churches and the Working Classes in Victorian England.* London: Routledge and Kegan Paul, 1963.

Isichei, Elizabeth. *Victorian Quakers.* Oxford: Clarendon Press, 1970.

Jackson, George. *The Old Methodism and the New.* London: Hodder & Stoughton, 1903.

Jalland, Pat. *Death in the Victorian Family.* Oxford: Oxford University Press, 1996.

Jay, Elisabeth. *The Religion of the Heart: Anglican Evangelicalism and the Nineteenth-Century Novel.* Oxford: Clarendon Press, 1979.

Jeal, Tim. *Livingstone.* London: Heinemann, 1973.

Jeffrey, Kenneth S. *When the Lord Walked the Land: The 1858-1862 Revival in the North East of Scotland.* Carlisle: Paternoster Press, 2002.

Jerrome, Peter. *John Sirgood's Way: The Story of the Loxwood Dependants.* Petworth, U.K.: Window Press, 1998.

Johnson, Dale A. *The Changing Shape of English Nonconformity, 1825-1925.* New York: Oxford University Press, 1999.

————. *Women in English Religion, 1700-1925.* New York: Edwin Mellen Press, 1983.

Jones, R. Tudur. *Congregationalism in England, 1662-1962.* London: Independent Press, 1962.

————. *Congregationalism in Wales.* Edited by Robert Pope. Cardiff: University of Wales Press, 2004.

————. *Faith and the Crisis of a Nation: Wales, 1890-1914.* Edited by Robert Pope. Cardiff: University of Wales Press, 2004.

Judd, Stephen, and Kenneth Cable. *Sydney Anglicans.* Sydney: Anglican Information Office, 1987.

Kent, John. *Holding the Fort: Studies in Victorian Revivalism.* London: Epworth Press, 1978.

Kent, Alan M. *Pulp Methodism: The Lives & Literature of Silas, Joseph and Salome Hocking, Three Cornish Novelists.* St. Austell, U.K.: Cornish Hillside Publications, 2002.

Kruppa, Patricia S. *Charles Haddon Spurgeon: A Preacher's Progress.* New York: Garland Publishing, 1982.

Kverndal, Roald. *Seamen's Missions: Their Origins and Early Growth: A Contribution to the History of the Church Maritime.* Pasadena, Calif.: William Carey Library, 1986.

Land, Gary, ed. *Adventism in America: A History.* Berrien Springs, Mich.: Andrews University Press, 1986.

Laqueur, Thomas W. *Religion and Respectability: Sunday Schools and Working Class Culture, 1780-1850.* New Haven: Yale University Press, 1976.

Larsen, Timothy. *Contested Christianity: The Political and Social Contexts of Victorian Theology.* Waco, Tex.: Baylor University Press, 2004.

————. "English Baptists, Jamaican Affairs and the Nonconformist Conscience: The Campaign against Governor Eyre." In *The Gospel in the World: International Baptist Studies,* edited by David W. Bebbington. Carlisle: Paternoster Press, 2002.

————. *Friends of Religious Equality: Nonconformist Politics in Mid-Victorian England.* Woodbridge, U.K.: Boydell Press, 1999.

Lawton, William J. *The Better Times to Be: Utopian Attitudes to Society among Sydney Anglicans, 1885 to 1914.* Kensington, U.K.: New South Wales University Press, 1990.

Lewis, Donald M. *Lighten their Darkness: The Evangelical Mission to Working Class London, 1828-1860.* Westport, Conn.: Greenwood Press, 1986.

Lincoln, C. Eric, and Lawrence H. Mamiya. *The Black Church in the African American Experience.* Durham, N.C.: Duke University Press, 1990.

Livingstone, David N. *Darwin's Forgotten Defenders: The Encounter Between Evangelical Theology and Evolutionary Thought.* Grand Rapids: Eerdmans, 1987.

Livingstone, David N., D. G. Hart, and Mark A. Noll, eds. *Evangelicals and Science in Historical Perspective.* New York: Oxford University Press, 1999.

Long, Kathryn T. *The Revival of 1857-58: Interpreting an American Religious Awakening.* New York: Oxford University Press, 1998.

Macinnes, A. I. "Evangelical Protestantism in the Nineteenth-Century Highlands." In *Sermons and Battle Hymns: Protestant Popular Culture in Modern Scotland,* edited by Graham

Walker and Tom Gallagher. Edinburgh: Edinburgh University Press, 1990.

Magnuson, Norris. *Salvation in the Slums: Evangelical Social Work, 1865-1920.* Grand Rapids: Baker Book House, 1990.

Marks, Lynne. *Revivals and Roller Rinks: Religion, Leisure and Identity in Late Nineteenth-Century Small-Town Canada.* Toronto: University of Toronto Press, 1996.

Marsden, George M. *Fundamentalism and American Culture: The Shaping of Twentieth-Century Evangelicalism, 1870-1925.* New York: Oxford University Press, 1980.

————. *The Soul of the American University: From Protestant Establishment to Established Nonbelief.* New York: Oxford University Press, 1994.

Masters, D. C. "The Anglican Evangelicals in Toronto." *Journal of the Canadian Church Historical Society* 20 (1978).

Mathers, Helen. "The Evangelical Spirituality of a Victorian Feminist: Josephine Butler, 1828-1906." *Journal of Ecclesiastical History* 52 (2001).

Maughan, Stephen. "Mighty England do Good: The Major English Denominations and Organisation for the Support of Foreign Missions in the Nineteenth Century." In *Missionary Encounters: Sources and Issues,* edited by R. A. Bickers and Rosemary Seton. Richmond, U.K.: Curzon Press, 1996.

McDannell, Colleen. *The Christian Home in Victorian America, 1840-1900.* Bloomington: University of Indiana Press, 1986.

————. *Material Christianity: Religion and Popular Culture in America.* New Haven: Yale University Press, 1995.

McEldowney, Dennis, ed. *Presbyterians in Aotearea, 1840-1990,* Wellington: Presbyterian Church of New Zealand, 1990.

McKinley, Edward H. *The History of the Salvation Army in the United States, 1880-1972.* 2nd ed. Grand Rapids: Eerdmans, 1995.

McLeod, Hugh. *Class and Religion in the Late Victorian City.* London: Croom Helm, 1974.

————. *Piety and Poverty: Working-Class Religion in Berlin, London and New York, 1870-1914.* New York: Holmes & Meier, 1995.

————. *Religion and Society in England, 1850-1914.* Basingstoke: Macmillan, 1996.

Moore, James R. *The Post-Darwinian Controversies: A Study of the Protestant Struggle to Come to Terms with Darwin in Britain and America, 1870-1900.* Cambridge: Cambridge University Press, 1979.

Moorhead, James. *American Apocalypse: Yankee Protestants and the Civil War.* New Haven: Yale University Press, 1978.

Nelson, E. Clifford. *The Lutherans in North America.* Philadelphia: Fortress, 1980.

Nienkirchen, Charles. *A. B. Simpson and the Pentecostal Movement: A Study in Continuity, Crisis and Change.* Peabody, Mass.: Hendrickson, 1992.

Noll, Mark A. *America's God: From Jonathan Edwards to Abraham Lincoln.* New York: Oxford University Press, 2002.

————. *Between Faith and Criticism: Evangelicals, Scholarship and the Bible.* New York: Harper & Row, 1986.

————. *A History of Christianity in the United States and Canada.* Grand Rapids: Eerdmans, 1992.

————, ed. *The Princeton Theology, 1812-1921.* Grand Rapids: Baker, 1983.

————, ed. *God and Mammon: Protestants, Money and the Market, 1790-1860.* New York: Oxford University Press, 2002.

Noll, Mark A., David W. Bebbington and George A. Rawlyk, eds. *Evangelicalism: Comparative Studies of Popular Protestantism in North America, the British Isles and Beyond, 1700-1990.* New York: Oxford University Press, 1984.

Obelkevich, James. *Religion and Rural Society: South Lindsey, 1825-1875.* Oxford: Clarendon Press, 1976.

Oden, Thomas C., ed. *Phoebe Palmer: Selected Writings.* New York: Paulist Press, 1988.

Oldstone-Moore, Christopher. *Hugh Price Hughes: Founder of a New Methodism, Conscience of a New Nonconformity.* Cardiff: University of Wales Press, 1999.

Orr, Edwin. *The Second Evangelical Awakening in Britain,* London: Marshall, Morgan & Scott, 1949.

Peel, Albert. *These Hundred Years: A History of the Congregational Union of England and Wales, 1831-1931.* London: Congregational Union of England and Wales, 1931.

Pelt, Owen D., and Ralph Lee Smith. *The Story of the National Baptists.* New York: Vantage Press, 1960.

Pierson, Arthur T. *Forward Movements of the Last Half Century.* New York: Funk and Wagnalls, 1900.

Piggin, Stuart. *Evangelical Christianity in Australia: Spirit, Word and World.* Melbourne: Oxford University Press, 1996.

Phillips, Walter. *Defending "A Christian Country": Churchmen and Society in New South Wales in the 1880s and After.* St. Lucia, Queensland: University of Queensland Press, 1981.

Porter, Andrew. "Cambridge, Keswick and Late Nineteenth-Century Attitudes to Africa." *Journal of Imperial and Commonwealth Studies* 5 (1976).

————. "Religion and Empire: British Expansion in the Long Nineteenth Century." *Journal of Imperial and Commonwealth History* 20 (1992).

————, ed. *The Imperial Horizons of British Protestant Missions, 1880-1914.* Grand Rapids: Eerdmans, 2003.

Price, Charles, and Ian Randall. *Transforming Keswick.* Carlisle: OM Publishing, 2000.

Prior, Oswald. *Australia's Little Cornwall.* Adelaide: Rigby, 1962.

Prochaska, Frank K. *Women and Philanthropy in Nineteenth-Century England.* Oxford: Clarendon Press, 1980.

Randall, Ian M. *Spirituality and Social Change: The Contribution of F. B. Meyer (1847-1929).* Carlisle: Paternoster Press, 2003.

Randall, Ian M., and David Hilborn. *One Body in Christ: The History and Significance of the Evangelical Alliance.* Carlisle: Paternoster Press, 2001.

Rawlyk, George A., ed. *Aspects of the Canadian Evangelical Experience.* Montreal & Kingston: McGill-Queen's University Press, 1997.

————, ed. *The Canadian Protestant Experience, 1760-1990.* Burlington, Ontario: Welch, 1991.

Rawlyk, George A., and Mark A. Noll, eds. *Amazing Grace: Evangelicalism in Australia, Britain, Canada and the United States.* Montreal & Kingston: McGill-Queen's University Press, 1994.

Reardon, Bernard M. G. *Religious Thought in the Victorian Age: A Survey from Coleridge to Gore.* London: Longman, 1980.

Richardson, S. P. *The Lights and Shadows of Itinerant Life.* Nashville: Publishing House of the Methodist Episcopal Church, South, 1900.

Richey, Russell E., Kenneth E. Rowe, and Jean Miller Schmidt, eds. *Perspectives on American Methodism: Interpretive Essays.* Nashville: Kingswood, 1993.

Robert, Dana L. *Occupy until I Come: A. T. Pierson and the Evangelization of the World.* Grand Rapids: Eerdmans, 2003.

Rosman, Doreen M. *Evangelicals and Culture.* London: Croom Helm, 1984.

Ross, Andrew C. *Livingstone: Mission and Empire.* London: London and Hambledon Books, 2002.

Rowell, Geoffrey. *Hell and the Victorians.* Oxford: Clarendon Press, 1974.

Sandeen, Ernest R. *The Roots of Fundamentalism: British and American Millenarianism.* Chicago: University of Chicago Press, 1970.

Schlabach, Theron F. *Peace, Faith, Nation: Mennonites and Amish in Nineteenth Century America.* Scottdale, Penn.: Herald Press, 1988.

Schmidt, Leigh E. *Holy Fairs: Scottish Communions and American Revivals in the Early Modern Period.* Princeton: Princeton University Press, 1989.

Scotland, Nigel. *"Good and Proper Men": Lord Palmerston and the Bench of Bishops.* Cambridge: James Clarke 2000.

————. *Methodism and the Revolt of the Field: A Study of the Methodist Contribution to Agricultural Trade Unionism in East Anglia, 1872-96.* Gloucester: Alan Sutton, 1981.

Sell, Alan. *Defending and Declaring the Faith: Some Scottish Examples, 1860-1920.* Exeter: Paternoster Press, 1987.

Sellers, Ian. *Nineteenth-Century Nonconformity.* London: Edward Arnold, 1977.

Semple, Neil. *The Lord's Dominion: The History of Canadian Methodism.* Montreal & Kingston: McGill-Queen's University Press, 1996.

Shaw, Ian J. "Charles Spurgeon and the Stockwell Orphanage." *Christian Graduate* 29 (1976).

————. *High Calvinists in Action: Calvinism and the City: Manchester and London, 1810-1860.* Oxford: Oxford University Press, 2002.

Shiman, Lilian L. *Crusade against Drink in Victorian England.* Basingstoke: Macmillan, 1986.

Sizer, Sandra S. *Gospel Hymns and Social Religion: The Rhetoric of Nineteenth Century Revivalism.* Philadelphia: Temple University Press, 1978.

Smith, Gary S. *The Seeds of Secularization: Calvinism, Culture and Pluralism in America, 1870-1915.* Grand Rapids: Eerdmans, 1985.

Smith, Timothy L. *Called unto Holiness: The Story of the Nazarenes: the Formative Years.* Kansas City, Mo.: Nazarene Publishing House, 1962.

————. *Revivalism and Social Reform: American Protestantism on the Eve of the Civil War.* Nashville: Abingdon Press, 1957.

Sobel, Mechal. *Trabelin'On: The Slave Journey to an Afro-Baptist Faith.* Princeton: Princeton University Press, 1988.

Stanley, Brian. *The Bible and the Flag: Protestant Missions and British Imperialism in the Nineteenth and Twentieth Centuries.* Leicester: Apollos, 1990.

————. "Christianity and Civilization in English Evangelical Mission Thought." In *Christian Missions and the Enlightenment,* edited by Brian Stanley. Grand Rapids: Eerdmans, 2001.

————. "C. H. Spurgeon and the Baptist Missionary Society, 1863-1866." *Baptist Quarterly* 29 (1982).

————. "Home Support for Overseas Missionaries in Early Victorian England, c. 1838-1873." Ph.D. diss., Cambridge, 1979.

Spain, Rufus B. *At Ease in Zion: A Social History of Southern Baptists, 1865-1900.* Tuscaloosa: University of Alabama Press, 2003.

Stock, Eugene. *The History of the Church Missionary Society.* 3 vols. London: Church Missionary Society, 1900.

Szasz, Ferenc M. *The Divided Mind of Protestant America, 1880-1930.* University: University of Alabama Press, 1982.

Talbot, Brian R. *The Search for a Common Identity: The Origins of the Baptist Union of Scotland, 1800-1870.* Carlisle: Paternoster Press, 2003.

Thompson, David M. "The Emergence of the Nonconformist Social Gospel in England." In *Protestant Evangelicalism: Britain, Ireland, Germany and America, c. 1730-c. 1950,* Studies in Church History Subsidia, 7, edited by Keith Robbins. Oxford: Basil Blackwell, 1990.

————. *A History of the Association of Churches of Christ in Great Britain and Ireland.* Birmingham: Berean Press, 1980.

————, ed. *Nonconformity in the Nineteenth Century.* London: Routledge & Kegan Paul, 1972.

Van Die, Marguerite. *An Evangelical Mind: Nathaniel Burwash and the Methodist Tradition in Canada.* Montreal & Kingston: McGill-Queen's University Press, 1989.

Vaudry, Richard W. *The Free Church in Victorian Canada, 1844-1861.* Waterloo, Ontario: Wilfrid Laurier University Press, 1989.

Voll, Dieter. *Catholic Evangelicalism: The Acceptance of Evangelical Traditions by the Oxford Movement during the Second Half of the Nineteenth Century.* London: Faith Press, 1963.

Wacker, Grant. *Augustus H. Strong and the Dilemma of Historical Consciousness.* Macon, Ga.: Mercer University Press, 1985.

————. "The Holy Spirit and the Spirit of the Age in American Protestantism, 1880-1910." *Journal of American History* 72 (1985).

Walker, Clarence E. *A Rock in a Weary Land: The African Methodist Episcopal Church during the Civil War and Reconstruction.* Baton Rouge: Louisiana State University Press, 1982.

Walker, Michael. *Baptists at the Table: The Theology of the Lord's Supper Amongst English Baptists in the Nineteenth Century.* London: Baptist Historical Society, 1992.

Walker, Pamela J. *Pulling the Devil's Kingdom Down: The Salvation Army in Victorian Britain.* Berkeley: University of California Press, 2001.

Walker, R. B. "The Growth Rate of Wesleyan Methodism in Victorian England and Wales." *Journal of Ecclesiastical History* 24 (1973).

Watts, M. R. *The Dissenters: II: The Expansion of Evangelical Nonconformity, 1791-1859.* Oxford: Clarendon Press, 1995.

Weber, Timothy P. *Living in the Shadow of the Second Coming: American Premillennialism, 1875-1982.* Rev. ed. Chicago: Chicago University Press, 1987.

Welter, Barbara. "The Feminization of American Religion, 1800-1860." In *Clio's Consciousness Raised: New Perspectives on the History of Women,* edited by Mary S. Hartman and Lois Baner. New York: Harper and Row, 1974.

Weremchuk, Max S. *John Nelson Darby: A Biography.* Neptune, N.Y.: Loizeaux Brothers, 1992.

Westfall, William. *Two Worlds: The Protestant Culture of Nineteenth-Century Ontario.* Montreal & Kingston: McGill-Queen's University Press, 1989.

Whisenant, James C. *A Fragile Unity: Anti-Ritualism and the Division of Anglican Evangelicalism in the Nineteenth Century.* Carlisle: Paternoster Press, 2003.

White, Ronald C., Jr., and C. Howard Hopkins. *The Social Gospel: Religion and Reform in Changing America.* Philadelphia: Temple University Press, 1976.

Wigley, John. *The Rise and Fall of the Victorian Sunday.* Manchester: Manchester University Press, 1980.

Williams, Daniel Day. *The Andover Liberals: A Study in American Theology.* New York: King's Crown Press, 1941.

Williams, Walter L. *Black Americans and the Evangelizaton of Africa.* Madison: University of Wisconsin Press, 1982.

Wilson, Charles R. *Baptized in Blood: The Religion of the Lost Cause, 1865-1920.* Athens: University of Georgia Press, 1980.

Wilson, Linda. *Constrained by Zeal: Female Spirituality amongst Nonconformists, 1825-1875.* Carlisle: Paternoster Press, 2000.

Wolffe, John. *The Protestant Crusade in Great Britain, 1829-1860.* Oxford: Clarendon Press, 1988.

———, ed. *Evangelical Faith and Public Zeal: Evangelicals and Society in Britain, 1780-1980.* London: SPCK, 1995.

Yates, Timothy E. *Venn and Victorian Bishops Abroad: The Missionary Policies of Henry Venn and their Repercussions upon the Anglican Episcopate of the Colonial Period, 1841-1872.* Studia Missionalia Upsaliensia, 33, London: SPCK, 1978.

Index